Islam as Political Religion

This comprehensive survey of contemporary Islam provides a philosophical and theological approach to the issues faced by Muslims and the question of global secularization. Engaging with critics of modern Islam, Shabbir Akhtar sets out an agenda of what his religion is, and could be, as a political entity.

Exploring the views and arguments of philosophical, religious and political thinkers, the author covers a raft of issues faced by Muslims in an increasingly secular society. Chapters are devoted to the Quran and Islamic literature; the history of Islam; Sharia law; political Islam; Islamic ethics; and political Islam's evolving relationship with the West. Recommending changes which enable Muslims to move from their imperial past to a modest role in the power structures of today's society, Akhtar offers a detailed assessment of the limitations and possibilities of Islam in the modern world.

Providing a vision for an empowered yet rational Islam that distances itself from both Islamist factions and Western secularism, this book is an essential read for students and scholars of Islamic studies, religion, philosophy and politics.

Shabbir Akhtar is Associate Professor of Philosophy and Religious Studies at Old Dominion University in Norfolk, Virginia. This political work is a sequel to his philosophical treatise *The Quran and the Secular Mind* (Routledge, 2007). He has written a number of articles and books on philosophy of religion, Christianity and Islam, and is currently working on a book on Islamic humanism.

Islam as Political Religion

The future of an imperial faith

Shabbir Akhtar

LONDON AND NEW YORK

First published 2011
by Routledge
2 Park Square, Milton Park, Abingdon, Oxon OX14 4RN

Simultaneously published in the USA and Canada
by Routledge
270 Madison Ave, New York, NY 10016

Routledge is an imprint of the Taylor & Francis Group, an Informa business

Typeset in Times new roman by Glyph International
Printed and bound in Great Britain by CPI Antony Rowe, Chippenham,
Wiltshire

British Library Cataloguing in Publication Data
A catalogue record for this book is available from the British Library

Library of Congress Cataloging in Publication Data
Akhtar, Shabbir, 1960-
Islam as political religion : the future of an imperial faith / Shabbir Akhtar.
    p. cm.
Includes bibliographical references and index.
1. Islam and politics. 2. Islam and secularism. 3. Islam and culture.
4. Religion and politics. I. Title.
BP173.7.A4925 2011
297.2'72–dc22   2010017592

ISBN 978-0-415-78146-6 (hbk)
ISBN 978-0-415-78147-3 (pbk)
ISBN 978-0-203-84182-2 (ebk)

Contents

A note on Arabic transliteration and on Islamic dates

Typically, I retain the final 'h' to indicate feminine nouns. Arabic has no upper case but I capitalize proper nouns and the initial word in transliterated titles of Arabic works. Some words can occur with an upper case (*Al-Qur'ān*) and a lower case (*qur'ān*). This is explained in the text. Elision of vowels is not indicated. I use the Library of Congress system for Arabic transliteration to indicate consonants unique to Arabic (ṭ, ẓ and ḍ).

Many words, notably Islam, Quran, Ramadan, Muhammad, hadith (Muhammad's traditional saying), fatwa, jihad, Shariah (holy law) and Shiite are being increasingly naturalized into English as Islam becomes part of the Western cultural landscape. In such words, the length of vowel, any diacritical dots, and glottal (') and guttural (') stops, are rarely indicated.

Islamic dates

Although our time frame is supplied by the common (Christian) era, dates are given in varied but consistent ways. An unqualified date always refers to the Christian calendar. I use the Islamic chronology of BH and AH (before and after the Prophet's exodus or *hijrah* to Medina). For seminal events, I offer Christian and Islamic dates, thus highlighting historical interactions between these religious superpowers. Dates of death only are given for classical scholars. For rulers, including all caliphs except the first four, only regnal periods are supplied. For important figures in modern history, I give dates of birth and death.

Introduction

I

Islam is associated with a misanthropic political vengeance and apparently motiveless malice exhibited daily in the world's crowded headlines. Its towering twin public countenances are a mystical faith of peace and a ferocious political ideology dedicated to world conquest through indiscriminate violence. Owing to this Janus-faced reputation, some European critics gave Islam the benefit of the doubt and were, as recently as 1989 when the Rushdie affair erupted, kind enough to eulogize it as potentially the best religion with the worst followers. Two decades later, practically all Westerners lament that Islam is the *worst* faith with the worst followers. Islam as political religion is now uniformly condemned as a resolutely intolerant, potentially totalitarian, unmanageably anarchic, dangerously subversive, irredeemably misogynistic, irrationally homophobic and avowedly imperialistic form of theocratic terrorism which aims to forcibly assimilate the secular and Christian worlds to its own obscurantist norms while rejecting offers of democratic compromise and eirenic accommodation.

Some Western extremists accuse Muslims of a new conquest of post-Christian Europe. Once God's continent, it is now renamed Eurabia or Europistan, conquered this time via immigrant infiltration and intimidation, not direct invasion. Such conspiratorial charges are supported by anxieties about the reach and purpose of Muslim, mainly Saudi, philanthropic donations to major Western universities. Is this a subtle attempt to monopolize and censor the study of Islam in the West, thus undermining secular freedoms of research, inquiry and speech?

Many non-Muslims sincerely wonder why Muslims, alone among religious believers, refuse to become citizens of a global political and economic order. This is a fair question. While we belong to many faiths, we remain a single humanity and share the planet. For those of goodwill who affirm the beatitude, 'Blessed are the peace-makers', the Islamic question is urgent, not merely theological. As an organic amalgam of secular and religious concerns, Islam resists secularization at a time when the gods of other faiths are competing to fall prostrate at the altar of secularism.

II

Two decades ago, during the Rushdie affair, I publicly argued that Islamic reform derives its authority from the attempt to resist and confront, not assimilate secular, political and artistic modernity. Religious reformers need religious, not intellectual, authority, in order to be credible to their co-religionists. That is why Sayyid Qutb and Ayatollah Khomeini and other activists succeeded in influencing the Islamic world while the exiled 'Muslim' intellectuals who plan to reform Islam, from the safety of their apartments in London and Paris, are ridiculed in the Muslim world. They are seen as resident stooges and puppets of the West as opposed to the Western-appointed puppets governing the Muslim masses in their own home-lands. Western-based Muslim thinkers who labour hard to create a so-called moderate – that is, politically impotent – Islam fully acceptable to the West, are dismissed as agents of the West.

Only a Muslim reformer who argues for strengthening Islam, not emasculating it, carries any weight with ordinary Muslims both in the East and West. Western non-Muslim readers should ask themselves whether they would prefer a legiti-mately empowered Islam which, historically at least, gave us peace, scholarship, political security and stability for millennia in several parts of the world or an impotent Islam that has recently given us terrorism and extremism as a substitute for politics and policies.

If this shocks you as a Western non-Muslim reader, ask yourself whether medi-aeval Christian reformers would have been taken seriously if they had proposed that Christianity should be reformed by becoming more secular. Or, alternatively, if they had pleaded that Christian dogmas should be liberalized through interac-tion and eirenic dialogue with Islam, then a powerful presence on European frontiers. If these had been their proposals, they would have been laughed out of court by the theologians of the Catholic Church. Instead, Protestant reformers showed that they were more truly conservative and committed Christians than their Catholic opponents. Moreover, the West's secular thinkers are suspect in the Muslim world today just as Muslim thinkers, especially Averroës and Avicenna, who virtually created the Renaissance in Christian Europe, were anathematized by mediaeval Europeans.

The type of reform proposed by westernized Muslims, including Muslim women who claim that the Quran gives women more rights and liberties than those secured by modern secular feminism, is tragically misguided. The West should support an organic, not an imposed 'colonial' reformation. For that to happen, Islam must confront secular culture, morality and philosophy. The crucial question is about the motivation and limits of such confrontation. Only such a stance could give Islamic reform, emanating from the West, any kind of religious authenticity in the West itself and perhaps some religious authority in the Islamic world. Like Daniel in the den, Muslims must face the lion, take on modernity on modernity's intellectual terms but without relinquishing the authority of the best of their tradition.

In this book, I recommend changes which enable Muslims to move graciously from their imperial past to a modest role in the power structures of a world in which their aspirations, even lives and property, mean little. I present proposals that modern Muslims, as conscientious and intelligent heirs of their imperial tradition, can implement. I recognize that my theme is academic and professional but also urgent and practical. Therefore, I write as a polymath who rejects the academic subdivisions of specialization which kill perspective by giving everyone a piece of the jigsaw puzzle but no-one the whole picture. By moving beyond mere scholarship and research towards insight and wisdom, a thinker can sometimes awaken a whole generation of his people. It is an open question, however, in which direction the awakened ones will march. In the absence of a clerical hierarchy in (Sunni) Islam, a Muslim thinker is always only an individual voice, crying in the wilderness unless that voice were to be amplified by reputation for personal piety and learning. Even if one had such advantages, genuinely innovative ideas take time to take root and seldom blossom within the life-span of those who propose them.

III

Western readers might be tempted to skip the bulk of the text and read only the chapters entitled 'A political religion' and 'An imperial religion'. Experts on Islam include an army of academic specialists (whose voice is sometimes wholly academic and hence practically irrelevant) but also veteran observers, including generalists such as journalists, with new wisdom to retail to their apprentices. These experts, like the drug companies, typically isolate one element from the whole plant. Invariably, they choose the opposed poles of political or mystical and then explain the remaining dimensions. In the pharmaceutical case, nature has the patent on the whole and wholesome plant while the artificial extract has toxic side-effects. The same applies to books, academic and general, featuring a uni-dimensional Islam. The attenuated faith bewilders Muslims since they are instinctively (if not intellectually) aware of their religion's complexity. They are forced to witness daily the biased vivisection of their sacred beliefs as they endure the prejudicial rigour of sensationalist analysis which spares all other faiths under a patronizing lenience.

We cannot comprehend the continuing *political* appeal of Islam without understanding it as the *moral* compass guiding a major segment of humanity. Moreover, Islam has intellectually challenging and appealing foundations; sympathetic non-Muslims recognize its early and classical history as exemplifying a successful experiment in creating and sponsoring a multicultural civilization. This is seen as proof of an empowered Islam's ability to be a force for the common good. Islam has patronized learning and scholarship: Muslim polymaths transmitted and amplified Europe's lost Hellenic heritage after recognizing and saluting it as one of the glories of the intellectual record of our shared humanity.

In view of several political alternatives, especially liberal secular humanism with its democratic underpinnings, why choose Islam? Western readers and scholars typically view Islam's political potential with alarm and do so in isolation from its appealing spiritual and moral aspects. They see this faith as a political nuisance, a religion that contains an elaborate ideological disguise for world domination.

'Islamo-fascism' best captures this Western exasperation, making Muhammad's faith resemble the totalitarian party's manifesto in George Orwell's dystopia *1984*. Some Muslim activists do fervently seek to establish a state where they can wield power over other Muslims. Their hidden love of absolute power is gilded with a veneer of justice and decency. Their secret aim is not to serve the interests of Muslim peoples but rather to pay homage to an abstract ideology marked by puritanical obsessions with social control of an imagined anarchic sexuality. Many are unable to cope with the free-ranging caprices of a modern world freed of ancient and often irrational strictures and inhibitions.

Our concern, however, is with ordinary and fallible Muslims who look up to Islam and identify it with moral good and political righteousness. We must assess this estimate of Islam as a conspicuously decent way of coping with life's pressures. Westerners dismiss *a priori* any suggestion that political Islam may contribute anything valuable to alleviate modern injustices and tyrannies. Dialogue with Muslims is often a monologue in which Westerners dictate their will. The West gave the world communism, fascism and now advanced capitalism disguised as secular liberal humanism, all in quick succession within one century. The next great global political paradigm may well be inspired by Islam's notions of political humility and economic justice.

IV

I clarify the aims and scope of this book through two substantive comments on defining Islam and two remarks about temperament and mood of inquiry.

Islam defies classification as a Western monotheism or even as a religion rather than an ideology. We know this from the invention of unnecessary words such as 'Islamism' or 'Islamist', created by analogy with ideological -isms such as Marxism (with Marxist acolytes). For other world faiths, we have no ideologically motivated neologisms such as 'Christianism' and 'Christianists'. (Judaism has an -ism suffix but is never classed as an ideology.)

I identify 10 features of Islam which jointly characterize it as a religion but as one distinguished by its political and ideological facets. Its originating (Meccan) facets are prophetic-historical, literary and potentially universal. At Medina, the faith enters its public and explicitly empowered phase: hence it's political, secular, legal and imperial facets. At both locations, for believers, it remains rational, ethical, and private (including mystical). These last three qualities, prominent in the initial Meccan phase, now re-emerge after the colonial onslaught that began three centuries ago. The first three (prophetic, literary and universal) endure as the essence of Islam's self-image. The political, legal and imperial dimensions, synthesized in secular power, actively fed the Muslim imagination from the time of Muhammad's establishment of an empowered community in Medina in the first third of the seventh century until the end of the Ottoman caliphate in the early twentieth century. The future of this trio remains uncertain.

This 'decimal' characterization of Islam equips us to predict its future development while defusing its currently tense relationships with rival faiths and ideologies.

I am not, however, defining religion as such. Thus, for example, Islam's political dimension is akin to the organizational one, common to all religions. Not all organization is coercively political: all faiths form communities but not necessarily states or empires. As for the standard facets of ethical, artistic (aesthetic), ritual, doctrinal and mythological, identified empirically by scholars of religions, Islam, no less than Christianity or Buddhism, has an accompanying art (including architecture), doctrinal scheme, mythology and rituals. But these do not distinguish Islam. Reading this book will help readers decide which facets are, were historically, and might therefore remain unique to Islam. Which are characteristic, distinctive or essential to it? Which are incidental and peripheral to it? This analysis of the evolving profile of an antique Islam as it moves into late modernity has practical and policy implications. Which facets of Islam's originating political axioms must continue to characterize it in the future? Might some of these evolve into apolitical forms?

Second, Islam is fully and authoritatively defined at its source. This is done inside the Quran, self-described as scripture rather than canonized centuries later. Islam was successfully established by the man who conveyed the Quran's message. Muhammad's meticulous and scrupulous attention to detail has left little scope for later developments that might radically alter his faith; no second patrons or secondary founders have arisen in later history. So defined are the originating axioms of the faith that no subsequent reformation has successfully undermined its original integrity.

The 10 facets of Islam mentioned above can be located in Quranic verses. Scriptural references will be given since competitive intra-religious hermeneutics merge into the political, not merely literary or theological, context of modern Islam as Muslims struggle among themselves and with outsiders to define and own their faith. The kind of Islam that Muslims want differs from the kind that Westerners and other non-Muslims would like to see emerging. This book negotiates between these opposed political aspirations for the future of a universal faith.

Third, I reject triumphalism and apologetic ambitions. Despite being a book with political and inter-faith relevance, I do not indulge the love of controversy for its own sake in order to score points. All faiths, in their origins and subsequent developments, have strengths and weaknesses. Thus, for example, Islam's early political successes became liabilities in later ages. The recession of fragmented late Islamic empires left exposed several Muslim minorities whose sufferings now constitute some two thirds of the daily world news coverage. About four fifths of all refugees are Muslims. By contrast, Christianity, born in weakness and persecution, later prospered and eventually become the most widely distributed and empowered faith on our planet, partly courtesy of Western colonialism.

Finally, the correct temperament of inquiry into the role of power is a subtlety we defer to the opening of Part II. Suffice it to say here that this work is neither detached philosophical reflection nor committed apology. I have tried to write a book that is strong but not strident, factually and historically accurate but not stale or predictable, precise but not pedantic, theoretical without being utopian or idealistic about practical implementation. The chapters dealing exclusively with power are scholarly and combative and some unsympathetic critics may judge their tone rather strident. I mention this here lest the occasional vehemence of my idiom be mistaken for dramatic dogmatism. Urgent themes do not admit of wholly academic discussion. Such inquiries are never merely professional and relaxed but rather sincere and urgent. Academic controversy is itself often translatable into practical forms, especially in the case of Islam. While Western commentators and publicists reject Islam as a false religion with a uniquely dangerous political potential, Muslim apologists defend it root and branch. I steer between Muslim activists' relentlessly polemical, abusively critical, zealously defensive perspectives on all alien convictions, on the one hand, and those of liberal Muslims, on the other, who write primarily to appease and please Anglo-American audiences and are therefore elated by Western praise and depressed by Western rejection.

V

I characterize Islam by identifying its five metaphysical pillars and its rejection of two other dimensions. The faith is grounded in an original *protology*: a doctrine of first things, including creation and nature, partly resembling the pre-historical materials in *Genesis*. A supplementary Islamic *anthropology* is embedded in the scripture. This pair constitutes an unverifiable metaphysical scheme which underlies a universal religious outlook with concealed moral, legal, political and imperial consequences. Third, a distinctive *eschatology* supplies sanctions to enforce the Quran's legal charter while also motivating believers to be privately virtuous. A *sui generis* Quranic *prophetology*, radically different from anything found in rival monotheisms, establishes a descriptive and normative *ontology* with combined ethical and political implications. Countless prophets have guided us in our daily moral conduct and encouraged us to struggle to establish a prosperous and just order on earth. Muhammad's enduring success as prophet and statesman ensures the stability of the building he constructed with these five pillars.

Islam has no *theology* and no *soteriology*. For theology, it substitutes law and ethics: we are given only to understand the moral and legal will of God, not to speculate about his nature. We are permitted to know what we need to know, not to know everything we wish to know. This simple arrangement offers salvation without a messiah; it requires no abstruse theology or saviour, only a prophet to warn us about the consequences of faith and rejection as we live out our probationary period on earth.

In Part I, we examine Islam as universal prophetic faith supported by revealed literary foundations. Chapter 1 portrays Islam as a prophetic faith in which confessing Muhammad as God's apostle gives anyone and everyone immediate access to membership of a universal community. Our account of Islam, a faith founded in the full light of history, seeks to sharpen and correct a vague and astigmatic view of its founder's political and sexual lives. In Chapter 2 we explore the Quran, the book which frames Muhammad's prophetic calling and makes Islam a literary faith. We summarize the teachings of this incalculably influential book, a manifesto for every Islamic utopia.

In Chapter 3, we probe Islam as religious globalization project engineered by Muhammad when he aimed to finalize religion as such. As the earliest historical attempt to take a perspective on the totality of previous faiths, Islam is a meta-religion which seeks to restore the world's original faith dating to Noah if not Adam. Muhammad finalizes sacred history in the seventh century; he supplies the missing brick whose placement completes the edifice and hence God's favour on humankind. We identify enduring tensions with earlier peoples of scripture, Jews and Christians, who resist Islamic claims to finality, concretely expressed in the early twin birth of a comprehensive legal charter supported by an empire. Islamic rulers relegated Jews and Christians to their corner as privileged communities of errant monotheists. In its phase of post-imperial decline, this view of fellow monotheists needs re-assessment.

A religion which claims to comprehensively direct human affairs cannot avoid entanglement, possibly conflict, with the modern political sector consisting of plural faiths in the framework of a separation of politics from religion. The theoretical and theological explorations of Part I secrete pragmatic, political and practical implications which are identified and assessed in the rest of the book.

VI

As we shall see in Part II, Islam is a secular, not a religious religion. Muhammad's temperament was neither ascetic nor inclined to tragedy. Therefore he succeeded religiously while enjoying life with a zest thought to be incompatible with faith. His behaviour with women alone, let alone his political adventures, disqualifies him in the eyes of his Christian critics. The Quran engages with the totality of life and the things of this world, a prerequisite of any politically active management of experience. This secular facet of Islam explains its sincerely but compulsively political, legal and imperial impulses.

Muhammad and his successors intended to conquer the world for Islam. In Chapter 4, we examine the twin birth of faith and empire which enabled Muslims to create a multi-cultural religious empire rather than, as in the case of Christianity, inherit a pagan empire and spiritualize it. Chapter 4 opens this inquiry into Islam's ineradicably political nature by examining the Prophet Muhammad's embrace of the power wing. The discussion aims to assess Muhammad's role as a statesman who established a nomo-theocratic utopia in Medina. We examine Christian and liberal critiques of Muhammad's Medinan ministry where the quest for power was incorporated into his faith's founding axioms. The Prophet's behaviour supplied the source of imitative piety for rulers in later centuries. Is this a problematic feature of original Islam? If so, for whom is it so? These questions are addressed conscientiously and not reduced to simplistic concerns for those Western policymakers who seek to uphold their economic and ideological interests in Muslim lands, often under the pretext of philanthropy and world peace.

In Chapter 5, we explore questions about the correct scope of modern Islam as private faith or public ideology. The theoretical and academic discussion in Chapters 4 and 5 contains a complete conceptual framework for an Islamic liberation theology. Although we briefly discuss the ideal Islamic state here, relevant pragmatic and policy implications are deferred until Chapters 6, 7, 10 and 11.

As we see in Chapter 6, Islam's political and legal aspects make it a secular faith concerned with, to use Christian terminology, the things of Caesar. These aspects continue to define Muhammadan Islam's aboriginal nature as the most pragmatic of world faiths. The law codes of the mediaeval past are no longer wholly applicable in any place but the canons are still in principle revered. In this chapter we assess classical Islamic jurisprudence as a preface to ways of moving beyond the inherited imperial tradition marked by its reliance on a holy law (Shariah) of total comprehensiveness operating in an empire constantly on the verge of expansion. This hardly reflects the situation of modern Muslims seeking to survive, with self-respect, in the face of an all-encompassing Western hegemony in which one goes west wherever one goes.

It has been about a century since the demise of the last Islamic dynasty, the Ottomans, history's longest lasting dynasty. In Chapter 7, we examine Islamic imperial history during the millennium when Muslim rule competed with Christian imperialism. After Muhammad, the world was divided between the circumcized and the baptized. At the dawn of the third Christian millennium, we note a resurgence of the rivalry between the crescent and the cross. We explore the justifications for religious imperialism and contrast it with the secular outreach for power and economic aggrandizement. Traditionally, Muslims developed only a theology of power since Muhammad left an undiluted legacy of success. We assess the classical caliphate and its limitations as we move away from empires based on religion into a world of nation-states administered on secular principles. This discussion sets the context for a final probing of modern issues of power and democracy in Chapters 10 and 11.

Let me mention why we examine these three facets in this order. Although Islam was potentially a political faith in Mecca, it found political expression only after Muhammad migrated to Medina. It emerged as a legal faith when he enacted laws and administered an empowered community there. The Quran's imperial insinuation is contemporary with Muhammad's apostolate but became explicit after his death. He ruled only the Arab peninsula but instructed his successors to create a univeral empire of faith.

VII

In Part III we consider how modern Islam seeks to maintain its rational appeal, ethical authority and spiritual grace in a sceptical, increasingly vulgar, shallow, cynical and materialistic age. Apolitical facets of the faith derivable from the Quran – the pedagogic, rational, ethical, aesthetic, mystical and philosophical – will become increasingly prominent as Muslim minorities world-wide interpret their Islam as a private faith devoid of the sanction of public power. How will modern Muslims living as minorities in Western democratic states, educating their children in the secular state sector, reconcile the duties of their faith with the obligations of citizenship? Can the liberal state accommodate Muslim needs – especially the urgent need for protection against gratuitous artistic provocation, itself a pre-requisite of attaining communal religious dignity?

In Part III, we move into the seductive world created by Western colonial modernity. This world, alien and alienating for Muslims, was born out of the Christian capitulation to secularism over the past three centuries when Western nations accommodated a politically truncated Christianity solely on secular terms. Though located in the ideologically defined west, the burden of the new secular condition falls on all peoples everywhere. Islam is emerging, in its post-imperial phase, as a religion in the Western sense of a private source of solace in the face of public adversity, as simply one more offer of self-help and spiritual hygiene. We examine the rational appeal and the ethical foundations of the sanity it provides for Muslims in a global, westernized and advanced capitalist world which values little except material possessions and the proximate promises of pleasure. Three chapters examine Islam as a privately practised rational and ethical faith.

In the Epilogue, we sketch Islam's political profile and predict its future evolu-tion. We examine the faith's contours in international politics, especially in conflict with some Western powers. How should Muslims deal with their current predicament of powerlessness? Is an apolitical Islam an acceptable compromise with the modern world or a betrayal of the faith's true nature? We note the emergence of democracies in Muslim nations. Is there a distinctively Western, particularly European, Islam about to be born? For non-Muslims, Islam's transition from public to private faith is wholly a matter of policy. For Muslims, it involves an agonizing, consequential and conscientious decision about the essence of their faith.

VIII

Although we analyze Islam's political-ideological facet, from various angles in the entire book, we focus on it in Part II. In its origins, theology and history, Islam is a proudly political religion. I therefore select 'political' to qualify it in the title of this book. For Muslims, juxtaposing 'political' and 'Islam' is redundant. The message of Muhammad was liberation: Muslims are militantly opposed to injustice and oppression.

The qualifier 'universal' could have been used instead since Islam is the last universal faith. As I argue in Part II, the religious universality of Muhammad's mission justifies its political and legal charter for society and not vice versa: Islam's moral ambition to unite the human family in God's name is more funda-mental than its quest for political power. However, calling Islam a universal faith does not highlight the link between its religious aspiration to universal appeal and its unique choice of coercively imperial option for achieving it. Other faiths, especially Christianity and Buddhism, cannot be classed as political faiths: even though their adherents aspire to universal missionary outreach, their *originating* dogmas are strenuously apolitical and pacifist. Therefore, despite the known risk of entrenching existing stereotypes, I feel obliged to underline Islam's political facet. I do not wish to mislead the reader about the dominant stress in this faith and in this book.

In Part I, the emphasis is theological and abstractly religious rather than political and practical though in Islam one cannot sharpen these distinctions. We explore the bases of Islam as a metaphysical and theological enterprise sustaining distinctively Islamic political embodiment. In terms of private versus public facets, Islam is characterized in Part II as public (secular, temporal, political, ideological, legal and imperial). In Part III, it emerges as private (rational, ethical, philosophical, mystical, ritual and artistic). As the Epilogue shows, however, a communal or political sense nestles beneath the surface of Islam even as privately practised, as opposed to publicly enforced, faith.

IX

The role of Muhammad is a major theme of this book. Although Islam is incorrectly called Muhammadanism, the centrality of Muhammad is fundamental to Islam despite the fact that he is, unlike the Buddha or Christ, not deified by his followers. We acknowledge his correct status by examining his life in the very first chapter. Throughout Part I, he is the bearer of an Arabic scripture with universal imperial import. Armed with his book, he becomes the architect of the first Islamic utopia. By exploring his standing as 'seal of the prophets', we note his contribution to the universality and finality of Islam.

In Part II, we examine Muhammad's credentials. These were, from the start, queried by Christians and Jews who are now joined in their doubts by liberals, agnostics and atheists. Those who reject all religion often single out Muhammad's faith as the world's most resolute enemy of art and free thought, an accusation made openly often enough but also sometimes hidden behind the veil of literature and media documentary. It is hard to imagine a more despised founder of a world faith. Muhammad's alleged delinquencies, through the faith he brought, outrage many Westerners and indeed adherents of other faiths who share 'bloody borders' with Islamic peoples. Muslims must acknowledge Muhammad's role as legislator-prophet entertaining an imperial vision of a single society under God. He was a general who led armies and, like Alexander before him, planned the conquest of the known world.

In Part III, Muhammad's role decreases as Islam becomes a private faith in which the Quran, Muhammad's legacy, becomes a guide to Islam as rational religion. He remains an ethical exemplar for believers but few can successfully imitate him in the modern world. His role is attenuated and residual although he continues to attract mystical devotion. In the Epilogue, we note the revival of Muhammad's role as just warrior-prophet, a role that appeals to Islamic activists enraged by determined, unprovoked and continuing Western aggression against Muslims. The Western animus against *Islam* is, as I argued during the Rushdie affair, mainly against *Muhammad's* posthumous influence. His role as statesman has a limited appeal but everyone must pretend to wear his insignia. As varied advocacies claim him, he emerges both as an activist who intended to conquer the world for Islam and also as a mystic who accidentally made the mistake of founding a world empire.

No-one can understand modern Islam without inquiring into the nature, extent and future of Muhammad's grip on Islam, from beyond the grave. Physically dead but ideologically alive, his influence will subside in some areas and increase in others. Is he dispensable to any facet of the faith? No Muslim reformer can intelligently address the problem of change and modernity without engaging with this anxiety. Rival Muslim apologists instinctively link to the mind and policy of their Prophet opposed modern advocacies, sifted through the Quranic filter: democracy or dictatorship, pacifism or militant radicalism, enslavement of women or their emancipation. They look for prophetic and scriptural touchstones of ancient pedigree while reading the newspaper headlines crowded with modern anguish. Nothing contemporary has any intrinsic integrity. It must gains its imprimatur, its seal of worth, from the revered past. The scripture can be convincingly read as supporting the classical tendency to condemn religious innovation as heretical while endorsing as normative the path trodden by Muhammad and the first and only perfect community.

X

This book contains a complete introduction to Islam, the life of its founder and the contents of its scripture. It also threads a schematic history of Islam into the entire book. Tracing this history will help the reader to see how Islam evolved from an empowered, legal and imperial faith into a private ethical and rational faith with residual legal and political features. Islam has a continuous history despite the trauma of colonialism which culminated in the significant wound inflicted on its body politic with the abolition of the caliphate in Turkey in March 1924 (1342 AH).

I divide Islamic history into two phases. The first and most politically empowered phase originates in 622 CE, the first year of Islam as political religion. It terminates in 1571. We explore Islam's version of ancient sacred history which culminated in the mission of 'Prophet-General' Muhammad whose legacy subsequently flowered into Islam's early (caliphal) and classical history. This phase contains the vicissitudes of the rightly guided patriarchal caliphates and the classical dynasties of the Umayyads and Abbasids. In 1258, the Mongols devastated Baghdad, the seat of the Abbasid dynasty. The next three centuries witnessed continuous disintegration culminating in the emergence of competing dynasties against the larger context supplied by Christianity's competitive colonial ambitions. Although the Ottomans conquered Constantinople in 1453, it was the expulsion of Muslims from Spain a mere 40 years later in 1492 that would finally decide the trajectory of modern Islam. Less than a century after the expulsion of Muslims from Western Europe, Ottoman maritime supremacy began to flounder. In 1517, an Ottoman fleet was decisively defeated at Lepanto at the entrance of the Gulf of Corinth. Islamic history from 622 to 1571 (through the Spanish trauma of 1492) supplies the hinterland to Chapters 1 and 3 of Part I and to all of Part II.

Observations about the second phase from 1571 to the present – the continuing encounter with the potent and colonizing Christian and secular liberal west – are dispersed into the final chapter of Part III and carried forward into the Epilogue. This second phase is subdivided into four periods, beginning with one of continuous decline from 1571 to 1798 when Napoleon's army occupied Egypt. The second period lasts from 1798 to 1924 when the last Ottoman sultan-caliph, Abd Al-Majid II, was deposed. The rise of anti-colonial Islamic radicalism dates to the aftermath of the abolition of the caliphate, a time of abject humiliation felt by Muslims worldwide. The third period lasts from 1924 to 1978 when a decisive reversal demonstrated the resilience of political Islam: Iran's Islamic Revolution.

Events since 1978, to turn to the final period of the second phase, are harder to assess since no period of history is as remote as the recent past. We note Muslim retreat and decay mixed with defensive militancy and resurgence. Islam shall remain a deeply held if private faith in Islamic heartlands and in the secularized democratic West. Indeed it thrives even in a secular world order. Interspersed with Islam's ad hoc participation and influence in international politics since 1978, we witness its periodic public revival inside Muslim societies. Provided that we are moving into a fairer world order in the near future, we shall witness, in the next 25 years, the complete domestication of political Islam as it subsides into a faith located mainly in the private sector.

Part I
The prophetic consummation

Islam as original and final religion

1   A prophetic religion

I

In the *kalimah* (word, statement) of faith, Muslims profess: 'I testify that there is no god except the only God and I testify that Muhammad is the messenger of the only God' (*Lā ilāhā illā Allāh, Muḥammadun Rasūl Allāh*). Both parts of this double testimony are in the present tense: believers affirm God's continuing uniqueness and endorse Muhammad as his current envoy. The creed does not claim that Muhammad is God's only messenger since Islam reveres all earlier prophets. Surprisingly, however, it does not claim his finality even though the prophetic office is abolished after the Arabian Messenger's universal mission (see Q:4:79; 21:107; 34:28).[1] Belief in Muhammad as the seal of prophets (Q:33:40) entails that he brought ultimate truth and confirmed it (Q:37:37). This controversial claim about the finality of prophethood defines and distinguishes Islam. It terminates divine revelation and implies that the prophetic office is the optimal method for the divine tuition of humanity. The latter view is contested by Christians who proclaim that God teaches and reaches deeper inside the human condition via initiatives of grace, atonement and incarnation.

Islam is fully defined at its source. The Quran contains, without prefatory attestation clauses, the separate halves of the declaration of self-surrender (*islām*). *Lā ilāhā illā Allāh* and its many variations thread the scripture (Q:2:255; 3; 2; 16:2; 18:110; 20:14; 27:26; 28:70; 59:22–3; 112:1) while *Muḥammadun Rasūl Allāh* is found only once (Q:48:29; see variations at Q:3:144; 33:40, 63:1). The Prophet's tradition states the total testimony of faith; it is best attested in the (authentic) collection of Muslim Bin Al-Hajjaj Al-Nisapuri (d. 875), a meticulous scholar from Khurasan in north-eastern Iran. Such attention to correct doctrine surprises us since Islam, a faith fortified with a law code, is correctly thought to uphold orthopraxy (behavioural conformity) rather than orthodoxy (empowered doctrinal conformity that rectifies and excludes alternative views). Correct belief, however, must support right conduct which by itself cannot redeem incorrect beliefs about God. Practical duties of faith are implicit in this profession although a clear majority of Muslims are no longer observant believers. Exceptions include mosque personnel: in setting an example for others, their publicly observed duty includes fulfilment of exacting ritual obligations.

Islam is a prophetic monotheism whose concise credo conceals lengthy practical, ritual, moral and legal entailments. Declaring a few succinct Arabic syllables places one within Islam's social ambit. Their denial, wholly or partly, suffices to make one an apostate. By affirming or denying the creed, one gives testimony – a legal act with legal consequences. This verbal testimony (*al-shahādah*, the evident; see Q:59:22) is Islam's first pillar. If uttered in the presence of two witnesses, it constitutes necessary and sufficient testimony: anyone who denies this sentence is not a Muslim even in name while anyone who affirms it, no matter how they subsequently behave, is indisputably a Muslim. Some individuals may profess the creed with the intention of deceiving the fellowship of believers (see Q:63:1–3) or as mere lip-service (see Q:49:14–17). These acts of perjury and insincerity respectively are reliably detectable only by God. Following Muhammad's practice as community leader, a person's confession of faith must be respected, within reasonable limits, even in times of war, even if they are a suspected hypocrite.

Another surprise: the essential creed does not mention the Quran which is self-praised as glorious (Q:50:1) but not as holy, the latter adjective being reserved for one of God's beautiful names (Q:59:23). 'Holy' was incorrectly adopted by analogy with the Holy Bible. Consider: 'There is no God but the only God and the Quran is the word of God' (*Lā ilāhā illā Allāh wa al-Qur'ānu kalimatu Allāh*). Muhammad is, after all, only a mortal messenger and, after receiving the whole Quran, perhaps dispensable. As his body awaited burial, some shocked believers, especially Umar Ibn Al-Khattab, refused to believe that the Prophet was only mortal. Abu Bakr Al-Siddiq then quoted the Quran (Q:3:144) to highlight the contrast between Muhammad's mortality and God's eternity. The quoted verse, revealed after Muhammad's brush with death at the battle of Uhud, affirmed the absolute mortality of even the final prophet.

Far from Muhammad being dispensable, the opposite is the case.[2] For modern Muslims, the confession is unnecessarily lengthy since the Muhammadan portion suffices for contemporary witness. The first Muslims were required to dethrone false deities before replacing them with the true God; the explicit disavowal of idols was originally the neophyte's only duty (apart from daily prayer). 'Muhammad is the messenger of the one God' improves on the ancient creed by highlighting the Prophet's centrality. It stresses the claim that sets Muslims apart from Jews and Christians, two groups united by their rejection of the Prophet Muhammad. Since Muslims see themselves as worshipping the same God as their fellow monotheists, Muslims are possessive only towards their Prophet. Hence the Persian adage: 'Do take liberties (lit. 'be crazy') with God – but be careful with Muhammad!'[3]

With Allah in first place, Muhammad and the Quran occupy joint second place. The Prophet said that his only legacy was the Quran and his example (*sunnah*), suggesting an organic and continuing bond between himself and God's word and hence God himself. The Quran framed Muhammad's prophetic career: he was called to be a prophet only after he was armed with the promise of the book. But Muhammad did not bring the Quran as we might now buy and carry a copy of it from a bookstore but rather brought it to the world in the sense of clarifying and implementing its message. His wife Ayesha called him 'the Quran incarnate' – or, more accurately, the Quran *inlibrate*.

Muslims revere Muhammad as the perfect man and the Quran forbids them to judge him (Q:33:36, 57–58). To concede embarrassment at his military exploits, for instance, which is popular with progressive Muslims in the West, is religiously inappropriate. Far from being judged by believers, Muhammad's conduct supplies the standard by which believers are judged. They are commanded to obey God's Apostle, to lower their voices in his presence (Q:49:2) and to bless him by joining in the divine and angelic blessings sent down on him (Q:33:56). Hence we have 'Peace be upon him' (PBUH) after every mention of his name, a pious requirement which awkwardly burdens devout publications.

How central is the Apostle Muhammad to Islam? The Quran describes him as a mercy to the worlds, a messenger who brings good news for all humanity, confirms and completes the message of previous prophets, a moral exemplar, a man of immense character, a lamp spreading light, and a recipient of superior grace (Q:2:119; 4:113; 17:87; 21:107; 33:21, 40, 45–6, 56; 34:28; 36:3–4; 68:4). His proper name occurs only four times and possibly a fifth as 'Ahmad' (Q:61:6).[4] This is misleading. Muhammad's role as prophet consumes him just as the secular roles of mother, waiter and teacher often drown out competing self-images. God often addresses him, in the vocative case, but only as 'Prophet!' (Q:9:73; 33:28, 45, 50; 65:1; 66:1).[5]

I want to record two further dimensions of this debate about the status of Muhammad. First, Islam is a prophetic religion with a mature prophetology which intervenes between a uniquely Quranic protology (doctrine of creation and first things) and a distinctively Quranic eschatology (doctrine of last things and judgment). Although its popular eschatology includes some confused messianic elements, Islam is not a messianic dispensation marked by external rescue and deliverance. We discern the political consequences of this stance in the penultimate section of this chapter. The finality of Muhammad's prophethood implies that God's tuition of humanity can find no resources beyond prophetic counsel, a view disputed by Christians as unduly limiting God's power. Christians protest '*Allāhu akbar*' (Greater is God) as they deplore the limited reach of holy law into sinners' lives. They propose a son coming in grace as a successor to a messenger coming armed with yet another law. Christianity is grounded in the Incarnation: engagement with human beings whose God volunteers to become more than the Lord who sends messengers armed with messages. Instead, he graciously comes in person – to suffer unjustly and willingly to redeem us wisely and eternally (see the parables in Matthew 21:33–22:14). We explore this antagonism between law and grace at the end of Chapter 6.

Second, as a postscript to the finality and indispensability of Muhammad to historical and empirical Islam, we note that Christian and Jewish creeds contain no reference to a prophet. Moses is redundant in Judaism; all that counts is the Torah at Sinai. The contemporary orthodox catechism for children instructs: *kabbalat ol malkhūt shamay'īm* (acceptance of the yoke of heaven) and *torah tzivah lanū mosheh* (the Torah was given to us by Moses). Note how the sentence begins with the Torah and relegates Moses to the end. This is no coincidence since the Torah is the sole saving agency even though Moses was Israel's greatest prophet. There is no Mosaic equivalent to *imitatio Christi* or *imitatio Muhammadi*. As for Christianity, Jesus is no mere prophet. Second Temple Judaism recognized Malachi as the last prophet. Prophecy died and apocalypse was born. The messianic yearnings of some ancient Jews found a terminus in Jesus the Christ. For those who chose to remain Jews, the Messiah (*meshiākh*), a human figure, from the House of David, will one day return to restore Israel to its former imperial glory. In a theological dispute of this kind, as in a traffic accident with many witnesses, everyone could be right – and everyone could be wrong. Jews themselves, exasperated by ambiguity and the anxiety of return, introduce a humorous note. A night-watchman, Jews muse, awaits the Messiah's arrival in case he arrives in the thick of night and feels himself to be unwelcome. The night-watchman has, Jewish humourists add, a low-paying but steady job.[6]

II

Muhammad's classical literary biography (*sīrah*, lit. journey) resembles a vita, the record of the life of Roman notables, especially successful generals. Muhammad lost only one battle (Uhud). Muslims would find alien the biography (*bios*) of the Greek hero whose life gravitated towards tragedy owing to some congenital defect of character or conspiracy of circumstance. Despite being orphaned in childhood, Muhammad was not cut out for tragedy. Unlike the New Testament writers who invented the *euangellion* genre to capture the good news of the salvation hero, *sīrah* was not a novel genre for the Arabs. Pagan poets and story-tellers sang of the exploits of the heroic warrior. None of these classical genres resemble our modern sense of analytical psycho-biography where we speculate about motivations for behaviour and the influence of subconscious forces during the formative periods of childhood and adolescence.[7] Jesus appears at 30, out of nowhere. Muhammad fascinated his contemporaries only after he became a prophet: his life begins at 40.

Ernest Renan (1823–92), a meticulous historian of Christian origins and no friend of Islam, conceded that Muhammad was the only significant religious leader who was born and lived in the full light of history. Muslims, we must add, indulged in little or no metaphysical speculation about their prophet's nature, making Islam a mundane religion. With most so-called founders of faith, we have only the fact of the legend: mythology replaces history. General Muhammad, however, mattered to his contemporaries – and they took note of him. He is known to Heraclius and to the Armenian chronicler Sebeos.[8] Think here of the Jewish case where hostile scepticism surrounds only recent Jewish history: even anti-Semites do not dismiss the Babylonian exile as a hoax. In the Islamic case, the reverse is true. Much mythology is written in the West about early Islam even though we know far more about the origins of Islam than about the origins of any other ancient faith. Liminal and marginal events in Muhammad's life are often elevated to central status while well documented ones, especially those located wholly in Islamic sources, are dismissed as legendary.[9]

For Muslims, Imam Al-Anbiyā' Sayyidnā Muhammad Ibn Abdullah (53 BH–11 AH; c. 570 CE to 632 CE) is 'The Leader of the Prophets, Our Master Muhammad, son of Abdullah'. He was born in Mecca in 53 BH and died in Medina in 10 AH. He belonged to the Hashim clan of the Quraysh, Mecca's main tribe, subdivided into a dozen autonomous clans. I am paraphrasing *Sīrah Rasūl Allāh* (*Life of God's Apostle*) by Abu Abd Allah Ibn Is'hāq, Muhammad's earliest biographer, born in Medina in 85 AH, died in Baghdad in 151 AH. Adi Ibn Hisham (who died in Baghdad in 218 AH/834 CE) revised this classical biography; his redaction of Ibn Is'haq is equally popular. Along with the Quran, these two works yield a common and indispensable framework for reconstructing Muhammad's life. All three were piled on my desk while I wrote the following succinct biography.[10] Scholars rightly value such primary sources for their chronological and linguistic proximity to the events they describe or document. Primary sources are not, however, free of bias. Ibn Hashim was no more a detached historian-biographer than were the New Testament writers of the Gospels and the Acts of the Apostles.

Muhammad's father, Abdullah Ibn Abdul Muttalib and his mother, Amina Bint Wahb Al-Zuhriyya, were pagans. Muhammad's father died before his birth. Early traditionists were embarrassed by the problem of making Muhammad a Muslim at birth before he became Islam's prophet at age 40. The boy Muhammad was therefore 'born already circumcised' (*wūlida makhtūnan*), presumably by angels. Tradition also claims that two angels took the prepubescent Muhammad away from his friends while they played together, wrestled him to the ground, removed his heart, cleansed it and replaced it – a spiritual open-heart surgery offered as a literal explanation of a Quranic verse (see Q:94:1). In his teenage years, God protected the boy from the temptations of alcohol and fornication. He may have participated in the obscure *fijār* (sinful) wars during which he probably learnt archery and horse-riding without necessarily participating in battle.

Muhammad began to receive revelations in 610 CE. In Chapter 2, we shall explore the inaugural revelation (Q:96:1–5) and its placement in the canon. Muhammad was shocked by the call, reluctant to become a warner. Public preaching begins with a divine order (Q:74:2) which is possibly the second revelation. The Qurayshi pagans threaten him and his few disciples; only clan-affiliation protects them from being killed. For the first three years, Muhammad preached only to family and intimate friends. A pagan woman named Umm Jamil wrote a poem mocking Muhammad by calling him *Mudhammam* (reprobate or blameworthy). It is a pun on 'Muḥammad' which meant the opposite (laudable). She wrote the poem after hearing that she and her husband, renamed by the Quran as Abu Lahab, 'father of [Hell's] flame', were condemned in a revelation. A verse refers to her as 'the wood-carrier' (Q:111:4) since she carried thorns and cast them in the Apostle's path. God sentences her to carry the wood as fuel for Hell-fire, a detail that sparked her fury. Armed with a stone pestle, she went to look for Muhammad so that she could smash his mouth to prevent further inspired utterances.[11]

Muhammad was born in a pagan culture which entertained nebulous memories of previous Arabian prophets. It was difficult enough for prophets to attain recognition even if their mission was among monotheists. A prophet should expect to have no honour in his native land of pagans. Mild early persecution gave way to torture of the poorer converts and slaves. In 614 CE, Muhammad ordered the first (the so-called 'lesser') emigration. The chosen haven was Christian Abyssinia (Ethiopia). Some Muslims went there during the years of intense persecution before the discovery of the Medinan refuge. Some non-Muslims have speculated, without evidence, that Muhammad sent certain potential political rivals to Ethiopia, effectively silencing all opposition. Uthman, later the third caliph, was among the Ethiopian exiles. In any event, a year later, the persecuted Islamic movement was strengthened on home ground when Umar converted to the new faith after hearing the opening verses of the Quran's twentieth chapter.

Nothing else was encouraging. A commercial boycott of Muslims for three years was followed by 'the year of sadness' in 619 CE when Muhammad lost his wife Khadijah and then his uncle Abu Talib,[12] his two most influential supporters. A missionary journey to nearby Ta'if was also fruitless.

After a dozen years of failure and frustration, the tide began to turn when some pilgrims came to Mecca and accidentally heard Muhammad preaching there. They came from a northerly city called Yathrib, mentioned by name uniquely at Q:33:13 and later renamed *al-madīnat al-nabiyy*, city of the Prophet. Having heard talkative rabbis in their native city, they recognized Muhammad to be a prophet and accepted him as an Arab Apostle of monotheism. At the next pilgrimage, a larger group came to ratify a pact. They vowed allegiance to the new prophet and offered asylum to him and his followers. Along with one preacher, they returned to Medina, thus enabling Islam to be preached there before the Prophet's arrival. The next year, at the pilgrimage season, 70 Muslim men from Yathrib signed a second pact. Islam was destined to become a community apart: a political monotheism had been conceived.

Dispossessed, isolated and stigmatized, the Muslims sold their possessions and secretly prepared to leave Mecca for Medina. The Quraysh feared that a man who is dangerous in their midst would be doubly dangerous when he departed. They could evade the clan caveat about bloodshed if a killer were chosen from each clan, thus making all Quraysh guilty of shedding Muhammad's blood. The Quran mentions a similar plot to assassinate the prophet Salih by evading the caveat of clan affiliation and protection (see Q:27:45–50). Muhammad's struggle mirrored prophetic travail in earlier times. Every Muslim left Mecca except Muhammad, Abu Bakr and Ali. Ali slept in Muhammad's bed on the night of departure, ready to die for Muhmmad. Abu Bakr and Muhammad were pursued in the desert and, as the Quran testifies, narrowly escaped assassination (Q:9:40).

A Jew spotted Muhammad as he arrived in Medina and called others, mockingly adding that the expected one had arrived. After the exodus (*hijrah*) to Medina, Muhammad became more than a prophet, teacher and social reformer. He became a law-giver, judge, prayer leader, army commander and head of state who received embassies. His personal roles as father, husband and friend are found on both sides of the *hijrah* divide.

Muhammad created the *ummah*, the fraternity of faith, by urging Medinan believers, renamed *Al-Anṣār* (The Patrons), to assist the impoverished Meccan *Al-Muhājirūn*

(The Emigrants) in settling in the new city. A solemn treaty with the Jews of Medina gave them equal rights in exchange for support of the infant Islamic community. The rabbis, however, expected a Prophet–Messiah who would grant them rule over Gentiles, not make Jews brothers of the despised Gentiles through a shared faith. They realized, presciently, that Muhammad was a dangerous man whose presence and principles would upset the communal balance in their city.

For two years in Medina, Muslims refused to fight, even in self-defence (see Q:2:216; 47:20). In 2 AH (624 CE), tension between Muhammad and the Meccans finally erupted as dispossessed Muslims, angry at their expulsion from Mecca, mocked and broke pagan tribal taboos. Ramadan is not one of the four months in which warfare is prohibited; the battle of Badr was joined on 17th Ramadan. Some commentators claim angelic support (based on Q:8:9, 12) and others cite a Meccan revelation (Q:54:43–5) predicting success. Muhammad shouted a verse (Q:54:45) at the end of the rout in which many senior Qurayshi leaders were killed. It was the first triumph for Islam as political faith.

During the confrontation at Uhud, a hill outside Medina, 50 Muslim archers were posted to protect the outer flank, a vulnerable pass, against the enemy cavalry. In the heat of battle, they disobeyed Muhammad's orders which had been given emphatically before the battle commenced (Q:3:121). Attracted by the prospect of booty which the archers feared others might obtain before them, they deserted their strategic position (Q:3:152). The Qurayshi cavalry, led by General Khalid Ibn Al-Walid, a disbeliever at the time, massacred the unprotected believers and even injured Muhammad (Q:3:144). Still nursing his wounds, he set out the next day with a remnant of his army to deter a full frontal attack on Medina. Although the Meccan chieftain Abu Sufyan returned disheartened to Mecca, the Muslims lost a battle which would otherwise have been an even greater success than Badr.

After this reverse at Uhud, the Medinan Jews were openly hostile to the Muslims. The Jews of the Banu Nadir tribe were therefore isolated, besieged in their walled towns, subdued and forced to emigrate. Some Arab Muslims hypocritically sympathized with them and encouraged them to resist Muhammad. But, at the last hour, with Muhammad poised to succeed, the Arab hypocrites betrayed the Jews (see Q:59:2–17).

In 5 AH, Muhammad participated in the Battle of the Trench (Persian, *khandaq*), also called the war of The Confederates (*al-aḥzab*), the title of the Quran's 33rd chapter. About 10,000 urban Meccans joined the desert tribes to crush Islam. After learning that the Quran was silent on military strategy, Salman, Muhammad's Persian companion, suggested a trench be dug around Medina. Muhammad joined in the effort. He used his hands, shared the scanty food and starved with the others. Like Alexander and Julius Caesar before him, Muhammad was never above his men. By sharing directly in their sufferings and triumphs, he boosted their morale. Alexander had once refused to drink water in the desert if there was not enough for his men.[13] These three successful generals led their men in battle and all three were nearly killed.

The Qurayshi mainspring was the cavalry. Unable to pass the trench, they showered the besieged city with arrows. In the midst of the siege, as the Muslims awaited the Meccan assault, the Banu Qurayzah, a Jewish tribe thus far loyal to the Muslims, went over to the enemy. As if to compensate for this loss, a bitter wind blew from the sea for three days and nights, an event cited as a divine favour (Q:33:9). The wind extinguished camp fires and overturned cooking pots and tents alike, demoralizing the miserable Meccans camped far from home. As the Meccans withdrew, the Banu Qurayzah took to their towers of refuge. They surrendered after a month. Their men were executed and the women and children were sold as slaves (Q:33:26–7).

After this battle, Muhammad led a pre-emptive strike against the hostile Arab tribe of the Banu Mustaliq. This expedition alarmed Medina's hypocritical faction, led by Abdullah ibn Ubayy. He marvelled at Muhammad's access to information, his resolute determination and his growing power. The hypocrites began to attack Muhammad's private life, mixing politics with sex. Returning from this expedition, while looking for a lost necklace, Muhammad's wife Ayesha was left behind and brought to the camp by a handsome soldier who happened to have separated from the company. The rumour was serious enough to warrant divine attention. According to reliable tradition, since God himself exonerated Ayesha (Q:24:11–20), she thanked only God rather than her husband and God.

Muhammad had a vision in 6 AH in which he entered Mecca, as a pilgrim, unopposed (see Q:48:27). Though only a dream, it alarmed the Meccan leaders. As one pagan cried out, 'By the gods, when Muhammad says he will do something, he does it!' In real life, 1400 Muslim men, attired in pilgrim garb, approached the Meccan sanctuary. The Qurayshi cavalry, frustrated by the last confrontation outside the walls of Medina, now donned their leopard skins, the pagan badge of valour, and swore to prevent Muhammad and his men from entering and 'defiling' the sanctuary.

Via a detour, Muhammad arrived at Hudaybiya, near the holy valley of Mecca. He opened negotiations with the Qurayshi custodians of the sanctuary (see Q:48:13, 24). The two parties agreed that there were to be no hostilities and a 10 year truce followed. The Prophet was to return to Medina without entering the shrine. He would, however, be allowed to perform the pilgrimage the following year, along with his comrades, when the Quraysh would evacuate the holy city for three days. For the duration of the truce, any tribe or clan could freely join either the Quraysh or Islam. It was additionally provided that deserters from the Quraysh to the Muslims had to be returned to the Quraysh; deserters from the Muslims could stay with the Quraysh. This caveat seemed prejudicial enough for Umar to oppose the treaty as insulting. The Prophet's wife, Umm Salama, calmed the Muslims, sensing that it was a victory in disguise. Although the conditions seemed humiliating, the Quran, during Muhammad's return journey, confirmed it as a signal victory (*fath*; Q:48:1).

As a result of Hudaybiya, for the first time, the two enemies met and argued, away from the battlefield. In intellectual warfare, Islam won more hearts than in all the previous years of conflict. The confused pagan narrative could hardly compete with the Quran's eloquent and coherent revelations. In 7 AH, the Prophet's dream was fulfilled. The Meccan pagans kept their word, withdrew into the surrounding heights and probably watched in awe as Muhammad entered Mecca to perform the new Islamized rituals of the Hajj, a ceremony now centred on an only God who tolerated no rivals.

On his return to Medina, Muhammad sensed that the Jewish threat remained. He led a campaign against the Jews of Khaybar, the Jewish stronghold in northern Arabia (Q:33:26–7).[14] The forts were individually reduced. Muhammad then exacted tribute (*al-jizya*; Q:9:29), payable to Islamic leaders, in exchange for protection of earlier monotheists by the new Islamic community. In obedience to the Prophet's death-bed command forbidding the co-existence of two faiths in Arabia, Umar expelled Jews from the Arabian peninsula but, after 638 CE, settled them among fellow Jews in newly conquered lands in Iraq and Palestine. (Umar was the first ruler to resettle Jews in Jerusalem since their expulsion by the Romans in 70 CE.) At Khaybar, a Jewish woman prepared poisoned meat which killed one of the Prophet's companions and which might have caused the illness that eventually caused Muhammad's death. She confessed her action but defended it: Muhammad had humiliated her people. The Prophet forgave her.

By 8 AH, the Meccans realized that Muhammad had outwitted them. Just as an athlete steps back only to jump higher, similarly, in the treaty of Hudaybiya, the Prophet foresaw the capitulation of his enemies. After two years, the Meccans broke this treaty by attacking a tribe allied to the Muslims. They massacred them inside the Meccan sanctuary where bloodshed was forbidden from ancient times. The Prophet, now freed from his treaty obligations, intended to attack Mecca. The city, however, surrendered and he declared a general amnesty. Personal enemies were pardoned and many became fervent Muslims. Only ideological enemies, especially poets who had lampooned the Quran, were taken to task. Muhammad ordered Ibn Salma to execute the Jewish poet-ideologue Ka'b Ibn Ashraf. This assassination of a poet was, for all its ruthlessness, a sincere if extreme form of literary criticism.

The Prophet quoted the Quran twice. He used Joseph's forgiving words to his cruel but eventually repentant brothers: 'No blame on you this day' (Q:12:92).[15] While smashing the clay idols, he thundered: 'We hurl truth against falsehood and it smashes its head and falsehood vanishes' (Q:21:18). There were barely a dozen casualties in this revolution, history's only bloodless revolution. One has only to look at the conduct of ancient leaders to note the contrast. To name only one, Alexander, uncritically eulogized as 'the great', murdered foreigners for pleasure.[16]

In 8 AH, Muhammad sent 3,000 men to Mutah in Syria when he heard that the Byzantines, Rome's inheritors in the Eastern Mediterranean, were planning to annihilate Islam. The Mutah campaign was unsuccessful but the Romans were impressed by the reckless bravery of the 3,000 men who joined battle with an army of 100,000 ferocious fighters including the elite Praetorian Guard. The three leaders appointed by Muhammad were martyred. General Khalid Bin Walid preserved a remnant by persuading the survivors to return to Medina. This was difficult since the Quran emphatically forbids retreat in battle, except as a strategy with the long-term intention of rejoining the battle (Q:8:15–16). The Muslims did re-engage the Byzantines only to break the backbone of their empire in 636 at Yarmuk, a mere four years after the Prophet's death.

In the meantime, despite the formal conquest of Mecca, Muhammad's troubles were not over. The pagan tribes from Mecca joined those of neighbouring Ta'if, the city that housed Allah's rival goddess *Al-Lāt* (lit. the only goddess), to avenge the loss of the Meccan shrine. Angered by the desecration of their idols, they retreated into a deep ravine in Hunayn (Q:9:25) and ambushed a Muslim army of 12,000 men and nearly routed it. Few Muslims remained firm-footed until the bloody end. But the eventual victory was total, the booty gargantuan since the pagan tribes had staked everything on this battle. Ta'if capitulated. Muhammad returned to Medina, to the delight of The Helpers (Ansar) who had feared that he might now return permanently to Mecca. The bond of faith was stronger than the love of one's native city.

In 9 AH, a report of another Byzantine army gathering in Syria reached the Prophet. He himself led the expedition to Tabuk in the extreme north of the peninsula but failed to locate the imperial enemy. The zealous and indefatigable but ageing Muhammad battled the heat of the day and the indifference of lukewarm and hypocritical followers. The defaulters who opted to stay at home are fiercely condemned (Q:9:42–110). This risky expedition to a distant land was the precursor of Islam's expansionist adventurism under the caliphs.

Although Mecca had been formally conquered, pockets of pagan resistance remained. Chapter 9 of the Quran has no declaration of divine mercy. It opens sharply, like an angry Pauline epistle such as Galatians, with a reprimand and declaration of hostility against polytheists. In the declaration of future Muslim immunity from polytheism (Q:9:1, 28), the pagans are forbidden to perform pilgrimage after that year. Only those idolaters who had ratified a treaty with the Muslims and subsequently had neither broken it nor supported Islam's enemies could enjoy protection until the end of the treaty's term. At its expiry, they were as other idolaters (Q:9:1–15). In effect, this proclamation irreversibly extirpated idolatry in Arabia although, as late as 1980, Khomeini issued his declaration of 'immunity from polytheism', insinuating that the Saudi guardians of the holy mosque are pagans (since they act as puppets of American and British 'godless' elites).

By the end of 9 AH, Muhammad had become the uncrowned Emperor of Arabia. He received embassies from the entire peninsula as tribal chiefs came to Medina to hear the Quran and swear allegiance to him. In the following year, he went to Mecca, 'the mother of villages' (Q:6:92), for the last time. From Mt. Arafat, he preached his farewell sermon of universal brotherhood of believers, asked the crowd to confirm that he had conveyed God's message, ordered those who heard him to preach to those absent (see Q:6:19), and affirmed piety as the sole criterion of human merit (see Q:49:13). Muhammad returned to Medina, fell ill and died on 8 June, 632. He is buried in Medina. Physically dead, his ideological life and greatness were about to begin. After 13 years in the Meccan crucible, there followed a decade of success, 'the fullest that has ever crowned one man's endeavour'.[17]

For all practical purposes, Muhammad died intestate although Muslims would say his bequest was the Quran and his noble example of life. On his death, his few remaining possessions were given away in charity. The Prophet had said that, unlike ordinary human beings, a prophet cannot be inherited by his relatives. Muhammad's daughter Fatima claimed her inheritance but Abu Bakr denied it to her by citing this tradition. There was only Muhammad, the prophet, not the man. To make matters worse, Muhammad died leaving no male heir although Fatima, through her marriage to Ali, gave him two grandsons, Hasan and Hussain. This situation was destined to aggravate later Shii-Sunni tensions.

Muhammad left behind virtually nothing by way of material goods since he spent generously in charity, especially during his last Ramadan. His ideological legacy is, however, vast and enduring. Although he forbade his followers to deify him, he is, even without deification, the most revered leader in world history. He led some 30 campaigns in person in his (successful) attempt to annihilate idolatry in Arabia. Morally, he replaced drunkenness with sobriety in a way never achieved in any society, before or since, by any faith. He raised woman from chattel to legal personality with moral dignity and a right to inheritance. By setting an enduring example for all believers who wish to live in faith, honesty and sincerity, he made universal faith-based brotherhood a practised principle of law and ethics and moved Arabs from polytheism and moral turpitude to the purest monotheism and rectitude. Muhammad the stateman transformed a fragmented tribal Arabia into a united people inspired by an ardent love of learning and scholarship. Within a mere two decades, he moved his compatriots from ethnic tribalism to history's only authentically religious empire. It is impossible to cite a comparable chronicle of success among religious or secular reformers.

III

Some Christians have condemned Muhammad as the victim of every temptation of the world, the flesh and the devil. He had women, used the sword and expected a sensual Paradise as his reward. By contrast with this lion of God, we have the innocent Lamb of God for whom mortal weakness was a form of divine strength. Orientalists attacked Muhammad's character by comparing it to Christ's but, revealingly, not to any prophets of the Hebrew scripture. Nor did they attack Islamic prophetology or theology – perceived by most Muslims as superior to an ethnocentric Judaism and an intolerant and incoherent Christian soteriology. Nor did Christian and Jewish critics condemn the ritual piety of a practised Islamic brotherhood which perhaps struck them as superior to the laxity and hypocrisy of much Christian observance. Many Western critics did, however, accuse Muhammad of religiously sanctioned self-aggrandizement: he appropriated the title 'seal of the prophets' (Q:33:40) and demanded total loyalty from his followers who must place him above their families (Q:33:6). Muslims see this as a divine gift and a divine imperative respectively rather than as the personal whims of a megalomaniac. Such disputes alert us to the permanently controversial reputation of Islam's Prophet.

Jewish and Christian critics see Muhammad as a false prophet who found the prophetic office all too comfortable since he was allowed to be violent and had access to as many women as he desired in both worlds. He was a debauched sensualist who used God's word to justify his secret desires. They grant that no-one, including Muhammad, suddenly became wicked all at once (*Nemo repente fuit turpissimus*). The Arab Prophet was gradually tempted and corrupted by lust, the sin closest to his nature as he aged. He had more than the quota of (full) wives allowed to others (Q:33:50). By the time of the revelation limiting it to four (Q:4:3), in the aftermath of Uhud in which many Muslims were killed, Muhammad already had five wives, in addition to the right to acquire any number of concubines taken in war.

In the seventh year after the Hijrah, the Quran itself prohibits him from taking any more wives 'even if their beauty (*ḥusn*) attracts you' (Q:33:52). The word *ḥusn* can also mean goodness; some puritanical commentators translate it as goodness, as if it were demeaning for a prophet to be attracted by female beauty. Muhammad boasted that 'among worldly things, perfume, prayer and women had been made dear'[18] to him. (Note the use of the theological past passive.) Muhammad would have regarded as degrading the view that women are snares and temptations rather than spiritual companions who can help one perfect one's obedience to God's laws and plans. However, feminist critics would allege, with some reason, that official Islam patronizes sexist inequities divinely sanctioned, corroborated by Muhammad's authoritative practice and perpetuated by a male religious elite.

The Quran's view of women and particularly of motherhood (Q:31:14; 46:15), as of sexuality more generally, is generous, liberal and charitable, in sharp contrast to the realities in much of the Muslim world. While the Hebrew Bible, on a Christian though not Jewish interpretation, convicts women as original sinners (Genesis 2:4–3:24), the Quran reverses the biblical narrative and blames Adam alone (Q:20:120–2) or both Adam and Eve equally (Q:2:35–6; 7:19–23). The Devil approaches them both (Q:7:20) or Adam alone (Q:20:120), never Eve alone. In the West, feminism was made possible only by the secular movement known as the Enlightenment which undermined the authority of the Bible and thus refuted the biblical patriarchy that had allowed Eve to be framed. The Quran has no misogynist pathology that must first be refuted before the seed of Islamic feminism can grow.

Muslims see monasticism as a religiously sanctioned form of sexism, degrading women as quintessentially evil, as hindrances to the life of virtue. Long before sex scandals in the Catholic Church, Muslims had already thought that the cloak of monastic celibacy concealed sexual perversion. The Quran explicitly rejects compulsory celibacy (Q:57:27). Muhammad taught that marriage enables and consummates the life of virtue. 'Marriage is half the faith', reads an authentic Prophetic saying. It is an act of nobility (*sharīfah*) which completes the faith by legalizing sexuality and enabling the righteous life. But Paul's opposed view of marriage as an earthly distraction from things godly has some echoes in the Quran, in the context of God's anger over calls for jihad going unheeded by married men with families (Q:8:28, 9:24, 63:9).

In Chapters 4 and 5, we examine Muhammad's alleged political delinquencies. Here we explore his attitude towards women, an attitude which, according to his Christian detractors, automatically disqualifies him from the elite spiritual life. I see Muhammad's treatment of his wives as an example of practical Quranic ethics. Since Muslims regard Muhammad as the model husband, his deportment yields moral and legal implications for contemporary reform and enhancement of women's rights. We now explore his marital life and briefly assess the character of his wives, strong and articulate women who influenced Muslim history. Both the first convert and the first martyr for Islam were women, facts that should check the glib assertion that Islam is a sexist faith by design. A Muslim social critic has even claimed that Islam is 'the only world religion founded by a businessman in commercial partnership with his wife'.[19]

Before his migration to Medina, at age 53, Muhammad had contracted two marriages. His first wife was the already twice-divorced Khadijah Bint Al-Khuwaylid to whom he remained monogamously married until her death left him widowed at 49. Khadijah became the first convert and sought Christian confirmation of Muhammad's calling. The Quran refers to her indirectly once in the context of a sudden and unique reference to Muhammad the destitute orphan whom God had enriched (Q:93:6–8). Is this an oblique reference to Khadijah's wealth? Khadijah and Muhammad had four daughters and two sons. The boys died in infancy, as did his only other son by the Coptic concubine Maryam. Hence the Quran's comment, 'Muhammad is not the father of any of your men' (Q:33:40), and the pagan taunt about childlessness (Q:108), a serious insult in a patriarchal culture which valued sons and often killed daughters at birth (Q:53:21–2; 43:16–19; 81:8–9). Two of the Prophet's daughters (by Khadijah) wedded two future caliphs: Ruqayyah married Uthman while Fatima was Ali's wife. Khadijah purchased the slave Zaid Bin Harithah at Muhammad's request and he freed him and adopted him as his son. Zaid will, as we see presently, appear in a scandal in the Prophet's life in Medina.

On the eve of migrating, Muhammad married the 55 year old Sawda Bint Zama who had been persecuted for the sake of the cause. At about this time, Muhammad also betrothed Aisha, his only virgin spouse. Aisha, the daughter of Abu Bakr, was only about eight when she was engaged although Muslims claim that the marriage was consummated in Medina some three years later. Non-Muslims allege that she was a child-bride and accuse Muhammad of the modern crime of paedophilia. None of Muhammad's contemporaries, not even his enemies, however, thought it remarkable.

To ensure privacy, Sawda and Aisha each had a mud hut (*ḥujurah*; pl. *ḥujurāt*; Q:49:4) adjoined to the Prophet's mosque in Medina. Sawda was threatened with divorce, possibly owing to Muhammad's lapse of desire. She offered to remain his wife while relinquishing her conjugal visit to Aisha in the nocturnal rotation. In an oblique reference to Sawda's dilemma, the Quran mentions marital desertion (*i'rād*) by a husband (Q:4:128) and commends mutual resolution of apparently irreconcilable differences. While men are permitted to have more than one wife on condition that they treat them equally (Q:4:3), the Quran adds, in the context of the Sawda affair, that it is beyond male competence to ensure equal treatment of multiple spouses (Q:4:129). This judgment about male incapacity for fairness between spouses, inspired by Muhammad's case, is a fortiori true of less scrupulous Muslim men.

Muhammad married two young war widows whose husbands fell as martyrs at Badr: Hafsa Bint Umar in 3 AH (625 CE) and Zaynab Bint Khuzayma a year later. Zaynab's husband was from the Al-Muttalib tribe for whom Muhammad was responsible in clan affiliation. Zaynab, famous for her charitable work, was affectionately called 'the mother of the poor'. Hafsa was, like her father Umar, headstrong and opinionated and often quarrelled with Muhammad. On one occasion, this lead to his month-long separation from his spouses during which he threatened to divorce all his dozen wives. The resulting political crisis, with tribal affiliations in the balance, was so acute that Umar threatened to kill his daughter. Hafsa was childless and often involved in marital intrigues and gossip involving her co-wives. The Quran hints at a scandal, nicknamed 'the honey scandal', but does not condescend to name the two wives whom it criticizes (Q:66:1–4). It is odd to find this domestic trivia in a book of eternal principles. To be fair, however, the same chapter of the Quran, perhaps for didactic contrast, refers to two (out of four) women judged perfect in the Muslim tradition: Mary and an unnamed consort of the Pharaoh, a woman who converted to Mosaic monotheism (Q:66:11–12). Hafsa treasured the manuscript of the Quran, entrusted to her after the Prophet's death.

Muhammad married his sixth wife Umm Salama as soon as Zaynab died at 30, within a year of her marriage. Umm Salama, a war widow of the second major battle, Uhud, was from the influential Umayya clan. She was reluctant to accept Muhammad's proposal and cited marital jealousy in a polygynous union and later protested gender bias in the Quran (see Q:33:35, revealed in response to her reservations). She was an older woman of the type whom we would now call an empowered and articulate feminist. Muhammad supported her and cared for her two children from a previous union. As an early convert, she had been persecuted by the Meccans before being allowed to migrate to Medina. The situation of female converts worsened so much that by the eighth year after Hijrah, Muhammad had to modify the terms of an earlier treaty: a new provision would allow Medinan Muslims to retain female convert migrants (Q:60:10) who fled to Medina from pagan persecution in Mecca. The migrant women came to the Prophet and took 'the woman's oath of fealty', an expression denoting the absence of the requirement to fight (see Q:60:12 where the jihad requirement is omitted).

The most complex case is that of the second Zaynab (Bint Jahsh), the Prophet's seventh wife. Critics accuse Muhammad of changing the laws of incest in order to marry this attractive woman who happened to be the wife of his adopted son, Zaid Bin Harithah. The scandal is acknowledged in the Quran (Q:33:37). This marriage was literally arranged in heaven (Q:33:37) and tempted Muhammad's witty wife Aisha to confront him and add acidly that while Muhammad laboured hard to please God, the arrangement was clearly reciprocal since 'Your Lord is also quick to please *you*.'

After Muhammad's last battle against his Meccan opponents, he opened a new front to prevent the Banu Mustaliq tribe from raiding Medina. At this stage, Medinan dissidents and hypocrites attacked his personal life. Until then, it was not considered remarkable for a man to find women attractive or for a chief to acquire several wives. The Quran rebuts Muhammad's accusers in the Zaynab Bint Jahsh incident and in the scandal of Ayesha's necklace, mentioned earlier. Ayesha's case led to legislation against traducing virtuous but careless believing women (Q:24:11–23).

Muhammad married Juwairiya Bint Al-Harith, the daughter of the tribal chief of the Banu Al-Mustaliq after their capitulation. Women were considered property in war and belonged to the victor. Muhammad could have retained her as 'what your right hands possess' (Q:4:3), a euphemism meaning concubinage, but instead married her in an attempt to win over the tribe through a peace treaty. She became close to Ayesha who tutored her in piety.

The Prophet married his ninth wife when he conquered Mecca. Umm Habiba (Ramlah) was the daughter of Abu Sufyan, an inveterate enemy of Islam who converted late and many would say hypocritically. Ramlah converted in the early years, in defiance of her influential father. She took part in the 'lesser migration' mentioned earlier. Many Muslims, including Ramlah's husband, died in exile in Ethiopia, since it was hard to send news of current developments on the Meccan front.

Muhammad married two Jewish women. Safiyyah was a Jewish princess whose male relatives either died in battle or were executed during the Prophet's final confrontation with the Jews of Khaybar. Acquired as a slave (concubine), her forceful personality was not content until she could finally marry Muhammad. The co-wives and other believers were suspicious of this daughter of a Jewish enemy despite her conversion to Islam. Muhammad treated her as an equal and instructed her to remind her Muslim co-wives, in friendly rebuttals, of her excellent pedigree (Abraham, Isaac, and Moses). Rayhana Bint Zaid entered Muhammad's life as a war widow. She was taken prisoner after the massacre of Banu Qurayzah in 626 CE (4 AH). Rayhana's husband was executed along with the other males of his tribe. The charge was treason against Islam. Rayhana eventually converted to Islam and Muhammad married her.

Muhammad's 12th wife was Barra Bint Al-Harith, a widow in her early 50s, best known by her two accolades. Muhammad called her Maymuna (blessed) since she reminded him of his Meccan victory. The Muslim community affectionately called her 'mother of the slaves' since she was devoted to improving their condition through manumission. A formal expiation for many sins was liberation of a slave, whether believing or disbelieving (see Q:4:92; 58:3). Like Khadijah, she proposed to Muhammad.

The Quran prohibits anyone from marrying Muhammad's widows (Q:33:53) and discourages potential suitors who might be waiting for Muhammad to die (Q:33:32). Critics allege that this proves Muhammad's sexual insecurity. The Quran gives the Prophet's widows the title of 'the mothers of the believers' to further discourage their remarriage.[20]

Only two of the Prophet's marriages were contracted in Mecca when he was not a leader of a growing community. Three of them (Khadijah, Aisha, Zaynab Bint Al-Jahsh) were possibly affairs of the heart. Most were acts of compassion: he offered livelihood to war widows. The majority of the Prophet's marriages were politically motivated. He wanted to contract and cement tribal alliances. Marrying for reasons of state was common in the ancient world. The Carthaginian General Hannibal (247–183 BCE) married the Iberian princess Imilce to consolidate Carthaginian power through diplomatic liaisons with conquered or friendly native tribes. Philip, Alexander's father, fought his wars through marital alliances and diplomacy to lessen his enemies' resistance and to ensure their docility after military defeat. Alexander contracted two marriages, in Sogdia and Iran, tempering his martial audacity with marital diplomacy.[21]

IV

A prophet is a human conduit who enables divine revelation to arrive in the human world and thus tutor humanity. The Quran's prophetology supplies its sole instructional method since God sends prophetic warning but no saviours. While God's nature and intentions remain inaccessible, he constantly clarifies his will for us by inspiring a series of prophets, patient men of probity, appearing at regular intervals and among all humanity. The prophetic enterprise is a unilaterally divine initiative rooted in God's mercy. It responds to human immaturity in moral perception and motivation although the Quran concedes that human beings were divinely created with innate limitations (Q:4:28).

A *nabiyy* (prophet) is an envoy who brings news of the unseen world. In Islam, he is a warner of divine penalty and bearer of good news; typically his mission is verbal and limited and introduces no new law. A *nabiyy* has privileged access to God but does not necessarily predict (or prophesy) the future, although the two abilities may coalesce in one man. He warns his community and, with the sole exception of Jonah (Q:10:98), arouses their anger. Typically, a *nabiyy* is a messenger who warns of imminent divine chastisement but brings no novel law or scripture to confirm precedents. A *rasūl*, however, is an apostle-prophet, such as Moses or Muhammad, sent to warn with the aid of a law that is binding until God annuls it through another *rasūl*. Moses and Muhammad alone are described as both *nabiyy* and *rasūl* (Q:7:157; 19:51). The passive participle *mursal* (one sent; Q:13:43; *mursalūn*, pl. at Q:7:6; 36:13, 16) often replaces the active form *rasūl* (pl. *rusul*). The word *rasūl*, but not *nabiyy*, can also refer to an angel of revelation (such as Gabriel); such divine messengers are called ambassadors (*sufarā'*, pl. of *safīr*; Q:80:15), a word the Quran reserves for them.

Prophets are created mortal (Q:14:11; 17:93; 21:7–8; 41:6) and constrained by a fixed life-span (Q:21:8; 25:7). They possess bodies which need food for survival (Q:5:77; 21:8; 25:7, 20); prophets marry and raise families (Q:13:38; 25:7). These selfless men lived modestly and moderately, not seeking personal benefits or power over others (Q:23:24). They were mortal and fallible in worldly matters but, as God's spokesmen, they were infallible expert witnesses to divine truth. Their credibility is based on their goodness, honesty and wisdom, all divine gifts.

Islam places the credentials of revelation in a morally perfect human personality rather than in a divine incarnation or in abstract faith in human reason expressed in deductive logic and syllogisms. Prophets are heroic leaders who are elected for the privilege of conveying God's judgment: they are not men of ideas but rather of action. They convey a message, not a thesis or a dream: they are, thank God, neither professors nor poets. Prophets are patient and determined radicals who fight and often die for the promotion of justice and virtue, all in the name of the holy one (Q:6:34, 162).

Prophets would never preach idolatry or recommend worship of any being except God (Q:3:79–80), let alone promote themselves as gods (Q:3:79–80). The Arabs and other communities before them expected prophets to be either superhuman or superhumanly assisted (see Q:21:3; 36:15; 54:24). Sinners refused divine guidance since the messengers who brought it were not accompanied by angels testifying to the truth of their claims (Q:6:8–10; 15:7; 23:24; 25:7). The Quran stresses the absolute humanity and unqualified mortality of Muhammad and of his prophetic predecessors, notably Jesus and of his mother. It condemns bitheism (Q:16:51) and interrogates Jesus about whether he had ordered his followers to worship him and his mother 'in derogation of the only God'(Q:5:118). One coherent form of the Trinity (amounting to tri-theism) is also declared anathema (Q:5:75).

Prophets were not exempt from sin or error, let alone impeccably innocent. The Quran concedes that Moses, in his anger, killed a man (Q:28:15-6) but is silent about the alleged adultery of David and other flagrant sins allegedly committed by various figures in the Bible. Some Muslim scholars hold that the sins committed by prophets were virtually always minor ones and even here God himself caused them to sin in order to teach a lesson to ordinary mortals. Nor were prophets above prejudice. Think of Noah's outburst that a disbeliever will beget only a disbeliever. This is placed in his own enraged mouth, not approved by God (Q:71:26–7). Noah is also corrected by God on a more understandable mistake. He lost a son in the deluge and argued with God that he had promised to save his whole family. A disobedient son, God replied, is not one's son and therefore not one's family (Q:11:45–7).

Since prophets were divinely guided, they were not politically fallible. They are therefore not good role models for democratically elected leaders. One is bound to wonder, however, whether Moses would have got out of Egypt in time if he had had to arrange for committees to meet and make resolutions.

V

Prophets are always chosen by God (Q:3:179); it is never a man's personal decision (Q:22:75; 27:59; 74:52–3; in the same vein: 2 Peter 1:20–21). Compare the strange view of the Jewish exegete-halakhist Maimonides: prophecy emerges naturally in those who have perfected themselves intellectually, morally and spiritually. God may abort its emergence; if he does not, it is inevitable.[22]

God chooses only men (and angels) to convey his messages to humankind (Q:12:109; 35:1, 32). Some special women, especially Mary and Elizabeth, and Muhammad's spouses, received revelation (Q:3:35–6, 47; 33:30, 32–4). Unlike the Bible, however, the Quran is silent on female messengers and probably rejects such a notion because it would have been strategically absurd to send a female prophet to warn a patriarchal culture where even male prophets were invariably expelled or martyred. By contrast, in the Hebrew Bible, we read of Miriam, Aaron's daughter, who was a prophetess and leader (Exodus 15:20), the prophetess Huldah who triggered a religious revival (2 Kings 22:14; 2 Chronicles 34:22), not to mention Deborah, a prophet-judge who led an Israelite army (Judges 4 and 5). The New Testament mentions four prophetesses, all unmarried daughters of Philip the evangelist (Acts 21:8), although these women did not experience combat or the travail of missionary travel.

Muslim apologists claim that jihad and prophethood are exclusive to men just as child-bearing is to women – both in virtue of biology. Feminists would retort that anatomy disables men from becoming mothers while no biological constraint or limitation hinders women from becoming prophets, priests and warriors. This objection is only partly true. Physical strength does to some extent limit women's participation in active combat. Male prophethood is a strategy of effectiveness, not an absolute divine preference that essentially links men to prophethood, just as women's biological capacity to bear children does not grant them a monopoly on compassion for dependent life or indeed even a greater leaning towards emotional nuance.[23] Historically, some of the greatest poets have been men and this remains the case today.

VI

Surah 26 portrays all prophets as brothers of their doomed peoples, emphasizing the link of common language and blood (see Q:26:161; 27:45; 50:13). Prophets teach only their own community and preach in their people's vernacular (Q:14:4; 41:44). Uniquely, Muhammad's universal mission finalizes all revelation (Q:4:79, 170, 7:185; 34:28; 61:9). Pre-Muhammadan messengers had limited missions but the content of their message, a deliberately stereotyped monotheism, was universally true. While the scope of such monotheism was ethnically limited, its message was *ethically* universal. In the final evolution of religion, Muhammad brought a universal message with a universal scope. His mission closes the prophetic chapter in sacred history, a view that is less dogmatic than it appears: no successful global religious movement has arisen after historical Islam.

God's messengers belong to a brotherhood (Q:23:51–3); all prophets support fellow messengers and previous ones (Q:3:81; 33:7–8). This is the uniquely Islamic doctrine of the indivisibility of prophethood (Q:2:136; 4:150–2). Muslims must believe in all divinely inspired messengers, named and anonymous (Q:2:285; 40:71), fortified by a scripture and law or sent with only a threat of direct divine punishment. The Quran comments on the careers of only a handful of apostles adding that not all are even mentioned in the scripture (Q:4:164; 6:34; 40:78). The dogma of prophetic indivisibility does not entail the equality of all prophets (Q:2:253; 17:55). Although God has caused some messengers to excel above others, their ranking is not given, a strange hesitation in an explicitly supersessionist religion. At inter-faith conferences, irate Christians use the Quran to argue for Jesus' supremacy since he was a prophet from birth (Q:19:30) while Muhammad received revelation at age 40 (see Q:10:16; 46:15).

The Quran's list of prophets is indicative, not exhaustive: Noah, Abraham, Jacob, Joseph, Moses, Shu'ayb (the prophet of Midyan, possibly identical to Jethro, Moses' father-in-law), David, Solomon, Jonah (*Dhū Al-Nūn*), Jesus, and Zachariah. Many others, including Isaac and Ishmael, John (Yahya), Job, and Enoch (Idris) receive only honorary mention (*dhikr*; Q:19:2–15, 54–5, 56–7, 38:41, 48). The Quran also proclaims often the preaching of two Arabian prophets, Hud (Q:11:50–60 and Salih (Q:11:61–68). An unnamed figure, to whom Moses applies for esoteric learning, appears as a super-prophet who breaks divine laws (Q:18:60–82). A mysterious prophetic elite is dubbed 'the power-prophets' (Q:46:35).

Although its accounts superficially resemble the biblical narratives of central figures, the Quran's prophetology and its rationale are totally different. Prophetology is the second most important theme in the Quran (second only to God's praise). Jews and Christians locate their prophetology in their mature theology and only incidentally in their scriptures. Both the chronology and the purposes of Quranic prophetology diverge from the biblical tradition. Thus, for example, the Quran paints a different picture of the lives of biblical figures such as Jacob, Lot and David, and vindicates them against some outrageous biblical accusations. The Islamic scripture also classifies biblical figures, especially David and Solomon, indifferently as prophets and kings.

The Quran incorporates a pre-Islamic Arab prophetic line unknown to the Bible. The clue here is in the Arabic names of the messengers unknown to the Bible. While the theophoric significance of Hebrew names (such as Yōsēf, meaning, 'let it increase') is lost in Arabic transliteration (Yūsuf), the Quran's own names of some messengers are fascinating. For example, 'Ṣāliḥ' means righteous. 'Hūd' is the root for Jew (Yahūd) and literally means guided; his people are the 'Ād (lit. rebellious). 'Lūṭ', the Arabic for Lot, means subtly hidden.

Unlike the Quran, the Bible distinguishes different kinds of prophets: suffering servants of the word (Jeremiah and Hosea), literary poet-messengers (Isaiah, Micah and Amos) and false prophets such as Hananiah who opposed Jeremiah (see Jeremiah 28). The Quran has no such categories, further evidence that Arab and Quranic prophetologies developed independently of the biblical tradition. Presumably, the Quran would recognize Jesus, Moses, Abraham and Muhammad as 'literary prophets' armed with scriptures but they could not, of course, take any credit as authors.

The Quran also avoids the biblical category of 'counter-prophet'. The concept of a false messenger contradicts the Islamic scripture's axiomatic liaison between divine truth and human apostleship. The expression 'false prophet' never occurs even as the disbelievers' description of any prophet; the Quran is content to say 'they rejected him' (Q:91:14). This is doubly surprising since a rival Arab prophet,

Maslama Bin Habib from the enemy tribe of Banu Hanifah, wrote a letter to Muhammad offering to share with him the title of 'God's Messenger'. Muhammad called him Musaylimah, a derogatory diminutive of his name, and insulted him as 'Musaylimah, the little liar'. The Quran does not even condescend to mention this false prophet who was killed in a sanguine battle at Al-Aqraba in May 633 CE, a year after the Prophet's death. Only Muhammad's biographers mention the rivalry between the two men, a spiritual enmity somewhat reminiscent of the suppressed hostility between Jesus and John the Baptist (Luke 7:18–35).

VII

Islam is the prophetic religion which terminates prophethood. The minority instinct, represented by Shiites, is centred on infallible imams who inherit Muhammad's charisma. It is not supported by the Quran and indeed it christianizes Islam into a soteriological faith in which the imams replace a divine saviour. In Chapter 4, we examine tragedy in Shiite history but it suffices to record here that original Islam rejects any messianic and apocalyptic politics in favour of a temporal and prophetic politics inside history.

Sufism is another christianization of Islam which explains why most Western converts opt for it. It may sometimes result in a deviant piety which compromises Islam's credentials as an activist prophetic religion. To explain, Sufism addressed reason and the heart, in Pascal's dangerous dichotomy. The eye of the heart yields intuitive and holistic wisdom, not merely knowledge or information, as the mystic moves beyond mere research and knowledge into wisdom. Sufism claimed to be a perfect amalgam of reason, emotion, imagination, experience, disposition, intuition and instinctively spontaneous faith.

Sufism is not a form of religion that can be pondered and understood before being methodically taught in ways that are publicly verifiable. A prophetic religion is, by contrast, to be taught and transmitted. Its preservation depends on scholarly knowledge and methodical rational reflection. These provide bulwarks, though not guarantees, against superstition, obscurantism and irrationalism. An intellectual, rational and literary faith which retains its spiritual power is a corollary of the prophetic self-image to which Islam successfully aspires. Since religion is already too full of fantastic claims, the last thing we need is a religious reason for being superstitious. This explains orthodox and traditional Islam's hostility to Sufi mysticism which is often dismissed, with much reason, as irrational, antinomian, politically suspect and anti-prophetic.[24] Sufis subtly suggest that the Shariah is imperfect since it cares for the exterior letter of the law, not the interior spirit. Modern Sufism is effectively a depoliticization and christianization of Islam, especially of Islamic law.

Sufism was largely anti-intellectualist, patriarchal and feudal. It went beyond mere books and instead supported a cult of personality, a feature that could inspire autocratic government. Indeed, the sheikh, for all his talk of poverty, was often a feudal ruler, living off the wealth of his devotees. For all their talk of radical egalitarianism, there is no spiritual path (*ṭarīqah*) named for an eminent woman mystic.

The political menace of cult of personality is looked at in Chapter 7. Here we merely assert that prophetic religion is the best religious and educational background to egalitarian democracy. In the messianic outlook, including its Shiite and Sufi versions in heterodox Islam, all politics are deferred as people wait for an external rescue from present distress. Messianism, the route of grace, and hence of unmerited salvation, is anti-democratic. It typifies those estimates of the human condition where large groups become convinced a priori of their social powerlessness. Individuals see themselves as helpless, their situation hopeless; they think they are incapable of shaping their individual lives (hence messianic theology and an escapist eschatology) and their societies (hence abdication of political effort). Politics reduces to private charity and bumper-sticker radicalism: people advertize their moral superiority and righteous indignation but do nothing. They experience a vague apathetic anticipation and expectation of change and liberation while making no realistic effort or struggle in the present, the sole arena for action. In Islam as political monotheism, the individual becomes, within limits, the architect of his or her own destiny. The passive apoliticism that places the whole responsibility on a divine (or human) redeemer is demolished.

Take an ancient example here. Pauline Christianity was an apocalyptic eschatology proposing an immediate and radical solution to the problem of sin and injustice. In this theology of escape and external rescue, one solved all human problems by relocating the human race in hell and heaven. The Quranic solution was a present-oriented ethical eschatology mediated through a prophetic monotheism. God demands that we humans do something about an evil order before God himself intervenes to do something drastic. Muhammad, despite fearing an imminent day of reckoning, nonetheless built his heavenly city on earth.

The practice of democracy, like prophetic politics, empowers the individual. The passive apolitical posture that lays the whole onus on the divine redeemer, Messiah, Sufi sheikh, Shiite imam or the long-awaited Mahdi is demolished in favour of individual responsibility. Again, the conspiratorial politics that demoralizes people by painting scenarios of the machinations of omnipotent malefactors is rejected by prophetic religion which instead emboldens individuals to step forward and lay hold of their own destiny. Messianic politics is simply lost sheep in search of a shepherd, hardly an apt comparison for the noble art of active political management. The picture of lost sheep in search of a shepherd is a politically demeaning image since man was made in the noble image of a creative and powerful God, not a weak sheep famed for conformity. In Islam, this was always the case. In Christianity, it was only with the Reformation that the gap between elite and popular piety was finally abolished, enabling a more democratic and empowered religious outlook.

As a postscript here, let me add that predestination, the sixth article of faith, runs contrary to a prophetic political faith that is individually empowering and socially liberating. For Muslims who are innocent of intellectual refinement – and that is legion – the doctrine of predestination collapses into a life-denying fatalism. In this book, I argue for a simplification of the creed, of the hierarchically arranged classical sources of law, and indeed of the articles of faith. The sixth article has no clear Quranic sanction. Some cite as evidence 'God made you and your works' (Q:37:96), a verse uttered by Abraham. There is firmer prophetic support but it is undermined by one of Muhammad's more famous comments: 'Tie the camel and trust in God'. This was said in response to the nomad who asked whether he should untie his camel and hope to God that it will not stray. Human effort precedes and supplements trust in God's actions on our behalf.

VIII

God is an educator who, like a strict but effective parent, knows both the blow and the word of authority and command. Discipline can bring intemperate demands and chastisement but a foolish lenience is equally wrong. God supplements prophetic tuition with his grace. The view that God will show mercy to us sinners should become neither a refuge for irresponsibility nor a pretext for neglecting his law. Disbelief in the divine mercy is cardinal infidelity, for, as the Prophet taught, 'God is more merciful towards his servants than is a mother towards her child.' But once the season of education is over, God wants the lesson learnt. Muhammad's master is compassionate yet vigilant as he watches over his servants from the watchtower (Q:89:14). The aim of revelation is not to impose, from the outside, unrecognizable duties, but rather to extract from within our nature an awareness of binding duties implicitly recognized. The scripture relentlessly calls its readers to think reverently, to bring their eyes close to the texture, opportunities and resources of their mortal life-span (Q:59:18–20).

The task of educating human beings would be a forlorn hope if the material with which a prophet works were unpromising. Scripture appeals to our higher nature which already acknowledges our duties and acknowledges all the more for failing to fulfil them. It is vital, if a religious ideal is to be viable, that it embodies, albeit in fairer form and more considered proportion, the very obligations which men and women are already to some degree able to meet. Effective ideals should mirror valid human hopes and potential rather than be an embarrassing reminder of the impossible.

The prophetic injunctions remain nonetheless new and demanding. Or else why must the divine spokesman cry in the wilderness or to the city's unheeding multitude? Sacred history is replete with rejection and conscious opposition to the moral ideals of our higher nature. The voice of the warning prophet does, however, eventually find its way into the consciences of those inclined to submission (Q:36:11). The devout are confident that the ideals which make us humane coincide with the ideals that our higher nature instinctively craves.

God is neither a tragedian nor a sentimentalist. The Quran displays a total understanding, without illusions, of human nature as it is. It firmly recommends the firm yoke of the law since we are are inertial in the pursuit of goodness while energetic in the pursuit of wanton pleasure. In quest of the vast estate of sexual desires, for example, human enthusiasm has never been dulled by the strict censures of religious law and morality. Indeed, the stricter the faith, the greater the sexual rebellion and anarchy it provoked. One has only to think of modern post-Christian Europe and of the hypocritically concealed sexuality in much of the Islamic world.

IX

The Quran rejects the Judaeo-Christian notion of sympathetic divine kinship: a God concerned for his people or for his faithful believers like a loving father for his children (Q:5:18). It repudiates the Christian doctrine of God as father. We see a vivid portrait of the good father in Jesus' parable of the prodigal son, unique to Luke's gospel, a tale that should perhaps be called the parable of the good father. In our more psychologically aware age, we know that fathers can be oppressors as well as kind saviours. It takes a whole lifetime to escape their doleful influence though Philip Larkin was using shock tactics when he wrote that your 'Mum and Dad – they fuck you up'. Nonetheless, as the lives of seminal figures such as Thomas More testify, fathers can determine a whole destiny.[25]

Paternity combined with divinity would have appealed to a patriarchal culture: the Arabs would have more readily accepted Muhammad as 'the son of Allah' than as his messenger. If Allah already had three daughters (Q:53:19–23), why not an only son? The Quran is compatible with an absolute divine kingship arrangement: a benevolent ruler treats his subjects like children who know only their wishes, not their best interests. God is the sovereign whose laws are promulgated and enacted by his spokesmen, the prophets, and their successors, the caliphs. Muslims do not demand *imitatio Dei* since what is required is obedience to God's will through obedience to his apostles rather than an imitation of God (see Q:4:59; 64, 69, 80–1; 24:51–2). Christians participate in God's own moral life by imitating Christ (Matthew 5:48) just as Jews observe and 'preserve' the Sabbath in order to share, by joyful association, in the divine holiness of the seventh day.

After the holocaust, Jews could be seen to struggle with God, no longer convinced that, as the original people of covenant, they still matter to him. The American Jewish thinker Peter Ochs observes that the utopian humanism of the European Enlightenment seduced many Jews away from their faith. But, he adds, a greater disaster lay hidden in the womb of history. During the holocaust, all the gods died as Jews also lost faith in humanity.[26] Through an incarnational Christology, Christians seek a human partnership with God. Muslims condemn this ambition as blasphemous mythology. *Et incarnatus est* is only fantasy. In the Quran's primarily legal relationship between creator and creature, tempered by mercy and love, God does not emotionally need humankind. Jews and Christians read this fact backwards into the character of Islam's God and dismiss him as cold and indifferent. Such a God could not be great. Muslims retort that such 'indifference' is not a denial of his greatness but rather its true quality. God's demands on us must override our conscience (Q:24:2) though we also know that, in his compassion, he would not make immoral or unreasonable demands.

A permanent stalemate persists between a prophetic monotheism which must arrest the divine engagement at the level of prophetic instruction and an incarnational theology which sees gracious possibilities beyond messengers bringing laws and divine punishment. Islam claims to fulfill, not transcend, the prophetic paradigm. Christianity fulfills the intentions of the law by transcending its letter while Islam claims to do the former without the latter.

To achieve an ecumene of prophetic monotheisms, post-Enlightenment Christianity must immediately disown rather than celebrate its secular legacies. Only then will it rediscover its monotheistic centre of gravity and reintegrate itself into the family of prophetic religions. Islam and Christianity, especially in its Catholic form, could form a coalition and thus forge a post-secular politics in which we counter the alienating processes whereby the poor become commodities and instruments in an usurious economic system that makes slaves of free humans through the pressures of mortgage and interest. The new paradigm unites formerly competing faiths to enable believers of different faiths to work together as they pursue the common economic and political good. They must show in practice a viable alternative to the liberal settlement which is essentially an indifferent inclusion of all and sundry so long as the economic hegemony of unfettered capitalism remains unchallenged.

This coalition of faiths would move us beyond an adversarial and agonistic 'democratic' politics that is contaminated by wealth in America and by inherited privilege in Europe. Only a new politics, informed by a reverent consciousness of our globalized world, can solve problems ranging from ecological collapse and pandemic health threats to economic upheaval and global political insecurity. The future, if there is to be one, must belong to the politics of prophetic faith.

2   A literary religion

Islam is a book-centred though not bookish religion. By ordering Muslims to go by the book (Q:6:155), the Quran makes Islam into a literary faith. Muhammad's oral inspirations were written in his life-time and codified as canonical scripture. These revelations supplied the fulcrum: Islamic ethics, law and spiritual authority have revolved around it ever since. The Quran is a normative scripture supplying the moral and legal foundations of the world's youngest universal faith, an axial text of a major language and its literature and a formative guide for a spiritual civilization stretching from Morocco to Indonesia and from southern China to sub-Saharan Africa.

Book centrality is found in Orthodox Judaism, focused on its Torah. Sikhism's scriptural compendium in Punjabi, the *Adi Granth* ('first volume'), is central enough to be named 'the seal of the gurus' although this stress on firm closure of canon may be due partly to Islamic influence. Sikhism, 'the sword of Hinduism', combines Hindu metaphysics and rituals with Muslim monotheism.[1] No known Jewish or Sikh societies have, however, been founded wholly according to the noble provisions of their scriptures. In Protestant Christianity, inspired by the Bible's dogmatic and moral sufficiency and expressed by the Lutheran Reformation slogan *sola scriptura*, scripture's authority is secondary: it witnesses the primary experienced authority of the revelation contained in Christ's sudden self-disclosure of divinity.

Unlike other scriptures in their ages of incidence, the Quran was in its own day influential political prose revealed to instruct Muhammad to establish a just republic. Its liturgical and legal provisions were immediately and scrupulously implemented by the Medinan community, the blueprint for the ideal political providence God intends for the entire human constituency. In the last decade of his life, the Prophet implemented in letter and spirit all Quranic edicts. As ruler, he stood, until his death, at the helm of his utopian republic. History knows of no other politically successful religion or ideology wholly founded by a man who framed his reformist career in terms of a guiding book. (Admittedly, a pamphlet can ignite a revolution while lengthy books can be useless.)

The Quran claims to reveal everything that believers must know and do in this life to earn entry into Paradise in the next. 'We have sent down to you [Muhammad] the book explaining everything – a guide, a mercy and good news for those who submit [to God]' (Q:16:89). The Quran mentions five of the six articles of faith (see Q:2:177). Faith (*īmān*) in God alone combined with acceptance of all inspired messengers, named or unnamed, belief in angels as God's supernatural messengers, acceptance of the integrity of all divine scriptures in their original form, these being named and definite, and a firm belief in the Day of Judgment fortified by the related conviction that 'the Resurrection after death be truth!'. The sixth article about fixed destiny is only ambivalent in the Quran. God created good and evil; fortune and misfortune are from him (Q:57:22–3; 113:2). Our actions are predestined in some sense yet we remain free to choose good over evil and will be held accountable for our choice (Q:4:78–9). Two further beliefs, both mentioned in the Quran, are held but not required as articles of faith: belief in the existence of elemental beings, the jinn, and in the efficacy of magic, a prohibited art (Q:2:100).

The Quran contains 'the clear message' (Q:29:18), 'guidance without doubt' (Q:2:2), self-evident in the light of reason, therefore unambiguous and universal. Islamic teachings are open, not esoteric; the Arabian Prophet's preaching is not addressed to a chosen or schismatic elite. Unlike Hinduism which forbade the lowest castes access to scripture, the Quran was, from the beginning, recited scripture that was heard by all. It was also unlike the Bible in Koine Greek or the version later locked in the obscurity of the Latin Vulgate which, ironically, never reached the *vulgus*. The Quran continues to live up to its name as 'the recital': the most liturgically rehearsed of scriptures, being constantly recited in its original language by over a billion people.

Muhammad answered Gabriel's third order to recite with 'I am no reciter'. Thus began the descent of instalments of Quranic recital, the reading of the illiterate prophet. The gravitas of this book is envisaged in a striking alternative inanimate reception: 'Had we sent down this *qur'ān* on a mountain, you would surely have seen it humbled, torn apart, out of the fear of God' (Q:59:21). The Quran often mentions mountains as symbols of stability but even mountains move when God descends on them as shown by the epiphany of Yahweh's descent on Mount Sinai (Q:7:143). The Quran descended on a man, albeit one with the spiritual stamina to bear the 'heavy word' (Q:73:5). This is one of the contexts in which Muhammad's character is commended in Meccan and Medinan revelations (Q:4:113; 17:87; 33:21, 46, 56; 68:4). Without Muhammad, we would have no Quran. But who is Muhammad minus the Quran? His life illuminates and clarifies the book while it motivates and guides his prophetic career. The Prophet's own words and actions interpret, explain and amplify the Quran's orders and doctrines.

II

Non-Muslims often tenaciously associate Islam with politically motivated violence even though, until its eclipse in the sixteenth century, it boasted a scholarly and intellectual tradition as distinguished as that of Judaism and Christianity. Arguably, no religion is more differently perceived by its adherents than by its detractors. Muslims, like Jews immersed in the Talmud, extol religious learning as a moral virtue. The Muslim transmission of Greek, Persian, Babylonian, Egyptian, and, to a lesser extent, Indian and Chinese wisdom and learning to the West crucially enabled the emergence of the modern West.

The inaugural revelation eulogizes the pen as the chosen instrument for the divine tuition of humanity (Q:96:4–5), an early hint that the recited Quran would become a book. One chapter is named 'The Pen' (*al-qalam*; Q:68:1) after an oath by the pen, a metonymy for the divine education of humanity through messengers armed with scriptures. The titles of two chapters (26 and 28) reflect literary themes: 'the poets' and 'the narrative'. The story of Joseph, related with much literary embellishment, is called 'the most beautiful narrative' (Q:12:3). While no chapter is titled 'The book' (*al-kitāb*) or 'People of the book' (*ahl al-kitāb*), words and phrases centred around the root *k/t/b* and its derivatives occur hundreds of times, reaching into an inexhaustible semantic field canvassed by Quranic philologists.[2]

The arts of the pen include calligraphy where much Muslim ambition was diverted given the ban on representational art. Calligraphy provides the visual parallel to the Quran's recitation: the eyes trace the gorgeous curves of calligraphy while the ear rejoices in the reciter's sensational display of the oral and aural beauty of its diction. The Prophet's legacy is entirely literary since all pictures and statues of the man are proscribed by Islamic law. Although some Sufis sing in praise of the Prophet and play musical instruments, in an annex attached to the mosque, the sole legitimate music of the mosque remains the melodious Quran. When it is recited live or conveyed by radio, going in and out of range, it reaches our ears intermittently, its potency and grave sublimity stoutly matching and challenging, if only temporarily, our profane drives.

There is no Quranic chapter entitled 'The sword' although the scripture refers often to fighting and killing. The arresting expression 'the revelation of iron' describes how this versatile metal supplies instruments of legitimate violence (Q:57:25). Notwithstanding countless references to bloodshed, Muslims regard *their* Islam as the religion of the pen, themselves a people of the book. The caliph's deputy, the vizier, carried the state emblem – an ink-pot, hardly a symbol of physical force. Oral reading or recital is the primal act of self-surrender. The first revealed word was 'Read!' (*iqra'*; Q:96:1), a masculine singular imperative addressed twice to Muhammad (Q:96:1, 3) and once to the sinner confronted with his open book of deeds (Q:17:14).

Muslims regard Islam as an intellectual faith with probative credentials supplied by the literary miracle of its Arabic scripture. The Quran's stress on literacy and on the absolute superiority of knowledge to ignorance (Q:35:20, 28, 39:9) is apparent in the ardent classical Muslim quest for knowledge, elevated to a primary religious duty. Sayings such as 'The ink of the scholar is holier than the blood of the martyr' and 'Seek knowledge even as far as China' are weak, and probably forged, but they contain intrinsically good admonitions compatible with the Quran's spirit. The Prophet's own thirst for knowledge is shown in his impatience to receive the revelation. He is told three times to be patient in receiving God's word (Q:19:64; 20:114; 75:16–19). The first reference is to his request for more frequent visits from Gabriel.

The founders of legal schools were, as we see in Chapter 6, considered imams in the sense of pillars of knowledge (*al-qawā'id al-'ilm*). The jurist Malik, renowned for his love of learning, said: 'When a man is ascetic (*zahid*) and fears God, God puts wisdom in his speech'. Again, 'Knowledge is in hunger' is an Arabic proverb possibly derived from a saying of the Prophet. Some scholars sold household goods to finance travel to further their knowledge of Muhammad's traditions. Again, Abu Hanifa, another jurist, was aloof from state authorities and lived modestly, preferring poverty and simplicity to state prestige and post. A recurring motif in Islamic hagiography is the scholar who eventually receives an offer of employment from the caliph himself only to decline it in order to maintain his piety and intellectual integrity.

III

Non-Muslims often condemn Islam as a faith of the sword brandished, not the word preached. It was a threatening presence on European frontiers for one millennium: from the Saracen to 'the terror of the Turban'd Turk' (Ottomans) as late as the nineteenth century. Europeans fantasized about the Saracen's black moustache shaped like a sword across his face. The word is, according to Christian scholars, a corruption of the Latin *Sarra a geniti* (emptied of Sarah) since Arabs were seen as the children of the Egyptian maidservant Hagar. Muslims surrounded Europe from the south (Spain, France, Portugal, Italy) and later, with the Ottoman conquests, from the East (Constantinople, Hungary, the Balkans, Greece and Vienna). Apart from subduing formerly Christian Mediterranean Africa, Muslim armies colonized the Iberian peninsula.

While dwelling in the smallest of the continents, Europeans have subjugated the adherents of every faith and race worldwide. By contrast, no non-European peoples, apart from the Arabs and Turks, have conquered parts of Europe. No scripture, apart from the Quran, openly challenges and rejects Christian dogmas. Western animus against Islam is not baseless. While civilizations cannot atone wholesale for past errors, Muslims have not even verbally apologized to Christians who lost the riches of Byzantium and the treasures of the North African church from Egypt to Morocco to imperial Islam. Regarding its Jewish populations, while Muslims practised a lenient ascendancy far removed from the focused brutality of Europeans in their treatment of Jews, virtually all Muslims, including educated ones, now indulge a shamefully casual anti-Semitism made increasingly inveterate by the challenge of an invincible Zionist Israel. Having conceded the Western right to apology for some relatively remote historical events, I must add that, in my opinion, the Christian west, in the past 500 years, abetted now by modern Jewry and secularized Westerners, has taken more than sufficient revenge for Islam's former occupation of parts of Europe and the holy land.

Politically motivated violence defines Islam in media coverage. Just as America remains a byword for crime, a national disgrace, so Muhammad's faith is tainted with the scourge of anarchic violence, seen by Westerners as part of an endless battle against decent and democratic (a codeword for Western) values. Muslims view things differently: they see themselves as the only ones challenging, albeit unsuccessfully, the West's worldwide cultural hegemony. The last great non-Muslim non-Westerner to effectively criticize the West was Mahatma Ghandi, a man who deserves his appellation of the great soul.[3]

While ancient linguistic borrowings from Arabic range healthily from 'arsenal' to 'algebra' and 'alcohol',[4] many of the words now being naturalized into European languages have violent connotations: fatwa and jihad are obvious examples. Unfortunately some Muslims abet this violent image. In many a *madrasah* (Islamic boarding school), the Urdu primer teaches the alphabet thus: *Jeem* (*J*) is for Jihad, <u>kh</u> for *khoon* (blood), *k* for Kalashnikov, and *tay* (t) for *tōp* (cannon).

In Western libraries, books on Islam are often classed under 'Terrorism' or more tolerantly under 'Politics'. Modern Islam has an image, as shallow as a mirror, reflecting more on the viewer than on the object. Books with titles such as *The Dagger of Islam, Sacred Rage*, and *The Holy Killers of Islam*, going back to the 1970s, invite such a classification as do more recent documentaries entitled *The Sword of Islam* and *The Fire of Islam*. This would be acceptable if we also had books and documentaries entitled 'The Sword of Joshua' or 'David's Slingshot: Target Goliath' or 'The Holy Killers of Christ' or 'The Buddha's Samurai'. But such sensationalism is reserved for Islam, the violent idiom ubiquitously associated with it: words such as 'bomb', 'terror', 'rage', 'dagger', 'sword', even 'spear' (anachronistic as it is), spice the title and trigger reactions that range from withdrawal and fear to anger and contempt from readers secure in the Western constituency, owing to geographical setting, ideological orientation and religious prejudice.[5] Neutrally defined terms of reference must precede dialogue; only a non-propagandist nomenclature can frame and thus conceptually enable healthy dialogue, a process that requires some parity in power. Words conceal power relationships and enable and eliminate options. One has only to call a Muslim 'terrorist' and 'militant' and it becomes justified to kill him along with his family even if he was only resisting Western occupation of his homeland.

IV

Judaism and Christianity are literary faiths grounded in revered scriptural canons. The Quran pays tribute to Jews and Christians by calling them 'people of the book' but also accuses them of sectarian parochialism (Q:2:89–91), of forging sacred literature (Q:2:79), wilfully altering divine writ (Q:2:75), maliciously concealing true scripture (Q:2:174), misreading or neglecting passages (especially those allegedly prophesying Muhammad's advent: Q:7:157, 61:6), and forgetting their scripture's potentially universal applicability and range (Q:2:75; 5:13). The Quran, as the last testament, offers to clarify and resolve such inter-faith controversies (Q:2:213; 27:76).

Are Christians and Jews 'people of the book'? The Quran, self-described as a heavenly prototype whose portions include the essentials of other heavenly books, claims to be the only complete and finalized revelation (Q:3:3–4; 119). Jews and Christians inherit 'a portion of the book' (Q:3:23). Since Jews and Christians do not make any revealed book the centre of their faith, the Quranic description is idealized and normative. Although Jews possess the Torah, in its presumed original Hebrew, allegedly containing some, if not all, of the words of the revelation sent to Moses, they usually prefer the Talmud for intensive study. In the Quran, 'the book' refers to revelation, not a humanly assembled compendium of dialectically opposed rabbinic rulings compiled over centuries. Christians cannot be a people of the book since their book, based on uncertain and fragmentary extant traditions canonized centuries later, is already in translation and thus lacks the *ipsissima vox Jesu* (the voice of Jesus) conveying divine speech. Islam demands this rigorous criterion for the transmission of prophetic messages. The Quran implies that the gospel (*al-injīl*), a word occurring only in the singular (pl. *anājil*) and with the definite article (Q:5:46–7), was given to Jesus just as the Quran was sent down on Muhammad. The Quran once uses *ahl al-injīl* (people of the gospel; Q:5:47) where *al-injīl* refers to some prototypical gospel.

Already self-described as revelation, the Quran was not canonized but rather codified some two decades after the Prophet's death. The Islamic scripture comes to us as a unified scripture, revealed over roughly two decades, addressed to a man fully known to his contemporaries and to subsequent history, a man who lived in two cities in the same country. It was written only in the language of the recipient and of the first audience, a living language that is still widely spoken. The period between its oral revelation and memorization and its final authoritative compilation is two decades. This contrasts sharply with the Bible: a religious anthology, the heterogeneous work of many hands, in several genres, in a trio of languages, in varied geographical locales, stretching over millennia.

The entire Quran had been recorded in writing by the time of Muhammad's fatal illness. Our oldest complete manuscript (or autograph to use New Testament critical terminology) probably dates to the very late seventh century of the Christian era. The vocalized, decorated, and phonetically written Quranic text, resembling the cantillated Masoretic text of the parts of the Hebrew Bible used by Ashkenazi Jews, dates to the mid-ninth century. Like the original Hebrew Bible, the Quran was written in shorthand as an *aide-memoire*. It evolved from an originally defective (unvocalized) script to a plenary text. Apart from a few variant readings that do not materially affect the sense, the text is invariant, defined and fixed. To edit the received Quranic text for any reason, including the wish to remove possible corruptions and errors in copying, was always seen as a wholly unthinkable liberty. The text has retained perfect purity; a unique version has enjoyed universal currency during the entire history of Islam, notwithstanding sectarian disputes about other matters. This privileged and enviable position of the history of its canon has one harmful consequence: Muslims are suspicious of literary diversity, an attitude with the political consequence that all authority is seen to reside rightly only in one canonical book given to one man.

V

Westerners find the Quran a closed book, its opaquely poetic passages meaningless, its prose too burdened by legalese and crude divine threats. Jewish and Christian critics see haphazard transitions and mismanaged narratives but nowhere the dis-cipline of relevance. Muslims extol the Quran's '*Arabiyyah* as God's language. It is among the world's least appreciated masterpieces. As scripture that has never subsided into mere literature, it presents countless literary obscurities which no translation, no matter how idiomatic, can entirely remove. As with all daring poetry, the Quran uses words and phrases with other than their conventionally correct or grammatically appropriate meanings. With its many neologisms and idiosyncratic usages, the scripture takes liberties with the Arabic language. Some obscurities lie in its poetic and elliptical form. Thus, for instance, even sustained accounts of Moses' life and mission and the tale of Joseph, the single longest continuous narrative, contain dialogue exchanges with little or no narrative as background or explanation.

Other obscurities delight only that elite readership conversant with Arabic and Persian poetry. Thus, for example, the complements of the Quran's oaths are sometimes omitted (Q:38:1; 50:1; 89:104); the sentence looks incomplete. In this rhetorical device of swallowing the sequel (*hadhf al-jawāb*), the reader is forced to reflect on the meaning and purport of the (initial) verses containing the oath. Again, the concluding clause is suspended to create rhetorical suspense (see Q:24:10, 20, 21 but cf. v.14). The economy of classical languages such as Arabic and Latin is most evident in violent contexts, where all languages become compressed once concision, directness and economy coalesce. The Quran has a compressed intensity in poetic and prosaic passages: translations are twice as long as the original while commentaries are vast. Thematically, the scripture telescopes all sacred history; Muhammad's enraptured soul must contain vast stretches of time. For some Western readers, such concision makes for incomprehensibility while the compensating rhetorical charms remain a bar to understanding the literal sense.

Moreover, most Western readers complain that the book's ideas are hyperboli-cally expressed and contain much mythologized history, including conflicting accounts of biblical events culturally dear to Jews and Christians nurtured on alternative sacred histories. For this readership, the Quran is at best an ill-informed paraphrase and an incompetent plagiarism of the Bible. More broadly, many non-Muslims do not find the Quranic message appealing. Its sensual paradise does not tempt them because it reflects simple desert tastes, as the American Catholic poet Robert Lowell complained. He was especially suspicious of Islam since 'Muhammad got religion in the dangerous years', during a mid-life crisis. Like some communists, perhaps Lowell thought that one must never trust a man above age 40.[6]

To Jews and Christians, the Quran remains a total enigma. The book is not domestically motivated by belief in a climax to an antique tradition of apocalyptic and messianic expectation. Muhammad as prophet, armed with his Quran, arises out of a historical vacancy. Even though Muslims claim to be insiders with respect to Judaism and Christianity, the Quran's claims do not flow from a prophetic continuum provided by existing monotheistic scripture. At the end of the chapter, Jewish and Christian scholars would not fail in their professional duty if they had the humility to admit that they cannot explain the Quran's origins.

The majesty of the Quranic recital, a powerful experience even for uncomprehending and disbelieving listeners, remains one of the world's least appreciated art forms. The voice control of accomplished Quran reciters is superior to religious singers such as Nusrat Fatheh Ali Khan or vocalists such as Luciano Pavarotti. When the Quran reciter changes pitch or inflects his voice to modulate the cadences, one can hear no stoppage or hiatus. The transition is linear and thus free of disruptions in tone. This emphasizes the duration of individual Quranic sounds: uniquely Arabian resonances and cadences conveying a challenging message. It is impossible to confuse it with other literary performances. The Quran's message remains, however, unlike the Bible in Western culture, venerated and obeyed, not isolated into mere admiration for its literary power or sentimental regard for its aesthetic merits.

VI

Muhammad's birth and upbringing in a culture steeped in literary pretensions introduce the polemical context of his mission and dictate the probative credentials of the book he brought. Arabic was not the language of philosophers and skilled dramatists; the reasons for its complexity and fecundity had to lie in its intrinsic genius. As a grammatically sophisticated language, pre-Quranic Arabic thrived despite being restricted to oral usage. Speech is a natural aptitude, a skill organically acquired by virtually all humans in all cultures; writing is a technological, therefore artificial, achievement and has emerged in some places at a certain stage of our history. Language, as speech, is the prerequisite of poetry, the supreme Arab art, extolled as noble and effective long before the advent of Muhammad.

In view of the Quran's prohibition of magic, poetry is gratefully saluted as 'the permitted magic' (*sihr halāl*). The Quran condemned *pagan* oratory as 'deceptively gilded speech' (Q:6:112). As tribal spokesmen, pagan poets were patricians who could prove influential opponents of prophets. Muhammad employed his personal orator, Thabit Ibn Qays Ibn Shammash, to counter the tribal boasting of the poets of the hostile Banu Tamim tribe. Ibn Shammash was an ardent lover of the Quran's beauty; his stentorian voice occasioned a critical comment from heaven (Q:24:63; 49:2). Along with most Quran lovers, he was martyred at the Battle of Yamamah, near Mecca, in 633 CE.

This regard for the subversive power of poetry is widespread among the ancients; we moderns find it strange since much poetry now is autobiographical, politically ineffective and boringly confessional. In his life of the mythical hero Theseus, the Roman orator Plutarch (d. 120 CE) writes that it is dangerous 'to incur the hostility of a city that is a mistress of eloquence and song',[7] referring to Athens. The German Protestant theologian Johann Georg Hamann (1730–88), who influenced Soren Kierkegaard, called poetry 'the mother tongue of the human race'.

Arab poets agonized over life's fleeting pleasures and lamented that it must terminate in death's humiliating defeat. The dislocation, transience and tragedy of mortal things inspired the sceptical wisdom of the itinerant tribes; their poets sang of the virtues of virility, the sole trait that enabled one to be a man in the face of the desert's arbitrary cruelties. The masculine virtues included personal and tribal honour, generosity of spirit as expressed in reckless courage, lavish hospitality for friend and foe alike and chivalry expressed as the duty to protect women and children. The poets, whether sober or intoxicated, could be playful and wistful, their themes earthy and erotic but simultaneously and inconsistently, like most poetry, craving for profound ideals that transcend the physical universe and its unavoidably humiliating limitations, especially our extinction in the finality of physical death and the depressing 'kenosis' of the body in post-coital exhaustion.

Arab pagan literary culture was rapidly replaced by a book that dominated Arabic literature for some 1400 years. The scripture's advent marks the eclipse of secular poetry although a few genres survived and even flourished. After the Quran terminated forever the secular Arab poetic canon, Arabic became the language of Quranic commentary and of jurisprudence while Persian became the primary language of poetry. Although the Quran is the most merciless editor of the pagan poetic canon, profane poetry was, like pre-Islamic mythology, in practice only partly discarded. The *khamriyyāt* genre extolled the pleasures of alcohol (*khamr*) even though the Quran, after equivocal verdicts (Q:2:219; 4:43; 5:90), prohibited the consumption of strong drink (Q:5:91), deferring its pleasures to paradise (see Q:47:15). The most famous *khamriyyāt* poets lived sober lives. Again, the poetry of the vagabond-poets (*al-ṣu'lūk*), expelled from society on account of their dissipation, was admired in urban centres while the genre of *tarḍiyyāt*, dealing with hunting, appealed to Muslim nobility in courtly palaces. The Sufi poets, a case apart, were allowed to use, with impunity, erotic and alcohol-related imagery.

Muslims admire the Quran's Arabic for its restraint and refinement. The effect of the recited scripture varied: some fell down on their faces in awe (Q:17:105–109) but others dismissed it as a forged fable (Q:25:4–5). This ambiguous response is found in the reception of all faiths even in ages of fervent faith. Thus a miracle-performing Jesus found most of his audiences unreceptive (Luke 4:24) while Peter noted that even though some were amazed at the marvel of Pentecost, others dismissed the miracle of glossolalia as a result of 'drinking too much new wine' (Acts 2:13).

The Quran attributes no miracle to Muhammad except the divinely produced and inimitable Quran (Q:29:48–51), an intellectual marvel displaying divine reason in fluent human speech. The scripture challenges humankind and jinn to produce something equivalent (Q:2:23; 10:38; 11:13; 17:88; 52:34). Islam's probative credential emerges out of an aesthetic challenge to poets. A literary faith indeed! Regarding its alleged inimitability of style and content, its incapacitation of the literary pretender,[8] we find widespread pagan presumption of capacity: 'If we so wished, we could have said something similar' (Q:8:31). Accordingly, the invalidity of human doubt about the revelation's divine provenance runs through the encyclopedic second surah (Q:2:1, 24). While believers say 'We heard; we obeyed' (Q:24:51) and errant monotheists declare 'We heard; we disobeyed'

(Q:4:46), the Meccan pagans mocked Muhammad and retorted 'We have already heard it all' (Q:8:31).

The Quran, the supreme achievement of the divine pen, twice notes its own everlasting spiritual and linguistic fecundity. If the ocean became ink, it would be consumed before God's words were exhausted even if God added another similar ocean for support (Q:18:109) where the word for ink (*midad*) echoes the word for support (*madad*). The inexhaustible nature of God's words is also expressed by imagining the earth's trees becoming pens to be dipped in an ocean of ink, with seven (to signify a perfect number) more oceans to replenish it (Q:31:27). This claim seems hyperbolic. Yet books such as the Quran and the Bible, like the lives of men such as Jesus (see John 21:25), can continue to fascinate us despite absorbing a life-time of study. Many exegetes of the Quran, already equipped with an encyclopedic intimacy with a scripture whose themes range from Moses to menstruation, still assiduously study it in their old age, only to find new treasures in the marvellous original.

VII

Illiteracy was common among the Arabs of Muhammad's time; even peripatetic poets could be experts in the oral language without knowing the use of the pen. After all, speech is natural while literacy is an art. Muslims believe that the archangel Gabriel infallibly dictated the revelations to an illiterate Muhammad who was appointed as the conduit of revelation: he brought divine speech into the human world (Q:2:97, 139, 189, 215, 217, 219, 220, 222; 109:1; 112:1; 113:1; 114). Muhammad received a revelation self-described as the literal, direct and immutable speech of God (Q:2:75; Q:9:6; 48:15) preserved in the book of God (Q:3:23). It is no paraphrastic inspiration diluted by later human additions but rather the facsimile of the divine words. The Quran is a revelation directly *from* God (Q:27:6; 32:2; 39:1; 40:2; 41:2; 45:2, 46:2, etc.) but not a revelation *of* God since it reveals only the divine will for us. God's nature is disclosed only where it bears on his moral and legal purpose for humankind.

The Quran is the book (*al-kitāb*) of revelation on earth and in heaven. As an earthly manuscript (*muṣ'ḥaf*) and, liturgically, as an oral recitation (*al-qur'ān*), it exists solely on earth. The oral revelations appearing within history as *Al-Qur'ān* (the recital) are celestial speech preserved in 'a guarded tablet' (Q:85:22), descending to earth as 'the glorious recital' (Q:50:1). The night of the Quran's initial descent is the night of power (Q:97:1–3), better than a thousand months of devotion (Q:97:3), a period of time which is, in the Prophet's commentary, considered an average human life-time. Grammatically, *qur'ān* is a verbal noun of the form *fu'lān* (based on the verb *fa/'a/la* as a template) which suggests continuous action, thus an eternal reading.

Although the Quran is reliably associated with Muhammad, he declined to claim its authorship. Secular cynics such as Nietzsche would say that our so-called great men were never great enough to own up to their own daring creativity and instead cravenly attribute it to a higher power. That aside, Muslims recognize only dictation (*imlā'*; Q:25:5) of revelation as being suitable for scripture; they maintain strictly the exclusively divine authorship of their scripture. God forbids that anyone should call a Quranic chapter 'The Book of Muhammad'. No human, not even prophetic, interpretation of the scripture is part of the scripture.

The Quran instructs Muslims to see Muhammad as a mouthpiece (Q:53:3–5; 75:16–19). At the moment of descent, God suspends the Prophet's capacities and faculties. While remaining sentient, he becomes a puppet (or robot) during the revelation. The verses descend on his heart to strengthen him in his mission (Q:26:194). Muhammad would go into a trance, often while doing something mundane such as eating a piece of chicken in his wives' kitchen. God would momentarily hypnotize and mesmerize him, programming him like a machine. The scripture contrasts *wahy* (revelation) with *hawā* (personal desire; see Q:53:3–4). This dichotomy indicates that the received text is infallible: no fallible elements can enter a work which is divine in its conception, design and delivery. Only the interpretation and implementation of Quranic imperatives bear the stamp of Muhammad's personality. This account of the Quran's inerrancy as literal divinity of diction has not been questioned by any authentic Muslim of the past 1400 years.

The Quranically imposed constriction of the Prophet's literary role inspired Islam's hostility towards speculative theology understood as theorizing about God's nature beyond his own revelation of his will. Naturally, every expression of the divine will, in human language, has a human context. The discipline of *sha'n al-nuzūl* (affairs of the descents) deals with the environment in which divine verses were received. The grammarian-exegete Abu Al-Hasan Al-Wahidi (d. 1075) penned an exhaustive commentary on the history, primary context and occasion of the revealed fragments so that believers could better comprehend their scripture.[9] While the Quran's silences, omissions and sense of priority remain mysterious, revelations were occasionally sent directly in response to human inquiry. For example, a woman complained to the Prophet that her husband had expressed his lapse of desire by saying 'You remind me of my mother's back', a pagan prelude to divorce. She had argued with the Prophet because he would take no action against her husband. God heard her plea and responded directly by abolishing the custom (see Q:58:1–4).

Most verses remain ambiguous and unclear without the aid of commentary on the occasion of their descent. Thus, take for example: 'There is not much good in their secret conferences – except for the one who orders charity, kindness and harmony among the people' (Q:4:114; see also Q:58:9–10). Is this a reference to one or more actual good-doers among the hypocritical conspirators in Medina? Or is it a divine description of the ideal assembly? From a sermon of the Prophet, we know the event that elicited this revelation.[10]

VIII

Before we survey the Quran's themes, we note those features which lend it a *sui generis* character. As a compilation with chapters and verses, the Quran dates to Muhammad's lifetime. Chapter divisions were orally preserved already at Mecca (implied at Q:10:38); Medinan verses (Q:2:23–4) suggest a written document subdivided into chapters. The word *āyah*, meaning a divine sign, refers exclusively to a Quranic verse. The word *sūrah* (pl. *suwar*; Q:11:13) is used solely to describe the Quran's 114 divisions and does not occur elsewhere in early Arabic literature (except in hadith narratives about the Quran). A *sūrah* is not a chapter in the sense of a body of writing centered on a single theme reflected in a title assigned by warrant of this dominant theme.

Each surah, except surah 9, opens with the Invocation ('In the name of God, the merciful, the beneficent'), probably the most recited group of words in the history of human speech. The surahs are named after some significant word in the opening verse. We see this naming system for scrolls of the Hebrew Bible which often take their Hebrew name from the first few words of the opening verse. Some of the Quran's surahs are named with single eccentric words or incidents, occurring anywhere in the surah, if these astonished the first audience. This ancient amazement persists in the reactions of Western readers who browse the Quran, while standing in bookstores, only to see that, for example, the longest chapter gives little clue to its encyclopedic contents since it is called 'The Cow' as if Islam also revered Hinduism's favourite animal. ('God forbid!' exclaims the devout Muslim since no two faiths could be further apart.)

The Quranic chapters are not arranged chronologically. Each chapter does carry a superscription indicating 'Mecca' or 'Medina' as the place of revelation. Some chapters are composite, containing revelations received in both cities but this is not indicated. Commentators suggest that the exordium (Q:1:1–7) was revealed in Mecca and rerevealed in Medina. As a summary of the Quran, it transcends the tale of two cities. In general, the Quran is, unlike the Bible, indifferent to secular history. It gives mere outlines of events in sacred history, offers no dates even for the life of Muhammad and contains only one vague notice of contemporaneous secular history (Q:30:2–6).

This is the best place to note the Quran's view of time. Linear temporality is restricted to the individual's life and to the progress of sacred history as it culminates in eschatology. In its accounts of sacred history as present guidance, the boundaries between past, present and future are malleable and permeable. History is not past spectacle but present guidance, a contemporary force altering the present, inviting to a new future beyond history but via the dynamic process called history. One can never tell if the time elapsed in any Quranic narrative is a few hours, a day, a year, a decade, a century or a millennium. Sinners on the Day of Judgment shall wake up confused about serial time thinking their whole life lasted a few hours of the day (Q:79:46). The disbeliever has no sense of purpose or of time (Q:30:55–6). Even believers have a confused sense of time and its passage (see Q:2:259; 18:25–6). To complicate matters further, human reckoning does not correspond to divine time measurements (Q:22:47; 70:4).

To understand the Quran's verses, to return to our theme, requires technical expertise. Like all profound and daring poetry, the Quran contains opaque passages employing familiar words bearing abnormal meanings. Such idiosyncratic usage is restricted to the Quran. Arabic lexicons record these restrictions, without offering comment or explanation. An astonishing liberty taken by the Quran is its meaningless verses composed entirely of disjointed letters of the alphabet. The opening verses of 28 chapters contain, or consist entirely of, these detached letters. One surah, uniquely, has two verses composed entirely of such letters (Q:42:1–2). These letters, in groups of one to five maximum, are part of the revelation. Reciters cannot omit them; uttering them, as a believer, earns one merit. Surah 19 was originally called *kāf hā yā 'ayn ṣād* while some Muslim poets still name the second surah as *alif lām mīm*.

Christians in the past speculated that the disjointed letters indicated a speech defect, perhaps a stutter, connected to – another disputed fact – Muhammad's epileptic fits. To be fair, epilepsy in the ancient world was nicknamed 'the sacred disease' and widely associated with divine and demonic possession. In any case, Jews, Christians and Muslims can all agree that another prophet, Moses, openly complained of his lack of eloquence and probably had some speech impediment (implied at Q:43:52). For Muslims, the Quranic letters cannot be interpreted or understood: their presence marks the Quran's uniquely arcane nature. These 'meaningless' verses are, by definition, *mutashābihat* (ambiguous or allegorical) as opposed to *muhkamāt* (legal, hence decisive; see Q:3:7; 47:20). The caliph Umar jailed a man, after flogging him a hundred lashes, for persistent curiosity about such allegorical verses.

IX

The Meccan–Medinan divide in Muhammad's biography is artificial and can moreover be exploited for polemical motives, as we shall see in Chapter 4. Muhammad's life was marked by a smooth transition followed by a return of the native. Nor is the divide helpful in classifying Quranic revelations. Some surahs, especially long or late Meccan ones, are composite. Some verses (such as Q:47:18) were revealed during the *hijrah* when the Prophet wept for his native city as he fled to Medina. Tradition classifies these as Medinan, preferring the journey's destination to its source.

The Medinan verses are not more mature than the Meccan although a few (nondoctrinal) verses were abrogated by later ones, often within the same city. There is no progress in the revelation since all is equally God's word. Thus, for example, precise inheritance rights (Q:4:11–2, 176) supersede the vague bequests to parents and relatives mentioned earlier (at Q:2:180).

The Quran is divided into 30 equal portions for Ramadan recitals. Surah 1 (Meccan) is a short summary of the Quran, used in all canonical prayer; surah 2 (Medinan), is a long summary, a compendium of sacred history, law and doctrine.

Out of 114 unequally long chapters, 91 were revealed in Mecca. About half of these comprise about a tenth of the book and range from surah 67 to the end of the book (with the exception of Medinan chapters 98 and 110). These Meccan chapters, memorized by millions and recited in daily prayers, are short and gradually become shorter; the final chapters consist of three to six short verses. The first third of the Quran (Chapters 1 to 9) is Medinan with the exception of chapters 1, 6, and 7.

The middle third ranges over an unbroken Meccan terrain numbered 10 to 46 (with the exception of three interposed Medinan surahs: 22, 24 and 33). These Meccan compositions decrease from very long to fairly long as they approach surah 46. The Meccan surahs resume from 50 to 56 and then from 67 to the end of the Quran.

Only four Meccan chapters (6, 7, 16 and 33) are substantial enough to compete with the longest of the Medinan chapters (if we exclude from comparison the Medinan chapter 2, incomparably the longest). Most Meccan surahs are far shorter than the 23 revealed in Medina; the component Meccan verses are also shorter and more poetic. Apart from the encyclopedic surah 2, the Medinan chapters are numbered 3 to 5 and consistently decrease in length. The next two Medinan revelations are chapter 8 (medium length) and 9 (long), together nicknamed *al-jihādān*, (the Jihad duo), and perhaps originally considered one chapter since chapter 9, uniquely, lacks an invocation.[11] The remaining Medinan chapters are 22, 24 and 33, chapters ranging from 47 to 49 and from 57 to 66 (apart from surah 64 revealed on the eve of the migration to Medina but classified as Meccan). Two short chapters complete the Medinan corpus: 98, considered very late Meccan, and 110 revealed during the farewell pilgrimage to Mecca and the last complete surah to be revealed.

X

The Quran is thematically and literarily a highly consistent scripture: all and only about monotheism and all as poetry. It contrasts with the Bible's varied literary formats and diverse contents where God speaks to his people through apostles and epistles, oracles and dramatic simulations, poetry and prose, and hymn and song. Islam is centred on one apostle who sends no epistles but simply hears the very words of God.

In Medina, as in Mecca, the message of Islam's homogeneous scripture is God's unity. Unique in his divinity, worthy of praise and obedience, he tolerates no partners in the sovereignty of the cosmos he created and sustains. When he intends to create a thing, 'He says to it, "Be!" And it is.'(Q:16:40; 36:82). No time elapses between imperative and fulfillment. This God demands that his creatures worship and obey him rather than merely vaguely profess to love him. His latest message is a complete monotheism on the theological, ethical, legal and political levels. The doctrinal and ritual entailments of this sovereign monotheism are dispersed throughout the Quran and expressed in a different tenor in the two cities. Suffusing the entire scripture is the conviction of divine unity, embellished with an astonishing variety of rhetoric and rhythm.

The Quran consists of 6,346 verses and mentions Allah 2,692 times.[12] The definite article is embedded in 'Allah' (contraction of *al-'ilāh*) making duality and plurality grammatically senseless. The Quran's use of the first person plural (when God speaks) indicates majesty, not grammatical or numerical plurality. Unlike in English, 'Allah' is never used metaphorically to mean an allegedly supreme reality seeking to usurp the place of the true God. The English idiom, 'Pleasure is his god', also acknowledges that by using god instead of God but classical Arabic lacks lower- and upper-case letters. Only *'ilāh* (god) can be used metaphorically (see Q:45:23; 25:43). Allah does not possess gender or sexual orientation although, as in classical Hebrew, *huwa* (the third person singular masculine pronoun) is used of him.

Allah is God's essential name; his other 99 beautiful names, culled mainly from the Quran, denote his attributes (such as mercy and justice) as these relate to his moral and legal will for us. God's names do not define or limit him but rather describe aspects of his nature as this relates to humankind. The Quran does not describe God's essentially unknowable nature. To utter 'God is Mercy' is to go beyond the sanction of revelation.

'There is no deity worthy of worship except Allah' (Q:27.26, 52.22) is the Quran's main message. Allah is incomparably great (Q:30:27; 42:11; 112:4). If his creatures reject him, the loss is wholly their own. Unworthy notions of God are condemned, whether held by Jews and Christians (who ought to know better) or by pagans (whose ignorance is only somewhat more condonable since all humans are congenitally aware of God's uniqueness). Muslims are iconoclasts: visual images and depictions of God and Muhammad are forbidden lest these stimulate idolatry. Since God is incorporeal, two- or three-dimensional depictions of him are incoherent. Against the Arab polytheists, Zoroastrian dualists and Christian tri-theists, the Quran firmly asserts God's numerically absolute unity (Q:112:1–4). The praise of God along with the petitions his human creatures should use in addressing him supply the Quran's doxological and doctrinal beliefs and fortify Islam's moral, legal and political foundations. These formulae of praise include pure adoration (Q:1:1–7; 2:286; 3:8–9, 16, 26; 14:40–1; 17:111; 18:1–3; 25:1–2; 112:1–4) and expressions of repentance and self-effacement uttered by prophets (Q:19:5; 21:87, 89).

XI

Classification of surahs as Meccan and Medinan does not adequately reflect the chronology of the revelation. Muslims are indifferent since the message is eternal and timeless although this valid curiosity is satisfied by the discipline of 'occasions of revelation' mentioned earlier. The Meccan period is subdivided into very early Meccan (before public preaching and the persecution it aroused), early, middle, and late (once the exodus date had been fixed). Knowing this sequence helps us to determine the emergence and evolution of Islam's legal and political dimensions. I shall classify the materials simply as Meccan (six themes) and Medinan (six themes) but indicate any which are exclusive to one of the two cities. Apart from very early Meccan revelations commissioning Muhammad as God's messenger, the Meccan and Medinan chapters jointly contain a dozen major themes ranging from educational and devotional, theological and liturgical, to historical and eschatological.

In the earliest verses, God, via Gabriel, the archangel and faithful spirit, reveals his will to a reluctant and terrified Muhammad (Q:81:19–21; also Q:53:1–10).

The first revelation (Q:96:105) was probably followed by Q:74:1–7 and other similar ones ordering him to be devoted to God alone (Q:73:1–9, 15) and to listen reverently to the weighty word descending in light installments (Q:75:16–19; see also Q:17:106). God reveals himself as Muhammad's omnipotent Lord and sustainer who consoles him (Q:93:3–8) just as he comforted earlier prophets. The new prophet's mission is confirmed with visions and portents (see 53:5–10, 13–16, 18; 81:23; see also 17:1; 18:60, 54:1–2). God occasionally rebukes him for his failings (Q:80:1–10) as he will continue to do in the Medinan period (see Q:17:74; 33:37; 66:1–5; see also Q:2:18:6, 22–24; 24:11–26 for milder or implied criticism). In the late Medinan period, just before his death, God's pardon of Muhammad precedes God's criticism (Q:9:43).

The early personalized revelations confidently predict eventual victory for Islam and everlasting fame for Muhammad. These prophecies (Q:93:4–5; 94:4) must have seemed incredible to impartial observers living in Arabia from 610 to 624. Non-Muslim critics dismiss these as self-fulfilling prophecies which prove the all too human Muhammad's sheer skill and will, his perseverance and mental equilibrium as shown in the hour of both eclipse and of victory. He was only a successful version of Julius Caesar.

Let us turn to the six Meccan themes. Two of these themes are found only incidentally in the Medinan pericopes. The first is the Arabic Quran's self-eulogy, its supremacy of literary taste and substantive authenticity (Q:12:3; 81:27; 39:23, 27–8), its inimitability and uniqueness (Q:10:38; 11:13; 17:88; 52:34; 53:4; 56:77–80), and its standing as confirmation and closing seal of previous scriptures (Q:12:111). We read pungent rebuttals of forged authorship (Q:16:103; 25:4–5), answers to accusations that Muhammad was an intellectually vain poet or madman or demon-possessed soothsayer (Q:15:6; 52:29–30; 68:2, 51; 69:41, 44–6; 81:22). These pericopes seek to convince us that Muhammad was not the author but rather the faithful transmitter of divine speech. This motif is largely restricted to the Meccan period but there is Medinan confirmation (see Q:2:23–4; 3:3; 4:82, 174; 5:48; 47:24; 59:21).

Second, God, our sole creator, has left ubiquitous traces or signs (*āyah*, singular; *āyāt*, pl.) of his beneficence and power in nature, human nature, history and society. These signs testify to his mercy and should elicit penitence, gratitude, worship and awe (55:1–25). The signs are natural routines which conceal divine favours and blessings and facilitate our tenure on this good earth. The range of the signs is immense: the arrangements of family and social life, the comforts and luxuries of settled urban and peripatetic nomadic existence (Q:16:10–11, 14, 66–9, 72, 80–1; 30:20–3; 36:33–7), and vessels of transport, including ships that sail in 'the two seas kept separate' (Q:25:53; 35:12; 55:19–24). The signs encompass the sheer variery in the colours of animals, including beasts of burden, all in a natural order made subservient to human beings (Q:14:32–4; 17:70; 30:46; 36: 41–2, 71–3; 40:79–81; 42:32–4). Horses and camels, the two noble animals of Arabic culture,[13] are among the signs (Q:16:8; 88:17) that should convince sceptics of God's creative genius. The charming humility of beasts of burden as they trudge home in the evenings is noted with restrained pathos (Q:16:5–8). Water, essential to human life (Q:21:30; 25:54), also regenerates a dead earth (Q:36:33–6; 43:11), a clear sign for the thirsty nomad. This gracious system of providential provision should daily evoke wonder and gratitude yet only the wise few take note.

By demonstrating the power of God in many locales, the signs convince sincere sceptics of God's power to raise the dead to life (Q:56:57–73; 75:36–40). Only the perverse remain unconvinced. This material is almost entirely Meccan (with rare exceptions at Q:2:21–22; 28–9, 165). Medinan revelations, addressed mainly to Muslims and to previous bearers of revealed scripture, presuppose the register of the signs.

A narrower sense of sign of God occurs almost equally in the Meccan and Medinan registers. To confirm their missions, prophets bring miraculous signs which are self-evidently probative. A prophet can request a sign for himself (Q:19:10; in the same vein: Q:2:260). Thus, Moses brought nine dramatic signs to the Pharaoh and his community (Q:7:132–3; 17:101; 27:12), each more humbling than its preceding sister sign (Q:43:48). Jesus performed many miracles (Q:3:46, 49), most of which are also mentioned either in the canonical New Testament or its associated Apocrypha.

Two argumentative themes, found with different emphases in both locations, link Muhammad's situation to past sacred history. Like other societies that were previously warned, Muhammad's pagan community rejects Allah, the only God, and compromises his worship. The Meccans casually dismiss the majestic Quran and its threats of accountability on an imminent and catastrophic day. Three social evils flow from and reinforce these sinful attitudes: excessive love of wealth, neglect of the marginalized and poor and zealous persecution of believers. All are time-honoured human patterns; equally God's method (*sunnat Allah*: Q:33:38) is to remain firmly judgmental against unjust societies.

The second of these polemical motifs: a quarter of the book consists of prophetic narratives which canvass the missions of some two dozen prophets. The Quran recounts the struggles of prophets against their unrepentant communities. In its countless destruction narratives, it notes the transience of *gloria mundi* in passages whose pathos, to the chagrin of Christian readers, never ripens into tragedy. We read of Moses' life-long struggle with the fickle and childish Children of Israel (Q:7:103–171), Abraham's iconoclastic jihad and personal growth (Q:37:83–111) and of Noah's anguish (Q:26:105–22). Exemplary accounts of righteous lives are interspersed with this adversarial material. Joseph is the hero of the Quran's longest continuous narrative (Q:12:3–102) as he rises from abandonment and slavery to riches and prosperity. The Quranic version of his story is not merely a combination of Genesis and Haggadah materials. It is a morality tale interrupted by motifs of God's constant care for his righteous spokesmen. Again, the life and chastity of Mary, *Maryam Batūlah* (Mary the devout), as Arab Christians lovingly call her, is recounted in two narratives of rare charm (Q:3:42–7; 19:16–29). Luqman, an African sage unknown to Hebrew wisdom, preaches to his son about the good life (Q:31:12–19).

The fifth type of material is late Meccan. It encompasses rudimentary self-defensive responses to Christian and Jewish claims of privileged access to divine truth (Q:6:146; 18:4–5) and materials prefiguring the detailed and system-atic critique found in the Medinan period. Polemical exchanges had already begun since the Prophet's Meccan detractors would visit Yathrib (Medina) to ask its rabbis to gather questions that would embarrass Muhammad: presumably he would apply for esoteric information from Allah only to hear nothing from heaven. Portions of surah 18 (vv. 9–26, 83–99) were revealed in response to Jewish prodding. Carl Jung wrote a commentary on this chapter because he was fascinated by the wandering traveller, named by commentators as Al-Khidr, the eternal man, exiled from ordinary life. The story is unique to the Quran (Q:18:60–82).

The final Meccan motif is judgment as history ends. Meccan passages describe in gripping poetry the terrors of the impending cataclysm, the resurrection, the final day, and the pleasures of *Al-Jannah* (The Garden) and the torments of *Al-Jahannam* (The Fire). This post-mortem eschatology contains vivid scenes of the promises and threats fulfilled in heaven and hell, often within the same surah (see Q:13:35; 14:16–17, 49–50; 25:11–14; 52:17–24; 55:35–44, 46–76; 56:12–38, 41–55; 69:25–37; 71:41–4; 74:26–31; 76:5–22; 78:21–5, 31–5; 83:22–9; 88:1–7, 8–16). Originally revealed at Mecca to convince the Prophet's pagan detractors, this material re-appears in Medina in simplified but shockingly brutal allusions (Q:4:56; 22:19–24). One Medinan verse (Q:47:15) mentions heavenly delights soon after noting the brutality of war (see Q:47:4). It adds one unforgettable detail of the torture that awaits disbelieving combatants once they reach hell. The Medinan periscopes about the next life are addressed to committed believers to reinforce them in their resolve to remain zealous and thus enter the Garden by avoiding the Fire (Q:61:12; 64:9; 66:6–8).

XII

The Meccan revelations motivate individual faith while the Medinan revelations offer rules for establishing an Islamic society. In Mecca, the believers were required only to repudiate idolatry and read the Quran in formal but private (as opposed to congregational) prayer. Such private piety concealed public conse-quences. The Meccan chapters, constituting some two thirds of the revelations, remind us that our creator has provided generously. Therefore, we should care for others by spending charitably rather than accumulating more wealth to satisfy our own lusts. Such moral knowledge does not save us from our greed and covet-ousness; the spirit of the moral law is futile without the legal letter to reinforce it. Even general moral principles, such as 'Do not commit injustice and do not be its victim' (Q:2:279) are placed in a context: in this case, the prohibition of usury. This renders them more usefully specific than, say, 'Do not harm others.' The Medinan revelations command the payment of compulsory alms in order to purify wealth while prohibiting gambling, bribery and commercial corruption (Q:2:188, 219, 267; 5:90–1) and the misuse of orphans' property (Q:4:2–10). They also institute the communal fast of Ramadan which inculcates self-restraint and cultivates moral awareness of the daily plight of the poor and needy (Q:2:183–5).

We can become victims of our idealism, immobilized by general commands. Meccan Islam was vague and resembled the imperatives of the Israelite prophets. Imagine Isaiah shouting these imperatives (Isaiah:1:16–17): *Chidlu hareah! Dirshu mīshpat! Ashru chamotz* (Stop 'evilling'! Endorse justice! Compensate (the) exploited!) Isaiah's noble and absolute but vague provisions were ignored until the rabbis, successors of the prophets, made more modest but practical demands on their people. The secret of the Quran's revolutionary success lies in its combination of the appropriately vague with the usefully explicit command.

The Meccan revelations provide general principles while the Medinan Quran fortifies it with ritual detail. Four of the five pillars are in Medinan verses. Canonical prayer called *salāh* (or *namaz* in Persian, Urdu and Turkish) is performed five times daily, alone or communally, but once weekly in congregation during the mandatory Friday assembly. The discipline of the Ramadan fast, regular payment of alms (*zakah*), and annual pilgrimage (*hajj*) to Mecca complete the rituals. Only the confession of faith and private (or informal) supplication date to Mecca.

In both cities, Islam tempers its idealism with practical sense. While confession and formal prayer are absolute and non-transferable requirements, there are exemptions for fasting and alms payment. When the Thaqif tribe of Ta'if capitulated, the Prophet allowed them to temporarily forego payment of the alms tax. There are specified exemptions from the Ramadan fast, some in the Quran (Q:2:184), the rest in the Prophet's traditions amplified by later law schools. And the pilgrimage, a duty owed to God, should be performed only when a believer, physically and fiscally healthy, has discharged his or her worldly duties (Q:2:196; 3:97).

Medinan chapters contain miscellaneous materials in the same chapter, telescoped to suit the faster pace of the revelation. Quranic law is compressed into the last decade of Muhammad's life. The legal permissibility of divorce (*talāq*), for instance, is established by the Medinan Quran (Q:2:226–33; 4:35; 65:1–7); its detailed implementation, utility, rationale, and limitations are implicit in the scripture but extracted, interpreted and clarified extensively by the Prophet's traditional sayings and practice and by the later law schools. Divorce involves unilateral male initiative. An arrangement called *khul'* (based on Q:2:229) permits the woman to divorce the man: she purchases her pre-marital freedom as her dowry is forfeited in the process. Incidentally, Muhammad never divorced any of his spouses.[14]

XIII

The Medinan stress is largely positively edificatory; a negative strain is the break from Judaism and Christianity. In Mecca, Muhammad inspired a small motley band of zealous neophytes who were harassed by their rich and arrogant pagan compatriots. In Medina, Muhammad was a charismatic founder-leader of an infant community for whom the Meccans posed a military threat. He was cautious of two more groups of resourceful enemies in Medina, the Arab hypocrites and the Medinan Jews, who combined their tactics and forces against him. The Quran engages in caustic polemical exchanges with his most determined opponents, the Jews. 'If 10 Jews had believed in me, all the Jews would have believed in me.' Muhammad reportedly said this when he arrived in Medina; presumably he could not persuade even 10 Jews to accept Islam.[15] The Prophet is referring to the quorum (*minyan*; Hebrew for number) necessary for public Jewish services. The Talmud promises that if 10 Jewish men pray together, the divine presence (*shekhīnah*; cf. *sakīnah*; Q:9:26) graces the occasion.

This argumentative Medinan material about inter-faith relations supplies the first of our six Medinan motifs. It is artfully braided with strands of positive doctrine that enable Islam to solidify into universal monotheism. The anti-Jewish and anti-Christian Medinan material is incorrectly dismissed by Jews and Christians as miscellaneous and unsystematic polemic. It is an organized, consistent, comprehensive and remarkably successful critique: empty Islamic rhetoric could not have punctured Christianity's hope of universally preaching the kerygma. Nor would it have been capable of making Christian-to-Muslim conversion the largest inter-faith traffic in history. Although the Quran intended to unite Jews and Christians with each other and both with Muslims, in practice, its message has caused inveterate and enduring conflict among the three Western monotheisms.

Second, after the Meccan birth-pangs, the Quran gave birth to Medina's Islamic community. The Meccan Quran already targetted the pagan political and religious ontologies as it anticipated the coming revolution in God's name. In Medina, this stress becomes explicit as God and his Messenger reform the power-structure that resisted their proposals. Motivating these political ambitions is the human praise of God – a theme which deepens as the Quran accumulates and reaches completion. The two most sustained contemplative passages were revealed in Medina during the Prophet's political phase (see Q:2:255; 24:35). This should check the hasty polemical judgment that dismisses Muhammad at Medina as merely an opportunist politician who had lost all interest in spirituality.

The Medinan Quran contains two sub-themes about Muhammad's evolution into a public figure as prophet–statesman. First, Medinan verses are addressed to Muhammad as prophet–leader of his community. He is ordered to convey guidance to other believers who are directly addressed as 'Believers!' (God never directly addresses pagans.) Muhammad receives moral exhortations, ritual instructions, prescriptive guidelines and legal precepts as he builds his Medinan utopia. Intoxicants, gambling and usury are banned, penal regulations specified, and the pilgrimage to Mecca, retrieved from pagan associations, is fortified with new rituals. The material also includes Muhammad's domestic life, his marriages and a few scandals, events covered in Chapter 1. This mundane material is set in the context of God's absolute sovereignty softened by his mercy and care.

Legal and exhortatory passages are now regularly wrapped in one or two of God's 'beautiful names', qualities that spiritualize and mitigate the unconditional imperatives. This trend started in late Meccan periscopes but becomes stereotypical in Medina. A Meccan verse on God's ability to ferret out the truth about our motives concludes with 'He is subtle, all-aware' (Q:16:31). Again, an account of human conception and progress towards strength eventually followed by senility concludes with: 'God is knower and mighty' (Q:30:54). These two divine attributes are chosen to emphasize, by contrast, the human being's inevitable loss of knowledge and power through ageing. In Medina, legal verses, especially about punishing sinners, typically conclude with a reference to God's compassion (see Q:4:16). A sub-branch of the sciences of the Quran offers a rationale for the choice of divine names for concluding such verses.

The twin sub-theme: Muhammad emerges as the true successor to Abraham, Moses and Jesus. Jesus' messianic significance, as understood by Christians, is denied. Abraham, an iconoclast like Muhammad, appears closer to Muhammadan Islam than to Judaism or Christianity. This Abrahamic connection is made in Meccan and Medinan revelations. Moses, the most discussed prophet in the Quran, received a book that resembled the Quran, a scripture approvingly linked with the Torah (see Q:2:108, 4:153; a Meccan reference at Q:28:48–9). Muhammad's troubles with his community in Medina mirror those of Moses (implied at Q:61:5). Some Muslims were reluctant warriors, a fact reminiscent of the Israelites' cowardice and hesitation about fighting their way through to Canaan (see Q:5:20–6). Narratives about Moses and the Israelites are not dominated by the motif of utter annihilation of communities amply warned, such as Pharaoh's people. Instead, we read of God's lenient treatment of the Children of Israel after justified chastisement (Q:2:47ff.)

The fifth Medinan motif, to return to our numbering, is Muhammad's struggle to establish a united and empowered community. While stereotyped attacks on Meccan pagans continue, the accusations are now directed at four groups: Medinan Jews (Q:4:153–161), Medinan Jews allied with Arab hypocrites (Q:59:11–17), Jews and Christians jointly (people of the book; Q:3:98–9), and Christians entertaining speculative and erroneous Christological dogmas that compromise God's transcendence (Q:4:157–8; 5:72–75). The first two translated into armed conflict in Muhammad's day; the second pair of confrontations still persists and plagues efforts at the ideological unification of our species.

The nascent faith chose prayerful orientation towards the Meccan shrine built by Abraham rather than towards Jerusalem. After God's disappointing experiment with both Jews and Christians, Muslims are elected as a 'middle community' on condition that they enjoin righteousness and forbid immorality (Q:2:143; 3:110). Jews had relentlessly but subtly mocked Muhammad and Islam through hint and linguistic humour, by playing on words, exploiting the similarity of the Arabic and Hebrew languages (see Q:2:104, 4:46). The Quranic rejoinders are caustic, mocking the claim that the after-life was solely for Jews (Q:2:80; 3:24). The rabbinate is declared an asinine institution, 'a donkey carrying tomes' (Q:62:5). Jews remained, however, one of the two privileged minorities protected inside Islamic hegemony.

The sixth Medinese thread is a secular eschatology inside history: the finality and completion of the Quran and thus Islam, the faith's glorious future and the imminent demise of its human architect. A few Medinan references to the Quran's status as divine revelation remain (see Q:2:1–2; 4.82; 24.1). Islam is now religion perfected, a meta-religion and corrector of previous faiths; the Quran is confirmer and guarantor of previous revelations and preventer of future revelations with, consistently, Muhammad as the seal of the prophets. Despite continuing to fear God's imminent judgment, as shown in Medinan verses (such as Q:22:1–2), Muhammad continued to build a secular order that would endure until 1924. History knows of no other case of a comparably enduring achievement that can be reliably associated with a known figure of antiquity. And it was a book that inspired the man. Islam is indeed a literary faith.

XIV

The Quran's enduring typologies transcend its historical advent. It alludes to many communities, often named by their creed: Jews and the Children of Israel, Christians, ('people of the gospel' only at Q:5:49), and collectively as 'the people of the book'. Also: imperial solidarities such as Byzantine Greek Christians (Q:30:2) and Persians (Q:16;103; 26:198; 41:44), Muhammad's ethnic contemporaries (urban Arabs and nomadic Bedouins), obscure contemporaries such as the Magians (possibly fire worshippers; Q:22:17) and the Sabians (Q:2:62; 5:71; 22:17), communities of various messengers, and universal groups such as Children of Adam and humankind. The religious typology is twofold: believers and submitters, in one group, and disbelievers, hypocrites and idolaters, as everyone else.

This neat typology is complicated by two factors. Firstly, the mention of 'The people on the heights' (mentioned only at Q:7:46–8, a Meccan revelation). These individuals are neither in hell nor heaven but are hoping to go to heaven. No grounds are offered for their optimism. (Is the Quran hinting at a purifiying purgatory like the one found in Catholicism?) Secondly, morally, of course, there are other typologies (especially the just, the unjust, and the rebellious) that overlap with the theological ones.

The themes of faith and disbelief permeate the scripture. Only hypocrisy is an exclusively Medinan motif (with Q:29:11 being the only Meccan reference, a very late one). The accusation is largely restricted to Arabs and Bedouins who pretended to embrace Islam. Although Jews and Christians are rarely called hypocrites (see Q:2:44, 85 for exceptions), they are occasionally condemned outright as disbelievers (Q:2:88–105; 5:72–3).

Faith (*īmān*) is a supernatural supplement to human rectitude and patience, a cause and a consequence of the fear of God (*taqwā*). The Quran distinguishes faith from the legal or nominal profession of submission (*islām*) to God's will (Q:49:14). Faithful believers are distinguished from mere submitters: we attain faith only after our constant effort and God's enabling grace.

Among the united ummah of faithful believers are elite sub-groups such as the Prophet's immediate family (Q:33:33). The Meccans who migrated (Al-Muhajirun) for the Islamic cause and their Medinan Patrons (Al-Ansar; see Q:33:6; 59:8–10), jointly constitute God's party (*hizb Allāh*; Q:5:56; 58:22), the vanguard of Islam. These are fearless and zealous believers who sell this life in exchange for the next. The Quran eulogizes other elite believers, some from past sacred history and a few whose identity remains a mystery: *al-sabiqūn*, the foremost (in virtue; Q:56:101), *al-muqarrabūn* (the ones brought close to God; Q:56:88) and *al-atqā* (the most pious; Q:92:17). The elect 'companions of the right hand' are separated eternally from the unfortunate 'companions of the left hand' (Q:90:18–9).

One rejects God by neglecting or rejecting his will, being ungrateful for his favours and by persecuting his messengers. This sin is *kufr* (literally, concealing [the truth]). *Īmān* and *kufr* are neologisms. The Quran was revealed to pagan Arabs with no existing monotheistic vocabulary. The New Testament, by contrast, inherits Jewish monotheistic nomenclature and also retains pagan terms such as *pistis* (Greek for faith), originally understood as loyalty (to Caesar). This was a central virtue for first century Mediterranean subjects of the Roman emperor. People had faith in Caesar while he was faithful to the imperial order and preserved its peace and prosperity.[16]

The Quran comes close to condemning hypocrisy (*nifāq*) as no better than insidious disbelief. The Islamic scripture has a richer exploration of hypocrisy in the religious life than all other scriptures, including the New Testament. The Quran encourages sincerity of intention and motivation in the inner life of the believer; it frequently condemns disbelief displayed as dissimulation. Apart from being mendacious, conniving and stingy, the hypocrites displayed a tepid, politically expedient, deviously external allegiance to God's eventually triumphant messenger (Q:8:49; 9:66–8, 73–87, 47:16–32; 63:1–8). They sowed dissension among the ranks of the faithful, especially in times of crisis. During the Tabuk expedition, for example, when the Prophet travelled north to locate a Byzantine army, the hypocrites complained that Muhammad was gullible – a serious charge during war when rumour abounds (Q:9:61; in the same vein Q:47:16).

Since hypocrites wore the carapace of faith, political opposition was, for Muhammad, always camouflaged as religious dissidence. All dissent was simultaneously theological and political, and therefore a political surrogate for a religious position. Religious dissent was never theologically pure: it disguised a hypocritical political stance. This attitude to opposition has shaped Muslim political culture.

Finally, denial or compromise of God's incomparable divinity is *shirk* – the sin of associating partners with God's unique divinity. The Meccan pagans already regarded Allah as the high god. They admitted, albeit reluctantly, that Allah was their supreme creator and sustainer, a pagan concession cited often in the Quran (Q:10:31; 23:84–9, 26:61–3, 29:61–3; 39:38; 43:9). In distress, pagans prayed fervently to Allah alone, never to his intermediaries (Q:10:22, 29:65). When the crisis was over, they reverted to idolatrous association of God with lesser deities (Q:7:189–90). By affirming God's uniqueness and investing his name with exclusive holiness and majesty, the Quran redirected, restricted and purified the pagans' allegiance. It is idolatrous to attempt to attribute God's qualities to anyone or anything else. We humans share with God his attribute of knowledge but not his omniscience, power but not his omnipotence, and virtue but not his absolute holiness. *Shirk* is Islam's only irremissible sin (Q:4:48, 116).

The contemporary reasoned denial of the existence of all supernatural beings has made idolatrous association anachronistic. Let me explain. One cannot be an idolater without believing in God. One may dishonour him, certainly, but that presupposes believing that he exists and is worthy of worship. Mecca's idolatrous sceptics and temporalists who endorsed the primacy and power of time (Q:45:24; 76:1) were hardly the hardened polemical atheists of today who aggressively deny God's reality and by implication his divinity and therefore exclusive divinity. Today's atheist may qualify as a disbeliever (*kāfir*) but not as an idolater (*mushrik*). The charge of idolatry is outdated: redundant against modern Muslims (and other monotheists) and inapplicable to atheists. The creed therefore, as I argued in Chapter 1, should be shortened to consist only of the second portion. This has the additional benefit of highlighting the Prophet's role in this literary faith centred on God's message as conveyed by God's last Messenger. In the next chapter, we examine the Muslim imperial aspiration to universal reach implied by the catholic scope of Muhammad's apostolate.

3   A universal religion

The Quran requires faith in a transcendent being who, as in Judaism and Christianity, is a supreme creator beyond the cosmos. Unlike the Bible, however, the Quran additionally seeks to transcend the empirical plurality of religions by achieving a perspective on all religion as such (Q:48:28; 61:9). I do not mean simply that Islam is a missionary faith seeking converts: proselytizing is hardly unique to Islam. Rather, it aims at the theoretical unification of existing religions, seeks to prevent the birth of future universal faiths and buttresses these ambitions with a vigorous commitment to the imperial universality of historical Islam. Although students of religions would concede that Islam is the earliest attempt to encompass religion in its totality, only for Muslims does its advent also complete the evolution of religious conviction. Muslims elevate their faith into a normative meta-religion, a supervisor of faiths. It becomes the world's only universal faith intentionally founded with a mandate to supersede existing 'revealed' and 'man-made' religions. While recent eclectic movements, such as Baha'ism,[1] also seek to finalize miscellaneous predecessor faiths, Islam remains the earliest meta-religion and the last and latest successful universal religion.

Muslims view Islam as the inheritor of the monotheistic project but simultaneously as an original faith that enhanced, corrected and perfected its monotheistic precedents. The two named ones are Judaism and Christianity (Q:6:156) but the unnamed ones must include the Persian variant called Zoroastrianism named after Zoroaster (Zarathustra), the poet–prophet of monotheistic ethical dualism. The Quran does not mention Zarathustra: it focuses on Israelite and Arabian prophets while omitting Eastern messengers. This is surprising since Muhammad's close companion Salman the Persian was a former Zoroastrian. There is a single Quranic reference to Al-Majūs, possibly Zoroastrian fire-worshippers. Judgment about them is deferred until the Day of Resurrection. Sitting next to idolaters, they are listed as the fifth in a list of six groups. The list begins with Muslims and Jews, mentioning communities in decreasing order of orthodoxy; Christians are cited towards the end of the sequence (Q:22:17). Muslim jurists and scholars of comparative faiths remained divided in their opinions about the status of Zoroastrianism even after they had decreed that the earliest varieties of Hinduism were, to the surprise of

Hindus and Buddhists, forms of revealed monotheism. This enabled Hindus and Buddhists to be honoured as 'people of the book' even though these communities were not mentioned in the Quran. Unfortunately, this honour came with a price-tag: to signify their protected status, these communities were now eligible to pay a tax.

Zoroastrianism certainly qualifies as a sophisticated moral monotheism, and, like its place of origin, serves as a bridge between East and West. Judaism, Christianity and Islam, acknowledged in the Islamic scripture, are also self-described as ethical monotheisms. Islam is additionally a political and prophetic monotheism – a complete and rigorous monotheistic ideology, absolute and unqualified, claiming the de jure right to influence behaviour at every level ranging from mystical and psychological to legal and cultural. This rigour distinguishes Islam's theo-politics and renders its theology theocentric rather than anthropomorphic. Judaism and Christianity are messianic and apolitical faiths which, according to Muslims, compromise God's autonomy and his numerical uniqueness.

All three Semitic theisms are exclusive: their only God is intolerant of rivals. This contrasts with the comprehensively tolerant 'monotheism' of polytheistic Hinduism which acknowledges the single supreme deity of every other faith. Judaism was, for much of its history, an ethical but ethnic monotheism; Christianity and Islam are *universal* ethical monotheisms although only Islam was founded as such. Muhammad brought the potentially universal message to the Arabs who then tried to make the message actually universal. Only an imperial Islam yearning for universality could have succeeded in a bipolar world of two previously established and appealing monotheisms. An apolitical Islam would have been universal only in name just as Buddhism, for all its globally relevant doctrines diagnosing the ills of our common humanity, remains largely restricted to Asia.

Islam's claim to offer universal guidance enables it to subtly downgrade its predecessors while effectively co-opting them. The Quran states that earlier revelations were perverted or misunderstood or imperfectly transmitted (Q:5:12–16). Muhammad brings no new message and claims no religious originality (see Q:21:24–5; 41:43; 43:45). 'Say: "My case is no innovation among the messengers"' (Q:46:9). Muhammad was merely ordered to restore the pristine religion of Adam and Noah, and, moving from pre-history to history, of Abraham (see Q:33:7; 42:13). Islam's religiously motivated conquest of the past undermines the need for novelty in the present.

II

What could qualify as innovative in an historical religion claiming to be a confirmation of precedents? Muhammadan Islam qualifies as novel partly by absorbing earlier influences while maintaining its distinctiveness just as seminal thinkers absorb the impact of alien stimuli without losing their own uniqueness. In the political, as opposed to narrowly doctrinal respect, Muhammad's case is a major innovation among messengers. After Muhammad, 'the seal of the prophets', there can be,

Muslims believe, no divinely inspired leadership. With the (Sunni) community as the universal faith's corporate guardian, any pious but fallible Muslim male may be appointed the titular leader of the faithful. Shiites object that members of Muhammad's family and their descendants alone inherited his divine charisma and that they alone are entitled to rule.

The Quran as finalized scripture aims to clarify and resolve controversies between Muslims and other monotheists (Q:27:76). Using the (intimate) vocative case, the Quran addresses the Children of Israel (Q:2:40, 47, 122; 20:80). During a dialogue with God, Jesus indirectly addresses his community about their mistaken notions about his alleged divinity (Q:5:116–19). The Quran attempts to unify existing faiths and transcend them into a super-religion that is complete, comprehensive and therefore eternal, all three qualities being corollaries of its universal and meta-religious standing (see Q:3:64; 5:3). Any post-Muhammadan attempt to perfect or amend or extend Islam is considered automatically deviant.

The unity of religion (Q:42:13) follows from God's unity and the continuity of prophets (Q:42:3). If we add the postulates of a monogenetic human race, unity of the prophetic family and a single universal faith, we have six appealing Quranic claims. Unity of religion could imply rejection of religious division and disharmony but also entail condemnation of religious diversity. Normative Islam's self-estimate as a climactic and ultimate religion revealed to correct and conquer all religions (Q:45:6; 61:9) guides the scope of its internal change, evolution and reformation and pre-determines a priori its perception of the rival duo of Judaism and Christianity. As a decisive and paradigmatic religion, Islam supplies the essential criteria of monotheistic faith, a view which infuriates Jews and Christians who are neatly dispossessed of their theological riches by an upstart faith indifferent to past history and present empirical data.

Islam intends to confirm previous revealed faiths and yet it differs in scope from any religion before or since. Some Westerners see Islam as a deviant religion: the world's first and only ideological faith motivated by a radical religious universalism that sanctions homogenization of ideologies and faiths and hence promotes religious imperialism. Islam's self-image as a religion eternally essentialized also ensures its perpetual confrontation with humanist polities: atheists and agnostics condemn it as a custom-made insult to otherwise universally shared and admired modern secular values in private and public life.

III

Theologically conservative and politically provocative Islamic claims are rooted in Islam's explicit and unique claim to universal finality. We can only appreciate the necessary limits of reform and revolutionary change and their tortured relationships with Islam's static inherited legal and imperial tradition against the background of this self-estimate: a finalizing meta-religion with an intentionally comprehensive scope determined from the first day of its twin birth as faith and empire. Organically gradual and internal reform, as opposed to the externally imposed variety, cannot be achieved without conceding this defining facet of the faith's formative self-image. Without comprehending this meta-religious axis of Quranic self-consciousness, we cannot discern the distinctive future profile of Islam as it struggles against liberal humanism, Christian evangelical outreach, and, most vitally, a mercantile capitalist globalism.

Before exploring further the Quranic stress on Islamic finality, we note two effects of this attitude, one cultural and one ideological. Many movements of thought and action gravitate toward climax and closure in Islamic civilization. This is evident in the awarding of honorific titles such as 'the seal of the saints' or 'seal of the theologians' or of martyrs. The coveted accolade of 'the seal of the poets' is awarded to the Persian Sufi Nur Al-Din Jami (1414–1492). The Prophet's grandson, Imam Hussain, is praised as the Prince of Martyrs. The Quran interdicts hypothetical speculation and speculative curiosity in doctrine and conduct (Q:17:36; 49:12) and implicitly discourages the open-minded philosophical attitude. Therefore, 'seal of the philosophers', an honour not coveted by Muslims, remains unclaimed. It should go to Ibn Rushd (Averroës). The inclination to close canons and finalize endeavour is both stimulus and constraint: it inhibits future efforts but also acts as a spur to (legitimate) ambition.

Second, Islam's meta-religious status explains its successful resistance to secularization, especially notable at a time of increasing Christian capitulation to aggressively polemical secularism. Islam's meta-religious self-estimate supplies the intellectual arsenal for Muslims to confront rather than accommodate secularism. Islam and secularism, as universal humanitarian liberalism, compete to be considered as history's culmination. The visceral urge to single out Islam for attacks that betray prejudicial rigour while shielding other – especially Eastern – religions under a patronizing lenience, is motivated by rivalry between these two totalistic visions of history's trajectory. Cyclical views of history as degenerative are not politically threatening while Islam's progressive and climactic view of the historical process is shared by its rivals, Christianity and Marxism, especially the latter with its utopian faith in the dialectics of materialism supported by the authority of history.

IV

In scriptural faiths, a sacred text is the source of all unqualified authority. Should all doctrine essential to a faith be contained in its textual foundations? Muslims, like Protestant Christians, believe so. Islam packs everything that is vital into the Quran and sunnah, its twin literary foundations, much as a pilgrim packs everything into one large bag. All else, including historical innovation and development, is declared inessential, sometimes heretical. At worst, it is reprehensible innovation (*bid'ah*), a Quranic word (Q:46:9). Less charged modern reformist vocabulary includes *ra'y* (opinion), *iḥdāth* (novelty), *ibdā'* (creativity). All imply redundancy in the face of an all-sufficient revealed truth.

The Quran stresses its intellectual finality and self-sufficiency. What are the consequences of this hermetically sealed universalism? A faith with a fixed canon encourages its adherents to look for and locate all significance in a single register, whether a canonical book or a revered personality. It enables obscurantists to resist novel enterprises such as democracy, philosophy and, to a lesser extent, science. A comprehensive religion tends to abort the possibility of autonomously competitive enterprises, particularly philosophy and science.

For devout Muslims, every significant belief and enterprise must find a basis in the Quran or at least in Muhammad's mind and policy. In giving us the final revelation through the final messenger, could God have overlooked anything seminal? Take Islamic philosophy. If it were as eminently useful as Muslim philosophers claimed, why did God overlook this enterprise when revealing the Quran? Even the Prophet's customary practice makes no mention of it. This was the undeclared motivation behind Abu Hamid Al-Ghazali's determined, meticulous and eventually successful assault on Muslim philosophers such as Ibn Sina and Al-Kindi, both of whom zealously assimilated cosmopolitan sources of human knowledge. Scandalously, they exalted the sciences of the ancients (*'ulūm al-qudamā'*), a euphemism for foreign sciences developed by pagans lacking the light of revelation. The Muslim thinkers retorted that the ancient pagans had the light of reason, a divine gift to our common humanity.

To be fair to Islamic orthodoxy, the Muslim philosophers, unlike Christian thinkers such as Thomas Aquinas, never treated (Greek) philosophy merely as theology's handmaiden (*ancilla*). Aquinas thought that theology perfects and completes philosophy, a view that implies the inadequacy of the latter. The Muslim thinkers' unqualified respect for the autonomy of secular reason coupled with their immodestly robust ambitions for unaided human reason understandably outraged orthodoxy. Ibn Rushd, to take the ablest culprit, effectively stressed the autonomous independence of philosophical thought from revealed religious belief while parading, as a pacifying tactical concession to orthodoxy, some religious-sounding phrases in his philosophical writing. Orthodoxy was too unimpeachably alert to be fooled by the philosopher's ruse.

While Ibn Rushd's legacy lies neglected, Al-Ghazali's fanatically pro-revelationist view has contemporary consequences. Muslims search for scriptural justification for every new idea, no matter how commonsensical or prosaic. Even common sense needs a divine warrant. Although we can easily mine scripture and find in it whatever we like, including common sense, it remains a waste of our limited quantum of intellectual energy. Moreover, it restricts creative departures: every new idea must appear under the moral if not doctrinal patronage of an older idea. In a meta-religious doctrinal scheme, one must conceal the novelty of an idea by presenting it under the patronage of an existing revealed text or normative prophetic action. To enable doctrine to evolve without exciting the charge of heresy, original claims must be presented as variations on something traditional. Thus, modern reformers supply an ancient *religious* justification for a new *morally* praiseworthy stance – such as family planning in poor Muslim countries – only by supporting their novel views with the Prophet's ancient authority. This disposition hinders contemporary reform by imposing an exacting demand on it: one must always locate prophetic authority for reforms that are already supported by reason informed by the revelation's core moral principles.

V

Islam's meta-religious self-image dictates a view of history and directs current political attitudes. Secularists condemn Islam's antipathy to history interpreted as that inescapable force which conditions and tethers all cultures and religions. They abjure Islam's ideologically motivated anti-historicism. This anti-historicism is not unique to Islam as religion. Christianity has it too in Soren Kierkegaard's claim that the central ambition of faith is to become contemporaneous with Christ, independently of one's location inside history. This is a religious way of by-passing history by creating its essential moment *anywhere* within history. Politically, however, Muslims and Marxists both intend to transcend history, within history. Muslim idealists add that Islam consummated history through its duplicable early seventh century utopia.

The Islamic self-image as comprehensive meta-religion revealed to terminate religious novelty has ambiguous political potential supporting as it does both an imperial thrust for universal domination and also recognition of plural pieties and diverse ethical systems. The Quran endorses the mutual recognition of tribes and groups as the very purpose of creation (Q:49:13), a vision that would support a progressive pluralist Islam. Its comprehensive vision enabled a multi-lingual and multi-cultural civilization in the heyday of imperial Islam. Jurists wisely permitted local custom (*'urf*) in conquered lands to become part of Islamic law. Indigenous customs were deemed valid unless these proved morally repugnant to the Quran or Prophetic traditions, criteria applied disinterestedly to Arab culture too in the merciless editing of pre-Islamic Arabian history.

The Quran asserts forcefully that sacred history has reached its climax: all religious dispensations, valid in their own day, must be transcended in favour of God's latest message. The Quran's meta-religious neutrality as umpire of world faiths contrasts with its zealous promotion of a historically established Islam which claims no monopoly of truth before its advent but claims it emphatically for all times subsequent to its appearance. Such a supersessionist claim accompanies every imperial religion. Expectedly, Islam and Christianity have competing colonial histories in which the globe has been divided between the baptized and the circumcised races.

Although historical seventh century Islam is the final religion fully established, Muhammad promised his followers that in every century, until the end of history, God would raise someone to revive Islam as universal religion. This secure tradition is found in the collection of the traditionist Abu Dawud Al-Sijistani. The conservative champion Al-Ghazali, eulogized as *ḥujjat al-islām* (proof of Islam), is informally regarded as the reformer (*mujaddid*) for the sixth Islamic century. Many claim the poet Allama Muhammad Iqbal (1877–1938), the ideological father of Pakistan, to be the latest *mujaddid*.

The benefits of the Prophet's promise for the perennial maintenance of universal Islamic identity hardly need proof or advertisement but few have noted the source of its massive strength. No faith which has fixed its eyes on progress and the future, rather than saluting only its tradition and the past, could entertain such a view. Only a faith which regards each generation as worse, not better, than its predecessor, could derive strength from posterity. In modern ideologies and faiths, including liberal forms of Judaism and Christianity, the past is a source of embarrassment, not of pride.

VI

Islam is a special case among world faiths. Islamic exceptionalism is rooted in the recognition of a unique ideological religion of universal import, conceived as a spiritual globalization project with an ambitious scope and latitude evident in its self-naming as an attitude, namely, devout resignation and moral self-surrender. An historical (as opposed to mythological) dispensation should be decisively linked with its founder. This is especially true for Islam since it was irrefutably established by Muhammad. Ironically, few founders of faiths belonged to their own belief systems. Jesus was not Christian, the Buddha was not a Buddhist and Marx was no Marxist! Muhammad was, however, certainly a self-professed Muslim who proudly upheld Islam.

'Muhammadianity' or 'Arabianity' would then reflect a generic link with the founder or his land and language. As it is, the Arabic word 'Islam' is the only clue to the ethnicity of its founder or to his aboriginal locale. Why associate a religion of self-surrender with any particular nation, land, person or language? Judaism, Christianity, Confucianisn, Buddhism, Hinduism and other faiths are delimited by their declared link to a revered person, tribe, place or ethnicity. Taoism (right way), Shinto (way of the gods) and Sikhism (quest or discipleship) may appear to be exceptions to this claim but these convenient labels were usually imposed by outsiders. In any case, all of these faiths remain completely identified with a limited ethnic setting.

All faiths have a self-image as somehow final and true. The Eastern faiths, being more ahistorical, do not use the language of finality. Jewish perception of Judaic finality is reflected in a self-image as exclusive custodians of prophecy, a genetic trait of a few Children of Abraham. God's word is essentially limited to Israel and there are no true Gentile prophets. Jews have, however, never seen Judaism as finalizing all previous manifestations of human religiosity. Christianity's stamp of finality and imperial consummation of history was imposed by its later patrons, Paul and Constantine. *Imitatio Pauli* is after all easier than *imitatio Christi* since we know much more about Paul than about Jesus. Paul wrote while Jesus spoke and the spoken word flies away.

As befits a faith motivated by globalization, the Quran describes Islam in catholic idioms: the religion of truth (Q:9:29), of God (Q:24:2; 110:2), of divinely created human nature (Q:30:30), and therefore the eternal or decisive faith (Q:98:5), the original faith to which the repentant sinner reverts rather than converts (Q:7:172–3). In its universal protology, the Quran praises Islam as the manifestly right and straight religion (Q:12:40; 30:30; 98:5), the conviction of our original and pure human nature. The postulates of divine unity and of human accountability to the divine are innate to human nature as such (Q:7:172–3). To reject God's sole sovereignty is to commit intentional perfidy to the submissive (*muslim*) aspect of our natural human endowment, whether we are believers or not. A secure tradition of the Prophet claims that every child is born submissive (*muslim*) to God's will. Jews, Christians, Zoroastrians and others pervert the child into other man-made faiths.[2]

Atheists would retort that children born in Muslim homes are natural-born atheists who are then subverted into an intolerant monotheism through a zealous indoctrination that starts early – a child abuse so prevalent that few notice it. There is justice in this charge. Indoctrination precedes education. The call to Islamic prayer is said in the newborn's ears just as baptism is performed on the unknowing child. Some pregnant mothers read the Quran to their child in the womb since the Prophet said: 'The mother is the first madrasah.' Muslim sages traditionally dated the child's life from his or her conception, not birth. Devout mothers chant the Quranic chapter named after Joseph, the handsome prophet, to ensure the birth of a beautiful child.

Muslim exegetes strenuously assure us that human diversity does not contradict our invariant and basic humanity. We can divest ourselves of cultural and linguistic particularities to embrace a universal religion, solely as human beings. Does anyone's *religious* identity however coincide with their abstractly *human* identity? By humanity, must we understand common humanity? If so, only the things we share with others make us human. And that implies that we are never essentially human in virtue of our distinctions. It would seem that our culture and ethnicity determine our moral and spiritual quest and are sometimes, as with faiths such as Judaism and Hinduism, identical with it. The Quran uniquely promulgates the pre-historical myth of the first assembly of the disembodied souls of the entire human race (Q;7:172–3) avowing allegiance to the faith of self-surrender (*islām*). It is designed to pre-empt a predictable challenge to its supra-historical and apparently unempirical vision.

What is essentially and therefore universally human identity? Is it a biological or an ethical or ideological identity? When we are born, we are automatically human only in the biological sense. The emergence of a social, moral and spiritual identity requires sustained effort located in linear time and in an ethnically specific rather than generically human community. Discerning how an authentically human and humane identity is assembled, mutually recognized or reciprocally denied is the joint task of religion, art and literature.

The challenge of an obstinate human diversity remains. While moral self-mastery is the central if abstract aim of all religions, the route to attaining this is unavoidably culturally determined. The Quran, for all its universality, contains ethical injunctions that are culture-specific. Its moral contents would be different if Muhammad and his contemporaries had been, let us say, totally indifferent to sexual pleasure but inordinately fond of intoxicants or games of chance. Admittedly, no human society has been totally indifferent to sexual pleasure but my point is that societies differ in the way they prioritize and curb the pursuit of different pleasures. A universal religion must accommodate human moral variety rather than theoretically insist that there is no such variety on the grounds that all we have in common is our common humanity. For when we consider the sheer variety of human moral schemes, our common humanity is no more apparent than our so-called common sense. Insofar as all moral schemes converge, they do so only in regard to vague directives such as 'Do not harm one another' or 'Be just'. Any actual moral scheme is more specific precisely because it reflects the moral opinions of some specific community. The moral variety of human beings, as expressed in concrete cultural ways, remains irreducible and therefore hinders the project of any universal faith. No religion has successfully united what class, race, gender, culture and language have put apart.

Major faiths are organized around universal themes such as sin (Christianity) or suffering (*dukkha*, Buddhism).[3] These categories are universal in application, capturing invariant features of our basic humanity. But the Quran's claim to unify all faiths conceals a different type of ambition. The Quran eulogizes the specificity of human languages and colours as a divine sign (Q:30:22) but does not regard this multiplicity as hindering the establishment of a single faith for all humanity. On the contrary, it underlines this variety as embedded in a universal monotheism which transcends such ethnic particularity to unite us in our shared humanity. Thus, the Quran's reference to multiple human tongues is no factual anthropological insight or a comment inspired by some idle speculative curiosity. Rather it aims to affirm the unique universality of Islam as final religion despite the persistence of some types of unavoidable specificity and variety. For unlike suffering and sin and indeed our ability to speak any language as such, the multiplicity of our languages is a contingent feature of human diversity which should not mislead us about the underlying unity of our humanity. Racists fall victim to this error in regard to the variety of our skin colours.

VII

In this and the next two sections, I focus on the trio of Semitic monotheisms by exploring how and why Muslims behave as insiders in the struggle between Jews and Christians. Unlike Christianity, Islam does not colonize the scriptures of a previous faith. For Christians, the Old Testament is mere background although Isaiah is quoted as though it were a fifth canonical gospel. Islam is neither the inherited universalization of an extant Abrahamic tradition nor 'Judaism extended' eastwards unto the Gentiles. Islam was founded as an imperial and patriarchal but not racial monotheism. While not ethnically Arab in conception or design, it inherited part of its wider Semitic culture. It was theologically unique, not merely a member of an existing 'Abrahamic family'. To mine alleged parallels between Islam and its rival Semitic faiths is misguided. It is, in effect, an excuse to put this latecomer in its place as an unoriginal appendix to the Jewish and Christian dispensations. Islam did not subside into a Jewish or Christian sect precisely because it was established as a novel and mature meta-faith of universal ambitions outstripping the scope of any existing faith.

Sympathetic Western scholars charitably locate Islam by mapping it against the dual co-ordinates provided by Judaism and Christianity on the common axis of Abraham. The patriarch whose divinely conferred name meant father of the nations (*ab raḥam*; father of the womb) has inspired a trio of competitive pieties. Jews and Muslims venerate him as a saint and iconoclast while Christians revere him as a man of faith accredited through faith, not works of the law. Ironically, the Quran's references to Abraham seek not to establish a link with Judaism but rather to disengage the nascent Islamic movement from its compromised older relatives Judaism and Christianity which are tainted respectively with ethnic exclusivism and egregious doctrinal error (Q:2:135). The Torah and the Gospel were revealed after Abraham (Q:3:65). 'Abraham was neither a Jew nor a Christian' (Q:3:67; see also Q:2:140). The Pharisees rescripted sacred history to claim him as a Jew. The denial of Abraham as a Christian makes little historical sense since he could plausibly be claimed only by Jews. The Quranic Abraham must mean the monotheistic template, rather than the man, just as Israel meant not only Jacob himself but the seed and prophecy of that house. Indeed the Quran once calls Abraham 'a nation (*ummah*) obedient to God' (Q:16:120).

Pre-dating Islam was the sincerely agnostic movement of the *ḥanīf* (Q:16:120), the rightly inclined freelance seeker who rejected official Christianity and Judaism as errant in doctrine and morals. The *ḥanīf* sought a private route to God. Abraham is often called a *ḥanīf* (Q:3:67; 6:161). God invited him to submit directly to his will (Q:2:231) rather than join an existing community of believers. Several verses subtly condemn Jews and Christians as idolaters while rescuing Abraham, 'the right-handed iconoclast' (Q:37:93), from that evil reputation by association (Q:16:120–3). The Quranic rebuke that the covenant with Abraham does not extend to the unjust (Q:2:124) is a diplomatic way of accusing Jews and Christians of disloyalty to their professed creeds (see Q:19:58–60). In any event, *al-ḥanifiyyah*, in honour of Abraham the *ḥanīf* (pl. *ḥunafā'* at Q:22:31, describing Muslims) could have been an alternative name for Islam. Many modern Islamic missionary and educational organizations proudly use that epithet.

The community closest to Abraham, apart from his own few followers in his lifetime (see Q:60:4–6), is Muhammad's populous community (Q:3:68). In the five daily prayers, the petition, whispered while seated on the ground, eulogizes Abraham and his people (*qawm ibrāhīm*; Q:9:70). The supplication links them as historical exemplars and precedents with Muhammad's community which is seen as the sole authentic inheritor of the hand of grace. The Jewish and Christian communities in the intervening centuries are rejected as insincere. Jews failed to 'preserve God's book' (Q:5:46) while Christians forgot the monotheistic covenant with God (Q:5:14). Some commentators think that 'the straight path of those whom you [God] have blessed' (Q:1:7) refers to this primordial Abrahamic community. Classical commentary on this verse is unimaginative: predictably it identifies Jews as intended by 'those against whom you are wrathful' even though God's anger has been kindled by countless others, including pre-Islamic Arab tribes who were annihilated for their sins. Plausibly, Christian communities are intended by the euphemism 'ones gone astray [doctrinally]'.

The Quran once, rather sentimentally, calls Islam 'the religion (*millah*) of your father Abraham' (Q:22:78) and condemns as fools those who reject this *millat ibrāhīm* (Q:2:130). It does not mention the institutions of this Abrahamic Islam which could have been inherited by Muhammad. The duties of canonical prayer, fasting, pilgrimage and compulsory alms define religion as such, being associated, regardless of historical development and evolution, with every prophet. Islam traces its origins not to Abraham but to Adam and Noah, both classed as submissive (*muslim*) apostles (Q:3:33; 42:13, 37:83). Abraham is once called 'Noah's partisan' (Q:37:83).

The pilgrimage, centred on the the Ka'ba (cube) in Mecca, is the only ritual with a specified historical origin (see Q:2:158, 196–200; 22:26–37). The original Meccan shrine was allegedly built by Abraham and Ishmael (Q:3:96–7). If Abraham the nomad existed, he could have travelled from Mesopotamia to build the Meccan shrine. He settled his offspring in an infertile valley near 'your holy house' (Q:14:37) and prayed for providential intervention in the form of 'fruits', a metonym for food, from a native population whose hearts God might soften towards alien monotheist residents. The Quran calls this foundation 'the first house of worship erected for humankind' (Q:3:96), eulogizing it as 'the house of excellent pedigree' (Q:22:29, 33). This is to remind its Meccan pagan guardians about its true origins. It was chosen as the site of the Holy Mosque after Jews mocked Muhammad as a false Gentile prophet and hinted that Islam needed the sanctity of Jerusalem, the Jewish sanction. In the very first year after the exodus to Medina, the prayerful orientation towards Jerusalem, adopted by default by the first Muslims, was changed to the Meccan sanctuary of Abraham, an alternative 'Jewish' sanction (Q:2:142–5, 150).

VIII

The Abrahamic connection, then, was not intended to make Islam part of a rather dysfunctional and artificial Abrahamic family. Jews and Christians bestow Islam with this membership as a compliment: Muslims are really like Jews and Christians, only somewhat misguided. The Quran argues that Christians were 'muslims' until they began to focus on Christ and thus went astray and became Christians. Their very name betrays their idolatrous error. This is patronizing though not insulting. Christians could retort that Muslims are merely bad or misguided Christians. It is a family quarrel, so everyone is right but partly wrong.

Islam was not founded as a departure from an extant but decayed institutional template. It did not arise as a reform movement inside the Abrahamic cult since that was unavailable as an organized faith in Muhammad's Arabia. Although Islam inherits no doctrine from the past (apart from the vague but fertile idea of monotheism), the Quran speaks modestly of Islam as merely the *muṣaddiq* (confirmer) of its precedents (Q:3:3; 5:48). Ritually, only the hajj, in its Muslim version, distinguishes Islam. Versions of the Islamic rituals of prayer, fasting and charity are found in virtually all faiths.

Note the contrasting origins of Christianity. Unlike Muhammad, Jesus belonged to an ancient culture of prophets and scriptures. Jewish heretics became Christians by retaining the Hebrew Bible but mutating its arrangement: Prophets (*Nebi'īm*) closed the canon. They re-interpreted the re-arranged canon, viewing it as a fulfill-ment of messianic prophecy in the aftermath of prophecy's cessation and the still birth of apocalypse. Muslims, unlike Christians, do not re-arrange or even read the scriptures of a previous sister faith. Christianity is rightly seen as a reform move-ment emerging slowly among the sectarian varieties of first century Palestinian Second Temple (post-Ezra) Judaism. Islam did not emerge as a moral reform movement inside a doctrinally related and practised local faith.

There are two possible sources of misunderstanding here. In claiming that Islam emerges as a new faith inside secular history, I am not claiming that it is theo-logically unrelated to its two monotheistic rivals. My point is that Islam is not simply a family guest who arrives late for the banquet. Muslims, Christians and Jews worship the same God but dispute his character and reputation. The Quran affirms that Muslims worship the same God as their fellow monotheists (Q:2:136, 3:64, 84; 29:4). Linguistic evidence also supports this theological claim. 'Allah' is probably from proto-Semitic *ilāh* and indirectly related to Hebrew *ēl* (god). It cor-responds to the Greek *ho theos* found in the Septuagint and the New Testament.

Second, the claim about the shared racial origins of Arab and Jewish Semites has religious but no ethnic significance in the Quran. The scripture mentions Ishmael and Abraham as among the Arabs' ancestors. They play this role, how-ever, in virtue of being co-founders of God's house in Mecca (Q:2:125–9). The devoutly resigned patriarchs pray for a submissive community (*ummah musli-mah*) to proceed from them (Q:2:128–9). Their prayer is answered in Muhammad and the Muslims as opposed to the racial grouping of all Arabs. Ishmael is men-tioned in perfunctory lists of messengers (see Q:2:136, 140; 4:163); two isolated verses praise him for standard religious qualities (Q:6:86, 21:85). We get a glimpse of a strict patriarchal disciplinarian of whom there is no shortage in oriental cul-tures. The Quran commends Ishmael for keeping his family on an exacting plane of piety by ordering regular prayer and payment of obligatory alms-tax (Q:19:54–5). Muhammad is similarly ordered to enjoin prayer on his household (Q:20:132). The Quran does not name the son who was bound by Abraham for sacrifice but Muslim tradition holds it to be Ishmael, the first-born, rather than Isaac (Q:37:100–7; cf. Genesis 22:1–14). The Quran's allusions to Ishmael, the gentle son, are inexplicit (Q:37:101–107); the pericope just mentioned goes on to affirm God's blessings on Isaac also (Q:37:112–3). The victim was therefore Ishmael, the Arab; the aborted sacrifice is commemorated in the '*eid al-'adhā* (festival of sacrifice).

IX

Ironically, while some Jews and Christians regard Muslims as fanatics, the Quran condemns the fanaticism (*ghuluww*; lit. undue emphasis) of these earlier peoples of the book. In virtue of their location in sacred history, Muslims must see Islam as a rational and universal replacement for a compromised Judaeo-Christian monotheism. In a long pericope (Q:5:72–82), Christians who deify Jesus and Mary are condemned as no better than disbelievers who worship idols that can neither harm nor benefit their worshippers. This formulaic condemnation of the vain worship of idols is standardly used to condemn pagan deities but is used here of the worship of Jesus and his mother.

I have explored elsewhere the ways in which Islam's offer of salvation differs from the Christian offer rooted in its Judaic inheritance.[4] The Quran rejects the dogma that blood cleanses us of sin or atones for our iniquities against a holy God, a view fundamental to the Torah (see Leviticus) and inherited by the writers of the New Testament. In the Letter to the Hebrews, written in Italy (Hebrews 13:24), not Palestine, we read an implied rebuke to those who hankered after the older sanguine but splendid dispensation centred on the Jerusalem Temple sacrifices: Christ abolishes the Levitical sacrificial system by offering himself as a sinless victim. The Quran would regard this as superstition. It associates this type of view with the pagan corruption of the Islamic pilgrimage: our piety alone, not the blood or meat, reaches God (Q:22:36–7; Q:6:136; see Amos 5:21–5). The slaughter of animals, a culminating ceremony of the pilgrimage to Mecca, provides food for the poor. It is not a propitiatory or penitential sacrifice but rather a prayerful, grateful and gracious commemoration of Abraham's willingness to sacrifice what he loved most. His piety terminated the need for animal sacrifice; instead we are to surrender and sacrifice our will and purpose to God, the meaning and message of Islam.

We have now reached a stage when Islam and Christianity should converge as prophetic faiths. Universal peace cannot be attained without reconciliation between Christianity and Islam. (Culturally and politically, if not theologically, modern Jews are on the Christian side of the divide.) Conservative Muslims might object here because the Quran occasionally forbids Muslims from taking Jews and Christians as allies (*auliyā'*; Q:5:51, 57–68). The context is variously war, interfaith tensions and verbal mockery of Islam by these fellow monotheists. The Quran orders Muslims to sever ties only with those Jews and Christians who oppose and mock them in matters of their faith. This need not mean permanent hostility. Enemies can become friends (Q:60:7); hostility is strictly restricted to those who oppose Muslims because they are Muslims (Q:60:8–9). Believers are equally forbidden to befriend pagan members of their tribe (Q:60:1–6, 13) or even to take their own brothers and fathers as allies – the same word (*auliyā'*) is used – if they prefer infidelity to faith (Q:9:23). Muslims are further commanded not to prefer the company of disbelievers and hypocrites to that of fellow believers (Q:3:28, 118–20; 4:144–5).

Islam's approval of Judaism and Christianity is shown by its special regard for Moses and Jesus, both divinely honoured (*wajīh*; Q:3:45, 33:69). Furthermore, the Quran starts the process of reconciling Jews with Christians and uniting them as 'people (*ahl*) of the book'. The word *ahl* is in the singular. Jews and Christians have never self-described themselves as a single faith in this scriptural sense. The unifying label 'Judaeo-Christian' is recent and inadequate since it ignores two millennia of focused brutality, the anti-Semitic chronicle of Western Christian history. 'People of the book' is a more historically responsible term for the Jewish and Christian ecumenical community.

Christianity must now rediscover and re-affirm its Jewish roots by disowning its Christological emphasis. The Christological emphasis is, even judging by historically approved Christian criteria, a distortion of Christianity. Early Christianity was constantly judged by its parent faith which demanded a rigorous monotheism. Jewish Prophetic, Pauline Messianic and Gnostic Christianities compete in the early Church. The crux of contention is Christ's nature. As the early Christians aware of their Jewish heritage realized, excessive emphasis on Christology was a compromise of that true monotheism which Jesus himself, a true son of Israel, would have never disowned. Hence we have the convoluted and Byzantine early history of Christian councils whose members hammered out dogmas that would preserve Christianity's monotheism and not merely relegate it to a part of its Jewish heritage. Why did anyone think, however, that Semitic monotheism could be successfully translated into secular Hellenic categories?

There were exceptions: heretics closer to the truth than to orthodoxy. Paul of Samosata (200–275 CE) taught a form of 'monarchianism' which upheld the rigorous inherited Judaic monotheism of Christianity. He served as bishop of Antioch (c. 260–9 CE) but a synod (held in 268) deposed him after incorrectly accusing him of teaching that Christ was solely human. Paul taught that Christ was born a man but, at his baptism, was infused with the divine *logos* (word), a view that resembles the Quranic portrait of Jesus as 'a word from God' (Q:3:45). Paul's subtle views are found embedded in his *Discourses to Sabinus*, fragments of which are preserved in an anti-heretical book attributed to Anastasius.[5] The Christian dilemma was that stress on monotheism left little room for a full-blooded Christology that made Jesus divine.

The challenging of Christology by Islam is rejected by Christians as criminally attenuating Christ's status but it has the unique benefit of not compromising monotheism. The Quranic account of Jesus is a 'Christology minus a divine Christ'. This seems paradoxical or incoherent only to Christians since Jews and Muslims endorse a human Messiah. The view that Jesus was, metaphorically, a son of God, like Adam (see Luke 3:38) is compatible with the Quran.

The Jewish and Jewish–Christian visions were originally parochial, unlike the Islamic one. The early Israelites were henotheists who recognized Yahweh as their tribal god while acknowledging gods such as Baal and Dagon as the deities of their enemies, especially the 'Philistines'.[6] The Hebrew God evolved ethically and became international but never became the sole universal God even with the advent of Jesus since his mission was restricted to the Israelites (Q:3:49; Matthew 15:21–8).

Islam is a convincingly universal version of a Judaic monotheism which could never remove its nationalist taint, now exacerbated by the very existence of Jewish Israel. Ethnic Hebrew narratives, such as the tale of Joseph, later percolated to a worldwide audience through Islam which elevated them to an organic part of its message. By contrast, in the Christian universalization of Judaism, such tales were merely an outdated supplement that had served their purpose only in an older covenant. Christianity was universal in scope but it was not a version of Judaism. The rabbis closed the Hebrew canon in Jamnia in 90 CE because they did not want the writings that later came to be called the New Testament to become part of the Hebrew canon.

To obtain the perspective of a third insider, the Quran mocks Jewish–Christian scriptural rivalry: 'And the Jews say the Christians have nothing to stand on while the Christians say the Jews have nothing to stand on. But they both read the same book' (Q:2:113). Christians contend that the Torah of the Messiah abrogated the Mosaic law (Galatians 6:2). The Quran calls Jesus 'confirmer of the Torah' but also affirms his right to relax Torah law (Q:3:50) but only since prejudicially harsh rules were imposed for some special iniquities of the Jews (Q:6:146).

The Quran, unlike the New Testament, can be seen as a universalizing supplement to the Torah (Pentateuch). The Muslim scripture then becomes the compendium of Western *doctrinal* monotheism, making the Bible redundant. Admittedly, the vast literary riches of the two testaments of the Bible are lost in the process. Muslims feel that they alone are preservers of God's true word since the universal gift of revelation had earlier been reduced to an ethnic inheritance. Imperial Islam universalized monotheism; the Quran globalized the otherwise ethnically limited heritage of the Hebrew prophets.

Muslims see Christianity as too other-worldly and view Judaism, especially American Judaism since 1948, as too *this*-worldly, little more than a worldwide fundraising scheme for Israel. And many Jews and Christians see Islam as a violent ideology which is the number one enemy of humanity. It is unfortunate that Jews and Christians are too myopic, owing in part to racial considerations, to join Islam in putting up a united front against secularism. If only we had even one *powerful white* Muslim nation! It would help Westerners to lessen their negative focus on Islam's political modernity and to see Muslims as neither hyper-enemies of Western civilization nor its unconditional admirers.

X

Let us leave aside the eternal family quarrels among Jews, Christians and Muslims and broaden our scope. Karl Jaspers coined the expression 'the axial age' to refer to the first millennium before Christ when visions of a universally transcendent reality were first created in places as widely separated as ancient Israel, Greece, India and China. Such a vague universal vision did not address the issue of the *de facto* multiplicity of regional faiths; indeed the faiths that arose in the axial age remained confined to their places, with no mandate for global expansion. Islam, however, founded as an intentionally universal faith aiming for comprehensive scope, speedily transcended its Arab confines.

The ancient faiths of Judaism and Hinduism have inspired internal moral reform movements (Christianity and Buddhism) which gradually became, as accidents of history, potentially global faiths. Many faiths won their way, by painfully slow struggles, only to triumph finally with the catalytic aid of monarchs who converted to it. Thus the Persian King Cyrus (d. 530 BC) patronized Zoroastrianism. Both Christianity and Buddhism ('the Christianity of the East') fortuitously found second founders and political patrons. Paul and Constantine, like Ashoka (nicknamed the

Buddhist Constantine), were religious and political co-founders or re-founders of *de facto* universal faiths. A secular authority buttressed a religious faith. Islam, as *de jure* universal faith, triumphed without the patronage of any monarch: Muhammad, as his own Cyrus, Ashoka and Constantine, founded a faith and the empire to sustain it.

Judaism and Hinduism are complex cases since there is no single founder. Both contained universal impulses that lay latent and dormant for centuries. Only at a late stage of their evolution, as a result of impersonal forces rather than the intended consequences of the behaviour of a seminal man of action, did the impulses towards inclusion burst out of the ancient vessel. This explains the birth of new and more energetic offspring whose appeal is enduring and universal. Christianity is remarkable in that its worldwide distribution was achieved at the twilight stage of its history, courtesy of secular colonial expansion.

The Quran condemns religious sectarianism as a human innovation (Q:6:159). Islam therefore begins as a universal, universalizing and imperial faith. As its classical age recedes, it inspires sectarian and ethnic movements. Shi'ism and sectarian groups in its margins, sects such as the Isma'ilis, distill a parochial version out of Quranic Islam. Only Sunni Islam has, in principle and in ritual practice, preserved the Quran's intended global ecumenical scope.

The Quranic claim that God's warners and prophets have been sent to all communities is intended to show that Islam was always the universal faith of all peoples in the human past. Therefore, it is unremarkable if it should be one in the future. Admittedly, the Quran's list of prophets is illustrative, suggestive and provocative (of memory), not comprehensive, detailed or exhaustive in scope. But its intention is to unify religions. The moral urge to include everyone in God's plan is a controversial issue in the theology of other faiths: theologians struggle with the injustice of God's apparently arbitrary if not scandalous decision to restrict salvation to one remote tribe in ancient Judaea or, more recently, to a group of prosperous Christian nations in Europe and North America. And he is the God of love. The Quran is the earliest document in world history to address the moral question of inclusivist pluralism. Humankind was originally one community, later ruptured by the preaching of God's messengers (see Q:2:213; 10:19). The appearance of Muhammad was intended to re-unify the human race by creating a universal monotheistic order. Instead, his advent has increased and embittered the conflict among the Western monotheisms and between religion and secularism.

XI

In this hiatus, I must note how the Quran presents itself purely as scripture universalized. It will equip us to see how Muslims intend to engage contemporary issues of race and ethnicity for a faith claiming universal finality.

Wilfrid Owen was reluctant to use the names of any individuals in his poems so that he could achieve a prophetic elasticity of application for them; he probably wanted to make his figures like allegories in a work such as John Bunyan's *Pilgrim's Progress*. It is a quaint way to introduce an aspect of the Quranic style of narration. Owen writes: 'If I thought the letter of this book would last, I might have used proper names'.[8] He hopes that the spirit of his poetry will survive after the names of heroes and battlefields are forgotten. The Quran similarly testifies to the most general archetypal truths about our humanity: each pericope has a mythic inclusiveness and completeness characteristic of scripture and of world-class literature, especially first class poetry.

By consistently subordinating the particular to the general, the incidental to the intrinsic, the Quran necessitates the need for interpretation and commentary. Its verses are marked by a sustained and studied ambiguity in choice of words; the scripture's commentary on incidents in sacred history and contemporaneous events seeks to attain the greatest scope and relevance through maintaining the maximal level of generality. A verse or an expression is to be taken generally unless it can be shown to permit of exceptions. Contemporaneous and ancient events are both described vaguely; the resulting elasticity permits different possibilities and, problematically, satisfies the aspirations of rival contenders. The scripture's widespread use of indefinite descriptions nebulous enough to denote several different personalities contributes to this plasticity of meaning.

Typically, individuals are identified by definite and indefinite descriptions rather than by name. 'The slave of God' *('abdullah* at Q:72:19) refers to Muhammad himself during his visit to Ta'if. Again, the complex indefinite description 'those who lower their voices in the Prophet's presence' and are therefore 'elected for virtue' (Q:49:3) can be made definite: it refers to Umar and Abu Bakr, the first two caliphs. Shiite readers claim to locate some favourable indefinite descriptions as intending to exalt Ali (see Q:9:19) and imply that he was among the few who truly understood Muhammad's mission. Sunnis are offended by the suggestion that Muhammad's disciples were no better than Jesus' disicples (as portrayed in the New Testament) and that Muhammad failed to inspire a populous community of sincere believers.

One Quranic allusion is a coded reference to Moses' teacher who taught him esoteric knowledge beyond prophecy (Q:18:60–82). Described as 'one of our servants ... whom we had taught knowledge from us' (Q:18:65), he is often identified with the wandering mystic Al-Khidr (lit. 'the ever-green man'). Carl Jung was fascinated by the wanderings of this enigmatic figure, seeing in him the wandering Jew exiled from the human condition.

The Quran's references to geography are also inexplicit. Its references to the holy land are certainly vague enough to intend Canaan or Palestine (Q:5:21; 7:137) but also Arabia, possibly Mecca (Q:27:91; 28:57, 85; 90:1–2; 95:1–3). *Al-Haram* (the forbidden or safe, thus holy) was a name for Mecca (see Q:28:57 where it occurs without the definite article). Again, 'Iram of the Pillars' (Q:89:7) is nebulous enough to refer to Damascus, Alexandria, or 'Ād. Places in the itinerary of the traveller called *dhū al-qarnayn*, the lord of two epochs (lit. the one with two horns), incorrectly identified with Alexander, are as mysterious as the traveller himself (see Q:18:83–98).

The Muslim scripture clarifies some doctrinal matters in interfaith relations but does not comment on factual controversies where we merely indulge our speculative curiosity. Thus, typically, Joseph is sold for 'a paltry price' (Q:12:20). It contrasts with biblical precision on such details (Genesis 37:28); the Quran regards these as incidental to faith and thus unworthy of comment. Again, Mary withdrew to 'an Eastern place' (Q:19:16), her labour occurred in 'a remote place' (*makānan qaṣiyyan*; Q:19:22). The comparative form of this adjective is used to describe the mosque (*masjid*) in Jerusalem as *al-aqṣā* (the most remote; Q:17:1), the traditional platform for Muhammad's departure to heaven. The mosque's location varies, in commentaries, from Jerusalem to heaven itself since there was no earthly mosque in Jerusalem until after its conquest by Muslims, six years after Muhammad's death.[9] *Masjid*, however, means any place of prostration towards God; used with the definite article, it refers to Solomon's Temple (at Q:17:7).

Consider this passage:

> On the day when the wicked one will bite his hands [to express regret], saying, 'Woe is me! I wish I had chosen a way with the messenger. Alas for me! I wish I had never taken such a one for a friend'.
>
> (Q:25:27–8)

The expressions 'the wicked one' and 'such a one' identify two specific men in Muhammad's day. Commentators take the indefinite descriptions to refer to any and every wrong doer and imposter.

Events in Muhammad's life are mentioned in a generalized and didactic way with no exotic or sensational colouring of the kind we might expect if we have read the adventures of Arab heroes such as Al-Antar or of scheming Scheherazade in *The 1001 Nights*. For example, the serious slander against Muhammad's young wife Aisha is related in a detached way and immediately recruited for moral and legal purposes (Q:24:11–26). The Prophet's wife, not mentioned by name, is the archetype of any chaste and virtuous but heedless Muslim woman whom licentious men and women might slander (Q:24:23). Not naming a woman was a sign of chivalrous regard for her. Devout Muslims still rarely name their wives when speaking to those outside the family circle.

Few in the Prophet's entourage are singled out by name (or epithet) for special comment. Zaid (Ibn Harithah), Muhammad's freed slave and adopted son, is the only Muslim named in the Quran (Q:33:37). It occurs in the context of a sex scandal already mentioned in Chapter 1. Zaid is at first described only as 'the one whom God had favoured and you [Muhammad] had favoured' (Q:33:37). From the rest of this long verse, the first audience could identify the recipient of this remarkable praise. Later in the verse, to avoid ambiguity, circumlocution and possible misidentification, he is also named.

Muhammad's paternal uncle, Abd Al-'Uzza, named to honour a female idol, belonged to Muhammad's clan. He opposed Islam and was given the derogatory epithet Abu Lahab, 'father of flame [of hell]' (Q:111:1).[10] He died a disbeliever but remains immortal since he has a surah named for him. Abu Lahab is the only enemy thus singled out for censure. Muhammad's other paternal uncle, Abu Jahl, in his lifetime called 'father of ignorance', was later vilified even more as 'the Pharaoh of Islam'. Named Amr Ibn Hisham by his parents, he was among the top leaders killed at Badr. An early revelation refers to him as hindering the course of piety of a servant (of God), that is, Muhammad (see Q:96:9–19).

XII

Apart from the time of Islam's earliest dynasty, the Umayyads (661–750 CE), there has never been an ethnic or secular Arab as opposed to a racially universal (hence purely human) way of being a Muslim. This dynasty is the first Arab nationalist movement, a neo-Byzantine rather than fully Islamic empire, and the earliest and only successful secularization of Islam. Its successor was the universal Islamic dynasty of the Abbasids (750–1258 CE) which made Islam into a universal moral system as merciless in condemning its own pagan past as that of the convert peoples. Ever since, even Arab cultural customs must be wrapped in *Islamic* dress to secure legitimacy. For example, the Saudis justify the absurd custom of banning female drivers by using specious religious arguments such as preserving society's moral purity, a quality so fragile that it is threatened by any freedom of movement for women.

Islam, unlike Judaism or Sikhism, is exclusively a faith, not an ethnicity reinforced by a faith. We see the larger point here if we compare the scope and substance of Islamic identity with the same concern in Judaism. Jews can affirm their religious identity by racial and by religious routes. That is why even nominal Jews are within the fold and boldly joke that they are not really Jews, only 'slightly Jew-ish'! This witticism is made possible by an accident of language, a Jewish casualness about identity and by the fusion of culture, race and religion in normative Judaism. It would be impossible to savour such a witticism in Islam even if language assisted us. 'I am only a Muslim because I am an Arab' is the closest one gets and it is senseless, even as parody or humour since Christians and Jews can be Arabs. Indeed Arabic was *a* language of Christianity long before it became *the* sacred language of Islam.

Arabs have seldom identified Islam with the affirmation of a racial creed. The Jews were *ethnically* a people before they met their God at Sinai. The Arabs became a people only after Muhammad introduced them to their God. The Arab tribes, the Bedouin and urban Arabs alike, were not united in virtue of their ethnicity but by Islam, a faith which contained a frontal attack on the priority of ethnicity (Q:9:23–4, 60:1–9). Islam created an Arab identity not by erasing the Arabic dimension but by transcending it in the name of a universal religion which required one to rise above tribalism and thus join the human family. As a prophetic, ethical, and universal monotheism, Islam, unlike Western civilization, its chief modern opponent, created a wholly religious rather than ethnic civilization.

Having said that, Arabs would have been too proud to embrace a divine revelation if it had been sent to non-Arabs charged with proselytizing them (Q:26:198–9). Imagine a 'Quran' sent to Persians who then converted the Arab tribes to Islam. The expression 'a Persian Quran' occurs uniquely at Q:41:44. It is intended as a racial joke to be savoured by Muhammad's contemporaries.

Judging by the success of the Prophet's mission, the Quranic outlook clearly appealed to most Arabs. The Quran addresses them as 'Believers!' rather than 'Arab believers!' or 'Arabs!' or 'Quraysh!' Even when extolling its Arabic character, the Quran never addresses Arabs as an ethnic community. The expression *ummah 'arabiyyah* is absent from the Quran. The scripture appeals to the Arabs' renowned sense of racial pride (for example at Q:21:10 and conditionally at Q:3:110) but never uses an ethnic form of address. It stipulates the conditions that make them an avant-garde community of truth: 'You are the best community ever raised for the benefit of humanity [because] you enjoin decency and forbid indecency' (Q:3:110). Unfailingly, it uses expressions with a universal intent, addresses its readers as believers and humankind and, less frequently, as Children of Adam. Muhammad addressed his fellow Arabs (qua Muslims) in a farewell oration, standing on the plain of Mount Arafat. He affirmed the moral and political solidarity of all Muslims rather than of all Arabs, adding that no human being is superior or inferior to another, except in respect of piety (see Q:49:13).

The Quran threatens the Arabs contemplating collective apostasy: God can replace them with others who would honour God and serve him more enthusiastically (Q:9:39; 47:38). It is impossible to imagine any community serving Islam with the enthusiasm of the early Muslims, the Prophet's noble companions. In later history, Iranians, Turks and Mongols converted and became passionate adherents, even patrons of Islamic resurgence. Afghans, Malays and Pakistanis today are more attached to Islam than most Arab Muslims. The prosperous Gulf Arabs are only nominally Muslims: Pakistani missionaries are dispatched to the Gulf countries to propagate Islam just as African Christian missionaries now visit the godless UK to proselytize a nation that once converted much of Africa to Christianity.

Islamic duties can be practised with excessive ritual precision betraying undue reverence for their Arabic dimension. Many non-Arab Muslims, including royalty, especially in south-east Asia, revere Arabs as patrons, not mere adherents, of Islam. This respect is fast decreasing as a result of tales of Arab racism retailed by returning pilgrims and by taxi drivers and labourers who speak of unrelieved rudeness from immigration officials and ordinary inhabitants of holy cities, especially Mecca.[11]

XIII

In closing this chapter, I note how religion is racialized and hence compromised by ethnicity even in universal faiths. Christianity and modern Judaism suffer from too close an identification with ethnicity owing to the colonial history of white Europeans and settler minorities in Palestine, South Africa, North America, Australia and New Zealand. European Christianity and evangelical North American Christianity are potent mainly as sources of Western racial pride and solidarity in the face of the immigrant threat.[12] When some right-wing commentators call America 'a Christian nation', the adjective is synonymous with white. Christianity becomes a source of acceptable racial pride rather than of true faith and conviction. Among African Americans, Christianity often reduces, without remainder, to culture and 'Churchianity'.

Third world conversions to Christianity, especially in South Korea and Pakistan, often express racial solidarity with the West: converts associate themselves with the secular (pagan) but powerful West rather than the poor but largely devout east. Most Christian denominations such as the (Catholic) Maronites in the Lebanon (associated with the French colonial masters) are despised by poorer groups such as the Shiite Muslims. Indeed, such resentment was the main cause of the civil war that ruined that nation. Copts in nearby Egypt are more assimilated and not seen as allies of an alien occident although dissident writers such as Nageeb Mahfouz are suspected of succumbing to liberal Coptic influences.

Islam, for all of its Arabic nature distilled in the Quran, potentially possesses an internationalist character. The struggle for the doctrinal universality of Islam, a shift away from its Arabolatry, marks Islam's fifteenth century. It will not be an imperial or territorial expansion but rather an internal intellectual opening of the range of Islam beyond its initial Arabic limitations. The Arabocentric focus will be lost as Islam grounds itself in lands distant from its Arab heartland and develops a theology, not merely law, alert to the local dimension. There is a precedent for this already in the case of the secularization of Turkey which was not a rejection of Islam but rather a rejection of Islam's Arab identity.[13] Turks wanted to become part of an affluent and progressive Europe, not of a poor and stagnant Arabia. The primary motive for Turkish secularization was ethnic, not religious. Turks were effectively choosing between ethnic, not religious, identities.

Only in its (orthodox) Sunni form does Islam retain its Arabocentric character. Iranian Shiites have long rejected Islam's Arabian stress. Although we owe most of the classical scholarship in Arabic to Arabicized Persians, they did not see Islam as an Arab achievement but rather as a divine one. Shiism originates as an early *Arab* sectarian tradition, later championed by Iranians. Eleven of the dozen Shiite imams are buried in (Arab) Iraq with only one, Musa Al-Kazim, buried in Iran. The great secret to Iran's ability to be the buffer which prevented Arabicization East of Iran is the magic of Persian language and literature. Equipped with the versatility and eloquence of the ancient Persian vernacular, Iranians withstood the Arab onslaught and maintained their cultural identity. Persian purists, especially the poet Ferdowsi in his encyclopedic chronicle of kings (*Shahnameh*), self-consciously avoided Arabic words in order to preserve the dignity of the Persian heritage against an upstart Arab civilization.

Muslims find an instructive parallel in Christian origins. In *Romans* and *Galatians*, Paul, the real if unacknowledged founder of Christianity and the sole founder of the Protestant variant of that faith,[14] forced Jews to scrutinize their self-image as people of exclusive covenant. He freed the nascent Christian movement from its Hebrew and Aramaic cultural and linguistic manacles; few today associate Christianity with Jews or Hellenized monotheists. Islam, however, has always been intimately annexed by and to Arab culture. Occasionally, some modern Arab writer will indulge a racist obsession with Islam's exclusively Arab genius and genesis, extolling it as an eternally valid divine vehicle of Islamic identity, integrity and unity.[15] Only an Arab-centred Islamic brotherhood can, we are told, redeem the Muslim world of its chaos. Such views lead many to see Arabs as 'the white men of the East'. They can, with impunity, racially denigrate other believers. Sadly, most white Western converts to Islam display the same racial superiority and arrogance that was traditionally restricted to Arab Muslims in their dealings with non-Arab non-white Muslims. In most Islamic organizations of south east Asian background, for example, one notes that white converts proceed directly, within a few months, from being neophytes to community leaders.

Tribal Arab Islam can be an incubus on the development of an enlightened Islam free of the inveterate racism and sexism of traditional Arab nations who pay lip-service to the Quran's just cosmopolitan vision. The Quran is not theologically Arabian, only linguistically so (inevitably) and ritually and culturally so (avoidably). Although the liturgical use of Quranic Arabic is sacred, all human tongues are praised as miraculous (Q:30:22), perhaps owing to the high threshold of abstract intelligence required for the acquisition of any language, a barrier that restricts it to human beings. The astonishing varieties of our languages, colours, cultures and religious rites are signs of God's genius and wisdom (Q:22:34; 30:22; 35:28). Nonetheless, the revelation consecrates aspects of Arab culture and promotes an Arab-centred Islamic brotherhood through the annual pilgrimage to Mecca, forever linked with absolute Abrahamic monotheism. Since God's House is in Mecca, the pilgrimage cannot rotate to different Islamic capitals each year – from Rabat in Morocco, facing the Atlantic west, to Jakarta in Indonesia, marking the faith's far Eastern frontier.

Part II

The twin birth

Islam as empowered religion

4 A political religion

Muhammad as statesman

I

In the late summer of 622 CE, a Jewish peasant from Yathrib, an oasis town some 200 miles north of Mecca, spotted two men heading towards the shade of palm trees. He recognized them: Muhammad and his staunch companion Abu Bakr (c. 573–634 CE), destined to become the first of the four 'rightly guided' republican caliphs who succeeded the Prophet. He knew they had escaped Meccan persecution to seek asylum in Yathrib, a city later renamed as *al-madīnat al-nabiyy* (city of the messenger). He was not prescient enough to know that their arrival marked the beginning of a new era of universal history.

The *hijrah* (migration) of Muhammad and his disciples in 622 is, apart from the (historically unverifiable) exodus of the ancient Israelites from Egypt to the holy land,[1] probably one of the world's most politically pregnant migrations. It capsulizes Islam as a tale of a prophet in two cities: powerless in Mecca, exiled but eventually powerful in Medina. The root of hijrah (*h/j/r*) is used in the Quran and is found in the naming of the group of emigrants (*Al-Muhājirūn*) who left Mecca. It is used in its literal sense once (Q:73:10) where it means to sever kinship ties, a traumatic decision in a tribal culture. Migration is a good idiomatic translation although it sounds too grand for a journey within the same country. Since Muhammad spent 18 months negotiating the terms of settlement for his followers, the orientalist description 'The Flight' is incorrect – although he was about to be assassinated on the eve of his departure.

Umar Ibn Al-Khattab (581–644 CE), the second caliph, credited with many judicious innovations, chose the time of Muhammad's migration for inaugurating the Islamic era.[2] Why commemorate a time of apparent defeat? Umar could have selected pivotal events in Muhammad's life: his birth, the inaugural revelation or when he scored his first victory at the confrontation at Badr, a small town southwest of Medina. Badr is a strong candidate since it is only one of two battles named in the Quran (Q:3:123), the other being the crucial ambush at Hunayn (Q:9:25). Badr is also alluded to often (Q:3:13; 8:5–19, 42–49) since it is Islam's first political triumph and hence proof of divine favour: it eradicated the flower of pagan Arab aristocracy and empowered the nascent faith. In world military history, it qualifies as that decisive battle which was engaged with the least total number of combatants: about 300 Muslims (equipped with three horses) versus about 1,000 pagans. The casualties were negligible: about 70 dead warriors and no civilians.

Umar chose the *hijrah* to date the Islamic era, a decision disputed by few Muslims.[3] This event neatly divides the Quran into Meccan and Medinan although the transition itself was gradual and fluid. It irreversibly and instantaneously transformed Islam from a persecuted ideology in a marginal peninsula to an embryonic imperial power. In moving to Medina, Muhammad did not move into the fatal obscurity of exile or the trauma of persecution and defeat. It was not his Jerusalem. An unarmed apostle taught an iconoclastic creed; an impenitent pagan city expelled him. Muhammad left his native city for the sake of his Lord who, even in the Meccan period, describes himself provocatively as 'the Lord of this house' referring to the city's central shrine. Muhammad took the high road to exile at 53 when he was too old to be a youthful idealist. Pathos permeates the opening couplet of the Quranic chapter called 'The City', referring to Mecca. 'I swear by this city and you are a free man (*ḥillun*)[4] in this city.' The love of God has a greater claim on us than the love of our birth-place. Islam condemns nationalism though modern Muslims are no less nationalistic than non-Muslims.

The *hijrah* was an exemplary decision for Muslim armies which, after Muhammad's death at 63, swept rapidly beyond the Arab peninsula into lands as distant as France and China, almost fulfilling the Islamic avowal to conquer the known world. A popular, possibly apocryphal but instructive, story of the Berber (Muslim) general Tariq Bin Ziyad, on the eve of the conquest of Spain in 711, illustrates this point. Overhearing his soldiers at night yearning to return to their motherlands, he burnt the boats that had almost brought them to the Spanish mainland, via the Jebel Al-Tariq, the rock named in his honour (still echoed in 'Gibraltar'). The *hijrah* of those who abandoned their possessions in Mecca was undertaken in the same spirit although Muhammad received divine reassurance of a triumphant return.[5] Muslim warriors saw themselves as extending Muhammad's witness to that almighty God to whom belonged the whole earth. Had the Apostle not left his native city for the sake of this God? Such imitative piety has appealed to many Muslims who, less dramatically, left home and comfort to venture abroad. For the sake of their faith, they abandoned the familiar coast which becomes home only after one has left it. The exodus to Medina still inspires Muslims to respect the duty to transcend local and national boundaries in the interests of a faith that is Arabian in origin but global in moral and spiritual appeal. Islam rejects the jingoistic motto, 'My country, right or wrong, left or right'[6] since God alone is great.

II

For non-Muslim historians, Muhammad was an Arab Caesar, a 'prophet'-emperor; Muslims would put the cautionary quotation marks around 'emperor'. Both would agree that his faith, a healthy twin birth of faith and empire, matured into a compulsively political and politically successful religion. Was the empowered portion of his prophetic career morally legitimate? This issue requires extended treatment since it involves a strategic theological concern unique to Islam. Muhammad Ibn Abdullah, a religious reformer and founder of a faith, dirtied his hands with the political muck. To assess his moral character and the achievements of his political militancy, we must command intellectual patience, inter-faith courtesy and skills of conceptual analysis.

These virtues are partly present in the work of the Anglican missionary–scholar and Arabist Kenneth Cragg whose critique of Islam's involvement with power relies on a multi-lingual scholarship buttressed by some 70 years of experience of the volatile Middle East. His major disquisitions are *Muhammad and the Christian: A Question of Response* and its sequel, *Jesus and the Muslim: An Exploration*.[7] Muslims wrongly dismiss or despise this intriguing mixture of insight and over-sight. Many Muslims and some non-Muslims accuse Cragg of being a missionary to Islam rather than to Muslims: a Christian hoping to Christianize and hence subvert Islam rather than crassly convert its adherents.[8] Cragg's largely articulate reservations deserve a reply at their own level of theological depth if not their stylized literary intelligence. His provocative but courteous criticisms enable us to sketch the contours of Islam as a politically aware religion. His agonized and searching thoughts force intelligent Muslims and non-Muslims to discern the ways in which, and the motives for which, Islam was from the beginning an ineradicably political faith.

Despite its avowed Christian axioms, Cragg's critique is largely didactic and objective, not polemical or propagandist. Cragg occasionally lapses from his own demanding standards of sincerity and objectivity. I then take him to task by iden-tifying the real (as opposed to professed) motives for his accusations and I expose his ostensible grounds as being merely motives. While I dispute Cragg's scholarly but combative characterization of political Islam and reject its policy entailments, I acknowledge that his writings deepen our theological understanding of normative Islam's political facet.

Cragg also wisely acknowledges in the very title of his treatise that Christians will have to take a stance on Muhammad, not only on Islam or the Quran. This is rare in Christian–Muslim relations. Thus, given the centrality of Muhammad to Islam, a document such as the Vatican's declaration of approval of Islamic mono-theism and of Muslims as fellow monotheists (who adore Jesus and his mother Mary) remains painfully silent on the status of Muhammad and the Quran.[9]

Cragg resembles earlier Christian polemicists in criticizing Muhammad for his decision to leave Mecca. He too alleges that this move politicized and therefore compromised and corrupted the Prophet's pristine Meccan Islam. At the water-shed of his prophetic calling, Muhammad betrayed his vocation. Unlike true servants of the word, he opted for force – a change of policy reflected in the Quran's partial alteration of style from moral preaching and private persuasion to political and legal injunction and coercion. This Christian reservation, historically inspired by a fanatical hatred of its rival, is in Cragg's work married to a thought-ful indictment of the Quranic–Muhammadan involvement with power which persists in our world where zealous Muslims produce unmanageably anarchic consequences for Western policy-makers.

Cragg questions Islam's unified enterprise of religious faith and temporal power. His accusations and reservations are theologically and politically consequential; he offers intelligent but partisan (Christian) grounds for accusing Muhammad of certain political delinquencies. Cragg condemns the Prophet's decision to recruit the political wing to achieve religious ends which, for Cragg, can never justify, let alone sanctify, the chosen secular means. Cragg's ancillary aim is to question the Muslim claim that the Shariah-based state delivers righteousness and justice in social policy.

In this and the next chapter, I show that Cragg's Christian critique misidentifies the political dimension of Muhammad's Medinan militancy. Allegations against Muhammad's political activities are exaggerations, their content nugatory. Cragg also misunderstands the Quran's perspective on tragedy and, more narrowly, on failure in the political lives of believers.

Bear in mind two points, one temperamental, one substantive. Christian thinkers are not the only ones in the grip of an ideological vision. Political issues connected with religion rapidly become intractable and expose the depth of other loyalties which secrete criteria congenial to judgments predetermined by unspoken theological assumptions. This disables impartial inquiry by precluding even temporary suspension of dogma. In inter-faith gatherings, doors are often slammed to make a point and to make an enemy. Our sustained argument will be broken by several reflective hiatuses which encourage intellectual patience, dispel misunderstandings and thus reduce prejudicial rigour against the opponent.

Substantively, we need a working definition of 'political religion' which shall be refined under pressure of inquiry. A faith can be political in one or more of four different senses; a continuum stretches from the nominally political to the robustly political.

Apart from religions that advocate monastic isolationism, all religions must have some dealings with the political order of their day. The level of engagement differs but indifference is not a viable stance. Thus, rabbis negotiated with Gentile rulers as Jewish communities struggled to survive in different lands. As a people with no army, until recent times, they adopted the Talmudic principle of 'the law of the land is law', a conciliatory and judicious maxim traceable to Mar Samuel who headed the academy at Nehardea (2nd to 3rd century BCE).[10] Believers must at least win the sympathy of the hostile political establishment. Again, owing to suspicion of subversion, Christianity in the pre-Constantine Roman empire barely survived: Christians were accused of being 'atheists', deniers of the Roman gods and indeed even criminals and cannibals. Countless Christians preferred martyrdom to submitting to 'the cult of the emperor' which legally obliged them to worship allegedly divine but shockingly depraved Roman emperors.

Second, most religious believers accept the moral obligation to challenge the unjust political and economic structures of their day. The preferred route is peaceful protest. Even monastic Buddhism is not without this type of political ambition. Radical Christianity, as liberation theology, is resolutely judgmental against oppression but still officially ambivalent about armed resistance. Islam shares liberation Christianity's moral credentials but is exceptional in clearly endorsing violence, even revolution, though only where chances of success seem high. Activist Muslims do not see Islam as simply a school of radical criticism and social protest – such as Marxism in the post-Soviet era – but rather as a virile faith which aims to endanger the rapacious material interests of super-powers. Additionally, Islam has inspired countless nationalist resistance movements against imperial intruders, foreign occupiers, and armed settler minorities in, for instance, Iraq, Afghanistan, Kashmir, Palestine–Israel, the Lebanon and elsewhere. In Chapter 5, we expound the liberation theologies of Islam and Christianity.

At the other end of the spectrum are the third and fourth variants, both unique to Islam. The Quran seeks to absorb politics into religion and thus sanctify it. Muslim jurists have developed a classical theology of temporal power. Islamic political ambition is typically embodied in the drive to establish an Islamic caliphal state whose power exceeds the merely social pressure of communal cohesion. Private piety is publicly and forcibly enforced through paternalistic legislation. The state, which upholds the Shariah, seeks to extend its power into private lives. Is the acquisition and administration of this power sufficiently democratic and hence accountable to an electorate? Or is it always autocratically acquired and then dictatorially applied? These issues and their countless ramifications engage us in Chapters 6, 7, 10 and 11.

Finally, Islam is the paradigm of religion born as imperial power. No other faith was intentionally founded to be a successful amalgam of faith and power. Although Muslims did not convert the world at the point of a sword, they did try to conquer it in the fastest and largely permanent conquest of recorded military history. Islam's imperial reach supplements its universal religious appeal and, often through Sufi mysticism, its peaceful potential for expansion and proselytizing. Pre-Constantine Christianity and both major varieties of Buddhism, however, are missionary faiths which extended their scope gradually by touching the hearts of many men and women, of great character, settled in lands distant from the original homes of these faiths. Their founders did not fight pitched battles in order to establish a faith that would quickly blossom into a religious empire.

III

For Muslims, Islam begins in paradise; for others, it began in Mecca when the first five Quranic verses were revealed in 610 of the Christian era. By 632, it had found adequate – Muslims say perfect – political expression in Medina as Muhammad the Prophet actualized God's political providence. Cragg's charge is simple and, discounting its nuances, a refined version of an older orientalist explanation for the backward nature of Muslim cultures. During the height of colonial penetration, subjugation and humiliation of virtually the entire Muslim world, the Victorian administrators of empire proposed that the Islamic unification of religious and political power hindered social progress. Many Westerners today correctly note that economic enterprise, civil rights and democracy are absent from virtually all Islamic cultures. Cragg's emphasis, however, is moral and theological: Muhammad as prophet acted treasonably to God's cause. In the hour of eclipse and crisis, he allowed the voice of his inner Caesar to drown out God's gentler voice – much as a man, irritated by unwelcome news bulletins or advertisements, uses the mute button to swallow the unpleasant messages. Eager to see Islam triumph, the Arabian iconoclast sought a short-cut. In matters of the spirit, unlike those of the flesh, Cragg warns condescendingly, we have no short-cuts or guarantees of success.

Cragg agrees with Muslims that the exodus to Medina is the fulcrum of the Prophet's life but interprets it as the juncture where 'prophethood culminates and rulership begins'.[11] Muhammad's tenure in the prophetic office terminated while he was still trapped in the Meccan quagmire. Exiled in Medina, he was no longer a prophet but rather a king or general implementing, with secular means, the religious commission he received in his native city. To be precise, however, as we saw in Chapter 1, the empowered phase begins late into the Meccan period itself as Muhammad negotiates with some representatives of the Medinan tribes after being informally appointed their arbitrator. While in Mecca, he negotiated the pledge of Medina. From 620 to 622, for almost 18 months, he played a combined religious and political role in the lives of the increasing numbers of Medinan converts. This historical detail has some bearing on the conceptual and theological dispute.

Cragg has religious reasons for sharpening the Meccan–Medinan divide. The divine message cannot legitimately be implemented in our world except through verbal exhortation, repeated enunciation and total trust in God. Muhammad's decision to leave Mecca betrays an unworthy and religiose desire to exploit non-verbal means to secure worldly success. His search for such auxiliary means indicates his impatience with the divinely authorized but limited arsenal available to genuine prophets. Cragg quotes with approval the Quran's address to Muhammad: 'Your task is to convey the message; it is for us [God] to do the reckoning' (Q:13:40 confirmed at Q:88:21–26). Both Meccan and Medinan verses support this view. It is no incidental emphasis born in a fugitive mood of despair but rather one embedded in the Quran's divine-human division for prophetic labour. In verses about Abraham, we read the same slogan (Q:29:18). Three (unnamed) prophets jointly make this claim (Q:36:17). The Quran's initial revelation (Q:96:1–5) was wholly centred on education. The Meccan scripture continued to instruct Muhammad that his only weapon is the Quran preached and that only only those inclined to fear God will heed the message (Q:25:52; 36:11; 50:45).

Cragg protests that the Meccan pagans did not have to wait for God to do the reckoning. The Prophet from Arabia did not bear the sword in vain: the Caesar in him did not let vengeance belong to the Lord. For Cragg, Muhammad's activism during his Medinan decade is, charitably interpreted, an unconscious and perhaps unintentional betrayal of the Gospels' more rigorous spirituality. Muhammad's political authority as statesman negates his religious authority as prophet. For conscientious Christians, reared on a diet of agape and divine atonement of sin, aware of Jesus' decision to drink from the cup of suffering in order to suffer willingly if unjustly, there must be 'an inescapable reservation of heart about the power dimension'[12] of the Arabian Prophet's post-*hijrah* activism on God's behalf. God's envoy is entitled only to take the wayward horse to water, not to force the animal to drink. Since Muhammad ignored this restriction, the Christian must return an adverse verdict on his militancy.[13]

In his indictment of political Islam, Cragg gives reasons for a prophet's refusal to drink from the cup of power. As political sanction chases it, the evil that rejects God's laws withdraws deeper into unconquered hearts still governed by profane norms; hypocrisy becomes their only refuge. Our impiety is concealed only from the public gaze since God is, as the frequent Quranic litotes has it, well aware of it (Q:11:123, 59:18). The religious mission to cauterize sin and perversity is a task beyond the scope of politically coercive weapons. Secular power builds only terrestrial, not spiritual empires. Ultimate human needs remain unfulfilled since no amount of power can accomplish love's task. Even where power seems to succeed, it fails: it generates compromise, contradiction and betrayal of the very principles it seeks to establish and follow. Love alone has the range and capacity for plumbing the depths of our inveterate injustice and perversity in order to reach faith's inner sanctum. The sword, preaches Cragg, can never replace the power of the message of love.[14]

For all his professed Christian caution against judging others, Cragg judges Islam and Muhammad. He mitigates this indictment, however, by conceding that Islam was a religious achievement which helped Muhammad realize his destiny as a reformer and offered spiritual pabulum to his followers then and since. Cragg cautions, however, that the Islamic story, given its spectacular temporal success, makes Christians wonder whether or not it is religiously authentic. Can religious truth, perennially short of sponsors in our evil world, ever star as the hero of a success story? Given that human beings reject God's laws – an uncontroversial claim for which there is ample Quranic support – the rapid and enduring success of Islam in this vile world needs explanation. That alone could reassure believers (of any faith) that a (true) religion can succeed worthily. Did Islam triumph by compromising Muhammad's prophetic credentials?

Cragg concedes that Islam has an authentic religious dimension, indeed a spiritual kinship with Christianity. This makes him suspect the political means used, especially when these betray loftier spiritual ideals painfully hammered out in Gethsemane. If Islam were a false religion, there would arise no moral problem about its political involvement or its secular success. If the message of a faith is genuine, however, we have a right to question the dubious political means used to convey it. These are fair reservations; Christians and Muslims alike have the right to their consciences.

Nor is Cragg opposed to militancy. He interrogates Muslims only about the kind of enthusiasm, the proper brand of zeal, so that we can all agree on the moral resources of faithful militancy. Cragg insists that a prophet must repudiate worldly power since faith has no fellowship with force. A messenger's only armour is the message preached; his vulnerability in the face of the profane anger thus provoked is part of his witness. What is religiously suspect about Muhammad is his decision to join the categorical divine imperative to do justice, shared by all theisms, with a militancy defined as profane physical power. In matters of moment, matters of the heart and spirit, 'Blood is no argument.'[15]

IV

These are preliminary thoughts; theological accusations have lengthy careers. The brevity of this characterization does not foreclose or beg any questions. We locate first the proper place of secular power in the messianic kingdom. The crucial event is Jesus' third temptation in the wilderness. Recorded in Matthew 4:8–10, it reads literally as follows:

> Again, the Devil takes him (Jesus) to an extremely high mountain and shows him all the kingdoms (*basileias*) of the universe (*cosmou*) and their glory and said to him: 'All these things I will give you if you fall down and worship me.' Then Jesus says to him: 'Go away, Satan. For it has been written: "You shall worship the Lord your God and serve him only."'

The Quran contains no passage parallel to this (or to Luke 4:5–8). We can certainly imagine Satan, a familiar and active agent in the Quran, approaching Muhammad to offer him the world's kingdoms on condition that he worships him. Would Muhammad's retort have differed from Jesus' response or from that of other messengers? Jesus' response, quoting Deuteronomy 6:13, is Islamic. What is our quarrel? Muhammad, unlike Jesus, accepted power as a means of achieving religious ends even though Christians reject such power as extrinsic to the divine arsenal. Although God is all-powerful, only his love and grace achieve triumphs over our recalcitrant hearts and wills. Christians interpret Christ's third trial to be the temptation to interpret the messianic chore as power-centred. Offered the cup of power, Jesus refused it since divine ends require divine means. Sinners need a divine but powerless Messiah and not, as Jews thought, and still think, a human, armed and militarily victorious redeemer determined to restore Israel to its former imperial glory. Christ chose the cup of suffering love in a 'tragic triumph'.

Muslim participants, offended by the suggestion that Muhammad 'chickened out' in the hour of crisis, often leave the conference hall at this point. They are troubled by Christian triumphalism: Jesus of Nazareth stood his ground while Muhammad retreated. We defer this attitudinal issue to the next chapter. Here we disentangle a skein of reasoning about two related substantive issues: the Islamic notion of prophetic mission and Jesus' ministry in the Quranic perspective.

Cragg admires Jeremiah and other servants of God's word because they preferred a worthy failure to an unworthy success. In the polemical context of Christian–Muslim rivalry, Cragg insinuates that Muhammad succeeded unworthily. Elsewhere he says explicitly that Muhammad's political career was tainted by secular power.[16] Does worldly success discredit a prophet's faithful activism automatically? Does then only political failure guarantee authenticity in religious mission?

Before responding, we amplify Cragg's case. He notes that the Quran is silent on the 'failed' servants – except for Jesus whose ministry is unpardonably attenuated. The Quran's reticence, suspects Cragg, betrays the shallow character of its model of piety which is internally coherent but blind to more gracious patterns. Thus, including Jeremiah in the Quran would 'have been to entertain an intolerable interrogation of Muslim assumption and assurance'.[17] As for Jesus, Cragg complains that the Quran re-interprets Christ's ministry and distorts it in order to align it with Islamic norms. Some Muslims, I suspect, do secretly think that God awarded Jesus spiritual honours and accolades, recorded in the Quran, as compensation for his political failure. Only Muhammad had the best of both worlds. A submissive (*muslim*) Jesus is spectacularly rescued from the cross, at the eleventh hour (Q:4:157). This frustrates the wicked intentions of the Jewish establishment while spiritually vindicating the *politically* failed servant of the word. Jesus' 'failure' is not allowed the last word; tragedy shall have no dominion.

Why does the Quran not mention the failed messengers? The scriptural choice of messengers whose careers are rehearsed is representative and indicative, not comprehensive and exhaustive. Many prophets receive no mention or only a brief allusion. Perhaps some prophets not mentioned by name or epithet in the Quran were failures by secular and temporal criteria. Naturally, all prophets would be recognized as true to their calling; God would never commission a messenger who might betray his trust or fail to discharge his duty. Most messengers, including Job, Zechariah and John, had no marked political ambitions. Joseph's case is unique among the prophets mentioned: he participated, for the sake of altruistic and righteous ends, in an oppressive infidel government. After his release from prison, he was rehabilitated as a minister of home affairs in the Egyptian monarchy (Q:12:54–6). God rewarded the long-suffering Joseph by plotting on his behalf so that he could lawfully detain his brother under the royal Egyptian law code (Q:12:76). Muslim moderates, forced to work with regimes they see as not wholly Islamic, often cite the precedent of Joseph to prove that it is legitimate to participate in power politics, inside an unbelieving regime, without aiming to overthrow that regime or seek absolute power for oneself.

The Quran does not identify success by a profane criterion such as political establishment. Even Muhammad is told that he might not live to see Islam empowered and established (Q:13:40; 40:77). He might be assassinated in Mecca rather than live to see Islam established with the sanction of power in Medina. His sincerity would not have been compromised had he died instead of escaping to Medina. Even so, 'failed' servants such as Jeremiah are not in the Quran. And Job, whose narrative is in the sacred volume, re-appears, like Jesus, eviscerated of the very features Jews and Christians regard as essential. Both Job's apologia (Job 31) and God's answer from within the whirlwind (Job 38–41) are unacceptable to Muslims: Job is unfit to be a prophet if he thinks there are no limits to his righteous self-justification and God the creator is not obliged to answer to creaturely interrogation. The Quran portrays Job as a blamelessly righteous servant of God (Q:6:84; 21:83–4; 38:41–4), affirming his Hebrew description as *tām* (perfect; *Iyyob* 1:1). The book of Job contains materials subtly subversive of monotheistic ethics: anarchic thoughts wrapped in mocking Hebrew poetry whose power translation drastically reduces. In the Quran, as we see in one dramatic hiatus after another in the tale of Joseph, the righteous are always rewarded and the wicked punished (Q:12:22–3, 51–7; 90, 100). God dominates in his moral purposes but 'most of humankind do not know' (Q:12:21). This alignment is allegedly flawless, appearances notwithstanding. Empirically, the decoupling of virtue from prosperity in our world is too widespread to be merely accidental just as the association of vice with prosperity is too prevalent to be merely coincidental.

Cragg claims that the Quran is reluctant to discuss the ministry of prophets such as Jeremiah because of diffidence about its own religious axioms. For me, however, as an insider, the Quran expresses, decrees rather, its normative convictions with sustained clarity and irresistible rhetorical force. It does contain anxious passages about prophetic failure. Like his predecessors, Muhammad is comforted often by his Lord (typically at Q:18:6–8). Such anxiety, however, indicates not diffidence about the truth of the vision on whose behalf it is felt but rather an ardent desire to see the appropriate ideals fulfilled in a recalcitrant world. This thirst for righteousness is not a worldly variety of anxiety.

The Quran then, does not veto the view that some of God's spokesmen remained political failures despite delivering their trust until their death, sometimes at the hands of militant sinners. Their spirituality is as complete as that of others such as Moses, David, Solomon and Muhammad, who exercised secular power. Neither political achievement nor political disability is a necessary condition of religious authenticity. Some Muslims may think that Jesus' spirituality remained immature since it did not blossom into secular triumph. This view is unworthy of the Quranic axiom that God ordains a career for a messenger, tailored to time, place and human capacity. 'God burdens no soul beyond its capacity' (Q:2:286) is a morally unassailable truth that applies to prophets too. They do enjoy the privilege of divine grace although this is an ambiguous compensation since it comforts them only after first greatly increasing their sorrows. As for Jesus, if God had willed, he could have been martyred on the cross, as Christians hold, rather than being translated into Heaven, as some Muslim authorities hold (see commentary on Q:4:157–8). Jesus could also have died and straightforwardly failed – all possible within Islamic parameters.

Although the Quran asserts that God exalted some prophets above others (Q:2:253), it does not suggest that political consummation is a criterion for assessing their worth in the hierarchy known only to God. Some Muslims, provoked by inter-faith rivalry, claim that their prophet is the best since he conquered both terrestrial and spiritual empires. This is a justified boast but its grounds are not religious. The religious view is that God granted a spectacular victory to the Arabian warrior–prophet (*al-nabiyy al-malḥama*), a traditional description not found in the Quran. Traditionally, in extolling Muhammad's spectacular success, believers noted with satisfaction that the wise and powerful God does whatever he pleases. He is bound neither by the whims of pagans nor by Jewish and Christian prejudices (Q:57:29). God's hand is not fettered: he apportions his grace as he wishes (Q:5:64).

Although there are no Quranic grounds for arguing that a messenger's commitment to *islām* is incomplete unless it culminates in political attainment, some Muslims, famously the late Fazlur Rahman, dismissed politically aborted prophetic careers as merely conventional speech-making. Rahman argued that given our perennially urgent need for divine guidance, it was imperative that divine messengers, especially the final one, should succeed.[18] It is difficult to assail this view from any credible angle. A messenger seeking to implement his message must will not only the right end but the appropriate means. Why should a prophet merely give speeches without any intention to succeed in practice? That would be to make a fetish of failure as if failure were the hallmark of religious authenticity. It reminds one of the surgeon who told the assembled crowd outside the emergency theatre that the operation was a great success but added casually that the patient had died.

Christians and Muslims, then, can concur that the essence of every prophet's vocation is resignation (*islām*) to God's inscrutable will. The unresolved issue here is whether or not worldly success can legitimately crown religious achievement. Some prophets' missions remained incomplete as they failed to arouse their community to repent in time; sinners even exterminated the warner and his dedicated group. For Muslims, the integrity of each messenger is a presupposition, not a result, of his mission: temporal success is the fruit, not the root, of religious faith. Islam rejects the presupposition that revealed religion is always allergic to secular triumph. The debate has reached a deadlock.

V

In this hiatus, we examine Cragg's inquiry into the ends of prophetic effort. What kind of victory suits religious truth?[19] Islam does not, I believe, exclude from the ambit of God's varied grace the victory exemplified in Jesus' ministry, as understood by Christians. Muslim polemicists mock it in shoddy pamphlets with superficially clever titles such as 'Crucifixion or Crucifiction?'[20] The Quran rejects the Christian imprint of grace on historical and doctrinal grounds. It imposes no absolute theological veto on a Christian interpretation of Christ's life and ministry. Jesus of Nazareth did not suffer in the manner required by Christian doctrines of atonement; he did not have to do so though he was ready to do so. If Jesus had been crucified, as many believers have been (Q:20:63–73; 26:34–51; 36:20–7; 85:4–8), the Quran would not have drawn tragic conclusions about the power of sin and the need for divine atonement. Crucifixion or no crucifixion, Jesus succeeded since he submitted his will to God's ordinance. He was a *muslim* (Q:3:51; 19; 16–36) apostle resigned to the will of his Lord and that suffices.

Cragg wonders about the kind of triumph appropriate to faith. In one sense: none is appropriate. God's views do not require the patronage of human victory understood as our acceptance of his word. The divine truth contains the guarantee of its own success and intrinsic worth. God's word cannot fail to be true in its claim to metaphysically secure status. At most, it can fail to be received by us – fallible, sinful men and women. So much the worse for us! The word of God must have the last word (Q:9:40) even in our imperfect mortal constituency. Whatever we may think, scripture is the ultimate truth about us and our world and, therefore, God's truth is independent of our response to his holy summons whether in penitent submission or in impenitent pride.

Cragg asks about the means employed by prophets to enable God's word to succeed in our perennially wayward world. Knowing that God's cause must ultimately succeed, how should a prophet crown his efforts with victory in our impious and perverse lives? God will win the war, if not all the battles, but we may reasonably enquire about his spokesmen's choice of weapons. Cragg compares Jesus' response to the crisis of Israel's hypocritical disbelief with Muhammad's reaction to the arrogant Meccans' rejection and scorn. Jesus diagnosed Israel's infidelity to be a malady in the soul, caused by an inveterate and perverse hypocrisy. Only a divine love, suffering unjustly in order to redeem wisely, could reach and cure it. Muhammad, it is claimed, interpreted rejection as necessitating social and political struggle.

Leaving aside the historical caveat that Jesus preached to Jewish monotheists while Muhammad addressed polytheists, these alternatives are false in fact and in implication. Islam intended to eradicate hypocrisy because God cared about the moral mischief caused by the inner self; and Christ's supposed repudiation of the political solution is not politically neutral. Was Jesus a revolutionary who transcended politics? In our kind of world, this is impossible. No-one can transcend politics. It is all politics since to opt out of politics merely serves a conservative political function. Muslims argue that we need an ethical politics, a moral force that enables positive management of our political instinct. No doctrine is more congenial to tyrants than the view that one can be a revolutionary without engaging in politics to secure legitimate power. Muhammad's choice of constructive and positive politics for the common good is unassailable on any credible grounds unless we judge even an honourable determination to do one's duty as merely concealed moral vanity.

While the Christian need for grace and theology sets different priorities than the Muslim need for law and the unification of creed and politics, neither Jesus nor Muhammad doubted the power of God's mercy, grace and love. Is victory attained through patience, prayer *and* political strife and struggle worthy of the spiritual life? Cragg re-iterates that preaching in alliance with patience and prayer exhaust the godly arsenal. The New Testament God has washed his hands of the dirty political side of the affair, despite his former militancy recorded in the Hebrew Bible, a scripture whose violent revenge fantasies (see Jeremiah 46 to 51 and Micah 4:11–3) must embarrass Christians since they must at least theoretically revere the whole canon. Traces of ancient Judaic militancy survive in the Christian Bible as we note in the anonymous ode to violent heroes of faith (Hebrews 11:32–4).

Christians who listen to the Islamic story note that it is a tale of limited violence resulting in great temporal success. The triumph of Islam is morally genuine only if it is a success worthy of faith. Cragg fails to note that to deny this is to deny Islam's *spiritual* as opposed to merely its derivatively *political* authenticity. The two are essentially related. Cragg claims to concede Islam's religiously genuine nature while disputing the political consequences of such a nature. Can these, however, be neatly distinguished, let alone forever separated?

VI

Muslims and Christians quarrel over the expression 'politicization of religion'[21] which describes how the divine arsenal was supplemented with profane power.

This phrase misleads Cragg into thinking that the inveterate opposition to Muhammad at Mecca politicized his initially purely religious faith, a reading that begs a question against his understanding of Islam as a faith which always incorporated and integrated the political dimension into a religiously comprehensive project. One cannot politicize such a faith any more than one can privatize a law code, the literal meaning of 'privilege' (law affecting an individual, derived from *privilegium*, from *privus lex/legis*). 'Political Islam' is preferable to 'politicized Islam' since the latter phrase implies an alleged degradation of a faith whereby a religion mutates rather arbitrarily into a surrogate for craftily concealed ideological, economic and political interests. Only Islam's detractors see it as no more than an elaborate disguise for achieving secular power.

Islam did not suddenly acquire its political temper from the rivalries and intrigues of Medina. The political impetus dates from an early Meccan revelation which describes Muhammad's God as 'Lord of this House', a provocative allusion to the cube-shaped sanctuary at Mecca, then patronized by the pagan Quraysh (Q:106:3). A later Medinan revelation calls this Meccan shrine 'the house of ancient pedigree' (Q:22:29, 33) in order to establish a direct link with the iconoclast Abraham. This early, pervasive and continuing stress on the only God's exclusive sovereignty shows that even Meccan Islam can be understood as a political monotheism. The attitude of obedience and submission to God the king has political overtones. Morally, only such a living God, not the impotent idol, can secure justice in human relationships. Muhammad's career began and ended as a political tale.

For Muslims, it is unfair to characterize God's political providence as extraneous to the religious ideal. An incomplete (though not apolitical or politically indifferent) Meccan Islam was merely completed and perfected in the Medinan crucible. Following earlier orientalists,[22] Cragg rejects this Islamic account and instead distinguishes a powerless Meccan Islam from the later empowered version which interpreted involvement with the recalcitrant political sector to mean the revolutionary overthrow of the pagan oligarchy. For Cragg, Medinan Islam was a falsely religious achievement: legitimate at most in its temporal context but not as a religiously commendable and permanent feature of an initially powerless but authentic faith founded in Mecca.

Cragg's assumptions are, naturally, Christian, indeed Protestant. One can politicize a faith if it is originally apolitical, hence the politicization of primitive Christianity under Constantine, or of Buddhism under Emperor Ashoka. Christian critics are tempted to smuggle alien and circumscribed conceptions of the 'religious' and 'political' wings into their study of Islam and then reject these as illegitimate liaisons. Western Islamicists usually isolate the political sector, understood in a pejorative and narrow sense rather than in the broader original Greek sense, and then condemn its alignment with the religious wing, also understood in a parallel restricted (contemporary Western) sense of religion as private solace. No human concern escapes the range of the Quran's jurisdiction; nothing human is alien to it. The law codes are accordingly inspired by this desire for radical inclusiveness and constitute the juridical equivalent of divine omnipresence in human affairs.

All faiths, including apolitical ones, must interact with the powerful establishments of their day. The New Testament mentions the Romans and the Sadducees; the Quran mentions the Qurayshi rulers. What makes Islam remarkable is its decision to absorb political community in order to sanctify it. Muslims who follow their Prophet's example do not see political institutions as extrinsic or irrelevant to the demands of 'private' faith. Cragg preaches, however, that while faiths may need to compromise with force as they become traditions, they should not do so in their origins.[23] He regrets that Islam, uniquely among faiths, unashamedly incorporates the power dimension into its originating ambience so that '… force has been so uncomplicatedly enshrined in the very canons of Islam via the patterns of the *Sīrah*.'[24] Cragg contrasts Christ's *sīrah* (biography) by noting his suffering out of love for sinners. To be fair, Cragg concedes that most Christians have readily betrayed their Master's teachings.

Cragg condemns the Muslim incorporation of power into Islamic canons without noting that the Muslim decision to include the political wing *ab initio* proves that such an involvement with power was seen as integral to faith and not, as he wrongly concludes, a compromise necessitated by later recalcitrant circumstances. Think here of Sikhism where the (10th) Guru Gobind Singh (1666–1708) reluctantly took up the sword in the face of determined persecution at the hands of Moghul (Muslim) rulers in the Indian Punjab. The Guru's own father had been martyred. It became a matter of survival. The pacifist faith of the (first) Guru Nanak (1469–1539) had to be politicized but only as a change of tactics that later changed the principles. Cragg's routine use of 'politicization' takes for granted an originally apolitical Islam, a demonstrably false *theological* assumption, not merely a controversial *historical* one.

Cragg rightly regrets our tendency to debase our professed ideals. Christians and, to a markedly lesser extent, Muslims, have done wrong in their respective, often competing, colonial adventures. It is a failing of our common humanity. Failure to live up to one's own ideals is, however, different from a failure to live up to someone else's ideals. In his indictment of Islam's position on power, Cragg presupposes, rather than establishes, the truth of the Christian position on power. He takes the latter as axiomatic. His accusation is therefore automatically reduced to the strange charge that Muhammad was unfaithful to (Christian) principles he did not profess. Cragg does not quarrel with Muhammad's failure to uphold his own professed principles; his quarrel is with the principles. The charge then is not hypocrisy but theological error. The accusation is neither moral nor political but rather religious and theological and therefore metaphysical. This is the true nature of the dispute and it is therefore impossible to resolve it since it has been lifted to a level beyond normal secular controversy.

Cragg, an Anglican Protestant, admits that in the light of absolute New Testament principles, those Christians who deploy secular means of acquiring power compromise their faith. One should add that the just war view, popular with Catholics, subtly betrays Christ's distinctively demanding injunctions to his followers. These later Christian moves are categorical if concealed departures from the absolute norm of *imitatio Christi* in matters of violence. Jesus did not physically resist militant evil even as he was led defenceless to the cross and he stopped his disciples from picking up arms even in self-defence (Luke 22:49–51). 'I have not come to bring peace but a sword' (Matthew 10:34) is meant metaphorically as its context (Matthew 10:35–6) makes clear. Correctly understanding Jesus' intentions, Tertullian extrapolated: 'The Lord, in disarming Peter, disarmed every solider'.[25]

Since the Quran, Muhammad's guide, recognizes force as in principle legitimate (Q:22:39–41), Cragg begs the question against Muhammad and Muslims when he claims that their use of force was equally compromising. While Christians compromise their integrity in using any coercion to effect reforms, Muslims compromise themselves – if we use standards intrinsic to Islam – only by *mis*using force. The Quran does not judge power as any more inherently destructive or venal than the appetite for sex, food or knowledge. We err only when we lapse from the ideal governing the correct recruitment and enjoyment of such putatively lawful facilities and resources. The Quran and the Prophet condemn only excess and prodigality (*isrāf*; Q:7:31; 40:43; *faḍūl* in Muhammad's sermons[26]). This moral error is discerned by reference to Islam's balanced religious ideals which guide fallible but educable sinners.

Muslims sympathize with Christians who attempt to be faithful to unconditional and unqualified New Testament imperatives. Such believers must necessarily see secular power as a temptation. It is indeed, for them, a temptation to be resisted: a principled and inclusive reservation about secular power defines primitive idealistic Christianity. The cited passage (from Matthew 4:8–10) does not sanction the repudiation of power as such but rather of idolatry – with the ulterior message that one should reject anything that comes from the Devil's hand, even something otherwise wholesome. Early Christians refused the protection of political sanction, fearing the venal influence of state power. Notwithstanding lengthy and brutal persecution under Roman rule from Nero to Galerius and, in the earliest years, the milder persecution by the parent Jewish establishment (Acts 5:17–8:3), Christians remained loyal to the ideals of the suffering Christ. Martyrdom, in passive non-violent resistance, as opposed to armed struggle in self-defence or the pursuit of empire, is prevalent in Christianity's first three centuries.

After Constantine, Christians eagerly compromised with the powerful principalities of this wicked world, often wielding the sword in practice while periodically decrying its use in their abstract theology. Since Constantine entered the Christian fold, the cross has doubled as a sword and as such continues to cast a long shadow not only over Europe but, via Western colonialism, over the entire world. There remains a pacifist Christian witness both today and in the past: Quaker, Mennonite and some progressive, mainly Baptist, African–American churches and also individual saints, scholars and activists such as Erasmus of Rotterdam, Martin Luther King and the eccentric St Francis of Assisi.

We conclude that Cragg is seduced by the misleading phrase 'the politicization of religion' which skews the debate by introducing a Christian squint. We may use this phrase to discuss the compromises of realpolitik but it can only be used in discussing Islam's originating norms if we acknowledge its limitations. Otherwise we beg the question against a faith that did not recognize any distinction between the religious and the political until the advent of an imposed and alien political modernity. For Cragg, Islam was contingently politicized owing to an avoidable confrontation with the Qurayshi establishment. Apart from the historical question of whether such a confrontation was indeed optional, his assumption denies a priori the viability of any theological reason for the inclusion of the political order within the scope of a divine sovereignty whose claim to sole divinity is shown decisively in its drive for comprehensive reach into creation.

We see this last point clearly by comparing 'politicization of religion' with the less sinister-sounding 'religionization of politics'. While both are imperfect descriptions of the Muslim involvement with power, the two phrases are not equally inappropriate. The latter expression describes a process closer to what the Islamic political ideal entails: the political life of faith is subjected to divine dictates and thus sanctified. We should avoid tendentious words and processes such as politicization and instead speak of a pure or theoretical Meccan Islam which later blossomed into the applied Islam of the Medinan utopia. We ignore the roots of Islam if we see Muhammad's prophethood as acquiring a political colouring after the exodus. Neither the Prophet nor his followers saw the move to Medina as a temptation that ought to have been resisted. We are bound to conclude that Muhammad's mission in Mecca was consistently ethically weighted. Even the Meccan Quran is not content merely to distinguish polytheism from monotheism. It already contrasts them as politically opposed alternatives.

VII

Cragg writes as though the Prophet's troubles were over after the *hijrah*. In Mecca, this caring man had voiced a jeremiad against affluent and influential men who occupied tribal positions of undeserved privilege. The wealthy and arrogant Quraysh ignored the just plea of the orphan and upstart Muhammad who had improved his lot by marrying a wealthy woman. After 13 years of earnest quest, pacific labour and anxiety, the Prophet found the 'short-cuts to ease the calling'[27] when he realized that power was the panacea. Jesus resisted while Muhammad succumbed to the temptation to take a detour, the easier option of using force to humble the haughty pagans. Christ drank from the cup of suffering by opting for 'the quiet strength of truth and the sure fidelities of love'.[28]

Was there an easing of Muhammad's travail in the post-*hijrah* decade? What impresses the impartial student of the Prophet's life is the continuous severity of his iconoclastic conscience, its stubborn if not masochistic integrity. The Quran, Muhammad's guide on both sides of the exodus divide, lays the axe at the root of every whim or desire that could attenuate or sell short the service of God or subordinate it to the mundane life. Temptations grew greater when the community became powerful in Medina; believers are accordingly warned against compromise and hypocrisy. The Quran cautions the infant community that though it has the decisive Badr victory to its account, this is only the beginning of their struggle against heavy odds (Q:8:65–6) which shall try their mettle and distinguish the zealous from the lukewarm. In the face of greater trials yet to come, God will demand ceaseless jihad, constant self-purification and struggle in his path. The self-vigilance implicit in this endeavour is incompatible with any 'short-cuts to ease the calling'.

It was in Medina that Islam's most ascetic rite was institutionalized and scrupulously observed. The canonical annual fast is an ordeal of abstinence that most Muslims still endure in Ramadan ('the scorcher'), the hot and dusty ninth lunar month. The fast was ritualized in Medina to mark retrospectively the Quran's first descent (Q:2:183–5). In the 'true fast' of Ramadan, no food, beverage or medicine, enters a body sealed off from sunrise to sunset daily. It was initially longer, lasting from the evening meal of one day to the evening meal of the next, 24 hours of complete self-denial in a humid and sultry climate (Q:2:187). To honour and please their Lord, believers were to shun physical needs and comforts, including sexual desire. And all this while actively fighting the Meccan pagans in pitched battles! The battle of Badr was won by the Muslims on 17th of Ramadan in 2 AH.

Again, in Medina, the Prophet trained the *ahl al-ṣuffah* (people of the verandah) – those saintly and ascetic men who were emulated by later believers searching for spirituality. About 300 poor men, including the famous *ḥadīth* transmitter Abu Hurairah, lived on the verandah of the Prophet's mosque lodgings so that they could closely watch his daily life. They sought to live, like Muhammad, in the active heat of a single pious emotion day and night. That is no mean achievement since in most of us the instinct for pious self-restraint ebbs and flows. The Quran condemns complacency, the illusion that one has ever done enough. Until his dying day, Muhammad fought for the cause of justice. He lived in holy poverty while being the master of Arabia. He prayed, repented, fought, taught, witnessed to God's glory, and prayed again in a sustained, vigorous and rigorous piety. These early believers, especially Muhammad their guide, knew they had miles to go before they finally slept. Only a prejudiced reader could discern an attenuation of religious demand or a drop in the moral temperature.

As for militant struggle against paganism, the Prophet saw it as a necessary evil, not as a short-cut or avoidable compromise. He taught that our final allegiance is to God. If force is required to secure justice and preserve witness to this God's truth, a prophet must use it. To ignore or discount violent struggle in that situation would be a venal compromise, a criminal marginalization of the things of God. The Prophet knew that while his message was intrinsically appealing, it was still bound to confront violent opposition. The Muslims were reluctant to use force even in self-defence; the permission for a modest use of defensive force is found only in the Medinan Quran (Q:22:39–41). Believers found fighting to be odious (Q:47:20) but God told them that he may put much good in something we humans perceive to be bad or unpleasant (Q:2:216). This is, incidentally, the verdict not only about violent struggle but also about married life (Q:4:19).

As any leader knows, sudden changes in policy induce cynicism among followers. If Muhammad had suddenly altered his policy at Medina by degenerating into a mere politician from an erstwhile righteous statesman, his disciples would have deserted him. Yet Muhammad's followers did not desert him when he began to battle the pagans even though some believers remained reluctant to use force. His disciples could see that Muhammad's policy was unified and consistent; strategies evolved but the goals remained unaltered. The Quran, as Muhammad's conscience, would have condemned force if it had seen its use as a betrayal of godly principles. Instead, it commended it. Hence the revolutionary slogan, 'Persecution (*al-fitnah*) is worse than slaughter' (*al-qatl*; Q:2:191, 217), revealed after Muhammad transgressed a pagan taboo against violence in one of the four holy months.

The Prophet is instructed to reject the pagans' offer of reconciliation through compromise on religious principle: the pagans would worship Muhammad's God for six months of the year if he and his disciples agreed to worship the pagan deities for the balance of the year. This is precisely a compromise. The Quran's verdict via Muhammad: 'To you your religion, to me my religion' (Q:109:6). This verse is ironically now seen as a manifesto for freedom of conscience and tolerance. Its original intent is intolerant and divisive. It suggests that Muhammad grew up in an atmosphere of tolerance of opposed beliefs so that the Quran's tolerance of Jews and Christians may partly reflect a culturally prevalent Arab *pagan* tolerance of religious difference.

The Muslims' unco-operative stance led to bloodshed, unhappiness and debacle. The rejection of compromise in matters of principle, as opposed to taste or strategy, is the Quran's hallmark (Q:3:139; 47:35; 68:8–9). It placed the bond of faith above that of blood, marriage and tribe. The resulting domestic friction severed tribes, separated spouses as Muslim–pagan marriages were forbidden (Q:2:221), and pitched brother against brother and father against son in open battle (Q9:23–4; 60:1–3, 7–13). This meant something in a cohesive culture where family unity mattered materially. Again, the slackening of alliances with the pagans caused commercial losses and poverty for Muslims (Q:9:28) This is hardly a religion of comfortable accommodation with sin and evil. To say *Allāhu akbar* while preferring one's own opinions and desires is to invite the charge of hypocrisy. For Muhammad, the rejection, not acceptance, of violent struggle would have denied God's supremacy. Is peace, even tainted with widespread injustice, preferable to justice secured through some limited violence? Muhammad was never seduced by such over-refined but cowardly hypocrisy that insinuates a devious justification for lapsing from the rigours of authentic idealism.

The abdication of political struggle would have been the more comfortable option for Muhammad. As with other Christian polemical arguments against Islam, Cragg's contention can be turned on its head. The refusal to engage in violent struggle against injustice is no less, perhaps more, compromising than a reluctant acceptance of its tragic necessity. The question of compromise is never resolved a priori but rather in relationship to an agent's perception of moral worth or lapse. Thus, Jesus and Muhammad used opposed strategies whose moral consequences and utilitarian aptness were grounded in their differing circumstances. If the Prophet of Nazareth rejected the political option, it is an insufficient ground for every prophet to do so. Jesus did so rightly perhaps given the straitened circumstances of his mission. Does that make it a normative precedent for the deportment of messengers placed in other predicaments? Why elevate an idiosyncratic but appropriate feature of Jesus' career to the status of an indispensable criterion for assessing the authenticity of every prophet's mission?

Since power is constantly liable to abuse, it conceals an ambiguous potential. The success that power brings must be worthy of faith. God does not approve of causes that betray his sacred purposes to profane ends. In the triumphant hour, the Quran instructs the Prophet to sanctify his success lest it should be claimed by an outwardly Islamic but inwardly idolatrous sovereignty (see Q:110). No ethical monotheism could approve of the spiritually sterile triumph of a merely political success.

VIII

The Quran generally emphasizes the individual's personal accountability to God as opposed to one rooted in our common humanity or shared political or ethnic solidarity. In view of this, Cragg attempts to discern a discrepancy in the Quran's view of collective evil. It is a subtle accusation, indirectly linked to any assessment of Muhammad's militancy. I shall explain.

Consider these two maxims. Firstly, the Quran's dictum: 'No soul, already laden, bears the burden of another' (Q:6:164; 17:15). The Christian notion of original sin is opposed to this view since it implies that we are born already bearing sin inherited from Adam. Cragg argues, in a heterodox commentary, that *peccatum originale* is misinterpreted as an individual act, committed by Adam, and then transmitted in a travesty of justice to all men and women. Paul does argue that Adam's individual sin becomes the generic sin of all humans (Romans 5:12) and that Adam's happy sin (*felix culpa*) gave us the gift of salvation through Christ. For Cragg, however, original sin is not historically inherited but perennially present in the shape of transcendent human perversity. We are all human and Adam is the typical mortal, the symbol of humankind in our collective pride and sinfulness, two traits for which we should all feel shame and guilt. Enigmatically, Cragg claims that 'this human solidarity makes for dimensions of human evil which a purely individual view of relationships is likely to overlook'.[29]

Cragg's meaning is unclear and his prose turgid. Perhaps he means that individual evil cannot be assessed fairly since it is unavoidably intensified by the collective evil of the social setting, a claim with Marxist overtones. Perhaps he means that entanglement in history and society is inevitable and that it makes us all accomplices of social, not merely individual, crimes. Thus private morals do not work in public life; politicians hide behind public roles. The private acts of public figures have public consequences; the social acts of all individuals have private effects. In a crowd, we lose our individual inhibitions. I am expatiating on Cragg's obscure observations. Can we rightly judge an individual without assessing his or her background and social limitations of class, gender and race? Such doubt about individual accountability in society is commonplace in university courses on the social causality of criminal behaviour – known as 'the depraved because I am deprived' legal defence – but it is not a concern we normally extract from scripture.

Cragg wonders: How can the Quran's author pontificate that 'no soul already laden bears the burden of another'? Islam's rejection of original sin, Cragg charges, obscures our shared human complicity in the evil of structures, aggregates of individual sin compounded by the sin of collectives, the whole structure transcending and thus obscuring personal guilt. Society sees to it that we all bear the burdens of others just as we are guilty of the sins of others, in virtue of being human and hence implicated by association. It is, perhaps, similar to John Donne's poetic thought that 'the death of any man diminishes me', that 'the bell tolls for each of us'. Perhaps entanglement in society inevitably makes one an accomplice of social, not merely individual, crimes. To confess complicity, a Christian might add, enables grace to enter and transform human nature and human history.

I shall speculate no further. Cragg regrets that the Quran's view of evil is, in general, 'very personalistic' – emphasizing private individual choices, a person's personal vindication or condemnation. Yet, adds Cragg, this Quranic model overlooks 'the evil of structures, of states and society, of collectives and institutions ...'[30] so that where 'motives of personal selfishness become corporate, or find excuse in the expediency to which things political and economic readily appeal, then the collective selfishness intensifies the wrong'.[31] Cragg approves of a Muslim writer who, like Cragg, experiences 'scepticism about the amenability of public "causes" to the moral restraints and standards that might weigh with private people'.[32]

Cragg either misunderstands or misrepresents the Quranic motto. Islam teaches that the divine reckoning that awaits the individual cannot be transferred or mitigated in view of racial lineage or group membership with the welcome implication that God is impartial. No soul is burdened beyond its capacity (Q:2:286) and no soul already laden can shoulder another's burden, not even that of a near relative (Q:29:12–3; 35:18). Naturally where others are the cause of our guilt, God will take that into account. Thus, for instance, God promises forgiveness to slave girls if their masters forced them into prostitution (Q:24:33). Others around us impose upon us burdens of pain and suffering – burdens that are not ours in their origins but ours only in the bearing. As employers and workers, lovers and friends and enemies, parents and siblings, citizens and rulers, we contribute to one another's sorrows. As members of families and groups, we routinely bear each others' burdens. In that sense, every burdened soul bears the burden of another. As social beings living in a web of interconnectedness, however, we bear only the burdens of pain and suffering imposed by others, not their sin. To bear the sin of others is barely intelligible; to bear the guilt of others is irrational, possibly incoherent. Thus Nietzsche's mockery of the Incarnation: 'a god come to earth ought to bear not only the sin but the guilt ... only that would be godlike'.[33]

'No bearer of burdens can bear the burden of another' (Q:6:164; 17:15; 39:7; 53:38; 65:7) contains a strict view of personal responsibility which is mitigated by Quranic references to the collective judgment of nations (Q:4:41; 13:11; 17:71; 45:28–9). The Quran rejects the Torah's notion of inter-generational justice where God visits on the children the sins of the fathers up to several generations. However, the actions of the righteous person can outlive them and their offspring might enjoy the benefits of their parents' piety. God can visit on the children the virtues of the fathers (Q:18:82). Relevantly, Islamic law does not recognize corporate legal persons such as the city, the university or the church. Only an entity with moral liability is considered a legal person.

Muslims hold that divine judgment is antecedent to grace: after just judgment, God, by his mitigating grace, saves some from the Fire. Unlike Christianity, there is no insurance policy for sinners. Redemption, atonement and substitution are rejected by the Quran. To think that someone else suffered for our sins and that we are redeemed by his blood is unjust. It is our self-surrender that merits salvation, not another person's self-sacrifice and merits, no matter how remarkable.

I have an ulterior motive for probing Cragg's elusive claim. Independently of our stance on the suitability of the Quran's view of accountability for the individual soul, we should note the unintended significance of Cragg's train of thought for his assessment of Muhammad's Medinan activism. Cragg reasonably if elusively suggests that collectives and groups develop their own momentum of evil, above and beyond the aggregate of individual evil, so that the consequences of private sinful actions are far from private. If this is the case, any effective way to deal even with individual, let alone collective, evil must be alert to the structural–public dimension of both types of wrongdoing. Like chameleons, societies can, in their resourceful adaptation to partial and piecemeal amendments, effectively resist just reform. Islam's Western critics deny, on a priori grounds, this strategic truth about the scope and resources requisite for social reform. Recognizing this would conclusively justify Muhammad's decision to alter not merely the recalcitrant consciences of individuals but also to revolutionize the underlying power-structure that resisted his preaching. No doubt, such forceful reckoning and engagement should respect the constraints of moral and religious principle. Political programmes require the energies of men and women who are long-suffering, working with and within individual minds and hearts, never against the promptings of individual consciences. The prior issue here, neglected by Muhammad's critics, is the recognition of the need to engage, rather than ignore or disown, the public dimension of wrongdoing.

If even individual evil has social dimensions, then no right form of piety, in its confrontation with such evil, let alone with structural and communal evil, can jettison political resources that enable one to eradicate the social, not merely the personal, consequences of both types of evil. This is especially true since collective evil is naturally aggressive and militant. Cragg concedes that evil assumes a structural aspect but denies simultaneously the need for a corresponding form of reckoning that is alert precisely to this structural dimension. This amounts to preferring an unrealistic and juvenile, possibly incoherent, model of righteousness, to the politically mature piety of Muhammadan Islam.

IX

In this interlude, we record a temperamental matter related to substantive political concerns in inter-faith relationships. Cragg is impressed by the confrontational environment of the Quran's incidence as reflected in its polemical exchanges and combative literary mood. The scripture's ambience is provided by militant impiety versus militant righteousness: the pagans passionately opposed the sacred cause. The forces of good and evil are entrenched in their positions: the Medinan Quran, like the Bhagavad Gita, was revealed on a battlefield.

Cragg rightly observes the martial mood in parts of the Quran. Suddenly, however, we read Cragg's wistful Christian musings, his hope that 'he might savour the message of divine transcendence in a constituency more congenial to its wonder', one less stubborn than Muhammad's Mecca, 'so that its quality might be known in a joyful availing of his word'.[34] This apparently innocuous wish is idle and misguided. There is only one constituency proper to God's message: the sinful human one, an arena never plastic to the ardent religious wish for the triumph of righteousness. This milieu was not congenial in the days of Moses or of Muhammad. It has not become so in the contemporary world; only the fool thinks it might become so tomorrow. Impiety has, does, and will always assume militant forms. This is unfortunate; but it is the way of the world – and one conclusively demonstrated, ironically, in Jesus' ministry. Did the world of first-century Palestine provide a congenial constituency where Jesus might have savoured a joyful availing of his word? Was his world lacking in the perversity and over-confidence of evil?

God works out his purposes in the real world, not through our daydreams. His realm of action is our 'life of the lower world' (*al-ḥayāt al-dunyā*; Q:14:27; 18:45; 47:36). If we attenuate the obstinacy of humankind or reduce the actual depth and real scope of our perversity, for purposes theological or practical, we are in effect longing for a constituency that has little in common with our world. We ask for illusions. Political reality does not reflect the wishes and slogans of any such irresponsibly pious will. These observations are crucial to any debate about the dilemmas of political violence. This harsh and indifferent world is not the only one worth describing – fantasy is rewarding – but it is necessarily the only one worth changing. A realistic scripture must therefore address itself to human beings as they actually are, not as we would ideally like them to be. There is no constituency more worthy of wonder than the real world.

There is a broader point here with serious implications. In these musings, Cragg wants to Christianize Islam by introducing accents of pathos and tragedy so that Muslims became more reflective in their piety and less hasty in their militancy. Thus he wants Muslims to develop their minimalist theology, not their extensive jurisprudence, so that they deepen their spirituality and aim to conquer their own souls, not other people's cities. He traces the standard Islamic impulse to its roots in Muhammad's militant interpretation of monotheism and notes its implications for the modern world. A more Christianized Islam would be a liberal Islam which the West can accommodate and one which would not, presumably, threaten Western political hegemony and economic interests.

Here Cragg has only to teach and preach to Muslims and has nothing to learn from them. Indeed, he does not consider the larger questions this raises about the style of Christian–Muslim dialogue and relations. Surely dialogue proceeds not by altering the character of the opponent but rather by sympathetic listening and compromise, by recording rift and difference and by respecting the consciences of one's opponents. Imagine if a Muslim were to Islamicize Christian origins by, for example, introducing somehow a measure of temporal success into a story of pathos and tragedy finally crowned by the spiritual triumph of the resurrection.

X

The war-poet Wilfrid Owen, born in 1893 and killed in 1918, wrote in a draft preface to a collection of poems published posthumously: 'All the poet can do today is to warn. That is why the true Poets must be truthful.'[35] Owen laments how little his own generation can do but remains optimistic about the future. Even so, we hear the note of inadequacy and despair which is made louder in speech if we stress '*All*'. Why is warning alone insufficient? The Quran calls Muhammad a warner sent to threaten the pagans with the penalties of rejecting the message; the pagans accused him of being a mere poet and ignored his warnings. Warning people is invariably toilsome and provocative; profane power confronted the Islamic cause on both sides of the *hijrah* divide.

The note of despair is justified because verbal warning alone rarely avails (see Q:54:17, repeated as a refrain at vv. 22, 32, 40). We may preach incessantly on behalf of just causes but the world seldom casts its vote for them. The words of reformers are acknowledged as praiseworthy but perverse opposition to truth reduces the size of their contemporaneous audiences. Recognizable moral superiorities attach to the petitions of good men and women; the excellence of their proposals are often acknowledged by their contemporaries and rarely dismissed by posterity. History records the lives of many 'bad' men who were later rebaptized 'good' men.

Our dismissal of the good cause is not due mainly to heedlessness (*ghaflah*), a frequent Quranic accusation. Heedlessness does not take the full measure of the variety of oppositions to the good, let alone their depth which goes far beyond *ghaflah* in the long reach of its roots, in the malicious quality of its motivation, and the tenacity of its perverse intention. The pagan opposition to a prophet's cause, a religious vision of the *summum bonum*, cannot be reduced to any casual, even regular or deliberate, neglect of religious norms. It is no mere indifference to justice and truth but rather a perversely determined, possibly conspiratorial and certainly sinister hatred of the good cause. As an intelligent and resourceful animus towards the just and equitable state of affairs, it leads to inveterate conflict: the Qurayshi establishment was determined to dislodge 'Allah and his Messenger'. Willful and cynical verbal rejection of God's message culminated in brutal persecution of the unprotected believers. The Prophet's activism is an instructive commentary on the pagans' range and capacity for militant injustice.

'All a prophet should do is to warn.' Cragg could have penned these words; the logic of his stance inexorably issues that verdict. Like the poet, the prophet and the preacher must also rely on purely verbal weapons. The pen had better be mightier than the sword since hearts are to be won using only the peaceful instruments in the prophet's arsenal: tact, persuasion, eloquence, endurance, patience and persistence. These have their limitations in a world whose enmity to truth is not lukewarm, intermittent, accidental or temporary but rather zealous, continual, determined and permanent. Cragg retorts that there is no alternative. An impulsive and impetuous militancy would compromise the moral quality of a prophet's allegiance to the divine cause. There is no way to ease the anguish: a prophet warns and people ignore him. He prays and suffers patiently in silence; the cycle is repeated. Many would concur with Cragg that contemporary Muslims are seduced into the impatient militancy of terrorism. The true man of God knows how to wait for victory, to cultivate patience (*ṣabr*), the most Quranic of the virtues.

Although Cragg's Christian view sounds magnanimous, it is acceptable only within limits since evil individuals can enter the territory of the faithful and threaten the warner's life. For Cragg, such helplessness is a liability of the prophetic office. To feel constantly vulnerable in the face of the world's scorn and physical power is not a weakness to be removed but rather the hallmark of the man of God living in our corrupt world. Muslims rightly question this extreme judgment. They condemn its apparent moral idealism and nobility since they discern in it an irresponsible pacifism and abdication of social duty.

The wrong type of militancy causes moral harm to the militants and physical harm to their victims. It is not morally self-evident, however, that good people should remain helpless in the face of aggressive wrongdoing, unable to intervene forcefully even to protect their own rights or those of other innocents involved. Granted that overwhelming suffering is an inevitable consequence of attachment to truth, it does not follow that the attempt to alleviate undeserved distress through armed defence is automatically a betrayal of religious principles. Why should suffering in total but humanly avoidable vulnerability be the only hallmark of a true prophet? Should the true man of God then plunge defenceless into the thick of battle only to be martyred by the ruthless forces of those who shamelessly foster an impiety unqualified by the mitigation of conscience and reject retrospective mercy for wrong inflicted? Put in these blunt terms, one can see the extremist nature of Cragg's stance on power.

XI

W.B. Yeats wrote in a letter dated April 1936: 'It takes fifty years for a poet's weapons to influence the issue.'[36] Why 50? Why not a more generous and less arbitrary estimate – a century, an age, a millennium? How long does it take for a prophet's weapons, as defined by Cragg, to influence events? Yeats is lamenting the unarmed literary warrior's keenly felt need for patience where others may opt for coercion and hasty militancy. The Irish poet is referring to his poem, 'The Second Coming', written in 1920, as a protest against the military cult of force. The pen is Yeats' only weapon; it is unlikely to achieve the influence he seeks. Patience is much needed. In 1940, a fellow sufferer, W.H. Auden, bitterly and correctly rejected his political poetry of the 1930s since 'poetry makes nothing happen'. More recently, weeks before his death, the Palestinian poet of resistance,

Mahmoud Darwish (1941–2008), lamented: 'I thought poetry could change every-thing, change history. But now I think that poetry only changes the poet.'

Suppose that a poet's or preacher's weapons fail to influence the issue even in 50 or 100 years. Powerful people may, with impunity, ignore the plea of the just messenger and do so indefinitely. Those who have ears to hear need not listen, as the Torah, the Quran and the New Testament concur. If so, patience is no longer the issue. Admittedly, Muhammad waited for only 13, not 50, years though one should add that he began his ideological career late in life. If the aim is to see truth triumph in a world forever addicted to falsehood and illusion, does it matter pre-cisely how long one waits before resorting to force as a last resort? Where goodness has knocked for admission long and hard, only to receive the contempt of silence, should one keep on knocking indefinitely? Or should one force entry so that, once in the house and after goodness has been heard, the miscreants may with impunity reject the message?

Cragg would reject these as shock, even terror, tactics although this reasoning is not restricted to Muhammad's case. Christians reasoned similarly in their defence of the recruitment of power after the first three centuries of persecution and weak-ness. Against Cragg's impractical proposal that only a powerless Christianity can be commended as genuine, one must reply that Cragg and other apologists would not be believers in this powerless creed if power had not, at a crucial hour, secured its future and made it prominent on the world stage. The practice of Christians is wiser than their idealistic theology of power. In his treatise *The Arab Christian*, Cragg contends that the enforcement of the Islamic juridical principle of protec-tion of monotheist groups, enshrined in the Quran and the Prophet's conduct, effectively deprived Middle Eastern Christians of the power needed to perpetuate their faith. The claim is ironic. Cragg often boasts that Christianity, unlike Islam, succeeds by abjuring political power. If so, the Muslim rulers did their Christian subjects a favour by supplying them with a presupposition of their faith: Christian political impotence ensured Christian authenticity. Cragg would reject such rea-soning as mockery presumably because he cannot believe in his own rhetoric.[37]

If men and women are to do good effectively, they must be able to act in asso-ciation. And no form of association, no matter how large, can afford to rest upon nothing other than community of purpose, implicit agreement of opinion and the cementing influence of shamanic leadership. If such associations, equipped solely with an intensely shared vision, are to survive attack by a hostile external world or subsist against the menace of internal dissension, these must count daily not only upon the fealty of members but also upon pervasive recognition of the need for struggle – including violent struggle – against profane forces intolerant of the common good. This is the Quran's reasoning in that matter of armed resistance and struggle (jihad) which alienates its Western readership.

What about pacific social protest inspired by meek individuals? Cragg argues that Muhammad did not encourage allegiance to humility, meekness and non-violent resistance to evil because such ideals would have inspired little enthusiasm among the early seventh-century pagan Arabs.[38] Yet even Islamic ideals, opposed to such pacific postures, did not automatically inspire enthusiasm. This explains the resistance to Islam even in its heartland in the Western Arabian peninsula containing Mecca and Medina. Potentially viable, appealing and practicable ideals are not automatically fulfilled; much depends on their perceived moral importance and on their ability to undermine or support vested interests. That is the case in every society. In the context of inter-faith rivalry, some Christian apologists see the continuing unpopularity of the pacifist ideal to be a sign of its supposed nobility. Muslims reject the view that impracticality and widespread lack of appeal are the hallmarks of genuinely religious ideals.

As for pacifism and its quiet protest against evil, one wonders whether that ideal has had much purchase in any society, including any Christian one. The morality of the Gospels has never been practised by any nation and has been especially rejected by self-respecting Christian nations, most of whom built empires through bloodshed. Even Judaism was not always a peaceful faith seeking accommodation among alien strangers. The wars mentioned in the Torah were aimed at extermination, holocaust and genocide. Judaism was an imperial faith for part of its long history, indeed a missionary faith until Constantine prohibited Jews from proselytizing. Gentiles had until then converted to Judaism to become God-fearers 'associated' with the seed of Israel.

XII

Muhammad, face to face with Pontius Pilate, would have given him a lot more to do than merely wash his hands. That Muslim boast, Cragg would retort, is the disabling defect of political religion. It answers the world on worldly terms. A prophet should 'stick to his guns': patience, prayer and trust in the Lord's ability to requite evil (see Q:2:45, 153; see the Christian arsenal at Ephesians 6:14–17). Islamic militancy, pontificates Cragg, is misguided: forceful engagement with opposed forces defeats the moral point of the engagement. Recruiting power must 'forfeit the very quality of truth and mercy which justified it in the first place'.[39] Christ saw this as a temptation to be resisted; therefore he succeeded. Muhammad sought to establish by the sword what his Lord professed to teach by the pen (Q:96:4); therefore, Muhammad failed.

I make three points of clarification before offering a substantive response. First, Cragg thinks that preaching seeks to persuade, not impose. The sinister ring of 'impose' cannot always, however, be contrasted with 'persuade' since persuasion can amount to imposition, admittedly non-violent, when for example, it appeals to prejudice and irrational sentiment. Propaganda, advertising and occasionally preaching are devious and insidious forms of persuasion, perhaps as harmful as outright imposition.

Second, Cragg points out that Muhammad's style of militancy frustrates evil but cannot redeem it. The distinction between the divine forgiveness of impiety, an expectation common to ethical monotheisms, and the redemption of impiety, central to Christian theism, is a subtlety requiring much sophistication even to comprehend. The Christian (originally Jewish) belief in atonement for sin and redemption for the sinner, for which there is no precise Islamic equivalent, resembles the shared religious expectation of divine forgiveness and forbearance of evil.[40] It is unclear, however, what redemption entails beyond forgiveness of a culprit. If it includes the culprit's contrition, there exists no *coercive* mechanism or facility for achieving what is an incoherent ambition. At best, then, this must mean a unilateral divine initiative which bypasses human co-operation and hence side-steps the problem of coercive versus voluntary repentance for wrong done. Muslims endorse redemption insofar as it resembles forgiveness, expiation and reparation among humans and, between humanity and God, reconciliation through closing the rift caused by sin. They reject, however, the Christian *mechanism* whereby God attains redemption for us by atonement of deserved sins. The Quran rejects it as metaphysically incoherent, theologically unnecessary and morally demeaning. This difference creates an enduring and volatile dogmatic deadlock between two religious superpowers.

I must explain the caveat about metaphysical coherence. An irredeemable residue of human perversity and evil persists. No intelligible move could entirely redeem it: the capacity to thwart divine purposes by opposing a prophet's divinely commissioned cause is an integral liability of the free human subject. This capacity generates evil and perversity that cannot be wholly redeemed. No mechanism can bleach out sin from the human fabric. At most, it can be opposed, subdued, and occasionally forgiven by God or his prophets. Some forms of evil cannot be fully redeemed so long as God respects the creature's autonomy and moral freedom. Unless we jettison the integrity of the cosmic struggle between good and evil by moving beyond both categories, perhaps into the realm of Hellenic tragedy, unredeemed wrongdoing, paradigmatically the Devil's, remains an irreducible residue.

Thirdly, Cragg sees a prophet's repudiation of coercion as an immediate deduction from God's wish to avoid compulsion.[41] He appeals to one Quranic verse: 'Let there be no compulsion in the faith' (Q:2:256). But the Quran condemns both compulsion and compromise (see Q:109). Cragg's claim entangles us in a question about deferred punitive measures against persistent disbelief, measures common to the eschatology implicit in Judaism, explicit in the New Testament, and central to the Quran. These measures are considered necessary to rectify errors in the moral government of this world where the righteous suffer while the ways of the wicked prosper. Put simply, we are talking about Hell. Some Christians, mainly liberal Protestants, have abandoned belief in Hell because they feel embarrassed by a 'God of the Fire'. Christian revisionists eviscerate Hell to a feeling of alienation from God without the physical terrors evident in the classical portrait. Jesus spoke openly of Hell and had no qualms about sending a lot of people there (Mark 9:43–9). When the reckoning happens, the Christian God may not be as eager as some modern Christian theologians to disown his threat of force and punishment.

XIII

It is time for a second reflective hiatus to help us take stock of our main contention. To Muslims, it appears that the stock Christian argument against 'political religion' is a synthetic contention manufactured solely to embarrass and bully Muslims. They do not disguise their quest for legitimate power in a world in which, tragically, the sword is mightier than the pen. It is, ironically, mainly Muslims who have suffered grievously at the hands of a Christian imperialist project that is wholly treasonable to the cause of Jesus. We address this concern in the next chapter. In the meantime, let us deepen our understanding of Cragg's central reservation.

Cragg writes: 'The Hijrah is not rightly seen as a lapse away from prophethood, but as its due sequence of obedience.'[42] This judgment, similar to others at crucial junctures in Cragg's contentions, requires further reading. Many admire Cragg's captivating style but, for analytical purposes, his prose is too ornate and distended. I assume he means that prophethood was not compromised but simply terminated at Mecca and that, in Medina, Muhammad implemented the commission he received at Mecca. Muhammad at Medina was only a statesman, not a prophet.

At best, what Cragg claims is true but irrelevant. Prophethood takes Muhammad's migration in its stride, unaffected by the move. God can reveal his will to powerful kings and to powerless prophets. Even Christian dogma does not veto it. Sustaining Cragg's doubt about the Prophet's post-*hijrah* activism is a false standard of success which Cragg gratuitously attributes to him. He insinuates, without evidence, that the unstated aim of Muhammadan religion is temporal triumph rather the victory of ideals such as piety and justice. (If even a scholar can argue thus, it is unsurprising that polemical journalists, such as Christopher Hitchens, routinely call Islam 'Islamo-fascism'.)

Cragg pontificates that Muhammad overlooked the spiritual axiom that hearts are not won by force. But if victory over paganism had been secured by force, it could hardly have endured. If we scrutinize the colossal but envisaged expansion of the Muslim enterprise beyond Arabia, we cannot credit that the Arabs, allowing for some hypocritical, timeserving and lukewarm allegiances to the new faith, remained largely unconquered by the Quranic message. One must not idealize the Islamic past: it had its quota of bloodshed, hypocrisy and compromise. Equally, however, impartial observers cannot overlook the sincere and heroic quality of Muslim conviction exemplified in zestful self-sacrifice, a feature of Muslim enthusiasm which endures even in our irreversibly secularized world.

Cragg presents us with a false dichotomy between spiritual authenticity and political success. A true prophet can aim at religious sanctity and secular success just as, according to Islam, conspicuous sanctity can incorporate matrimonial sexuality. The Quran orders human beings to be aware of the limits set by God in order to attain individual and social surrender to his absolute but merciful will. That is the human share in the affair. It is God's prerogative to crown our endeavours with success – a prosperous and just social order. If he does not, the believer bears it patiently. We may legitimately seek success; there is no religious veto on it so long as it is worthily attained. A God worth revering would not be the one to render vain our efforts – a claim for which there is ample scriptural support (Q:2:112; 12:90; 47:4–6).

Cragg hastily concludes: 'There can be no doubt that the Prophet's militancy ensured his cause, and ensured its compromise.'[43] Is worldly success, then, even when attained inside the boundaries of moral and religious scruple, automatically a betrayal and a compromise? If a cause must fail in order to be authentic, only then is Cragg right to accuse Muhammad, the successful politician, of unpardonable compromise. But why should revealed religion be allergic to temporal success? Given the contingent tragedy of Christian origins, rejecting the liaison between faith and power is a pardonable enough prejudice. A condonable prejudice is nonetheless a prejudice.

Cragg wonders whether or not moral preaching and political activism, the word and the sword, are compatible. Certainly; nor need Cragg move outside Christian history to recognize this truth. The deeper questions here are: Is the morally constrained use of force ever legitimate? Can armed struggle be a valid part of a struggle to mobilize Muslims, whether in self-defence or, more problematically, in pursuit of empire? With dramatic dogmatism, Cragg asserts that the Islamic duty was to succeed politically, at all costs. He adds that coercion and power were required to attain political security for Islam in seventh-century Arabia – and this as if Muhammad's Arabia were alone in sustaining the link between physical power and worldly triumph.

For polemical motives, Cragg shelves the pertinent issue: What is the intended scope of Islam? How can we competently gauge its many dimensions and explore its facets in order to do justice to its political character *as a faith*? Is it indeed, as Muslims claim, a comprehensive system of practical rituals and moral ideals aiming to reflect and implement the divine will on earth? Could such a system omit the political sphere, so massively distinctive of our nature and cultures? The Quran aims to bring the political order inside the purview of divine dictates and thus to purify it. Why is this ideal an unworthy one for God, his prophets, or believers generally? Cragg must explain why this ideal is worthless instead of assuming that his position is axiomatic and paradigmatic for revealed religion as such. What entitles a Christian critic to judge as unacceptable all patterns of piety where piety is organically combined with polity?

XIV

We must now explore another dimension of this disagreement. While there is no harm in hoping for success, believers must be ready to encounter intractable and large-scale failure, even tragedy. These are normal casualties in the religious battleground. This fact forces us to inquire into God's own character and, therefore, into the most elemental dimensions – doctrinal, temperamental, ethical and political – of opposed but related theisms. Which outlook is truer to life and historical experience? Is Islam equipped with resources for a fruitful engagement with failure and tragedy in our sacred history? If not, what are the political implications of that deficiency?

The Christian temperament differs from the Islamic one and feeds on a different conviction about the scope and presence of tragedy in creation. Cragg laments that Islam lacks the accents of pathos familiar to readers of the New Testament and of the Hebrew Bible, especially the Book of Job. True enough; but it is a further question whether or not this amounts to a deficiency. Islam rejects tragedy. When Greek writings were translated into Arabic, under Abbasid patronage, in early ninth-century Baghdad, the tragedies were left untranslated. For myriad millions, Islam reversed and frustrated the Christian-Hellenic will to tragedy after its entrenchment in pagan and theistic minds for millennia. It is an open question, however, whether that is progress or regress.

What would an Islam with tragedy look like? Cragg investigates: 'It is fair to ask how the revelation might have been if there had been a Karbala inside the Koran.'[44] The Karbala tragedy – in which the righteous Husayn was martyred by cruel Yazid's forces – actually occurs in 680 AD, about 50 years after the close of the Quran. Muhammad's widow, Umm Salama, the last of his wives to die, heard of the tragedy just before her death in that year. To answer Cragg's hypothetical question, the revelation, in its dominant mood and axioms, would have retained its incorrigible optimism by absorbing the tragic episode into a larger picture of religious certitude and political confidence.

Some incidents of failure fall inside the Quran's 23 year incidence and a couple are mentioned in it – though none is as traumatic, especially in Shiite experience, as Karbala. Now, Muslims had won Badr against heavy odds. God, notwithstanding Napoleon, is not always on the side of the strongest battalion. 'How many a time a smaller party has vanquished a larger one, by the permission of God' (Q:2:249). Muslims were defeated at the next battle which was joined in 625 (3 AH) on a hill, Mount Uhud, just outside Medina. As in the later ambush laid by a pagan tribe in the valley of Hunayn, the Muslims took keen pleasure in surveying their military prowess. The Quran cautioned them that victory was only with God's help (Q:9:25–6). After the reverse at Uhud, the sequel to Badr, the Prophet's camp flew their flag at half-mast: the pagans reasoned that if Badr had proved Allah's prowess, Uhud refuted it. The Islamic deity was not always mightier than Hubal, the imposing idol credited with the pagan victory.

The Quran drew different conclusions. In the face of pagan derision, it explained the defeat (Q:3:121–75) and counselled Muslims about patience and endurance in the hour of eclipse and trial. 'So what if you are killed or die in the cause of God? Forgiveness from God and [his] mercy are far better than all the things men hoard' (Q:3:157). It did not concede that failure was irreversible, innate or permanent – the ingredients of tragedy. Instead it drew, if we may enlist a discrepant ally, Nietzsche's lesson from the military school of life: 'What does not kill me, makes me stronger.'[45]

An astute general, Muhammad was out in the field the very next day, injured and bandaged, leading a remnant of his army, hoping the Quraysh would hear of his survival. A friendly Bedouin told the Meccans, led by Abu Sufyan, that Muhammad and his disciples were still ready to fight. Abu Sufyan saw the huge camp-fires blazing for several days, on the outskirts of Medina, and reasoned that the Muslims were strong enough to defend the city. Muhammad's tactic probably saved Islam from annihilation. Uhud is the only battle General Muhammad lost; even in defeat, like other great tacticians such as Julius Caesar and Hannibal, he tried to salvage it.

What lessons did Uhud teach? Failure broadened perspectives. God meted out difficult days to try the mettle of the pious and honoured them by taking martyrs from their ranks (Q:3:157; 33:23). The causes of defeat included greed for booty by a group of archers (Q:3:152–3). Satan was cited as actively involved (Q:3:155). God used the opportunity to purify the mixed intentions of believers (Q:3:140, 154), to test their mettle as they faced defeat and death (Q:3:142–3). As for suffering, pagans suffered too; moreover, believers could at least hope for God's grace and help while the only sequel for disbelievers was doom (Q:4:104). Apart from trust in God, one needed only patience, understood as an active and strategic acquiescence with misfortune and defeat, awaiting final and assured vindication, with God's permission and assistance. A chilly hour in June is no more the end of the summer of success than a bright day in December is the end of the winter of discontent. Success and failure are equally didactic; Uhud taught what Badr could not. The only cure for failure is success – and this is promised (Q:3:121–6, 139, 160).

The minority instinct about tragedy is represented by the partisans of Ali (*Shiat Ali*), prominent of late in Iran and Lebanon. Cragg approves of the tragic dimension of Shiite history which informs an allegedly more profound, certainly more pessimistic, theology alert to dimensions of pathos, consuming grief and permanent secular failure. Shiites have a history of minority standing within Sunni hegemony. They offer a corresponding catalogue of suffering dating back to the controversial episode of the alleged usurpation of the right of Ali, Muhammad's cousin and son-in-law and an early convert, to succeed Muhammad and thus make Islam a family business![46] The alleged denial of Ali's right was relentlessly compounded by subsequent defeats at the hands of Sunni dynasties. The legacy of tears, epitomized in the martyrdom of Husayn in the Karbala massacre, perpetrated by Sunnis against the Prophet's line on the 10th of Muharram (58 AH), is still fervently commemorated. No witness of this inveterate if irrational grief, re-enacted annually in Shiite passion, reminiscent more of Christianity than of Islam, can remain unmoved by its telling and melancholy clue to the cruelty of political rivalry in religious dress.

This is an intra-Muslim historical topic that we shall not explore further. We note only that Cragg misrepresents the significance of suffering in Shiite theology since this stream of dissident piety is within the Islamic ocean in its attitudes towards political success and failure. The concept of tragedy, which lacks a native Arabic equivalent, has no place in ancient or modern Shiite thought. For Cragg, tragedy feeds on the contemplative spirit which effectively atrophies our drive for activism as we realize that human beings are, in virtue of original sin, incapable of moral and political perfection.[47] This assessment, independently plausible though it is, remains an anathema to Shiite theologians. Modern Iran has given the post-colonial world the only revolution in the name of Islam; the late Ayatollah Khomeini is the first man since the Renaissance to establish a theocracy anywhere in the world. Could such dramatic activism have inspired Shiite masses and leaders if they had thought that, given the innate limitations of human nature, the political facet of faith is extraneous to, perhaps even unworthy of, true religion?

In the Arab Middle East too, only secular political movements, such as the Fatah (victory) movement in the West Bank, entertain tragic and resigned perceptions of their predicament of enduring political impotence. Where Islam inspires and consoles people, as in grass-roots movements such as Hamas or Hizbullah, an unaccountable sense of hope reigns despite circumstances which give no warrant for it. Hamas and Hizbullah daily prove this resilience and inveterate optimism.

Shiite and Sunni scholars concur that the Quran's executive function (which guides administrators of empire) survives the death of Muhammad as its unique revelator. The Medinan polity was not a state in our sense but it was an empowered and politically autonomous community that all Muslims see as a blueprint for a perfect society reflecting God's intended political providence. Shiites concur with Sunnis that the apparatus of government should survive the Prophet's demise. The schism is not over the legitimacy of the continuation of Islamic rule but rather over the choice of the right person to head the faithful community-effectively a practical difference embedded in a sectarian theology of leadership. Who should have been at the helm of Muslim political destiny after the Prophet died? Should it have been Abu Bakr, as Sunnis claim, or rather the less experienced younger man, Ali? Both groups accept the involvement with power as being integral to Islam. Neither Sunnis nor Shiites think it tragic that Islam tried to conquer the world. It is non-Muslims, especially Christian polemicists and evangelists, who see a successful Islam as the greatest tragedy that has befallen the human race.

XV

The original Muslims' activist drive had Quranic warrant. The pagan order must be subverted and annihilated in the name of God. The Quran condemns Muslims who might settle for a premature peace where residues of injustice and pagan ignorance stain the order (Q:3:139; 47:35). That would be immoral compromise and betrayal of the cause of God and his messenger. Little of the old pagan system was to be spared. The litany of pre-Islamic sins ranged from a denial of orphans' and widows' rights to infanticide and indiscriminate and disproportional atrocities committed against members of alien tribes. Even the remnants of paganism were irreversibly transformed: anarchic pagan energies were systematically released, sublimated and channelled in the service of the new cause. Reckless courage was disciplined and then rebaptized as the courage to be martyred for God's sake; devotion to the pre-Islamic pilgrimage to Mecca was purified of its idolatrous associations and the cleansed city declared the hub of the Muslim universe. No recidivism or relapse into paganism undid Muhammad's efforts. Martyrdom and the Meccan pilgrimage, retrieved from pagan Arab energies, remain basic to Islam up to this day.

The Quran was merciless in its onslaught on the contemporary sinful society's individual and structural defects and injustices. The result was a transformation so total and irreversible that to call it 'revolutionary' is to employ too lenient a vocabulary. It is however the right word given its welcome accent on the Islamic commitment to power and polity deployed to ensure, sustain and maintain justice.

Let justice be done though the heavens fall! Indeed, our commitment to do justice maintains the divine balance (*al-mīzān*; 55:7–9; 57:25) so that the heavens stay in place only if justice is done on earth. Ali, the fourth caliph, once remarked: 'Government can endure despite infidelity (*kufr*) but not despite injustice (*zulm*).'

Through its legislative verses, the Medinan Quran secretes political assessments although 'political' here does not intend international or imperial power relations. Nor does it intend the narrow modern significance in which politics is contrasted with spiritual matters. Quranic politics is not a delineation of struggles for place, post and prominence as ambitious people jostle for influential positions. Such worldly ambition exists among Muslims, of course, but it is not a Quranic ideal. (*Al-siyāsah*, modern Arabic for politics is not used in the Quran.) The scripture intends to subordinate perverse worldly ways to God's ways and thus ensure the triumph of an impartial and benevolent divine sovereignty. The Quran is not political as in 'All is fair in love and war' although its contents partly relate to politics, understood pejoratively. The impulse behind its authorship is, however, more moral than political (or legal). It is supplied by the first commandment of ethical monotheism: seek holiness by sanctifying every event of your life in order to obtain God's mercy and grace. The Quranic conception of politics transcends mundane political providence by introducing a transcendent standard of humility. Genuinely religious as opposed to restrictedly political categories ensure that the pursuit of power does not make Muslims into fanatics for the Islamic cause. Rather, Islam's just and spiritual cause recruits, harnesses, restrains and sanctifies the will to temporal success and thus rescues it from collapsing into a secular realm marked by profane and unbridled fanaticisms which can lead, as Orwell has tutored us, towards the totalitarian terrors of power for its own sake.

Islam's de-secularization of politics has, contrary to Western misconception, resulted in toleration, not bigotry, in justice, not caprice. Precisely because theirs was a political creed by design, not accident, Muslims were obliged by the precise letter of their holy law, not merely by its vague spirit, to tolerate their minorities in a way which proved impossible in Europe, until Christianity's eventual collapse. Hence, for instance, owing to this aboriginal political dimension of Islam as established by Muhammad, no civilization has been more appreciative of its Jewish populations, often admired as learned and industrious fellow monotheists. Christian heretical minorities were also welcomed into the House of Islam. Both were regular victims of focused brutality in a Europe consumed by confessional politics. Had Islam renounced politics, the fate of Jews and of some minority Christian communities[48] protected by the Islamic *imperium* would have been calamitous, as we may judge from Europe's treatment of the interior dissident and exterior infidel in its high ages of faith. Religious enthusiasm in devout societies will *perforce*, to rehabilitate an apt archaism, spill over into the political arena. It is only if that realm is governed by ethical controls grounded in the religion itself that abuses, inevitable given our common human fallibility and sin, stand any chance of being checked.

XVI

Success corrupts; power is a dangerous gift. Mindful of failed European experiments with religious government, Cragg warns Muslims of the dangers of a theocratic polity that claims to be the noblest humanism but in practice invariably degenerates into an inflexible totalitarianism. One thinks of the ultra-purists such as the Taliban in Afghanistan. Those who claim divine guidance seldom accept human criticism of their policies and, once entrenched in power, rarely relinquish it without the additional inducement of exile or assassination. Critics emerge, however, even in a political order whose citizens appear uniformly submissive and united. The opposition has good grounds for its doubts since rulers are tempted to usurp divine prerogatives, arrogating to themselves what belongs only to God. Lest it be discerned and challenged, opposition often grows insidiously, as in Muhammad's own day, sponsored often by intelligent dissimulation. Such tactical hypocrisy only further contaminates politics.

As we shall see in Chapter 7, to invite a pious man to rule absolutely is in effect to ask him to become a megalomaniac. We moderns rightly expect accountability rather than perfect virtue from our rulers. The apparatus of government must be accountable to the whole Muslim community since the ruler's claim to be accountable to God directly or to his Prophet alone is in practice meaningless and ostentatious piety. Only regular accountability to ordinary citizens can prevent the caliph or sultan from abusing his powers. Otherwise, a ruler can elevate himself into an absolute despot, the only check then being his private conscience – a faculty too weak to fight his inner demons.

These are the menaces of political religion as Cragg reminds Muslims although they hardly needed his reminder. Islam, a paradigmatically political religion, embraces power as a means of securing social justice and corporate amelioration. The faith encourages social change but Muslims, as the agents of such change, must review often the dangers of political religion. The reminder to be aware of the liabilities of power, coming from powerful outsiders and rivals, however, strikes modern Muslims as ironic and strange since they are members of a populous but weak and wounded, indeed powerless, civilization in constant decline for some 500 years. Not only are about four fifths of the world's refugees Muslims, most of those killed, assassinated, wounded, exiled or displaced daily, anywhere on the planet, are Muslims. If anything, the warning should be about the dangers of powerlessness. If power corrupts, so does powerlessness. We shall defer this theme until the final chapter but we can provisionally agree with Cragg: nothing that he says here about the moral perils of political entanglement is alien to Muslims. The Quran is alert to the menace of recruiting power in God's name and appeals often enough to believers to be discriminating and alert in the execution of his designs (see Q:4:83, 94; 49:6).

Cragg asks why the Quran is confident about the truth and validity of its cause.[49] Why were early Muslims never diffident that their cause and God's holy cause coincided? Cragg speculates that a faith lacking in the stress on failure and tragedy attracts votaries who are impulsively self-assured in their militancy. Cragg confuses two separate anxieties. As for the Quran's confident tone, all Semitic sacred literature is aristocratic in temperament. God asserts and commands; he does not try to persuade through argument. Being morally and metaphysically perfect, God has no reason to doubt the righteousness of his cause. For Cragg, the Islamic scripture is not the word of God but the product of an inspired but fallible and largely misguided human authorship; neither the Quran nor Muslims, however, proceed on Cragg's presuppositions.

Cragg's scepticism speaks prejudicial rigour. He conflates the confidence of the Quran's author – a description that keeps the issue an open one – with the confidence of believers, including Muhammad. Thus the Muslims' confidence and God's confidence are treated as though the two were equally blameworthy. Muslims are mortal and fallible, a significant truth in the politics of faith. For God, however, and only for him, to believe in something is automatically to know it. As for believers, the Quran and the Prophet's traditions emphasize the requisite interiority of motive and purity of intention when engaged in jihad on God's behalf. The Quran is unimpeachably alert to the ways in which people seek to arrogate to themselves God's rights and prerogatives. Did the early Muslims identify their selfish interests with the altruistic cause of faith? Did they strive for the establishment of Islam or merely for booty and plunder? It is difficult for anyone tolerably well informed of the history of early Islam to retain a choice in answering these two questions. Scholarship, however, is not above partisanship; it easily collapses into polemic and propaganda when its producers are in the grip of rival visions.

Political life often degenerates into a pursuit of ends that are, in inception and consequence, lacking in moral purity. Since the struggle for power has been and remains intense among adherents of all faiths and ideologies, including those who claim no interest in the benefits of that indispensable facility, we do not expect moral risk to be absent. The purity of motive demanded by the sincerely religious life often conflicts with the need for diplomacy and forceful sanction necessary in our compromised world. This is not an avoidable dilemma. Social reformers, such as Muhammad, having embraced power, can at best do their best to ensure that, for the sake of establishing socially fair power structures, dirtying one's hands is morally more beneficial than keeping them clean. This reduces inevitably to a choice between evils; it is not a choice concerning which one can plead indifference or immunity.

This coin has an encouraging side. The need to enact faith in social forms enables believers to put their words into action which is more salutary than idle hopes and wishes felt in a fugitive mood at the close of evening. Such action may occasionally be wrongly motivated or be sincerely motivated but have disastrous consequences. Inaction, however, rarely fails in either respect. Ordinary men and women need realistic ideals, enjoining appropriately practical action. They do not need impossible ideals which are an embarrassing reminder of those imperfections of which we are aware and all the more so for failing to eliminate. The liabilities and limitations of private salvation in a politically unredeemed world are displayed fully in the hour of practical action. To perfect oneself, to secure one's own salvation and that of one's little club, is only to cut the first sod while contemplating the vast and untended field of duties to the planetary community of our species.

Sadly, as we see in the final chapter, the alternatives to legitimate power reduce to either political day-dreaming or terrorism. Among the affluent and powerful, lucky enough to be living in politically secure societies, mainly in the ideologically defined Occident, we note many varieties of unwarranted cheerfulness fed on a diet of supposed personal salvation. Such a feeling of private solace carries its possessors very lightly through the callous indifference and colossal cruelty of the real world. It dulls the pain that conscientious human beings feel when contemplating the vast panorama of contemporary evil follies, perverse fanaticisms and militant oppositions to goodness, probity, equity and integrity. Nor is this merely an indictment of conservative Christians and affluent right-wing Muslims. Members of the left-wing liberal Western academic class are no better when they mistake their own affluence for a universal condition. Even Cragg, a bishop sympathetic to the travail of ordinary people, remains nonetheless – to make a fair ad hominem point – insulated by layers of privilege. He is a white male ensconced among the religious and educational elite of an important nation.

XVII

Warning without sanction rarely suffices to remove injustice because establishments seldom part voluntarily with their privileges, let alone effect just reforms that would curtail their existing interests in an unjust order. This is the case today as it was in the past. The task of reformers such as Moses, Muhammad or Marx, is therefore to assess the dangers and risks of an improper deployment of power and weigh it against the benefits of a morally and strategically correct recruitment of that facility. This is the only relevant task; the view that power should never be used, that all its employments are always wrong, is a subtlety best reserved for exchange in the footnotes of theology journals and in lengthy papers presented at conferences in the convention halls of academe. Meanwhile, in the real world, all cultures, including Christian ones, instinctively seek and, in the Christian case, usually enjoy, the sanction of political power. It is our moral duty to legitimize the employment of power by qualifying force: making it authoritative, rational, constrained and discriminating, limited in scope and accountable to an electorate.

Muhammad recognized power as part of the religious arsenal in a world where impiety brazenly embraces militant forms. He was commanded to hold his ears and eyes close to the texture of real life in order to discern the true scope of human perversity and injustice established by coercion. Enabled and inspired by the Quran, he sought to achieve an empirically validated assessment of the actual, as opposed to desired or imagined, relationship between ideal and reality, between divine demand and the human will to subversion, between the imperative of justice and the determination of unjust powers and principalities to resist and reject it. Faith is as faith does; and it can do little without the power to protect its heritage and ensure its future. In his native Mecca, Muhammad boldly proved that the prevalent political ontology – the existing pagan power structure – was neither right nor eternal but rather corrupt and mutable. By exposing the Meccan shrine's true pedigree, as a shrine built by Abraham (Q:2:125–9), he radicalized his political ontology. The result was a revolution for the sake of monotheism, through the instrumentality of power.

Any acknowledgment of the necessity of social power as a means alters the nature and purpose of this debate. At most, the critic can quarrel with Muhammad's actual political strategies; even the unsympathetic critic cannot reasonably censure his attempt to gain legitimate power. The Prophet's career, despite its extenuating profession of faith as his guiding principle, remains subject to independent moral appraisal. This assessment can only be fair, however, if it rejects negative a priori judgments and the prejudicial rigour that routinely singles out Islam for rebuke while shielding other faiths, especially Christianity, behind a patronizing lenience. The just estimate would take the full measure of the Prophet's professed religious principles and goals. The propriety of his employment of the political arm must not be exclusively assessed on exterior theological bases that beg the question against the Quran's model of piety which achieves comprehensive scope by uniting faith with power.

Muhammad, unlike other seminal religious figures in the Western and Eastern faiths, risked his reputation for personal holiness by soiling his hands with the political muck. To seek merely personal purity, to avoid contamination by the world, is a form of selfishness, doubly odd in those who claim to be denying the self. Muhammad took a great and heroic risk; he succeeded. As a prophet–statesman, he had a surprising genius for diplomacy and the calculating, almost utilitarian and pragmatic, realism of politics; his attempt to subdue the Quraysh and unite the other Arab tribes of the entire peninsula was part of a master-plan executed with precision, foresight and patience. With its barely few hundred casualties, the Islamic Revolution in Medina was the least violent in history.

Muhammad's entry into Mecca in 630 (8 AH) was virtually bloodless. The city surrendered. A few individuals were executed, all for offences against God, especially the denigration of his message. There was a general amnesty for any who had harmed and injured the Prophet in his capacity as a fellow human being. Muhammad soberly recognized that where men and women are addicted to the logic of coercion, any negotiation with the militant calumnies of evil must be supplemented with a confrontation in the sphere of physical power. In modern parlance, the threat of forceful sanctions combined with diplomacy and economic pressures can ensure mutual deterrence – although the use of sheer force must remain a last resort, to be used as a last resort. At the end of the chapter, however, believers must enter fully into peace (*silm*; Q:2:208), the wholesome peace of submission (*salām al-islām*).

Cragg's point, severely Protestant and wholly out of touch with the realities of ancient history and of recent memory, is that the very enlistment of the political sector, irrespective of its potential for legitimate and morally excellent reform, is sufficient reason for entertaining a permanent moral reservation about Muhammad's style of religious commitment. It is a judgment at once too absolute and *in extremis*, trapped in a dogmatic vision that sets itself needlessly insoluble political dilemmas.

Cragg's words should be mollified by the qualifications brought by experience, political practice, and historical contingency. Islam's laudable realism removes the necessity for that false antithesis of rendering unto Caesar the things that belong to Caesar at the expense of the things that rightfully belong to God. One must of course never deny Cragg's reminder about the corruptibility and menace of political religion as it tries to usurp divine prerogatives. The Quran obliges believers to cultivate the God-mindful spirit in which political tasks are to be undertaken. This duty is transparent in its ethical scheme which schools the political temper for a comprehensively religious vocation.

Having explored the hinterland of Quranic political theology and Muhammad's activist role, we must now begin to ascertain Islam's status as a contender in today's political order. In the next chapter, we probe the implications of Cragg's Christian assessment of Muhammad as failed prophet but successful politician. The policy entailments of these derivative issues – especially Islam's standing as private faith or public ideology – are carried forward into Part III and the Epilogue.

5 A secular religion
Faith or ideology?

I

In Chapter 4, I contended that Muhammad introduced religious principle and the leaven of mercy into politics and thus cleansed it of its Machiavellian ruthlessness. Machiavelli cared only for pragmatism in politics, rejecting Christian political norms as juvenile, idealistic and perfectionist. We must stop hankering for a virtuous utopia, he argued, and accept that we are politically imperfect and 'imperfectible'.

The taming of our power instinct through legal constraint and the amelioration of our plight through coercive intervention are twin themes that interest all who seek a self-respecting identity rooted in legitimate empowerment. The Quran's final imperative, the liberation of vulnerable and marginalized peoples, differs however from the merely moral absolutes of the New Testament. While much Christian criticism of society is exclusively moral, the Quran's reservations are legal and structural, hence political. Christ's charisma appeals to those on society's outskirts – orphans, widows, lepers and tax-collectors – now newly invited to his table, hosted by a liberal divine host who replaces a tribal Yahweh. The Christian appeal to the social periphery, through its kerygma of everyman's emancipation, marks it as a universally ethical monotheism. Islam's political monotheism, however, additionally challenges the power structures that patronize the inequities and iniquities which make some unfairly vulnerable to others. Domestic Western protest against the excesses of capitalism is theoretical and metaphysical, not practical or political. Among faiths, Islam alone formally condemns a usurious economic order (Q:2:278–80) that strangles poor people. Objects of exploitation must become, by God's grace, agents and subjects of history (Q:28:4–6).

Against the largely contrasting backdrop of canonical Christian views of power, we inquire into applied Islam's liberating potential for humanity, as it inspires Muslims to struggle to establish a divinely willed society. Notwithstanding most Western ideologues and polemical atheists, Islam is neither a fascist nor totalitarian ideology but rather a dynamic and evolving moral commitment to engage and defeat economic and political oppression. Christians reject the Islamic struggle as deficient in the New Testament emphases of love, forbearance and the transforming power of suffering for the sake of justice and truth. This is an absurd contrast. The Quran does not veto the stress on forgiveness, love and conscientious regard for others' rights. Equally, Christians can join Muslims in struggling to establish

God's Kingdom on earth in ways that go beyond the pious platitudes and fantasies of the apolitical imagination.

For Muslims, justice is a structural public obligation that flows from private religious confession. The Quran links faith with justice. Thus, 'God sent down the book and the balance so that humankind may rise up to justice' (Q:57:25). This literal translation, with its descent–ascent typology, underlines the correct order of priorities: the believer's prayers and the self-restraint are preparatory. Reading scripture, learning and obeying its demands, and purifying one's heart, eventually enable one to rise up to implement justice, the end of true faith. Believers are ordered to be just (Q:5:8). In the original, the imperative is direct, the verb transitive, the message succinct. Justice is next to godliness (Q:5:8); injustice is to be avoided even if the heavens fall (see Q:4:3). Injustice is blasphemy against God. The Quran condemns worshippers who divorce religious observance from the duty to feed the poor and care for the dispossessed (Q:74:42–4; 107). Fulfilling standard obligations – five canonical prayers daily, fasting one month annually, giving alms once yearly and a pilgrimage once in a lifetime – supplies only the means. The preacher content with preaching piety in the private sector invites the charge of indulging conventional rhetoric and promoting a selfish salvation.

God himself is not neutral in the struggle between justice and oppression. He votes too for God's party (*ḥizb Allāh*; Q:58:22), contrasted with the Devil's party (Q:58:19), a Quranic version of the two-party system! The scripture contrasts the oppressors and oppressed (Q:14:21; 28:5) and eulogizes God as the King of 'the masses' (Q:114:2–3).[1] This reading is no illegitimate annexation of God to one's personal political agenda. The cause of justice is not anyone's private business or some vigilante concern. It is a universally human and wholly public cause. Muslims have the correlative obligation to establish a just society on earth. The just are the true peace-makers.

Justice as due balance or impartiality also features prominently in the sayings of the Prophet. A righteous indignation about injustice is a vital part of the prophetic representation of God's quality as lord of requital (*dhū al-intiqām*; Q:3:4; 14:47). The Prophet warned believers that the selfish pursuit of power (*ḥirs*) differs from the selfless pursuit of power (*quwwah, ṭāqah*) for the sake of establishing justice for all. Presumably, envy motivates people to become political. Those who are, as Muhammad was, naturally without envy, will be indifferent to political power. The Prophet preached that oppressed individuals, whether human or, for rhetorical effect, animal, can all seek redress. This is the doctrine of *radd al-maẓālim* (restitution for the wronged): the Prophet (Peace be upon him) prayed for pardon for his people, and received the reply: 'I have forgiven them all but acts of oppression, for I shall exact recompense for the one who is wronged, from his oppressor.'[2]

II

In his revolutionary Christian phase, Leo Tolstoy mused: 'Everyone wants to change humanity and no-one wants to change himself.' He gave away his money to the poor while wandering in Moscow's slums one night. But he did not address the general question he himself posed: 'What is to be done?'

The duality of changing society and changing ourselves lies inside the heart; the choice between revolution and repentance is not exclusive. Nor is it a single event. That is why the dichotomy between peace (through internal transformation) and conquest (through external suppression of enemies and territorial expansion) is false and pernicious. 'Purify the heart – and the institutions will follow.' But equally: 'Purify the institutions – and the heart will follow.' Which order of priorities is truer to life's political dimension? A just order is impossible without a collective purity of hearts while an individual pure heart is no bulwark against an unjust order. The Islamic verdict on the relationship between social power and private faith, introduced in Chapter 4, is part of a topical debate in our power-conscious and ideologically charged world. Can we balance the reform of individual hearts with the requisite structural changes (within nations) and thus secure single standards of international justice?

One Christian approach argues for a change of individual hearts and minds while deferring the transformation of evil structures to the trinity of patience, prayer and the future. The opposing strategy, popular with Marxists, is to place one's bets on changing the infrastructure that perpetuates social evils while hoping also for a wild card. This card, hard to come by in the post-Cold War era when Marxists are dealing close to the bottom of the pack, represents the gamble for widespread individual purity of revolutionary commitment – considered superfluous only by tough-minded Marxists who have blind faith in a pre-determined classless utopia.

These contrasting views are of course both mistaken. We must change human hearts while revolutionizing those power structures which lodge and perpetuate injustice. This was the Prophet's procedure as he founded the Medinan polity. Most Christians emphasize reform of private consciences; those with socialist leanings see such conscientious reform as a preface to revolution. Given their reservations about our sinful nature, and a fortiori about human beings as political agents, Christians cannot consistently believe in a heavenly city on earth. The Christian hypothesis of the political 'imperfectibility' of our humanity is not implausible. Collective hope that historical advances will comprehensively improve the human lot confronts the sobering insight that each age finds itself beset with novel problems which are as, and occasionally more, formidable than those recently resolved. Many Christians regretfully conclude that the best we can have are decent individuals who work humbly for the common good within a social, political, and legal order which seldom spontaneously respects Christian restraints and values.

Christians remind Muslims and Jews: 'Law does not change the heart.' Martin Luther King reminds us all, 'But it does restrain the heartless'. Quranic legislation formally protects society's powerless victims. Christians confronted with injustice, rather than those theorizing from afar, accept a liberation theology especially for 'Third World' countries. Such theology has received little support from orthodoxy. Muslims, by contrast, have a scripture whose only theology is liberation theology. The Quran endorses laws and political mechanisms, revolutionary if required, that protect us from each other's callousness and avarice. With its sanguine view of human nature, a view that dismisses original sin as unjust and superfluous, the Quran teaches that the self-accusing soul (Q:75:2) can struggle against social wrongs without being fatally tempted by the sinister possibilities of power. While Islam attempts to redeem the political sphere, redemption as a political notion is foreign to Christians. The lexicographer Samuel Johnson, speaking on behalf of Christendom, mused in his only surviving couplet of poetry: 'How small of all that human hearts endure/That part which laws or kings can cause or cure.'[3]

Laws and kings can actually cause a great deal of suffering. Muslims are more troubled by the tragic limits that powerlessness imposes than by power's sinister temptations. Powerlessness is a demoralizing experience which atrophies the active moral conscience. Apolitical religion corrodes believers' hearts as they wring their hands in impotent despair in the face of brazen oppression. Thus, for example, one must wonder about the inner state of officially appointed Muslim scholars and jurists who refuse to endorse even verbal protest against the oppression of fellow Muslims within their states, let alone endorse armed intervention against the brutal persecution of Muslim minorities worldwide. Can we compromise fully with evil and still be capable of prayer? Is such a conjunction morally achievable?

III

At the end of this chapter, we shall examine the moral virtues of political religion, a dimension of empowered faith Christians are religiously obliged to ignore. We begin by comparing and contrasting with Islam the dominant Christian stance on power and polity, including the associated liberal secular humanist stance that emerges from it. Our final and practical goal, deferred until Part III and the Epilogue, is to find a role for the legacy of classical and imperial Islam in the contemporary democratic system.

Christianity, in its originating dogmas, aims to remain aloof from political ambition. I argued in Chapter 4 that the Muslim stance on power, exemplified in Muhammad's embrace of the political arm, is morally, theologically and practically defensible. We now clarify the Islamic stance further by assessing Christianity's alleged moral right to resist facing the Muslim tribunal of accusation on charges of political delinquency and irresponsibility. Practically all Christians, perhaps virtually all Westerners, entertain triumphalist sentiments with respect to the continuing Muslim involvement with power which dates from the foundation of the faith, with the example of Muhammad himself for emulation. The conceit is that while Muslims eagerly dirty their hands, Christian origins are undefiled by the muck of political life.

This Christian triumphalism has not been directly challenged by any important Western writer. George Orwell's political journalism, however, contains the germ of a critique. 'The distinction that really matters', writes Orwell in his essay 'Lear, Tolstoy and the Fool', 'is not between having and not having the appetite for power'.[4] He claims that people who are opposed to armies and police forces are 'nevertheless much more intolerant and inquisitorial in outlook than the normal person who believes that it is necessary to use violence in certain circumstances'.[5] Orwell is disturbed more by creeds that dictate thought and bully people through dogma than by creeds whose adherents threaten physical sanctions to maintain the tranquility of the realm. He suggests that creeds such as pacifism and anarchism, which apparently uphold a complete renunciation of power, insidiously encourage a dictatorial and inquisitorial intervention into people's hearts and minds.

We can apply Orwell's insight to our inter-faith concerns: those who endorse the primacy of the spirit of the law can be more intolerant, in practice, than those who care solely for the letter and leave conformity with the spirit to each person's conscience. Orwell concludes:

> For if you have embraced a creed which appears to be free from the ordinary dirtiness of politics – a creed from which you yourself cannot expect to draw any material advantage – surely that proves that you are in the right? And the more you are in the right, the more natural that everyone else should be bullied into thinking likewise.[6]

In its repudiation of physical power, (modern) Christianity resembles pacifism and anarchism. Muslims admit that they care for power but add that its pursuit should be dispassionate. Islam acknowledges and regulates what in Christianity was originally ignored and later implicitly disowned. We find in the Quran and in Muhammad's traditions the supplementary and salutary stress on sincere intention in politics. Muhammad preached that the best action is the one preceded by the best intention (*niyyah*), a word that does not occur in the Quran even though the scripture often orders pious motivation for action (see Q:4:135; 9:18–20, 112; 59:18). Many Muslims, notably Rumi in his *Mathnawī* (Couplets), celebrate the moral subtlety and discernment of the fourth caliph Ali who, in the heat of battle, was posed to deliver the coup de grace to an enemy host. Suddenly, as Ali sat on the victim's chest, he spat in Ali's face. This angered Ali and he therefore stayed his hand as he recalled the Quranic injunction to kill only for the sake of righteousness (*fi sabīl allāh*; Q:9:111), free of the rancour and indignation that nourish personal vengeance.

This contextualized stress on sincere intention and pure volition is absent in unqualified New Testament imperatives. Christians have intractable problems with unconditional imperatives such as 'Judge not that ye be not judged' (Matthew 7:1), 'All who take up the sword shall perish by the sword' (Matthew 26:52) and 'Whosoever among you is without sin, let him cast the first stone' (John 8:7).[7] Such aphorisms are impractical and morally untrue unless we mention the intentions of their teacher or the nature of their audience. The aphorisms can rightly be addressed only to a person under the yoke of passions such as anger, an emotion that the Romans stigmatized as 'madness for a short time'. Impartial judges pass legitimate judgment on wrong-doers without being themselves condemned for it.[8] Many men, including Muhammad, have justly drawn the sword without therefore perishing by it; even more have cast stones without feeling obliged to ask themselves whether they themselves were sinless. Judges and executioners, in Christendom, have never been hindered in their professions by these New Testament absolutes.

IV

While many Muslims privately relish Islam's laudable realism concerning human nature and the social order, they regret that such candour about the need for power leads more devious people to accuse them of being war-mongers, though that accusation is harder to believe after recent world events in which Muslims are overwhelmingly the victims of direct Western aggression. The Quran's social pro-gramme engages fallible and hypocritical human beings who often disown the very ideals they preach. Although its defining involvement with power is a corol-lary of this presupposition, this does not lend Islam exceptional status since all viable faiths and ideologies presuppose the failings of our common humanity. In acknowledging their willingness to employ force constrained by moral scruple derived from, and sanctioned by, revelation, for the sake of just causes, Muslims are more frank than the adherents of rival faiths and ideologies who, ironically, often enjoy the beneficial sanction of superior power.

The Christian apologist replies that Christianity, unlike Islam, does not incor-porate the political kingdom into its originating self-definition. This is a weak response: non-Christians are validly concerned with the Christian interpretation of this disavowal of politics as shown in the behaviour of self-professed Christians inside history's vicissitudes. Empirical Christianity is more relevant than the per-fect Christianity formed by Western idealists and romantics for whom it is now simply a source of racial pride. Muslims do not regard modern Christian attitudes, influenced by their liberal secular backdrop, as any more authentically Christian than mediaeval Catholic and Byzantine theologies which accepted temporal power as a moral imperative. The history of the mediaeval papacy, the last surviv-ing Western feudal institution apart from the ancient European universities, does not convince non-Catholics that Catholics are merely sanctifying the political realm. (Has the Papacy, which has outlived the caliphate and survived modernity, compromised with the secular world much more than the Islamic institution did?)

No religion whose votaries conquered nearly the entire globe, including its uninhabited extremities, and recently colonized parts of space, in the hope of saving others (and presumably themselves), can truthfully claim an indifference to power unless one indulges some private sense of humour. Official Christianity, both Catholic and Protestant, has historically sought authority over the powers temporal. Its associated colonial policy-makers managed subjugated peoples in a way that permitted an unremitting search for unfair privilege for the ruling elite. Whole nations were impoverished to enable corrupt secular cliques to indefinitely milk resources and enjoy undeserved affluence. A sincere Christian may concede that the deportment of these colonialist Christians is treasonable to the cause of a powerless Christ whose kingdom was not of this world. If so, that itself is a mel-ancholy comment on the radical failures of Christ's followers and a confirmation of the futility of impossibly difficult ideals.

Reality is reluctant to reflect the slogans of Christian apology. Official Christianity, like reactionary state-sponsored Islam, often abets and seconds cruelty and injustice. We note it in Catholicism's enthusiastic association with venal state structures in the Catholic Americas and the Catholic Orient (Philippines). The Spanish civil war is a chilling example of Catholic complicity with fascism. Moreover, original Christianity's apolitical doctrine is custom-built to legitimize oppression since no doctrine is more congenial to tyrants than the view that religion has no political entailments. Christianity is easily prostituted by unscrupulous rulers who sense that the New Testament stance on power lends itself to misuse. Passivity in the face of gross injustice and provocation cannot be morally preferable to the limited use of force. Oppressed men and women need much patience if their attempt to recruit force against blatant injustice depends on the supply of a coherent theology authorizing its employment. Although Western Christians congratulate themselves on their renunciation of power, the moral truth is that in the pursuit of justice in our kind of world, clean hands, rather than bloody ones, are sometimes a better indication of callous indifference.

For most Christians and pacifists, power translates into the images of Orwell's *1984*: the rubber truncheon wielded by hooded guards, the massive iron boot descending on the upturned, vulnerable and petrified human face and endless networks of convoluted barbed wire. This is, however, not only the ethos of power but also that of weakness. It depends on whether one is the guard or the prisoner. Which side of the barbed wire one is on decides one's view of power. Orwell, the prophet with honour in his native land, opposed the abuse of power as men and women indulged in 'doublethink', the hallmark of intellectual and hence moral indolence and dishonesty. This moral slackness is the opposite of the exacting reflection (*tadabbur*), repentance and self-scrutiny that the Quran inculcates from cover to cover (see Q:4:82; 47:24). Power can become an end in itself, as it did in the police-state of Orwell's nightmare. The challenge, however, is not to renounce legitimately acquired power but rather to use it for morally worthy ends – something only reflective communities can achieve.

To renounce limited force in the struggle against unjust rulers is sometimes immoral and not merely an unsuccessful strategy. Notwithstanding Christians and other apologists for non-violence, even religious sanction cannot sanctify such a moral absurdity. One should remind the oppressed to imitate Christ in his voluntary powerlessness. One can do so, however, only as a counsel of perfection and a supererogatory demand, not a routine prerequisite of inter-personal engagement. For though one may laudably turn one's other cheek, we should intervene where other people's cheeks, and much more, are being enthusiastically slapped.

Secular humanists condemn religion precisely because of such reactionary scruples that serve a conservative political function. Muslims cannot endorse the Christian attitude of effective passivity and acquiescence in the face of grossly provocative and violently enforced injustice. Why should we have expected, for example, black Christians in the former South Africa to have endorsed non-violence against a regime that was zealously violent? Oppressed peoples are oppressed enough already without feeling the extra moral weight of external accusers suggesting that the powerless should also abdicate any militant resistance to injustice. Reproachful Christian judgments that implicate Islamic doctrine in encouraging gratuitous belligerence are rightly ignored by committed Muslims; they accept the Quran's verdict demanding indifference to unfair profane verdicts as the final proof of the strength of the believers' moral fibre (Q:5:54). Such indifference to the consciences of others is sometimes culpable but its culpability depends on whether the accusers are just or unjust. It is not immoral to ignore the consciences of oppressors, assuming they have any. Conscience is the right to be right, not the right to be wrong.[9]

V

The Quran's attempt to sanctify the political dimension of life, its decision to incorporate power into Islam's originating ideals, explains classical Islam's tolerant ascendancy and humanity. Rulers enforced the juridical principle of *al-dhimmah* (the responsibility; Q:9:8, 10), the protection of monotheistic communities mentioned only once in the Quran along with a single reference to the protection tax (*jizyah*; Q:9:29). The principle is enshrined in the Prophet's practice. He pledged protection and honourable treatment for Jews and Christians. Being a Quranic imperative, the legal protection of Jews and Christians was, for Muslim rulers, a duty, not a merit. Hence we have the haven created by imperial Islam for communities of Jews, Eastern Christians and religious refugees fleeing from a Christian Europe steeped in violently intolerant enthusiasms. When Catholicism was re-imposed in Andalusia, Jews usually preferred migration to Muslim lands. We can imagine their alternative fate if mediaeval Muslims had abdicated their political obligations by pleading indifference to temporal power.

Present Christian and Western unease about Islam as political religion is informed by specifically European experiences of theocratic rule. Just as the Christian experience of religious government has been invariably toxic, the Muslim experience of secular administration, imposed by Western powers, has been even worse. Under the Ottoman regime, the longest lasting dynasty in history and a genuinely Islamic order for all its defects, the Middle East experienced no major conflict for 400 years (from 1517 to 1917). That is the longest period of continuous peace for the holy land.[10] Since 1917, however, secular colonial modernity, imposed in myriad forms, has presided over the unrest for which the region is now a byword.

Christian theocratic violence – inquisitions and crusades – and Christian imperialist violence are both betrayals of Christ's unambiguous pacifism. The view that heretics, unless they recant, should be excommunicated and then exterminated is found in the documents of the Holy Inquisition. In a far cry from Christ's 'Love your enemies and pray for those who persecute you', Thomas Aquinas recommends excommunication and capital punishment for the heretic:

> [I]t is a much graver matter to corrupt the faith which gives life to the soul, than to forge money, which nourishes the temporal life. Therefore, if forgers of counterfeit currency and other criminals are immediately sentenced to

death by the secular authority, there is even greater reason that heretics, once convicted of heresy, be not only excommunicated but put to death.[11]

In St Peter's Square, St Paul, a Roman citizen, stands by a sword to indicate his execution by decapitation. Paul's association with the sword differs from Constantine's who did not bear it in vain. 'In this sign, conquer' indicates the shift from the cross to the sword, from martyrdom as non-resistance to evil to martyrdom in pursuit of empire. Paul, like Jesus, was the passive victim of the sword, not its wielder. Constantine was the first influential Christian wielder of the sword. In these two phases of Christian history, Christians change from being victims of violence to its agents worldwide. Christianity remained restricted to Europe for about a millennium. Potentially a universal faith, its actual universality was achieved through worldwide colonial expansion. Christianity was first Europeanized and then globalized while Jesus was racially rehabilitated in decorative art.

Beginning with the Reformation, Christianity sanctioned by kingship, inspired Europe's confessional wars. Modern churchmen contritely acknowledge the religious fervour that contributed to the excesses of colonialism, including the church's brutal attitude towards conquered non-Christians. According to Catholic canon law, with the coming of Christ, every office, governmental authority, lordship and jurisdiction was forcibly taken from 'every infidel lawfully and with just cause' and granted to the faithful through the agency of Christ the almighty.[12] Muslims wish to forgive but find it hard to forget the aggression sponsored by the Church triumphant.

To feel the force of the forced evangelization of the Americas, let us listen to a typical voice of mediaeval Catholicism: the bull *Romanus Pontifex*, dated 1454, barely 40 years before the final expulsion of Muslims from the Iberian peninsula. Pope Nicholas V (r. 1447–55) gives Portugal's Alfonso V the right to 'invade, search out, capture, vanquish and subdue all Saracens and pagans whatsoever, and other enemies of Christ wherever they live', in order to appropriate 'their kingdoms, dukedoms, principalities, lordships and goods, both chattels and real estate' and to 'reduce their persons to perpetual slavery and to take for himself and his heirs their kingdoms'.[13] Again, the Conquistadors, 'rapacious aggressors, fully supported by the Church',[14] rapidly conquered South America, destroying civilizations and exterminating indigenous peoples, with mass conversions literally at the point of the sword, the accusation Christian apologists ironically level at Muslims who subjugated many peoples without insisting on their forcible conversion to Islam.

Given Europe's deplorable record of religious intolerance, one can sympathize with post-Enlightenment theologians who fear to enter the corridors of power. Understandably, since the Peace of Westphalia (1648), secularized Westerners have been reluctant to allow religious zealots to define the content of political ethics. Non-Europeans have, to say it gently, behaved with far greater political humility than European Christians.

Two features of original Christianity facilitated a colonialist interpretation of that faith notwithstanding its founder's pacifism. Christianity was made exclusivist by the dogma of the Incarnation, a claim denounced by the Quran as blasphemous mythology (Q:5:17, 72–3). The Incarnation made Christians relentlessly hostile to Judaism and Islam, faiths whose adherents typically regard their faiths as the best but not the only paths to salvation. Second, the appointment of an empowered and infallible interpreter in the guise of the one Church fostered doctrinal rigidity and hence encouraged regular inquisitions (lit. examinations). Mediaeval Muslim society was, compared with the Christendom with which it marched in triumphant imperial reach, conspicuously tolerant towards dissident Muslims and towards non-Muslim confessional minorities. We read of isolated instances of persecutions, heresy trials and mild inquisitions. Even hostile historians, however, of whom there is no shortage in the case of Islam, cannot find what can rightly be called the genocidal instinct which broke surface with regular and predictable frequency in Christian and Christian-ruled lands right up to the very late-twentieth century.

The uniquely ascendant lenience of imperial Islam derived from two factors: its political self-consciousness which made tolerance of diversity the sign of a mature and pragmatic faith and second its theological position as the eschatological climax of the world's sacred history. These facets of the faith, and the tolerance they spontaneously engendered, account for the phenomenally rapid expansion of a religion that began its career relatively late in world history. Reductionist explanations for the largely unaccountable rise of Islam, offered by *engagéd* rival Western monotheists, are the result of zeal, not scholarly objectivity. Some fair-minded Jewish and Christian students of Islamic history, scholars whose good-will and ability are indisputable, endorse the traditional Muslim account.[15] Agnostic Western historians, however, are far more objective than their religious counterparts. And they are unanimous that the conduct of Muhammad's successors in every land, particularly in locales with resident Jews and Christians, especially in Jerusalem and Egypt, was scrupulously benign and conspicuously just in an age noted for its religious fanaticism and apocalyptic zealotry, not for its diplomacy, judicious secular compromise and pragmatic strategy.

Agnostic historians often contrast the tolerant and liberal attitude of Islam with the politicized barbarity of official Roman Christianity and the brutal tribalism of imperial Judaism. Islamic tolerance was in part the continuation of a pragmatic local tradition. Arab pagans were tolerant. This tolerance is found in other oriental cultures too, such as the Persian lenience towards Jews, noted at the close of the Hebrew canon in the Jewish arrangement of the Tanakh (2 Chronicles 36:22–3). This tolerance brought rich rewards for Muslims: economic benefits via tribute and, culturally, an efficient administration of Islamic empire by talented Jews and Christians.

VI

Christians say that, with God, nothing succeeds like failure! That was, as we saw in Chapter 4, the essence of Kenneth Cragg's critique of the Islamic success story. With God, perhaps, failure does count but in the human world that is rarely the case. Islam, like other belief-systems and ideological solidarities, including Christianity, desires and sometimes secures, the enabling sanction of power. Muslims developed no theology of powerlessness since the God of Islam was not crucified and Muhammad left only a legacy of undiluted religious and temporal success.[16]

The Prophet succeeded though he might have failed. For Cragg, the *hijrah* and its politically successful sequel were necessitated by the failure of the Prophet's verbal campaign against the Meccan idolaters. The political character of Medinan Islam therefore is due solely to this initial Meccan intransigence rather than to Quranic doctrine about a comprehensive divine sovereignty made incarnate, as it were, in the political providence of an empowered utopian Islam. If Muhammad had won the perverse pagan heart, he would not have migrated to become the sultan of Medina. The historical sequence of exile and triumphant return, which gave Islam its political baptism, is contingent, not necessary. Cragg's proposal of an alternative Islamic history, however, naïvely assumes that it was optional for the pagan Quraysh to resist the political monotheism of Islam even though, even in Mecca, Muhammad's preaching fatally threatened their economic interests.

What is at stake here is not the contingency of history but rather a conceptual anxiety about the adequacy of an account of Islam which neglects its power dimension, a facet viewed as integral by Muhammad himself. This concern is addressed obliquely in Cragg's discussion of Islamic statehood[17] where he admits that 'to diagnose the religious blight of statehood … is not to deny the inevitability of the political order'.[18] Cragg concedes that all groups and clubs, religious and secular, whether cemented by race or faith, seek and sometimes enjoy the power sanction. (Christians often deny this truth in polemical exchange when they are putting their faith on display for the admiration of outsiders.) Cragg adds that, in the overwhelmingly Muslim Middle East, Jews empowered themselves after millennia of precarious stateless survival. He does not add that the very survival of Jews in Arab lands is courtesy of lenient Muslim rule. Cragg also concedes that Arab Christians recognize that political power is indispensable.

This is reasonable enough until Cragg gratuitously singles out Islam for its supposed view of the state as an end in itself suggesting that Muslims are committed, with Machiavellian callousness, to the state and worldly success.[19] Cragg approves of Jews and Christians seeking power in the Middle East but opposes the Muslim quest even for legitimate empowerment because, he insists, Islam lacks the self-critical temper which characterizes Judaism and Christianity. Cragg here abets the stereotypical and confused assessments of Islam's political dimension. We need not press to fine detail Cragg's self-serving rhetoric to discern the falsity of such claims. All empowered communities, religious or secular, often neglect to be self-critical even though the demand for a tolerant and self-accusatory temper is part of the ethics of all responsible, including religiously motivated, politics.

Countless Quranic passages commend self-criticism, personal repentance and social equity. As a translator of the Quran, Cragg is bound to know them.[20] Here is a typical Quranic plea for cultivating a self-accusatory temperament:

> Believers! Be resolute in the doing of justice, as witnesses to God, even though it [the evidence] tells against your own selves, your parents or your

relatives, whether it concerns the rich or the poor, for God is nearer to both [parties]. Do not follow your own desires lest you pervert the truth. Yet if you do decide to act in bias and prejudice, [note that] God is well aware of your actions.

(Q:4:135; in the same vein: Q:4:3; 5:8; 49:9, 13; 59:18–9)

Cragg ignores the moral double standard he creates. Let me explain. True religion must, in its very originating norms, as Cragg asserts in his critique of Muhammad's statesmanship, exclude the political wing. However, Cragg simultaneously permits the followers of avowedly powerless creeds to enjoy power nonetheless. It is, however, hypocritical for Christian apologists to condemn Muslims' avowed *de jure* quest for legitimate empowerment while conceding its *de facto* necessity for non-Muslim communities who do not officially concede the need for power. Thus, Christians are not obliged to follow the apolitical teachings of their faith since these teachings are impossibly noble; Muslims must not follow the political teachings of their faith since these are pragmatic enough to acknowledge as right in principle what everyone else is allowed to take for granted only in practice. Such convoluted reasoning in support of this moral double standard is neither easy to understand nor appealing. Muslims dismiss it as devious political manoeuvring for power by those who cannot candidly admit it in their theology.

We counter Cragg's views simply by recording the Muslim stance. The state is subordinate to the demands of revelation; the political establishment is not a god or an ultimate reality beyond negotiated compromise. Muslim devotion has, as the creed proclaims, no terminus other than God. Ultimate allegiances are not satisfied by serving derivative realities: the object of our worship is God, not our beliefs about God or the state which enacts his laws. Therefore, where polity compromises piety, the former must be reprimanded. Piety demands a polity for the full expression of religious conviction; it can justly subordinate and discipline the state when it betrays or disowns the righteous intentions or goals for which it was created. We cannot behave autonomously in the political life; we must obey the higher rules of faith. *Allāhu akbar* is no mere slogan; it is interpreted as literally true.

As an Anglican, Cragg welcomes the post-Enlightenment ideal of church–state separation and believes that Muslims wrongly allow religion to be co-extensive with the political establishment. Christians uphold secular statehood because it is '... an invitation to a humbler posture on the part of religion, a call to serve society from within and not from above'.[21] The secular state nourishes religious ambition through the suitably modest role of discharging voluntary charitable duties. Can the humility of such service, however, safeguard us against the power of the unjust state? When secular states sponsor oppression and injustice, no religion with so narrow a function can effectively oppose them. Worse, such states could recruit religion itself for a conservative role to legitimize the evil that secular politics generates. Witness here the reactionary and quasi-colonial role played by official Catholicism in Latin- and South America or evangelical Christianity's conspicuous contribution to bigotry and intolerance in America's republican government.

Cragg's recommendation of secular statehood is motivated by an unjustifiably optimistic estimate of the extent to which secular unions and groupings are amenable to moral constraints. In an era that has seen the arrogant and casual brutality of two 'world' (or rather European) wars, Hiroshima, and, in a twenty-first century not even in its teens, the increasingly darkening shadow of nuclear holocaust, one has every right to doubt the axiom that only secular postures of power can nurture political humility. Most of the tragedies of the previous century, our most violent so far, were caused by secular and nationalist ambitions though these were occasionally camouflaged as religious. The hubris of power when it rejects accountability to transcendent forces is not any more pardonable because its source is secular. Inquisitions are not the monopoly of religious enthusiasms. Orwell's *1984* is a critique of *secular* totalitarianism. Big Brother was modelled as neither the Pope nor an Ayatollah.

There is no a priori reason why humility in politics cannot obtain in theocratic government. Humility and self-critical temperaments are not exclusive to secular democratic polity. Theocracy, properly implemented, is government under the aegis of the most radical humility, a virtue nowhere more apposite than in our accountability to God. When a Byzantine emperor visited Umar, he was surprised to see that caliph, dressed in rags, sleeping in the mosque portico. The same Umar once lost a camel and tried to find it. Asked why he did not send a slave to do so, he replied that he himself was the most abject of slaves. The ruler serves others rather than lording it over them, a view shared by Christians (Mark 10:41–5) – though even self-consciously Christian emperors (such as Constantine and Charlemagne) ignored it. Umar, history's only philosopher-saint, serves as an outstanding model of political self-effacement. Nearer our day, even hostile critics noted that after deposing the secular Shah who dwelt in indolent luxury, Ayatollah Khomeini lived in a small and inconspicuous dust-coloured home that foreign journalists had difficulty locating.

Any polity, religious or secular, can deteriorate into absolutism once hubris strikes an alliance with arbitrary power in deference to the conviction that power is only power when it is absolute. Our potential for abusing power is not wholly constrained by any form of government; the corrupt will creates the circumstances for its own exercise. There is, however, no reason why the political nursery cannot be one place to nurture the virtue of humility. Muslim history is replete with examples of soldier–saints who combined the ordeal of politics with the process of self-denial, aided by the recognition that human power can never be absolute as long as God alone is great absolutely. Thus, for instance, Abd Al-Qadir Al-Jaza'iri (1808–83), a ruler whose title reflects his fame as Algeria's national hero, combined armed resistance against the invading French with a personal jihad against the private (apolitical) passions of his lower self.

'To study Islam both in its history and its theology, is to encounter the most resolute and unperturbed of all faiths in placing trust, and finding pride, in political religion.'[22] Cragg does not stop to ask whether the trust is well-placed or the pride legitimate. Islam as political religion reflects the Quranic conception of *deity* as holy sovereign, not some independent or arbitrarily autocratic Muslim conception of *polity*. We serve only God; and we serve only him in our political life too. There would be reason for shame, not pride, if the political arm were embraced for its own sake rather than for furthering the designs of revelation.

VII

Cragg cites the emergence of sizeable Muslim minorities without a state, for example, as in India, disputed Kashmir, Israel–Palestine, liberal humanist Europe and Christian North America. He asserts that Islam can survive without a state. He is right. Possibly Iran, Saudi Arabia and Sudan apart, there are no Islamic states and yet we find devout Muslims in countless majority-Muslim nations. Cragg's enthusiastic recommendation of stateless (domesticated) Islam, however, hides a Western manifesto. He mistakenly suggests that only an Islam devoid of state establishment and recognition could teach Muslims political humility. Cragg is desperate to produce some supporting Muslim voice, no matter how marginal; he quotes approvingly the claim of an unknown Indian Shiite author who asserts that Muhammad did not found a state (defined here as empowered community). (Lest credibility be challenged or parody suspected, I quote directly the Indian author cited by Cragg.[23])

This dispute is partly verbal. We define the state as an organization with resources of violence superior to those of civil society. Muhammad headed a civilian community that was legally autonomous, socially united and therefore easily mobilized against external enemies. Cragg cites his obscure author, however, to show that Muhammad never sought to empower his community – a demonstrably unhistorical claim. Such baseless speculation discredits its author and any who approve of it, making scholarship collapse into a partisan pursuit of power interests.

A stateless Islam teaches Muslims something more time-honoured than political humility: the liabilities of political impotence. Powerlessness corrupts and absolute powerlessness corrupts absolutely. Some powerless Muslims, in their desperation, will resort, as a last resort to terrorism thinking that if people do not care, there are ways of making them care. Powerful people do not need to demonstrate on the streets or hijack aeroplanes or become what cynical Western newscasters call 'suicide bombers'.[24]

I am not claiming that Muslim populations need a state to bolster their faith. Cragg's priestly forbears who presided over the Inquisition in re-conquered Spain knew well enough that Muslims do not lose their faith solely because it is not externally enforced. The destruction of the Islamic *ummah* by colonial powers has not led to a mass crisis of faith or even a minor leakage from the vessel of Islam. As private faith, Islam has survived far better under secular administration than has Christianity. To feel secure in one's private faith, however, does not mean that one can protect and perpetuate one's heritage in a precarious world with its contending empowered ideologies. Every community needs power to ensure its legacy. Judging by Western outrage over 'radical Islam', one would think that that requirement was unique to Islam.

VIII

We have examined Cragg's position in isolation from broader contemporary concerns such as Christian–Muslim relations and Christian liberation theology. To deepen our awareness of Islam's stance on power, we must assess some types of Christian entanglement with temporal power. Islam and Christianity are called missionary religions but 'missionary' is a polite term for 'imperial' just as 'secular' is a euphemism for 'pagan'. These two global religious superpowers interact directly today and have competitive traditions of colonial adventurism. Their rivalry is integral to the contemporary Islamic involvement with power. Islam is the political and religious competitor of Christianity, the world's most widely distributed and populous faith. Battles between the crescent and the cross regularly erupt in places as far apart as Nigeria and the Philippines while Beirut's streets and forbidden zones confirm that Christian–Muslim rivalry is not restricted to the footnotes of academic journals.

The neo-orthodox theologian Karl Barth once joked that he read the Bible in one hand and a newspaper in the other. Christians, Muslims and Jews who adopt his style of reading find that their scriptures contain relevant verdicts about politically motivated violence against suffocating oppression, the search for social and international justice, the scourge of global poverty, organized urban crime, and the curse of unemployment which makes many settle for 'Home is wherever one has a job'. Which text, the sacred–eternal or the profane–ephemeral, should determine our world view? Can we interpret newspaper headlines in the light of revelation? Does the Quran supply a reverent and relevant perspective on our planet's irately competitive voices? Does God still care enough to liberate the oppressed through the appointment of new liberators?

Barth's style of reading the newspapers must have inspired Christians attending the Medillin Conference in Colombia in 1968, the Vatican II of Latin America. These Catholic thinkers wondered about the correct moral response to the accelerating marginalization of vast populations condemned to live in perpetual poverty and social degradation. The problems were all the more pressing since prosperous Western Christian nations both now and historically were largely responsible for this moral outrage. The cross and the sword had been constant companions in the vast historical enterprise of occidental aggression, not least in Latin and South America. Injustice was a scandalous condition that must be remedied since it was contrary to the will of a loving God and in any case injured human dignity.

The reasoning here resembled the Marxist analysis of the political uses of charity. Private charity is the enemy of revolutionary politics. Oppressors would at best give charity as a salve for their consciences. Powerful people enjoy being charitable since charity makes them feel and look good. They choose how much charity they wish to dispense and control the scope of their philanthropy. The poor should realize, however, if they are thinking straight, that they need justice, not charity. But to allow for justice, the powerful would have to sacrifice some power. In a just society, private virtues such as individual generosity to the poor are virtually superfluous. On the other hand, no amount of personal generosity can resolve the structural problems of a society based on unjust distributions of power and wealth.

Five years after the Medillin gathering, the Peruvian theologian Gustavo Gutierrez published *A Theology of Liberation* which inspired and guided a revolutionary initiative in twentieth-century Christianity.[25] Gutierrez shouted that liberation from the personal prison of sin is incomplete without the further liberation from unjust structures of power and prestige. He argued that to distinguish between politics and religion or, equivalently, to stay aloof from politics, as many of his conservative Catholic colleagues did, was already a conservative political act that practically perpetuated the unjust status quo. Private religious salvation is worthless when we live in public distress. Like Gutierrez, other liberation theologians preach the liberation of oneself and others from all oppression: the private burden of sin, naturally, but also public forms of tyranny, including political, economic, legal, sexual, racial, patriarchal, environmental and even 'religious'. In Latin America, Christian compassion was directed at the continuing political and economic suppression of already impoverished masses; in the South Africa of the day, the white ruling elite's brutal crackdown on legitimate black majority rights evoked the theologians' revulsion just as the mammoth task of eradicating spectacular poverty in South Asia continues to engage their sympathies.

Liberation theology was based not on the secular truth that injustice exists in the world, a political analogue to the first noble truth the Buddha taught, though we hardly need anyone to tell us such truisms. Christian liberation theology was founded rather on the Christian insight that God suffered too and therefore sympathized with suffering humans. Liberation theologians did not meditate in the detached setting of academia – as arm-chair or bath-tub theologians – but rather lived in the messy milieu of ordinary life. Their theology was spontaneously generated at grass (or rice-) roots level,[26] inspired by direct knowledge, even experience, of the deprivations and tribulations of small, poor and isolated communities professing the Gospel of compassion in the face of armed callous witnesses. This movement, dubbed 'poor theology' by admirers and detractors alike is a religious programme of liberating the world's voiceless and oppressed masses by exercising a 'preferential option for the poor'. Critics dismiss it as unorthodox and hence 'poor' in a different sense: it is unfaithful to the unarmed Christ's teachings since liberation thinkers interpret the Gospel, heretically, as effectively authorizing armed socialist resistance to armed oppressors.

The indictment of liberation theology by orthodox Christians resembles their indictment of the Muslim entanglement with power. Conversely, the rejoinders of Christian liberation theologians to their orthodox co-religionists resemble the Islamic critique of official Christianity's irresponsible withdrawal from the political sector. Christian liberation theology is in effect an Islamization of an originally apolitical Christianity. The hero of liberation theology is not Jesus of Gethsemane but some political activist resembling Muhammad of Medina or Judas Maccabaeus.

Traditional Christians object that liberation theology devalues religious reflection by exalting political action: dogmatic Christianity, offering salvation, is reduced to humanist idealism, a Christian-sounding appendix to a secular declaration of human rights. What is the point of religious meditation, however, if it does not affect our practical conduct or, worse, immobilizes us? Equally, what is religious about activism unrestrained by revealed absolutes and moral scruples? To balance reflection with appropriate action marks a mature monotheism. Granted that Christianity is not solely a declaration of the rights of humankind, are not all ethical monotheisms concerned, minimally, to secure these? And granted that Jesus was not an armed warrior, why should his (alleged) passivity in the face of militant evil be the only truly religious episode in his ministry?

Recent research has modified the traditional Gospel picture of a pacifist Jesus in order to explain events such as the forcible expulsion of the money-lenders from the Temple. It would be a digression to speculate about the relationship between Jesus and the Zealots, mentioned in the New Testament, or between him and the Essenes who are not mentioned. It suffices to note that neither of these groups explicitly repudiated military force against the Roman occupiers of Judaea. Recent biblical scholarship has given conservative Christians second thoughts about the received portrait of the historical Jesus.[27] The great prophet has been steadily rehabilitated into his native Judaism and therefore Islamicized so that he re-emerges as a reformer of shamanic charisma, a revolutionary challenging institutions and individuals who degrade and dispossess others. The Jesus of the canonical Gospels, however, did not resort to violence.

Some Christian thinkers have revised the traditional Christian attitude to power in view of recent cases of irresponsible Christian pacifism, especially as shown in the Catholic Church's refusal to sanction violent resistance to Hitler's regime. The just war precedent has been supplemented by new thinking that unites many Protestants and Catholics. Let me briefly record this tradition before exploring this matter further.

For the first three centuries, Christians refused to be soldiers, and declined any public office that required the violent administration of justice. The just war doctrine, associated with Augustine (354–430), was an extension of the biblical order to love one's neigbour: one had to protect the weak neighbour. The Christian ruler was obliged to protect his subjects against aggression. The just war doctrine in effect offers the conditions under which Christians may break the Hebrew Bible's commandment to kill. A legitimate authority can wage war if there is a just cause and all non-violent means have failed to achieve redress or justice. The sole intention is to restore peace; there is a reasonable probability of success and the principle of proportionality is observed in combat so that non-combatants are spared. In a nuclear age, one must add, such conditions are hard to satisfy and one can perhaps speak only of a just peace rather than a just war.

The Hebrew Bible added realism to the idealism of the Christian (New) Testament so that its radical new imperative to 'overcome evil by good' was effectively relegated to purely personal realtionships and thus no longer applicable to public ethics. Paradoxically, while the just war doctrine minimized the use of state force to contain violence, it also enabled the conscientious use of massive violence: 'just cause' need not be defined as self-defence against foreign aggression but could be interpreted as the defence and extension of the Christian witness to the whole world, a view with imperial consequences. Indeed, the just war doctrine makes the Christian ethics of war identical to the imperial Islamic stance – though origins and rationales obviously differ.

Catholic thinkers such as Father Peter Mayhew speak for many Christian denominations when they claim that force is sometimes necessitated by the intransigence of evil: war is tragically often the only way to ensure a hearing for peace.[28] Between the extremes of absolute principled pacifism and unconstructive, motiveless violence, we must embrace the justifiable option of violent revolution for the sake of an enduring and just peace. Constructive violence, motivated by mercy rather than malice, has been central to the Islamic defence of Muhammad's militancy. It resembles, as we saw earlier, the just war doctrine although Catholics cannot convincingly claim New Testament support for it.

Muhammad's restrained militancy, by contrast, is directly based on the Quran (Q:22:39–41). Christianity's just war tradition, especially as developed by the papal court theologian St Thomas Aquinas, is a politically motivated revision of a Christianity that was apolitical in its originating impulses.

Mayhew concludes that where injustice persists despite lengthy pacific protests, the pursuit of justice obliges Christians to endorse limited violent options. He demonstrates that the pacifist interpretation of the New Testament ignores its equally forthright and more time-honoured emphasis, dating to the Israelite prophets, on the need to secure social justice by confronting the forces of communal wrongdoing which usurp others' legitimate rights. Many powerful conservative voices oppose Mayhew's radical Christian stance. Martin Luther articulated the prevalent and still influential post-mediaeval view about Christianity's proper role in the political realm. Today, it is promulgated by European churches such as the established Church of 'England' which is misleadingly named, like other institutions in the United Kingdom.[29] It is both broader and narrower than its name suggests: a worldwide communion, courtesy of British imperialism and its residue, the Commonwealth. It is also mainly the church of one privileged class, not of the whole nation.[30]

Martin Luther's influential division of politics into the 'Two Kingdoms' depoliticized Christianity. The state was to be governed by secular laws while the church was ordered by the gospel which contained the divine promise.[31] While the state reigns supreme in secular matters, Christians should build a kingdom that is not of this world by withdrawing from politics in order to maintain a fellowship of love where compromise with secular power is unthinkable. The two kingdoms, like Rudyard Kipling's imagined east and west, are never to meet though in both cases there is inevitable interaction. There emerges a mutually supportive relationship between the established faith of a nation and a political order that is far from Christian. In this dangerously mistaken view, patriotism is mistaken for piety. It reaches its culmination in republican America. It is a far cry from the robust views of the French reformer John Calvin (1509–64) who thundered from his pulpit in Geneva (from 1541 until his death) that the Church of Christ should be a thorn in the secular flesh constantly piercing secular powers, forcing rulers to know and acknowledge their duties and limits.

The identification of institutional Christianity with exploitative Western power structures, particularly capitalism, rightly angers modern liberation theologians. Christianity is far easier to practise in a socialist than in a capitalist economy. Any Christianity which can support Margaret Thatcher's policies in the United Kingdom or Ronald Reagan's in America must be opposed in spirit to Jesus' teachings. If this Christianity is merely treasonable to the cause of Christ, its effects on Third World peoples are catastrophic. It is a standing reproof to Western Christians that they never effectively opposed the racist behaviour of settler minorities not only in the past in lands colonized by Westerners but also in modern nations such as Israel (under its right-wing governments) and the former South Africa.

Contemporary European and American Christians confine their faith and its universal claims to a social ghetto from which it poses no threat to a capitalist economic system which most Christians acknowledge to be unjust. An established Christianity is domesticated by its upper- and middle-class domains, many churches reduced to 'hatch, match and dispatch' (birth, marriage and death) function. The secular establishment applauds this truncated Christianity because Christians humbly acknowledge their limits and rarely ask questions that might awaken memories of that poor, derided, outcast, crucified God who came to earth at the sight of human hubris. This post-Enlightenment Christianity, willingly confined to the private sphere of piety, silently legitimizes the established order which, in turn, manipulates it for its secular ends. In North America and Europe, official Christianity is a civil religion, promoting both liberal and conservative sexual views but tending to endorse uniformly right-wing stances in foreign policy.[32] Faith has here won a Pyrrhic victory over the secular order – particularly true of the established Church of England, described by cynics as the ruling party at prayer and as the most profitable of Britain's nationalized industries.

State establishment compromises Christianity by controlling its moral passion, emasculating a force that might check the excesses of secular hubris, power and avarice. The Church of England, torn between its desire for worldly power and its Christian commitment to powerlessness, has betrayed the mission of its Master; the clouds part to reveal how its kingdom is of this world only. When Christ returns, he will feel more comfortable among the despised and impoverished British Muslims than among the Anglicans, whose presence among the poor grows more tenuous by the decade. Anglicanism is not the establishment of the faith of Jesus and his disciples but rather its manifest subversion. Whether or not such a church should be disestablished is for Anglicans to decide. Muslims would only remind Christians that worldly privilege and Christ's cause are not natural allies; Christian values are not those of bourgeois capitalism. Muslims challenge European and Western Christians to remain the custodians of God's word, not merely the nervous defenders of their institutional and class interests in a convenient marriage of throne and altar. The purpose of wedding religious restraint to political ambition is to ensure that, in politics, the world does not get its way, every day. At least on Sunday (or Friday), God should be at the helm of our destiny as political creatures. 'Seek ye only the political kingdom' is heretical but not so if we seek the political kingdom as a prelude to the heavenly one.

IX

The virtue of political religion – a cardinal virtue characteristic of Islam – is its honesty about the periodic need for force in a constituency imperfectly malleable to just demands. This is no different from our recognition of the need for secular legislation which also presupposes that we all need the yoke of the law. Muslim political involvement, taking its cue from the Prophet's activism, is direct and sincere. Muslims refuse to be victimized by arguments employing an alien logic, especially when the premises of such arguments lead to tolerance of gross injustices. In opposing injustice, however, Muslims should not seek to impose their beliefs by force. The Shariah grants conscientious liberty and ensures the right of minorities who also aim to walk in the paths of righteousness. The Quran: 'Had it not been for God's repelling some men by means of others [through the law], cloisters and churches, synagogues and mosques, in which God's name is abundantly mentioned, would certainly have been destroyed' (Q:22:40).

There is a positive side to political religion which Muslims, unlike Christians, readily acknowledge. Christianity does not provide a habitat for the flourishing of what the Greeks knew as the political virtues. It would be a parody to claim that Christians have no involvement with power: unless they are cloistered, Christians too must interact with temporal powers and principalities. That is, however, far from the full-blooded participation in the political life which alone can nurture the virtues of the civic life. Active citizenship alone can cultivate the political virtues. Islam allows the sea of faith to flow into a political estuary since the rejection of the active political life freezes at its source one spring of morally excellent conduct in community. Civil society is the chief nursery of the distinctively political virtues.

Political demands enlarge the sphere of religious duty. I do not claim that piety is unattainable unless one lifts one's aspirations beyond the local charities of the self, family and neighbourhood. Only political participation, however, provides occasions for developing qualities of character whose value and benefit are not limited to civic life. Many virtues are engendered by one's involvement in local, national, international and even imperial citizenship, particularly the virtue of vigilance about the rise of militant evil aiming to injure the common good. If good men and women leave the civic field free for the miscreants, the miscreants are bound to gain power. For evil to triumph, it is more than sufficient that good men and women should do nothing to prevent it from doing so. Abstention from a corrupt system is not the best rebellion against it.

Muslims admit that the social evil that righteous political engagement seeks to abort may itself seek the patronage and protection of the religious establishment. Where the political virtues flourish, there the political vices also build their nest: venal religious personnel seek personal aggrandizement by exploiting the gullibility of ignorant believing citizens. The political life can beget a spirit of impiously calculating realism and an unscrupulous opportunism which jointly make for callousness of heart – killing honour by habituating conscience to devious manipulation and immoral compromise. These are the risks. The Muslim mind, schooled in the humility of the Quranic lifestyle, concedes that the piety which welcomes power as the effective instrument for enacting religious truths must constantly face the divine tribunal. The political life, even more than the sexual, needs vigorous internal devices for monitoring its abuses.

Muslim rulers are afraid to tamper with Islamic law which places firm and clear limits on the ruler's authority. Those who abuse power and perpetrate injustice may be certain that they will be overthrown and humiliated so long as courageous Muslim jurists and scholars can show that rebellion and revolution are preferable to a stable but corrupt order. Unlike Marxists, Muslims do not wait for history to patronize just causes.

The question of the use and abuse of power is part of a larger one. Should one completely forsake a facility, a natural resource or aptitude, for fear of its potential abuse? Resources such as the appetite for material comfort, knowledge and sex, can be enjoyed moderately but also indulged as recreation. The knowledge that gives us refrigerators and antibiotics also gives us bombs and bullets. The gender division that perpetuates the human heritage, with its diverse paraphernalia of love and romantic tenderness, also leads to private vulnerability and public exploitation. Should one abjure a resource solely because it can be abused? If so, given that knowledge is liable to misuse, should one preach that ignorance is bliss? Following the Quran, Muslims do not bet on every horse. If a facility has little benefit but causes much harm, it should be completely abjured. This is the reasoning in the case of Islam's ban on intoxicants, especially alcohol, a prohibition that has prevented Islam from becoming a more thriving universal faith. Not only do Muslims consider an absolute veto on power, knowledge or sex unrealistic, they trust that the morally constrained recruitment of these natural resources and impulses produces on balance more good than harm.

6   A legal religion

I

The Prophet Muhammad's 'companions' were his 'disciples' since they followed the 'discipline' he imposed. Jesus' disciples were more like companions since no legal discipline was required. (In Spanish universities, to the delight of professors, students are called *discipulos*!) Christians regard the law as worldly, secular and therefore inferior to the religious gifts of grace and truth (John 1:17). Secularism, understood as an autonomous world view with atheistic foundations rather than a political ideology compatible with religious faith, could only have grown out of a dispensation divested of sacred law: a faith concerned solely with the things of God, a religion that vacated the secular realm. Once armed with a holy law, a religious faith can compete successfully both with political secularism and with secularism understood more broadly as a comprehensive ideology underpinning atheistic humanism. Hence we have Islam.

By insisting that the intentions of ethics must remain unfulfilled without the supplement of legal coercion buttressed by political power, Islam affirms the need to enforce virtue in a scheme where secular crimes are simultaneously sins. Only a legal–political, not merely moral, compass can envisage the full range of good and evil. Coercive measures to punish transgressions are required by the intransigence of unreformed human nature. Its private moral promptings must be supplemented by the *lex divina*. The legal and political order supplements internal forms of moral coercion (derived from conscience) with external force, thus penalizing evil conduct through immediate mundane sanctions and deferred eschatological ones. The holy law motivates individuals who would otherwise suffer from moral inertia and thus leave undeveloped their potentially virtuous nature. The effects of the holy law on conduct are immediate: fear of present and deferred sanctions is more effective in motivating people than academic reasoning and patient education of moral dispositions.

The *lex divina* is situated between the privacy of ethics and etiquette, on the one hand, and state empowerment, on the other. This ambivalence dictates Islam's vacillating destiny as privately binding or publically enforced faith. The Quran's affirmation of our original righteousness provides a rationale for Islamic law. God made human beings only potentially virtuous by granting them a self-accusing spirit (Q:75:2) and a perfect nature (Q:30:30). He also created them congenitally prone to evil (Q:12:53 spoken by Joseph). Most human beings flout divine laws; few of them desire a self-motivated moral life through spontaneous submission to God's will. The Quran affirms the necessity of law which implies that we need more than to merely recollect innate moral truths in order to be virtuous. Islam's paternalistic legislation presupposes continuous re-enforcement, proof that we are only potentially virtuous. The Quran is not an academic treatise and therefore does not address the theological puzzles that arise from our dual natural heritage. Instead it offers a practical solution for our recalcitrance to virtue. It gives us the Shariah.

This word, which alarms many Westerners, occurs only once in the Quran (Q:45:18) and normally means the sacral law but some commentators use it to mean all revealed ordinance just as 'Torah' can mean law as well as revealed guidance generally. The Quranic context is the triple gift of scripture (*kitāb*), commandments (*ḥukm*) and prophethood (*nubuwwah*) vouchsafed to the Israelites. Muhammad receives the culminating Quran, inherits previous sacred laws through a final '*sharī'ah* of (divine) command' (*'amr*; Q:45:18). These words secrete a combined legal and moral import. The verb *sha/ra/'a* (to ordain) is the opening word of the verse ordering Muhammad to re-establish the primordial faith (*al-dīn*), that dates to Noah, and to allow no divisions in it (Q:42:13). Two other words, *shir'ah* (law) and *minhāj* (programme of action), occur in a combined ethical and juridical sense (both at Q:5:48 uniquely). Their context is supplied by a pericope (Q:5:41–7) about the binding nature of the Quran's predecessors, the Torah and the Gospel. The Quran instructs Muhammad to advise Jews and Christians to judge their affairs by reference to laws found in their own scriptures. The Quran, in its dual role of confirmer–custodian (*muṣaddiq–muhāymin*) of previous scriptures, shall be the umpire:

> And to you (Muhammad), we revealed the scripture with truth, confirming scriptures before it and as their guarantor. So judge between them by using what God has revealed and do not follow your own whims which may diverge from the truth that has come to you. For each [community] we have appointed a divine law (*shir'ah*) and a precedent (*minhāj*). Had God willed, he could have made you a single community. But he wishes to test you by means of the things he has given you. So, compete with one another in virtue. To God you shall all return and he will inform you concerning your differences.
>
> (Q:5:48; see Q:9:29 for a later, less tolerant passage)

The holy law (Shariah) is a divine gift. It does not evolve organically from a primitive social setting but rather predates the social order it governs just as revelation predates the sacred society it creates. The Shariah is, in Kantian terminology, the radically noumenal and thus transcendent law capturing God's moral will (or legal mind). Only the given (or positive) order of law, called *fiqh* (understanding), is humanly created and thus accessible as social phenomena.

The Shariah is consecrated by a divine imprimatur; its parameters and some of its contents are divinely and therefore eternally fixed. One puritanical view that arises out of this theory of sacred law holds that there is no humanitarian purpose to the Shariah: Islam is simply a selfless worship of God and total obedience to even arbitrary divine imperatives. This view is unfaithful to the moral character of the Quran's God who does not intend any hardship in the faith (Q:2:185, 4:28, 22:78). Countless passages confirm divine compassion for believers although Quranic requirements such as fasting and jihad are arduous.

The Quran will continue to judge the putative justice and righteousness of legal innovations. The reformer must ask: If law is grounded in God's infallible will, how can democratic procedure alter or vitally modify its essential content? Laws evolve for varied reasons but all reform and alteration presupposes the fallibility of human wisdom. What is legally permitted need not be just. But in a system of revealed law, such ordinance is by definition just, thus leaving no gap between justice and legality. The concept of an unjust law presupposes a secular and fallible background. Only the interpretation of core Islamic law is conceded as possibly unjust (since it is administered by human judges).

If the content of laws evolves towards greater justice, then those laws were previously partly unjust. If just laws evolve towards greater injustice, they were initially partly unjust. In either case, the evolution of fully just law is incoherent although its implementation is another matter. The democratic evolution of law is grounded in the political perfectibility of human rational capacity which already presupposes the fallibility of the former. Muslims reject only the dogmatic secular view which upholds the total autonomy of law. In secular and religious systems of law, human casuistry and ingenuity can always secure devious escape from any laws, just or unjust.

II

Some 500 Quranic verses, out of a total of 6236, have prescriptive content; only about 200 have directly legal import. Such statistical data is misleading: law was sufficiently central to Islam for most of the classical commentators to be trained as jurists. Jurisprudence, theoretical and applied, was inspired by Quranic exegesis and the Prophet's customary praxis (*sunnah*). It pre-dates the development of hadith criticism and sciences of the Quran, two subjects retroactively integrated into jurisprudence when the four (Sunni) schools began to solidify in the late ninth (Christian) century. These schools formalized an already functioning legal system. The law schools were schools of interpretation of diverse legal precedents, based on the Quran and Muhammad's practice, both later amplified by analogy and deduction.

Islamic scholars are not theologians but jurists; sacred jurisprudence is the master discipline which monopolizes the correct interpretation of the faith's imperatives. Devout Muslims must be law-abiding; private religious belief is not distinguished from legal instruction and neither is distinct from the social order. The politicization of law, in the sense of the emergence of a hierarchy of sources of legitimate authority, occurs in Muhammad's own time when the community was admittedly a voluntary civilian group attracted to and cohering around the shamanic charisma of God's messenger. It had no centralized violent means to enforce its will, let alone destroy an independently created civil society. It was not a nation-state. To implement the newly revealed commandments and to enforce the legal will of the divinely guided republic, Muhammad relied on the Quran's persuasive force, his own inspiring example and the intelligent resourcefulness of his ardent followers.

The Quran's optimism about the faculty of reason impressed scholars who laid the moral and philosophical foundations of the comprehensive and fundamental discipline of jurisprudence. Muslim jurists, often elevated to saintly status as shown by their title of Imam, demonstrated that applied Islam, founded on Quranic doctrine, provided practical and spiritual knowledge that satisfied the canons of a reason untainted by our capacity for sin and error. The sacred law is rationally justifiable and comprehensive. It includes reason as a source of legitimacy but not at the same level of primacy as the Quran interpreted by the Prophet's praxis. This was part of the rather modest view of post-revelation reason as wholly instrumental, never seminal. The sacred law covers ritual obligation, moral regulation and extends to etiquette. This *shumūliyyah* (radical comprehensiveness) testified to historical Islam's relevance to all times and places, the mark of the universal dispensation finalized.

III

The Islamic state is a manifestation and an instrument of power, the power of the Shariah. It is a theo-nomocracy with God as king or sovereign (*malik*; Q:59:23; 62:1). The Islamic state is not a clerical theocracy since classically Islam has no priesthood. (The political office of ayatollah as supreme jurist is a modern innovation and restricted to Shiite theology.) The pursuit of justice is absolute. It transcends the Shariah and reflects the character of God as just master. The Shariah is a means to an end and is judged by its ability to administer justice. As a substantive, humanitarian and universal virtue, justice transcends all legal systems and faiths. For Muslims, it is furthermore a metaphysically absolute ideal ordained by God.

Justice is defined in Islam as due but not absolute regard for human freedom and equality. The pursuit of absolute freedom is condemned as license. Muslim radicals can concur with the Marxist analysis of bourgeois laws as concealed instruments of class control and class warfare, parading as harbingers of fantastic freedoms. The rebel despises the law but the law creates the rebel (as criminal) before also catching and punishing him. So much for absolute freedom!

The option of giving or withholding consent to the state is part of the political mythology of secular liberalism. In practice, no citizen has such a choice. The liberal state ensures obedience by permitting and encouraging the individual to believe that he or she has a real option to refuse the state's orders. In Western societies, the correct relationship between religion and politics, between church and state, has been legally (coercively) imposed, not freely sanctioned by private morals or the conscience of citizens although most Westerners imagine that they had a choice in the matter. The *de facto* reality of the self-defined state as absolutely sovereign is a *fait sociale* which resolves this elemental issue through a dogmatic declaration of laicism. No religion or religious institution has the right to interfere with the sovereignty of the state – proclaims the state. The authority of the state is grounded in the monopolist claim of the state: it claims to be the sole final regulator of the behaviour of its citizens. It expresses its sovereign character simply by claiming it; this claim is not rational but assertive and dogmatic. Like the God of the mature Semitic monotheisms, the state simply exists. Conservative apologists explain *ex post facto* the state's sovereignty as the will of its citizens – to preserve the myth of absolute liberty professed by democratic polities.

The liberal secular state has a monopoly on politics as coercion. Who gave it that right? The Western nation-state, through its *potestas*, dethroned God and put itself in its place in an act of coercion, not reason. The liberal state arose by destroying the sovereign, sometimes literally. Liberal statehood was the antithesis, not the fulfillment, of sovereignty. Apart from the human sovereign, God was the unstated competitor against the state, not merely a willing partner who had agreed to take a second place in the queue, for the sake of the tranquility of the kingdom. Through its legal and political mechanisms, the European state actively removed God from the public arena and kept him in his private space. Hegel was right (and for once intelligible) when he proclaimed that the state has moved to occupy the functional place of the deity. More charitably, the secular state actively replaces a sovereign God with a sovereign good.

In principle, the modern state need not mention religion at all; statesmen can leave unanswered the question of the role of God's law, thus diplomatically avoiding conflict by shelving the issues. Western European states declare their policy: religion is a private matter with which the state is not concerned and which should not manifest itself in the public sphere.

Islam's confession, 'There is no god except God', dethrones the state as God. In the Muslim world, the dethronement of organized institutional religion was, in recent centuries, attempted in imitation of Western models. It has now been actively reversed in several Islamic theo-nomocracies. God is the true and sole sovereign of the ummah, its source of authority and one indispensable source and enabler of legislation and moral virtue. For Muslims, the test of divine sovereignty is the power to legally revoke, in the name of God, secular law itself. The religious right to rescind the secular right to legislate is the rival moral and legal foundation of the Shariah.

Muslims charge that, in secular legal codes, God's rights (*ḥuqūq Allāh*) over his human servants are neglected in favour of absolute human rights (*ḥuqūq Adamī*). Islam, as a juristic monotheism, claims to balance these sets of rights. The Quran is not fully compatible with a secular notion of human rights and does not deliver the same set of rights. Thus, for example, even the *de jure* rights of Muslim women – and these are remarkably extensive in Islamic law though not in Muslim practice – differ from those secured by a Western feminism determined to achieve maximal rights for women while, from certain viewpoints, potentially neglecting the rights of the family and the legitimate grievances of men.

The Quran contained revealed legislation and the *sunnah* was fixed by Muhammad's lifestyle and approved by God. Both were imposed on believers: authoritative by

the fiat of revelation, not by consensus or individual ratiocinatic
Muhammad's traditions, the first four caliphs and the four
schools, together define what most Sunni Muslims see as the
binding tradition. The righteous elders (*al-salaf al-ṣāliḥ*) i.
companions and the generation which succeeded them. In pt,
actions are considered normative. We can better assess this claim aftc.
the scope and sources of Islamic law.

IV

Islamic law contains rules for governing the relationship between human beings
and their creator and also between members of the community. It ranges over matters
private and communal, secular and temporal. The Shariah covers all departments
of life but its provisions for governance and social justice apply only where the
government is Islamic. As Muslim law developed, it was implemented by a *qāḍī*
(judge), appointed by political authorities. This judge dealt with family law (divorce,
inheritance, marriage, rights of orphans) and administered charitable trusts (*awqāf*)
and civil disputes. The *mufti* gave expert legal rulings (fatwas) which were privately
sought and rarely implemented.

Acknowledging God's greatness affirms divine authority for human justice:
legal justice here and moral justice in the next world. In this dispensation, the spirit
matters in law and in ethics. This spirit is concretely expressed in interior human
intention that is fully discoverable only by God. The Prophet taught that the intention is material to the act. The best action is the one preceded by the best intention
(*niyyah*).[1] The acts comprising ablutions are, for example, invalid unless accompanied by the intention of doing ablutions. Washing one's face and arms lacks
religious merit if done solely to remove dirt, a rational rather than exclusively
religious ground. Concealed intention matters in ethics and in law but never to
such an extent that it turns law into ethics. Nonetheless, the demand of mercy
triumphs over the letter of even the just law.

We now canvass Islamic jurisprudence before returning to the question of the
relationship of law and ethics, from a wholly theological angle, at the end of this
chapter. Jurists are arbiters and supervisors of all knowledge since the revelation
of the law has epistemological priority. God has ordained a holy law – where law
is metonymy for knowledge of matters absolute and final, hence all significant
knowledge. This serves as an antidote to human whim and wantonness, the uncouth
barbarism of the pagan age of ignorance (see Q:5:48–50).

The Shariah, as law in the abstract, has purposes (*maqāṣid*); as fallible jurisprudential scholarship, it reduces to *fiqh* (understanding) with sources or principles
(*uṣūl*) and various dendrites (*furū'*). Its aim is to understand the Shariah. The branches
of fiqh are *'ibādāt* (worship, that is, ritual purity, prayer, almsgiving, fasting and
pilgrimage) and *mu'āmalāt* (interpersonal actions, encompassing family, mercantile and criminal law). *Uṣūl al-fiqh* (the principles of law) categorizes all action for
its legal liability. Every action, whether moral, legal, spiritual or neutral occurs
on a continuum of five axiological categories. The polar extremes are absolutely

ligatory (mandatory) and absolutely forbidden (prohibited) actions; in between lie ctions that are commendable, neutral (permissible) and reprehensible (detestable but permitted).

'Sources of law' establishes the hierarchy of juristic authorities. The Quran and the Prophet's custom, both authorized by the Quran, qualify as common denominators of every school of law. Consensus (*ijmā'*) is deduced from the prophetic tradition that 'Muhammad's ummah will never agree on an error'. Analogical reasoning (*qiyās*) is an application of unaided reason (*'aql*), the supreme and distinguishing divine gift to humanity. This branch includes the study of complex rules for extrapolating novel norms from agreed sources and for extracting new judgments. Two general areas of legal reflection supplement this training. The first is the theory and rationale for *ijtihād*, the exercise of personal or independent judgment beyond revelation.Grammatically, *ijtihād* shares a root with jihad; the two words mean, respectively, intellectual and physical struggle (or effort). The second desideratum is establishing the law's moral and pragmatic purposes: the preservation of faith, life, knowledge, lineage and wealth.[2]

The Shariah presupposes that justice is achieved through law, not only through morals. Accordingly, it covers commercial, criminal, domestic and political affairs and extends to devotion and moral conduct; it covers areas Western legislators consider concerns of private hygiene and social etiquette. It treats the act of apostasy, considered private in secular Western law, as treason against the state. Conversely, it privatizes one transgression that is public in Western law: in cases of homicide and manslaughter, parties may settle out of court and the family of a murdered victim may accept blood money as compensation (Q:4:92) and forgive the perpetrator 'for God's sake'. The *lex talionis* (law of equals; Q:2:178–9) applies only to murder (Q:17:33). It replaces the pre-Islamic tribal vendetta with requital (just retribution). The Quran also improves on the Mosaic law: 'If any one remits the retaliation by way of charity, it is an act of atonement (*kaffārah*) for himself' (Q:5:45).

For extreme (*ḥudūd*) offences, the Quranic punishments are deliberately brutal being intended to serve as exemplary deterrents (Q:5:38). Intentional murder, public corruption, treason, publically declared apostasy, piracy and highway robbery, rape and adultery are seen as attacks on the fabric of society and therefore merit capital punishment. Amputation of hands and feet (for theft and public disorder) and flogging (for false witness and fornication) suffices; execution and exile are stipulated for the vague offences of public disorder and declaration of war on God and his Messenger (see Q:5:33, 38; 24:2). Stoning to death (for adultery) is found only in the Prophet's traditions although some scholars speculate, on the authority of the caliph Umar, about a lost or abrogated 'stoning verse' to punish this serious transgression.

Substantial evidence is required for conviction in all cases, especially those crimes with specified Quranic, and therefore inescapable, punishments. Where evidence was inadequate, jurists obeyed the maxim, 'It is better to be mistaken in forgiveness than in punishment.' Islamic legal culture treats the judge as judge by granting him absolute discretion but expects him to exercise mercy as part of his professional duty. This is harder in the decidedly statutory jurisdictions of Western legal practice which are so restrictive that only the most senior judges exercise discretion, and even then privately fear they may have acted *ultra vires*.

Judged by Western criteria, Islamic procedure seems unfair since there is no due process, no jury and no prosecution or defence. Judges investigate, call witnesses from both sides, interpret the law and determine the verdict – all *in camera*. Fair procedure can, however, lead to unfair, usually pre-determined, outcomes if one allows for the kind of casuistry that secures, especially for the rich, release from deserved penalty. Equally, an apparently unfair or hasty procedure may result in a fair outcome if the system is independently predisposed to be just.

Is the Shariah fixed and permanent? Or does it evolve in response to empirically determined needs and challenges? The Quran is now a closed legal canon but legislation was fluid during Muhammad's lifetime (Q:4:15; 65:1). After closure, a later verse could still repeal an earlier one because a Quranic verse can annul the authority of another Quranic verse although such abrogation is restricted to legal and prescriptive verses, not to doctrine. The history of Islamic law pays attention to social nuance and responds to the needs, including political needs, of Muslims. Since colonial modernity interrupted Islam's history, its law lacks a continuous and indigenous evolution that could organically reflect the Muslim condition.

V

Unlike modern Christians, Muslims still study sacred history and their Prophet's customary practice in order to extract the legal significance of these realities rather than to indulge a theological curiosity. Prophetic history and prophetic praxis are grounds of juristic authority. All Muslims see Muhammad's behaviour as normative; devout and sinful Muslims alike intend to copy as much of it as possible. By contrast, Christ is, except in the case of saints, more admired than emulated.

A man's greatness is most realized in his absence. The posthumous hadith literature was inspired by the Muslims' loving but receding memory of their noble Prophet. The principal hadith scholars and editors had died by the early fourth Islamic century. The curiosity about Muhammad's actions and views, however, dates to the early second Islamic (eighth Christian) century when written sources of hadith began to compete with oral traditions. The peninsular Arabs had conquered the more literate Arabs of Syria and Iraq.

The authenticity of hadith materials can be classified either on the basis of contents (*matn*) or on credentials based on a transmission chain (*isnad*) attesting Muhammad as the first speaker of a narrative. Two definitively authentic (*ṣaḥīḥ*) compendia are based on thematic content: Sahih Bukhari compiled by Muhammad Ibn Ismail Al-Bukhari (d. 870 CE), and Sahih Muslim collected and edited by Muslim Ibn Al-Hajjaj Al-Qushayri (d. 875). Bukhari's manual is the most influential book in Islamic history, competing with the Quran's (theoretically) incomparable authority. The remaining four collections are collectively called *sunan* (singular, *sunnah*) although they are sometimes included with the two authentic collections and then known as the six trustworthy ones (*ṣaḥīḥ sittah*). The voluminous *sunan* corpus contains collections authored by Abu Dawud Al-Sijistani (d. 888), Muhammad Ibn Majah (d. 896), Abu Isa Muhammad Al-Tirmidhi (d. 893), and Ahmad Ibn Shuayb Al-Nasai (d. 915). The only important traditionist who also founded a legal school is Ahmad Ibn Hanbal. His compendium *Musnad*, as its name implies, is arranged around chains of transmission, not themes. It is not one of the canonical six.

The categories of *ṣaḥīḥ* (sound) and *ḥasan* (good) hadith are a basis of law. All are *mutawātir* hadith: narratives with multiple, including parallel, chains of authoritative testimony amounting to a textual transmission of the Prophet's praxis. The third category includes narratives too weak to acquire legal authority. Like apocryphal scripture for Protestants, this material is approved and useful for teaching and moral admonition. A weak (*ḍa'īf*) hadith is inadmissible as law but may be morally enlightening and historically informative. The remaining categories include forged traditions (which are rejected) and rare and exceptional narratives which are cautiously accepted but not used for legal or moral guidance.

The Prophet's non-verbal practice, consisting of his actions and tacit consents, is reported as anecdotes about events or situations involving his participation. These include verbal approval or rejection. Non-verbal reactions include facially expressed anger (typically turning away his face in disapproval). Prophetic silence meant approval. More broadly, in a ruling derived from a Prophetic tradition, a virgin's silence signifies her assent to a marriage proposal. In most Eastern cultures, silence has approbative power.[3]

VI

What was the political background to the emergence of Islamic law? The caliphate was first based in Medina. The first three caliphs ruled from there but Ali left Medina to quell insurgents in Iraq and unwittingly moved the caliphate to Iraq. Basra and Kufa, in modern Iraq, were two early Islamic centres of learning. Both were founded during Umar's rule. After Ali's assassination, his son Hasan relinquished his right to be caliph in favour of Mu'awiya; the caliphate was moved to Damascus in 661.

Four extant Sunni legal schools (*madhhab,* singular) and one major Shiite school together constitute Islam's legal corpus. It is an encyclopedia of scholarly industry and pious meticulousness of legal reasoning competing in size and sophistication with Talmudic compendia and with Catholic canon law (taken separately). The four canonical Sunni schools recognize each other's authority since they differ only in emphasis and detail and can therefore, like the four Gospels, be harmonized. The Sunni schools concur on some four-fifths of the legal substance.

The Hanafi (Kufan) school, Islam's first legal movement, has the largest number of adherents, guiding a third of the ummah. Abu Hanifah, the theologian–jurist who informally founded it, lived in Kufa from 80 to 150 AH. As with all truly influential men, he didn't write anything. Like Socrates, but unlike Jesus, he had excellent disciples. His chief disciple, Yaqub Al-Ansari, affectionately called Abu Yusuf (d. 798/176 AH), later became a judge and a scholar of comparative fiqh.

Along with Muhammad Ibn Hassan Al-Shaybani (d. 804/182 AH), he developed the master's flexible oral dispensation into a coherent system, supplementing it with a supple essay in legal reasoning. Both disciples lived in the intellectually vigorous period of early Abbasid rule when Islamic philosophy was founded. The school is politically conservative and opposes revolution even in the face of despotism. It was the official school of the Abbasid (763–1258) and Ottoman (1281–1921) empires.

The secret of Hanafi supremacy lies in its principle of *istiḥsan* (choosing the best). Confronted by a choice between equally authoritative rulings arising from equally authoritative sources, Hanafis exercise equitable legal discretion. Jurists elect the principles which promote the law's *moral* purposes. The Quran permits the need for choosing the best (*aḥsan*) among valid alternatives (Q:39:18). A partial exception is permitted to an otherwise general and absolute principle because of moral considerations arising elsewhere in the corpus of the Shariah. Thus, the totality of the law's purposes is considered and rulings arising out of this totality are preferred to a single absolute principle taken in isolation. For example, the Quran rules absolutely that guardians must hold in trust and not transfer to orphans their wealth until they reach the age of discretion and sound judgment (Q:4:6; 6:152). This implies that an orphan minor may not make a bequest, while still a minor, regarding his or her wealth. But suppose the orphan dies before reaching legal majority. Since anyone can die at any time, a minor can make a bequest for his or her wealth to be spent charitably, in the event of death, an event that automatically removes fear of poverty, the sole motive for keeping the orphan's wealth in trust in this world. This Hanafi legal device was rejected as too liberal by Al-Shafi'i, the founder of a later school.

The second school was informally established by Imam Malik Ibn Anas (93–179 AH/795) who lived in Medina. His *Kitāb Al-Muwaṭṭā'* (The Book of the Beaten Track), the earliest collection of Islamic law, reflects accurately the spirit of Muhammad's utopian society in Medina. When Muhammad died, there were, as tradition puts it, '20,000 weeping eyes'. The witness of these 10,000 companions in Medina was the source of Maliki law. Such an extensive witness meant that recourse to analogy (*qiyās*) was hardly needed: the large corpus of legal texts made it redundant. The first school to use analogy was the Hanafi one. In Malik's *Muwaṭṭā'*, we find no use of analogy but plenty of judgments from the people of Medina: Muhammad, naturally, but also the four rightly guided caliphs and some Umayyad caliphs and governors such as Mu'awiya, Marwan, Abd Al-Malik and the fifth righteous caliph Umar Ibn Abd Al-Aziz.

More so than later jurists, Malik encouraged the effort to deduce sound legal opinions by the exertion of independent personal reason (*ijtihād*). (It is no coincidence that the philosopher Ibn Rushd (Averroës) belonged to this school.) Maliki jurists were guided in their independent intellectual effort by *istiṣlaḥ*, the principle of discerning the intended good of the Quran's and the Prophet's injunctions in relation to the empirical demands of public welfare. The principle of *al-maṣālih al-mursala* (public welfare unlimited) deals with matters not explicitly covered by the Quran and the sunnah.[4] In the absence of a definitive precedent or judgment, a legal verdict that enhances the public good is permitted so long as it does not contradict an existing judgment. This caveat ensures that the new verdict departs, as narrowly as possible, from tradition: a juridical principle cannot directly contradict a deduction from the supremely authoritative sources of the Quran and Muhammad's authentic custom. The Malikis accommodated the public interest on condition that innovative laws were consistent with core sources and moreover promoted the five purposes of the law. In practice, though not in theory, all schools of law and all Muslim leaders, especially the caliphs, applied the principle of public welfare while risking, from their ultra-conservative critics, the inevitable charge of reprehensible innovation.

Imam Al-Shafiʻi (150–204 AH) was born in the year that Abu Hanifah died. Al-Shafiʻi inherited Abu Hanifah while anticipating the work of the anti-philosophical thinker Abu Hamid Al-Ghazali whose rational theological achievements provide a religious analogue to Al-Shafiʻi's legal achievements. A basic difference between Abu Hanifah and Al-Shafiʻi is in method. Abu Hanifah studied specific cases and then generalized until a coherent method emerged. This inductive approach contrasts with Al-Shafiʻi who established his method a priori and then dealt with specific cases on the basis of existing rules. His deductive method began to predominate after the eleventh century. It has led to authoritarian imposition of pre-ordained rules and replaced an empirically responsive pursuit of mutable but legitimate interests in varied cases. It is an open question as to which of these men is closer in spirit to the teachings of Muhammad although Abu Hanifah is historically more proximate.

The youngest school is named eponymously for Imam Ahmad Ibn Hanbal (164–241 AH). As the most conservative in ethics and theology, the Hanbali confession attracts the least number of adherents but exercises great influence as the official school of plutocratic Saudi Arabia and is therefore the legal expression of Wahhabi traditionalism. This sect is self-described both as Salafiyya (righteous elders) and as Muwahiddun (Unitarians as opposed to polytheists). Its members follow the strict and legalist Hanbali dispensation. Since the thirteenth century, beginning with the decline of classical Islamic civilization in the face of determined Western assaults, Hanbali conservative legal ideology has continued to attract many Muslim conservative reformers who were born into more liberal legal schools. The Hanbali school is ferociously insular: its adherents only theoretically and reluctantly accept the other three schools.

The sixth Shiite imam, Jafar Al-Sadiq (83–148 AH/699–765 CE) was a contemporary and possibly a teacher of Abu Hanifah. (The Shiite assertion that Jafar was poisoned by the Sunni caliph Mansur Al-Abbas is groundless.) The Jafari school, the legal system of the Islamic Republic of Iran, is politically conservative. Khomeini was a legal innovator who flouted many of its laws to promote a revolutionary spirit in Iran. Sexually, however, it is far and away the most liberal Islamic dispensation, enthusiastically enjoining temporary marriage and artificial contraception. Shiite legal orthodoxy incorporates the rationalist school, the Muʻtazilah, who rejected all hadith narratives and emphasized greater reliance on individual reason.

We have surveyed the extant legal schools. Some schools died in their infancy, others merged with larger ones and a few were aborted. The Hanbali school absorbed Al-Zahiriyyah, the literalists, a school which died out with the end of Muslim rule in Spain. Founded in Iraq by Dawud Khalaf in the ninth century, the Zahiri school spread to Iran, Mediterranean Africa and Islamic Spain and lasted for 500 years despite fervent orthodox censures. The polymath and historian Abu Jafar Al-Tabari (839–923 CE) was persecuted in Baghdad for trying to establish a legal school which would have rivaled the Hanbali and Shafiʻi systems. Judging by his tendency towards uncritical description and comprehensive recording of narratives and incidents, including a juxtaposed recording of contradictory materials, it would probably have been an eclectic school borrowing generously from its rivals. The result would have been an amalgam notable for its generous range rather than novel content.

VII

Al-Shafiʻi's *Kitāb Al-Umm* and Malik's *Kitāb Al-Muwaṭṭā*' are comprehensive compendia of Islamic law and, taken together, regulate the entire range of Muslim experience in pre-modern times. Al-Shafiʻi ranked the Quran first; the Prophet's customary practice (which was, in this context, reduced to authoritative hadith) was in second place. Universal consensus came next. He relegated analogical reasoning (*qiyās*) to fourth place. For Malik: the Quran, then *sunnah*, *'amāl* (actions) of the Medina people, including their mutually respected differences, and finally the consensus (*ijmāʻ*) of the Medinan believers. Al-Shafiʻi opted for a consensus of the whole community, though in practice he limited it to its learned members. Malik restricted it to the Medinan community. 'My community cannot agree on an error' probably meant the universal, not some local *ijmāʻ*. Jurists approved of the silent consensus *(ijmāʻ sukūtī)* best demonstrated by Umar who prayed a burdensome optional prayer in Ramadan as though it were canonical and no-one objected. This prayer remains legally supererogatory; in practice it is treated as canonical.

Al-Shafiʻi and Abu Hanifah saw *qiyās* as indispensable for adjusting and adapting to new circumstances arising beyond the early community. This was only to be expected in a rapidly expanding empire. One could generate an indefinite number of legal verdicts from a finite set of authoritative materials. Consensus could also generate new but far fewer laws since, unlike individually exercised analogical reasoning, it required agreement among many.

Qiyās will be the central method for Muslims developing a legal response to secular modernity. It is a rational technique which works by isolating the intention behind an existing authoritative judgment. Thus, if intoxication by wine is prohibited by the Quran and by the Prophet, then intoxication by other means is also forbidden. Why? What is being forbidden is not wine but rather intoxication. Why is intoxication forbidden? It interferes with the performance of timed prayer (Q:4:103), a matter that is of no concern to the dwellers of paradise where wine (and therefore intoxication) is permitted. On earth, intoxication by all and any

means is forbidden. Wine happened to be the prevalent means of achieving ine-
briation at the time of the Quran's advent. The analogy could be extended to any
substances that cause intoxication and indeed any that cause any bodily harm.
Jurists failed to get cigarettes banned since smoking cigarettes does not cause
intoxication. (The Sikh gurus explicitly forbade smoking cigarettes.) Although
smoking clearly causes harm, perhaps some jurists secretly thought that it would
be unwise to be too strict. Believers need to be able to indulge a little too – on
earth. Smoking is thus disapproved (*makruh*); it is permitted but reprehensible.
It resembles divorce which the Quran permits albeit as a last resort.

VIII

The Quran is the first and supremely authoritative manual of Islamic law. It specifies punishments for certain offences. These penalties are neither negotiable nor
subject to juridical discretion. Yet, even a clear Quranic verse needs interpretation
as to its range of applicability. The Quran is an opaque text despite its repeated
self-description as a clear one (Q:12:1). Its allegorical and allusive passages are
confessedly figurative and evasive (Q:3:7); its terse exhortational Meccan passages
are opaque even to believers. Medinan verses contain unambiguous penalities and
clear judgments (*nass al-kitāb*; see e.g., Q:4:3; 24:2–9). Even these judgments,
including the brutally precise ruling to cut the hands of male and female thieves
(Q:5:38), require interpretation. Despite being the clear ruling (*zāhir al-kitāb*) that
must be taken at face value, a judge must decide its scope of application before
implementation. Does it apply to children and pregnant women who steal? Does
it, as Umar wondered, apply during times of famine.

This is the problem of general and specific application – the question of legal
qualification of Quranic verses which occur both in unrestricted and qualified
versions. For example, the Quran order believers to flog 100 times any male or
female believer who fornicates (Q:24:2). Another verse (Q:4:25) stipulates that
for committing *zinah* (fornication), believing slave girls should receive only half
the punishment of free women. Thus, a slave girl would be flogged only 50 lashes.
The reduction is not in virtue of her gender but her lack of freedom. This is itself
puzzling. More understandably, the Quran addresses the Prophet's spouses to inform
them that their punishment for the vague sin of 'open obscenity' is double that of
other (free) women but adds that their reward for virtue is also doubled (Q:33:30–1).
This doubling of reward and punishment is justified by the fact that the Prophet's
wives are special women providing role models for the community's female believers
(Q:33:32–3).

Although some purist Islamic sects have discounted the *sunnah* in order to zealously safeguard the unique centrality of the Quran, it remains the second source
of law in all schools of law. Some modernist reformers, such as Sir Sayyid Ahmad
Khan (1817–98), the Anglophile founder of India's Aligarh Muslim University,
elevated the Quran alone to universal and eternal status while dismissing the Prophet's
practice as historically conditioned and local. In general, however, the record of
the Prophet's practice, once sifted and cleansed of fabrication, is revered even by

liberal reformers. All jurists regard it as co-extensive with the Quran as source of positive law. Al-Shafi'i was the first jurist to note this forcefully but later jurists concurred while earlier ones assumed its truth. Al-Shafi'i showed at length that the Quran enjoined Muslims to obey the Prophet. Disobedience to God and to his Messenger coincided: one could not claim to obey God alone.

The final purpose of holy law is to please God by carrying out his commands and avoiding the forbidden. Obedience to a prophet is the legal basis of society (Q:3:32, 132, 47:33) since a prophet, especially one bearing a scripture or a law, establishes new institutions and confirms old ones. All prophets, especially those fortified with a law, were sent to be obeyed (Q:4:64) and they invariably called on their peoples to obey them (Q:3:50, 26:108, 110, 126, 131, 144, 150, 263, 179; 43:63; 71:1–4).

Obedience to Muhammad as God's final messenger has legal and moral significance: imitating him is morally praiseworthy and his conduct and words are a material source of law. 'Take what the messenger gives you and reject what he rejects for you' (Q:59:7). Obedience to the Prophet is a direct and indirect divine order (Q:3:132; 4:63, 68, 79; 7:157; 8:20; 24:54; 33:6; 48:8–9, 13, 59:7; 64:8). The order is direct in the Medinan revelations but implicit in Meccan revelations (such as Q:7:157). We read gentle and conditional pleas to follow Muhammad, upheld as a role model who will help get one closer to God (Q:3:31–2; 4:64; 8:24–9; 33:21). There are threats for disobeying Muhammad's orders (Q:24:63; 4:114 and mildly at Q:9:25). One should love and honour him (Q:48:7–8), bless him (Q:33:56) and lower one's voice in his presence (Q:24:63; 49:1). Since the Prophet Muhammad is closer to the believers than they are to their own souls (Q:33:6), loving him is a duty, not a meritorious option. Finally, authentic hadith collections (of Al-Bukhari and Muslim) also confirm the necessity to obey God's last apostle.

Originally, Muhammad's authority, unlike that of the Quran, was immediate since it was not interpreted. Today, both are interpreted. Muhammad implemented God's laws but God himself did not do so. The Shariah expresses the abstract will of God through the concrete will of Muhammad (as messenger of God). If Islam remains tethered to the past, it is owing to Muhammad who is known to us with clarity. Was Muhammad's combined temporal and spiritual authority in Medina a circumstantial one or a binding precedent for all believers at all times? The Quran, for all its theoretically supreme but abstract authority, is not a formidable hurdle to reform and appropriate compromise. Individual hadith narratives can, however, be used as polemical hand-grenades. One can thereby validate any of one's own preconceived views, whether liberal or conservative. Owing to the variety and ambiguity of even authentic hadith narratives, Muhammad can, for example, appear as both a pacifist and an imperialist.

Muhammad was, as Al-Shafi'i noted, mandated by the Quran to be a supreme authority. Elevating Muhammad's authority to the level of the sancrosanct suggests that the Quran's authority is only theoretically supreme. In practice, an established Muhammadan practice is far more influential even if it contradicts the moral spirit of the Quran, though not its letter. Muslim jurists use Muhammad's customary practice to interpret all the Quran's imperatives, simple and complex.

Muhammad is infallible only as God's Prophet: regarding only matters of faith rather than mundane issues. His infallibility derives wholly from the fact that he is a messenger of an infallible God. No (fallible) believer can judge him (Q:33:36) and no-one, believer or otherwise, should malign him (Q:33:57–8).[5] And if Muhammad sounds like a controlling megalomaniac, recall that there was in Muhammad's day no coercive authority (such as a police force) to enforce the leader's will.[6] Moral persuasion was the sole motivator.

IX

Are the Quran and the Muhammadan exemplar separate sources of law when in practice both are considered equally infallible? Muhammad's legal and moral verdicts are treated as being no less authoritative than the Quran. Infallibility of judgment does not admit of degree any more than a unique thing can be almost unique or fairly unique. If both Muhammad's authentic custom and the laws of the Quran are infallibly just, it is a good ground for making these into a single source.

If the Quran and *sunnah* coalesce, there emerges a vast amount of material, often contradictory and in need of judgments of abrogation and prioritization. How is this in principle different from dealing with contradictions within each of these sources? The difference is practical: conscientious jurists have a much greater body of conflicting material to assess. If the internal conflicts prove irresolvable, we can ignore the imperatives contained and rely on reason exercised critically and independently in the aftermath of revelation. We may need to discount the Quran and the *sunnah* but only where their guidance is made suspect by internal incoherence and contradiction with 'internal' ranging over the Quran and Prophetic custom combined.

I propose that there is only one source of law, the Quran and the *sunnah*, seen as a joint corpus. The Quran has to be interpreted for legal content; the *sunnah* must first be determined as authentic before being mined for positive legal content. The other items are not infallible *sources* of law but rather fallible *methods* of reaching legal verdicts. No method is used to create the primary legal sources since these are considered revealed. The two revealed sources are to be supplemented by secondary methods for extracting judgments. The richer the (primary) sources, the fewer the (secondary) methods needed.

Analogy (*qiyas*) is a method, not source of law, since it contains no content. It is not a textual or otherwise authoritative source of law but merely a means for generating novel legislation. Unlike the fixed and infallible sources, analogical ratiocination provides a continuous source of novel legislation. Analogy, rejected by stricter law schools, is a fallible and limited method for generating new laws based on existing ones.

X

Some progressive Muslims, considered apostates by the majority of believers, argue for the abolition of the Shariah. I recommend a replacement of the quadruple (Sunni) canon with a single contemporary school of law operating with a simplified hierarchy of sources. In this essay, we are simplifying all dogmas: the creed, the articles of faith and the legal system. We reject the confused and complex classical hierarchy of several sources of law in favour of only one valid source and one valid means. The Quran, combined with the certified (or authentic) prophetic *sunnah*, is jointly interpreted as one source of existing legislation. The means is the unaided reason of competent believers – a ground or source for both analogical reasoning and consensus, two specific methods for extending, supplementing and eliminating some of the existing laws.

I am proposing that legal discretion (*ijtihād*) must now be reborn as the *de novo* examination and determination of legal matters unencumbered by the accretions of inherited doctrines and later precedents. It must be formulated solely in the light of the continuing relvevance of the purposes of the holy law, purposes that both transcend and underpin the sacred legislation in all ages. This should enable Islamic law to evolve internally and generate novel ordinances without exciting the charge of heresy.

No single factor better epitomizes the closing of the Muslim juridical mind than the fact that the four legal schools are made to remain valid through continuous piecemeal changes, despite being foundationally fixed mediaeval canons. Their legal algorithms liberate the modern Muslim from relying on his or her own initiative; decision-making procedures become redundant as believers become brain-dead robots. It resembles the consequences of the proliferation of road signs which, contrary to the intentions of the Ministry of Transport, sometimes encourage accidents as drivers no longer rely on their common sense and judgment. The ritualizing of complex conduct, through reliance on law, started the stagnation of the creative powers of the Muslim mind and conscience. The legal schools unintentionally spelled the end of Islam as a contemplative and ethically alive and active faith. Ironically, the very foundation of these schools and the supple essays in legal reasoning thus produced both witnessed to the creative genius of the orthodox Muslim mind under the joint tuition of the Quran and Muhammad.

XI

A modern Muslim must concede the role of independent reason and conscience. Islam cannot, however, be reduced to a solely *ethical* monotheism. As a juridical monotheism with an ethical component, it views law as ultimate even though it concedes that the moral aim of the law can never be fully achieved by any mechanism once we permit freedom of the will, the creature's privilege to flout the law. Christianity offers a purely ethical monotheism that has fulfilled and thus transcended the law. In the Torah, the protocol and the letter of the law counted more than its spirit and the ethical motivation of the actors. Yahweh teaches his people a lesson in exact observance when he kills two enthusiastic sons of Aaron for offering unauthorized holy fire to him (Numbers 10:1–7). Significantly, this incident is not in the Quran though some sanguinary episodes from Israelite history are corroborated in the Muslim scripture (see Q:2:54). The Quran unfailingly emphasizes interiority of correct motive (*niyyah*), a frequent word in the Prophet's sermons though, surprisingly, absent from the Quran.

In the law versus grace debate between Muslims and Christians, Muslims emphasize that God, through his prophets, teaches human beings, those promising but wayward students. Islam recognizes no resources greater than the prophethood that institutes law as guidance. Does law, with its auxiliary intention of justice, achieve its professed purpose of making us virtuous? Does divine legislation fulfil the divine intention that inspired it? Or do we need something more than the institution of prophethood for teaching and guiding humanity? Is that higher institution sonship, understood not as a physical relationship (cf. Q:6:101) but rather an abstract divine relationship to humankind, characterized by the divine initiative of suffering and gracious love? Do we need a God who comes rather than brings, who gives himself to us in unconditional love? Christians argue that our condition craves the grace and love that only a morally resourceful and sensitive God can supply.

Muslims see human beings as promising but heedless and wayward disciples, as disobedient students who learn only through repeated exhortation and devout attention to excellent example. They often fail miserably. This double potential, the grandeur and triumph of the believer, and the historical evidence of radical communal failure, permeates the Quranic portrait of history. It is the cornerstone of the Islamic philosophy of history as a legal and moral process directed externally by God and his prophets.

Islam and Christianity have different theologies rooted in different anthropologies. Islam has no original sinners though a Christian might quip that 'unoriginal sinners' are no different. Whether aboriginal or historical, sin is a reality no theism can convincingly deny. Christians contend that, in view of our innate sin and perversity, Islam overestimates the educative influence of religious and legal institutions. Evil is inveterate, not only a film on the surface of personality. It reaches into the heart and cannot be removed by external action or repeated profession. Islam, it is alleged, for all its forceful condemnation of idolatry and hard-heartedness fails to recognize the true depth of the perversity that flouts the holy law. No evil act could be more inveterately rooted than the perversity that fathers it.

Whatever our verdict on this matter of sin, Christianity can cure human recalcitrance no better than Islam or Judaism. We are as free to reject the grace of Christ as of Allah or of Yahweh. Human perversity is an irreducible feature of our constitution. Apart from God's coercive grace, nothing can conclusively cure it. No saving action done by God can necessarily save free sinners from the hold of sin.

As we saw in Chapters 4 and 5, the Christian Arabist Kenneth Cragg disagrees. He contends that the logic of Islamic prophethood (*risālah*) itself demands Christ's saving actions. Messianic Christianity is the natural terminus of prophetic religion and sonship the successor to prophethood. Cragg laments that Islam limits its moral potential when it terminates the divine engagement with humanity at the jejune level of law and prophecy. Arbitrarily it arrests the movement of divine grace and love into a created order designed for precisely this fulfillment which comes after the preliminary (and admittedly merciful) divine initiatives embodied in the law and the prophets. Christianity goes beyond revelation to incarnation.

These are not crude criticisms but rather subtle in temperament, style and substance. The step towards sonship, however, described as natural by Cragg, is not even intelligible. It is incoherent. Cragg never debates the alleged incoherence of the Incarnation and the unintelligibility of the related doctrines of the Trinity and Jesus' sonship. He writes exclusively about the Incarnation's rich moral potential, suggesting that Muslims unwisely reject suffering divine love, wrongly dismissing it as an offence to God's dignity. But granted, for the sake of a case, that the Incarnation contains a unique ethical significance absent from Islam (and Judaism), we must wonder whether the doctrine is coherent. Only after we establish the coherence of the Incarnation can we assess its moral potential.

It is a further issue whether or not the Incarnation, if coherent, could either ease our travail in fulfilling our obligations or drastically cure the perversity of radical evil. The prior conceptual question, which Cragg fails to identify, heads the agenda. More broadly, he does not answer Muslim and Jewish charges: the irrationality and demonstrable incoherence of normative Christianity's distinguishing dogmas, the impracticality of its deceptively noble ethics, and the implausibility of its gracious promise of unconditional salvation divorced from works of the law.

If the Trinity is incoherent, the Incarnation and sonship are also incoherent. Three divine persons, the Father, the Son and the Holy Spirit, are each considered God but each remains distinct from the other two. Thus, the Father is God but is not the Son or the Holy Spirit while the Son is God but not the Father or the Holy Spirit. Finally, the Holy Spirit is God but neither the Son nor the Father. Assuming that there is only one God, the Trinity implies:

i   Christ must be his own Father and his own son;
ii   The Holy Spirit is neither Father nor Son yet he is both;
iii The Son was begotten by the Father but existed before he was begotten;
iv   Christ is as old as his Father;
v   The Father is as young as his son;
vi   The Holy Spirit proceeded from the Father and Son but he is as old as his 'parents'.[7]

These are absurd propositions. Even Aquinas, a reputable theologian notwithstanding his posthumous reputation as the Papacy's apologist, cast this dogma into the realm of mystery. In this context, one can see why the arrival of Islam is the true marker of the end of early Christianity: millions of Christians left the convoluted complexities of their dogmatics to embrace Islam's simpler creed. Even if the Trinity and the associated Incarnation have the moral benefits claimed by Cragg, an omnipotent God could and should have devised a solution that was coherent and yet equally effective.

God's supreme greatness is not at stake here. That conviction is shared by the trio of Semitic monotheisms. *Allāhu akbar* is no monopoly of Islam although Muslims regard modern Jews and Christians as paying only cultural lip-service to

God's greatness. Christians and Muslims understand divine supremacy differently. What makes God great? For Cragg, Muslims misunderstand divine greatness when they deflect the puzzle of human perversity into the legal dimension, where rejection is subdued, not redeemed. We examined political aspects of this charge in Chapters 4 and 5 but we deferred a broader inquiry.

Cragg contended that Muhammad's recruitment of the political–legal wing was a natural corollary of his belief that prophethood exhausts divine resources for teaching sinners.[8] God has warned through his spokesmen; sinners disregard and ignore. Cragg suggests that when divine education fails to cure our perversity – once the pen runs out of ink – Islam's God must opt for force to enforce his will. God must succeed but God's party has run out of the only arsenal that they are permitted to use. If they resort to force, the message is not taught but enforced. The sword then becomes mightier than the pen and all the more mighty for being the only weapon that remains. Only in a crudely coercive sense do God and his spokesmen have the last word.

The Christian God, argues Cragg, is above this kind of greatness. When his message fails to educate, his long-suffering grace pre-empts premature punitive options. Though we failed the examination, refused to learn the lesson, God redeems this failure through the greater initiative of a love that suffers unjustly to redeem the unjust. It is predictably human to resort to force in the face of spiritual failure. Divine ends require divine means. The weapons and techniques of Muhammad's activism must be carried backwards into the character of his God. *Allāhu akbar* is denied internally by the Muslim refusal to allow God to be greater than merely the omnipotent Lord who dispatches moral and legal instruction manuals for us humans and punishes us severely when we fail to learn and implement them. God should frustrate the will to impiety by redeeming and rehabilitating the evil which it fails to cauterize through the merely educational initiative of prophethood. Only a God who can accomplish this feat ought to have the last word.

Cragg correctly emphasizes that multiple and vehement exhortations, condemnations of perversity, threats of punishment, and edificatory speeches do not suffice. Human beings continue to flout the law. Nor do villains and miscreants care about the exemplary goodness of the saint or martyr. In the face of enforced religion, perverse sinners withdraw deeper into the privacy of their hearts; rituals such as prayer and fasting cannot eliminate hypocrisy. Even collective piety, impressive on account of numbers and ostentatious passions, need not be genuine after the thrill of the public gaze subsides. Piety, once achieved, as hagiography shows, carries further temptations and trials: the moral excellence of sainthood does not preclude insidious inner tendencies to self-righteousness and, with a further twist of the spiral, a deeper kind of hubris, this time under the aegis of an apparent sanctity.

Certainly, our perversity and the disturbing scale of rejection of divine purposes are not disputed theses of religious history. Can we, however, cure this perversity by any mechanism other than preaching the law? It is incoherent to look for an external rescue from the plight created by human recalcitrance to divine law. God warns; we disregard. God punishes and destroys. This must be the typical divine–human interaction since human beings, created free, have an inner, often dominant, tendency to do wrong. Nothing can cure it in most of us – although God mysteriously cured it, by his grace, in the case of prophets and reduced it drastically for saints. God's greatness consists in doing what is possible. The divine gesture in the Incarnation is metaphysically incoherent, though we understand the moral stresses that demand it. Christians are obliged to demonstrate the coherence of this move which sets Christianity apart from other Semitic monotheisms.

Independently of our verdict on its coherence, the humility in the Incarnation is irrelevant to the problem of reducing recalcitrance to divine law. Setting excellent examples, human or divine, does not ease the individual's moral strife. Besides, obeying the law is easy enough – for God. True, Christ was both man and God. But we are simply, plainly, men (or women). We need an uncomplicatedly human exemplar. And even this does not curb our desire to sin though it does show us that high spirituality is humanly possible and fully compatible with our fallible and mortal humanity.

On earth, though not in heaven, human perversity is bound to have the last word. We are in a rut: human recalcitrance persists and so does the divine demand. The law makes theism juridical and paternalistic as it regulates the relationship between free humans and a demanding sovereign deity. Although God is a kind teacher, he wants the lesson learnt. Divine law shows that God means business. The face of obligation may, however, justifiably look stern so long as its final intention is not degrading or immoral. Moral constraint differs from moral freedom not on account of the absence or presence of external restraints but rather owing to a liberating awareness of the source and nature of limitations and of the moral worth of the ends these serve. Revealed law prevents our natural passions from becoming strong enough to be autonomous. 'Greater is God' is a moral denial of the autonomy of our lower nature. The holy law merely uses sanctions to implement this ethical truth.

7   An imperial religion

I

Non-Muslim historians marvel at the Islamic chronicle: with no standing army and hardly any institutions, the early Muslims overthrew two gargantuan centralized empires. After uniting the newly converted Arabian tribes, the four caliphs took the unified programme of an empowered faith to the world. How did an Arabian religion rapidly expand into a universal civilization that became multi-ethnic, intercontinental and poly-racial? Muslims assimilated and Islamized the cultural products and bureaucratic hierarchies of the defeated empires of Byzantium and Persia; caliphs enthusiastically employed talented Jews and Christians to build a multi-lingual, multi-legal, poly-ethnic and religiously plural but nonetheless Islamic civilization. Muhammad's faith was an imperial monotheism which built and enriched many cultures while eliminating only those local customs which were judged theologically erroneous or morally depraved.

In this chapter, we trace Muslim colonization of lands. A point of nomenclature: imperialism can mean remote control conquest while colonialism is direct hegemony. We shall ignore this distinction for now but will bear it in mind in Section V below. We shall assess the caliphate, Islam's earliest imperial institution, which survived into the twentieth century. Investigating classical Islamic notions of legitimate power enables us to sketch the relationship between a post-imperial faith in decline and a secularized legal and political modernity.

In Muhammad's day, Christian Abyssinia (Ethiopia) was an independent regional power while the Persian Sassanids competed with the Roman Byzantines on the world stage. It was a bipolar world divided between the rival duo of Christian Byzantium, successor to the Roman imperium and Zoroastrian Iran, ruled since the third century by the Sassanid dynasty. The capital cities were Constantinople and Ctesiphon, the latter about to be replaced by Baghdad, the seat of the Abbasid dynasty. The Arab peninsula was marginal to the high society of the early seventh century. Few of royal blood had heard of Mecca or Medina.

A Quranic revelation, dated to seven years before the Hijrah, predicts and promises a victory for the Christian Byzantines within a decade or so (Q:30:2–6). Islam too will enter world politics: five years after the Hijrah, once Muslims had been tested in the crucible of persecution and fear, the Quran promises to empower them (Q:24:55). It predicts Islam's eventual imperial reach (Q:61:9) and mocks those who reject Muhammad's mission (Q:22:15). We read in a famous authentic hadith: 'Every prophet was sent to his own people; but I am sent to all humankind.' The Quran eulogized Islam as the true, completed, decisive and eternal religion (Q:48:28; 98:5); accordingly, Muslims interpreted this finalized universality to be a divine mandate for imperial expansion (Q:48:28). The theological foundations of Arabo-Islamic imperialism are contained in Islam's self-image as religion perfected. Muhammad sent epistles and emissaries to Roman and Sassanid emperors, inviting them to embrace Islam. A sincere, simple and dynamic Arab religion with virtually no institutions rapidly defeated the lethargic and bloated bureaucracies of the Roman Byzantines; Muslims annihilated the Sassanids who had been internally enervated by their convoluted and torpid royal inertia and externally weakened by perpetual skirmishes with their Byzantine rival.

Islamic imperialism was a corollary of the appealing view that all humanity is one family with a common monogenetic origin and a common political future as one community under God and caliph. Islam's egalitarian spirit was no doubt universally appealing. From his base in Medina, Muhammad had militarily challenged Mecca's pagan oligarchy. The Islamic enterprise spread speedily from its native Arabia to lay claim to an international heritage inside the worldwide web of lands and peoples. The Islamic belt today extends from Morocco and Senegal to China and Indonesia. No world faith has successfully and peacefully assimilated such a vast range of cultures and races and done it so rapidly and largely permanently. Nor was it, unlike the Mongol hegemony, sheer conquest without any moral and artistic contribution.

Islam is a compulsively political and politically successful faith. Indeed, it succeeded too much, too early. 'Early to blossom, early to wither' is as true of civilizations as of individuals. In the final chapter, we note the tragic consequences of these early successes for modern Muslim minorities worldwide: as Islamic empire receded and fragmented, vulnerable Muslims were left to struggle and survive among hostile non-Muslim nations. The Muslim masses still see Islam as a single fraternity despite the many nation-states created arbitrarily by Western colonialists as they formally withdrew. The pain of any Muslim minority is noted and shared by the universal community of believers although, for racial reasons, Arab Muslims generally remain indifferent to non-Arab Muslim suffering.

Islam corresponds to both Christendom and Christianity. As empires based on religion dissolved, nation-states emerged, first in Europe and then globally as a result of European colonial intervention. The imperial Muslim tradition resembles the mediaeval Christian west until the time of the Treaty of Westphalia (1648) which enforced the maxim '*Eius regio, cuius religio*' (whoever's region, his religion), first formulated during the Peace of Augsburg (1555). These four Latin words created the political map of modern Europe by endorsing the disintegration of Christendom into many individual states under sovereign national rulers rather than the single dominion of the Catholic Church. The Peace of Augsburg killed the imperial *corpus Christianum*. A nation of citizens divided into religious groups replaced a religious empire divided into ethnic groups and nations.

Is Islam a disguised form of Arab imperialism? Are there different types of colonial and imperial hegemony? Can we compare Arab imperialism with the English, Spanish, Dutch and French varieties? How does Islamic expansion compare with European imperialism, including Christian imperialism? Is Islam's attempt to establish God's sovereignty worldwide any different from the aggression of European nations in their scramble for Asia and Africa? We seek to answer these questions in this chapter.

II

The Quran is consistently self-described as a revelation to all humankind (Q:4:79, 170; 6:19; 7:158; 14:52; 21:107; 34:28; 38:87; 61:9; 81:27). It affirms both its universal mission and its standing as 'an Arabic Quran' (Q:12:2; 20:112; 39:28; 41:3; 42:7; 43:3). While addressing and correcting the condition of one ethnic community in history, it continues to speak, Muslims would contend, to the human condition of the human race. The Meccan Quran already orders Muhammad to preach a universal message (Q:6:19, 90; 7:158; 14:52; 21:107; 34:28; 36:70; 38:87; 81:27). Medinan verses bluntly affirm its expansionist intentions (Q:3:138; 4:79, 170; 61:9).

Despite its potential for universal expansion, the Quran was originally addressed to Muhammad and heard only by his people (Q:43:44). Its few non-Arab listeners included Bilal Ibn Rabah (d. *c.* 641), a slave of African origin, living in Mecca, persecuted for his conversion to Islam, and later bought and manumitted by Abu Bakr. He was the first muezzin. (The Malay word 'bilal' means muezzin!) In the nineteenth century, the historical Bilal became a potent symbol for African liberation struggles against Western colonialism. It was a surrogate struggle between two faiths: Islam as imperial liberator and (European) Christianity as colonial slave-master. Another foreigner was a zealous Zoroastrian named Rouzbeh. Born in Persia (in the same year as Muhammad), he is better known as Salman Al-Farsi (d. 657). He converted to Christianity before he met Muhammad and ended his spiritual quest by embracing Islam until his death. The Prophet renamed him Salman (one who is safe) and affectionately called him 'my family'. Salman might have translated the Quran into Farsi. If so, he would be its first translator into any language, the man who started the intellectual expansion of the Muslim message, predicted by the Quran (Q:6:19).

Four Medinan pericopes (Q:2:191, 217; 8:30–40; 9:28) are of special interest in modern debates about the scope of Islamic empire. Referring to Meccan pagans as *de facto* guardians of the Holy Mosque in Mecca, these verses order fighting and killing all pagans in the environment of that mosque. The prohibition of pagan access to the Holy Mosque (Q:9:28) is followed by a verse ordering Muslims to fight Jews and Christians (Q:9:29). These verses were interpreted by Muhammad and his political successors to mean fighting the whole world of infidelity and errant monotheism. Although the political bifurcation between the House of Islam and the House of War (*dār al-islām* and *dār al-kufr*) is not in the Quran, it is implied by its many sharp divisions between faith and rejection, sometimes expressed in deceptively mild language (see Q:59:20). The Prophet and his immediate successors all understood such verses to have universal, not local or restricted application. Quranic exegetes always extract the general meaning of a verse rather than the specific meaning suggested by its occasion of revelation. This is done regardless of the content of the verse, so long as it admits of extrapolation and generalization.

Although it would go against the weight of revered tradition to restrict the range of application of such imperial verses today, not all contemporary Islamic currents flow in the same direction. Virtually all modern Muslims want only a domesticated faith with some measure of political autonomy for Muslim nations. They reject as idealistic and unrealistic any calls for an expansionist jihad to terminate disbelief wordwide. Jihad was a religious duty entailed by Islam's commitment to universalism. It was not primarily a political requirement of the state. Muhammad and his successors intended to conquer the world in God's name, to create an empire that would be ruled by an Islamic fraternity, a religious aristocracy. The Quran's sanguine anthropology upholds the political perfectibility of human nature and the reformability of corrupt power structures. It rejects the low Christian estimate of our capacity as political beings. The Muhammadan imperial project failed because it was militarily too ambitious. Its foundations were theologically consistent and still appeal to activist Muslims. We explore this theme in the final chapter.

III

Islamic political history starts in 622 when Muhammad and his dispossessed disciples migrated – to use a grandiose verb for a move within the same country – from their native Mecca to Medina. The first phase, 622 to 660 (1 to 38 AH), encompasses the political careers of the Prophet and his four rightly guided successors who ruled from Medina. The conquest of north-west Africa was intended as a base to launch an invasion of Spain, Portugal and the southern portions of Italy and France. This phase terminated in 1258 with the wanton Mongol destruction of the Abbasids, the first universal Islamic dynasty. The only important intermediate date is 732. The place is Poitiers. If Badr was a decisive victory that made Islam an imperial faith in embryo, the defeat of Muslim armies at Poitiers in 732 ensured that Europeans would remain uncircumcised. Though a minor battle, it is profoundly significant in its consequences and looms large in the modern French nationalist imagination. It was the first battle Muslims lost in one century of uninterrupted victories. For Islam's first 1000 years, Christians fought internal religious wars while Muslims expanded their empire. The roles have been reversed for the past 500 years.

Abu Bakr Al-Siddiq (*c.* 573–634), a Qurayshi, was elected the first ruler of the Islamic state. He cemented the political structure he inherited from Muhammad by defeating separatist revolts (during 'the wars of apostasy') and killing false prophets, especially Maslama Bin Habib. To prevent civil war in the peninsula, Abu Bakr identified an external outlet for Arab energies and started the process of expansion into Iraq and Syria. Muslima defeated a Byzantine army at Ajnadayn in Palestine in the summer of 634, just before the death of Abu Bakr, the only one of the four exemplary caliphs who was not assassinated.

The Umayyad dynasty (661 to 750 CE) was an Arab dynasty headed by Mu'awiya, its first caliph, who ruled (from 661) from Damascus which had been part of the Eastern Roman empire centred on Constantinople. This shift from Medina to Damascus secularized Islam: a move from the Prophet's city to a centre of Graeco-Roman civilization. The Umayyad rulers adopted many courtly and administrative practices of this antique imperial tradition but made no attempt to Islamize them. The dynasty quickly died out but a branch survived in Spain until 1492.

In 762, the Abbasids founded Baghdad, as their new capital. Like Rome, Baghdad grew from village to empire but, unlike Rome, in a mere few decades. It was located east of Damascus, Medina and Mecca, 'orienting' the Muslim temperament towards the Orient. Think here of St Paul's missionary cry of 'westward ho!' from Jerusalem to Rome. The turn eastward meant that imperial Islam would inherit little of the republican and democratic spirit of European pagan antiquity. Instead we would have the oriental penchant for treating rulers as potentates, encouraging their megalomaniacal tendencies, a problem that still persists.

Within 200 years of Muhammad's death, Arabs became a minority within Islam and this has remained so ever since, their percentage shrinking continuously. Today, a mere 15 per cent of all Muslims live in the 22 Arab nations. From the time of the Medinan polity, through the 80 years of the Umayyad dynasty and until the early Abbasid period, the Arabs were a minority ruling class quarantined from their subjects. The Muslims were an army in exile, an efficient military machine that functioned and fought with ferocity. The conquerors lived in garrison cities such as Fustat, precursor to Cairo. The Persians, Egyptians, Syrians and Iraqis saw the conquests as a mere change of masters; many welcomed the new rulers and converted. Some desired to associate themselves with the rulers by changing their names to reflect an Arabic addition. Such Arab patrician patronage enabled non-Arab converts to be 'Arabicized': the neophytes attached themselves as associates or clients to a tribal lineage and thus appropriated Arab language and culture. As clients or relatives (*mawali*, pl.; Q:33:5), they assimilated both universal Islamic and ethnic Arabic ideals.

This background complicates the sense of 'Arabian', an adjective which can intend and qualify a territory, a culture, a language, and a racial ideology. The Levant and Mediterranean Africa were subdued by Arab Muslim armies during the middle- and late-seventh century and became Arabic-speaking lands. But this was a constructed colonial identity, not an organic ethnicity. In their Eastern expansion, the Arabs failed to colonize the Persians, Indians and, at a later stage, the Malays. All became devoutly attached to Islam but retained their languages and those customs that did not contradict core Islamic strictures.

IV

This chapter could have been titled 'Islam as liberating religion' since Muslims interpret their chronicle of conquests as the world's emancipation from the darkness of paganism and the corrupted monotheisms of Judaism and Christianity.

The word for conquest (*fath*) literally means 'opening up' and supplies the title of surah 48 where it refers to an apparent defeat that foreshadowed eventual victory (Q:48:1). The Quran's first surah, *al-fātiḥah,* literally means 'the opening' or 'conquest' (of paganism).

What is the Quranic mandate for religiously motivated conquest? In a mystical verse, we read that at the beginning of sacred history, humanity was offered the trust of the heavens and the earth. While the heavens, the earth and the mountains rejected the offer, humankind accepted it since human beings are foolish and vainglorious (Q:33:72). Despite the angels' temporary reservations and the Devil's permanent doubts, man is appointed God's deputy (*khalīfah*; Q:2:30) on earth. He assumes rule over nature on condition that he accepts rule under God. Any reading of political autonomy that dispenses with God as sovereign is anathema to Islam. The right to be an imperialist in nature is conditional on the duty to be God's servant. We are nature's trustees and custodians, not its usurpers or proprietors. In a political setting, the ruler is entitled to rule his subjects on condition that he remains accountable as a servant subject to the Shariah. Islamic leaders have, however, often denied this double status as ruler–servant, claiming to be accountable only to God rather than to the community of faith.

1992 marked the 500th anniversary of the fall of Muslim Spain and yet no Muslim thinker wondered on that occasion about the legitimacy of Islamic imperialism. Muslim apologists have never felt obliged to justify the use of force in the service of extending the witness to Allah's dominion beyond the confines of the Arabian peninsula. Muhammad's contemporaries thought imperialism to be nothing remarkable. It originated with the biblical Assyrians who depopulated vast tracts and resettled their subject peoples in distant lands to diminish the love of the fatherland and hence lessen chances of rebellion. Earlier colonial adventures directly affected the rise and spread of Islam. We have a document prepared by Alexander's secretary, Eumenes, dictated to him by Alexander (356–23 BCE) as he lay dying in the summer heat in Babylon. The top item on his list was the conquest of Arabia, a peninsular subcontinent that had been spared occupation by the Greeks and Persians.[1]

Modern Muslim apologists attenuate early Islam's political ambitions by claiming that the classical jihad was a defensive undertaking rather than an outreach for universal conquest. In fact, many territories were acquired either by force or by truce, including peaceful surrender. The House of Covenant (*dār al-ṣulḥ* or *dār al-'ahd*) is intermediate between the Houses of War and of Peace and includes Christian nations who paid nominal tribute. All schools of law endorse jihad, in defence of existing Islamic territory, as an individual duty (*fard al-'ayn*) incumbent on all Muslims. Jihad, in pursuit of empire, is also a collective duty (*fard al-kifāyah*, lit. duty of the sufficiency), a vicarious obligation performed by a select group in order to render blameless the rest of Muslim society.[2] Only a caliph can declare or authorize the offensive jihad. The whole (able-bodied) male community must not, however, go to war. A contingent of scholars should remain at home so that they can advise the fighters about the Islamic lifestyle once they return to civilian life (Q:9:122).

Jihad permanently remains a collective duty when Islam is ascendant and reaching for imperial extension; it becomes an individual duty only when an existing Islamic territory is threatened by non-Muslims. Even war is permitted against a state that is oppressing its Muslim population (Q:4:75; 8:72). Jihad is directed against infidels and apostates while tribute (*jizyah*) is levied on resident male Jewish and Christian adults who exchange the right to proselytize Muslims in exchange for defence of their lives and property during war. The tribute can be paid in kind: a literate Jew might undertake to teach a group of Muslim peasants. Women, children, monks and rabbis are exempt from such taxation. In this arrangement, conquest enables, not compels, conversion. It is a substantive distinction which historically comforted conquered Jews and Christians though they remained subjects who never graduated to become citizens of the Islamic state. In theory, they did not enjoy suffrage although in practice many rose to high office. Their situation resembles that of America's permanent residents – aliens with 'green cards' – who cannot vote or hold government office but nonetheless thrive and prosper in its free economy.

V

'We English have one advantage over other nations: we are not foreigners.' This colonial witticism implies that while no-one is a foreigner in their own land, it is remarkable not to be one in other peoples' lands. This was the signal achievement of British colonization as it annexed a quarter of the world. The United Kingdom, an island of 120, 000 square miles, ruled over nine million square miles, a fact and feat that delighted the devout Christian imperialist Rudyard Kipling.

European colonial rule was regal, clothed in the mystique of arbitrary pride of power. Islamic rule, in principle, was meant to be freed from worldly ambition, to become a robust witness to a style of rule where pride of governance was founded on humility of service. Where we dominate, we bring submission too. As with nature, so with politics: the scientist studies nature as a causal system but, on the way to the laboratory, visits the mosque, as a grateful penitent. Believers understand the natural world so that thay can thank God and thus rule the world in order to serve the King of Kings.

Political humility excludes various sources of hubris: the ethnic pride in land of national or patristic allegiance, the mundane pride of worldly success, the imperial pride of absolute power undiluted by accountability, and the Semitic pride of exclusive and unconditional covenant. The *ummah muslimah* is a multi-lingual and poly-ethnic society of peoples, based on the revolutionary requirement of freely chosen belief in one God. It is motivated by a political monotheism inspired by a hierarchy based on a quality that cannot be inherited. Piety is never automatically an attribute of status, rank, birth, position or achievement. Moreover, the arbitrary circumstance of nationality, an accident of birth for the majority of citizens, was replaced in favour of a revolutionary view of human nature as monogenetic, descending from one species, but distinguished by levels of piety. What peoples and tribes believed was the factor that decided allegiance and conferred imperial citizenship. The new commonwealth was not multi-racial. That was considered a fraud: there is only one race, the human race, biologically rooted in one species. Rather, the Islamic community was multi-lingual, multi-civilizational, but mono-ideological.

The group that coalesced around the Arab Apostle was set apart from the rest of humanity by its vision of a noble humanism practised 'in the way of God'. Arab colonization of lands was an expressly religious movement, coming on the heels of the Messenger's demise and in professed obedience to the Quran's imperial dictate: 'It is he [God] who sent his messenger with guidance and the religion of truth so that he may cause it to prevail over all religion while pagans resent it' (Q:61:9; also Q:48:28).

Many Muslim rulers were just conquerors who lived permanently among the indigenous peoples and brought them within the fold of a collectivist faith. That explains why other nations, especially the Turks and Iranians, the Pakistanis and the Malays, have each had separate love affairs with Islam and often became its passionate adherents, though, unlike Arabs, never its patrons. Voluntary conversions were commonplace; ordinary people, unlike their corrupt rulers, generally welcomed their new Muslim masters. The aim of Muslim imperialism was to impose Islamic law. Religious minorities were tolerated, even embraced, for Islamic reasons.

This systematic conquest of territories and peoples in an attempt to establish God's universal sovereignty differs morally from the aggression of nations whose ambitions were divorced from scruple and benevolence. The Islamic narrative contrasts with the imperialist initiative of European nations. Theirs was a calculated attempt to achieve power, without any attempt to transform it into morally acceptable authority. The expansion of the European design worldwide was started and finished at a time when Christianity's restraining moral influence was almost zero. This did not prevent the formal alliance of the Bible with the bullet in the most determined enterprise of unmitigated cruelty and hubris in recorded history. It did prevent the European scramble for Asia and Africa and other lands from achieving the dignity that revealed religion may otherwise have conferred on it. One cannot imagine an enterprise more completely treasonable to the cause of Jesus of Nazareth.

We cannot introduce nuance and detail about the varying levels of racism and exploitation among the different imperialisms of European origin. The common factors are few. The resources of countless peoples were systematically plundered and the peoples reduced to poverty and dependence. The colonialists, despite being colonizers rather than remote control imperialists, had no intention of settling in the lands they acquired. When they decided to grant independence – as if anyone has the right to grant anyone else what is a human birth-right – they returned to their European sites. They created synthetic nation-states whose government was placed in the custody of venal elite sympathetic to Western ideals of capitalist exploitation and secular laxity in morals. As Western colonialists physically receded, they remained committed to their protégé states ruled by their agents who ensured that the citizens remained poor and dependent. Former colonies thus remained appendages of the departing powers. The whole process was cynically dubbed 'independence'. These crimes and inequities of the recent past sustain inequalities of opportunity in the present. Continuing immigration to the West is, as I know from my own experience, one of the economic consequences of Western imperialism.

British and, to a lesser extent, French imperialists modelled themselves on the central city-state which received wealth siphoned off from the rest of the colonies. It is no coincidence that most British imperialists were trained in the classics and dreamed of the glory and grandeur of Rome and Greece. Roman imperialism spawned several imitative Western imperialisms. Arab imperialism, as Islam, was *sui generis* and generated no imitative imperialism. Nor was it located in Mecca as the mercantile hub of the Islamic empire.

Europeans conquered much of the globe. In Islamic lands, they began with commercial expansion and exploitation, followed by armed invasion, occupation and conquest. They ruled some Islamic territories for centuries and some for a few decades. A few – Turkey, Afghanistan, Iran and Saudi Arabia – were never colonized. Europeans have, incidentally, never formally ruled any Islamic country for as long as Muslims ruled parts of Spain.

British colonialism is a case apart. English chains of class identity – gilded fetters for some but mainly heavy irons for the workers – were transported worldwide, including white nations. The deleterious effect of British colonialism on *white* colonies has not been noted. Canadians, to take a prominent example, lack a national identity since they never formally repudiated British colonial influence. Unlike the Americans, they missed out on revolution. Australians remain ambivalent about the republican ideal.

Imperialism must always rely on a racial aristocracy. Thus, a poor uneducated white boy or girl from West Virginia can torture an upper class Iraqi general. It is no coincidence that non-white nations had to struggle violently for independence while some white nations (such as Canada and Australia) were peacefully granted independence. The racist paternalism of British imperialism is also apparent in its unduly draconian laws to keep non-white natives in line.

There are motives, not grounds, for the conceit that those who founded their 'democracies' on bloodshed can teach others the art of government. In 1956, Tunisian Muslims refuted the stock French justification for governing North Africa. The Tunisians asked: 'Are the French ready for self-government?'

VI

We shunt our train of thought now to Islam's first imperial institution, the caliphate. The Quran appoints Adam as God's 'deputy (*khalīfah*) in the earth' (Q:2:30). This is not an appointment but rather an endorsement of human political capacity. We are beings to whom political power can be trusted; it would be wrong to deduce any particular pattern of government from this endorsement of the dignity of political office. In the Quran, only two men are called *khalīfah*: Adam and David (Q:38:26). Neither was a caliph in the Islamic sense of a temporal ruler succeeding a prophet – although David was a king.

The caliphate emerged *ad hoc* to replace the temporal aspect of Muhammad's prophetic office. Muhammad was the seal of prophecy; none could succeed to his spiritual authority. After revelation ended and prophecy ceased, the prophet's deputy or successor (both covered by *khalīfah*) was a human and fallible leader. He was God's representative insofar as he ruled righteously by following Quranic guidelines. The four caliphs who succeeded Muhammad are called rightly, rather than divinely, guided. The caliphate is not a constitutional office since no legal document of early Islam provides for it. It is an innovation, albeit a praiseworthy one. The variety of forged traditions about this subject suggest that many in the early community felt the need to supply the caliphal office with some prophetic-traditional (if not Quranic) authority.

The caliphate contained innately religious credentials conferring both political and religious authority. The dichotomy of *sacerdotium* and *regnum* (church and state) was invalid. The caliph headed the governing institution which combined mosque and state. He did not see himself as a dictator or autocrat. Sovereignty belonged to God and derivatively to the Shariah in virtue of being God's law. The caliph was not a sovereign but a civilian subject of the state, subject to Shariah law. His authority did, however, come ultimately from God and he was therefore not necessarily accountable to public opinion. Like the Catholic Church, the caliphate is not a democratic institution reflecting the laity's views. Both are governed by the autocratically exercised authority of charismatic leaders. The caliph was not required to be a jurist or a theologian but he had to be a virtuous soldier and was often called by his military title of *amīr al-mu'minīn* (commander of the faithful).[3]

Classical Islam demanded heroic virtue rather than accountability as a test of the competence of its rulers. Rulers headed armies and risked death; the caliph had fortitude, courage and strength of character. General Muhammad set the example by leading his armies, including the Tabuk campaign, towards the end of his life. He was nearly killed in the confrontation at Mt Uhud. The Ottoman sultan Murad IV (r. 1623–40) was the last Muslim ruler to lead his army in person. In 1638, he appeared beneath the walls of Baghdad, heading an army that defeated the Persian governor stationed there.

The caliphate both unified and divided the Ummah. How can a fallible caliph be a deputy of an infallible God or even infallible Prophet? This was the Shiite objection to the Sunni theology of fallible human leadership which endorsed the united republican caliphate. Lasting from 632 to 661, this was a patriarchal but consultation-based appointment. In the dynastic rule of Mu'awiya which followed the end of the righteous four, the Muslims were an elite group of Arab rulers united in religion and ethnicity. Mass conversions among the ruled masses during the next dynasty, the Abbasids, sundered the ummah by creating ethnic diversity inside a single religious fellowship. The caliphal office was the most potent symbol of unification, providing a unique locus of legitimate political, religious, and temporal authority, among populations in conflict on other matters.

While the caliphate was not required to be based in Medina, caliphs had to be of Qurayshi descent, certainly in the early days. The caliphate moved from Medina to Damascus, to Baghdad, Cairo and finally to Istanbul. In 1918, the British and French forces defeated the Ottoman sultanate. An antique symbol of Islamic unity, identity and political integrity since June 632, the caliphate survived until its abolition by secular Turks in March 1924. Foreign colonizers abetted domestic modernists in abolishing this pivotal institution.

VII

The genesis and genius of Islamic civilization lies in its Shariah, a mix of law and jurisprudential scholarship. Muslims have produced little independently ethical or political thought. Apart from the musings of the philosopher and musical theorist Abu Nasr Al-Farabi (d. 950 CE), the sole extant classical source is the work of the judge–jurist Abu Al-Hassan Al-Mawardi who was born in Basra in 974 CE/362 AH and died in Baghdad in 1058/448.

Al-Mawardi's treatise *The Rules of Governance and Faithful Guardianship* (*Kitāb Al-Aḥkām Al-Sulṭaniyya wa Al-Wilāyat Al-dīniyyah*) was compiled at the request of an Abbasid caliph to defend the supremacy of the caliphal office.[4] The treatise is effectively an *ex post facto* endorsement of the actual inner workings of Abbasid power. By Al-Mawardi's time, the caliphate had become a constitutional monarchy.

The treatise treats the first Muslim community of Medina as utopian and relevantly normative and then describes the rights and duties of those entrusted with power. The author discusses the selection of the khalifah and the way he should appoint ministers in central government, amirs for the provinces and the army, imams for mosques and various judges and court officials. Also listed are the duties of those who collect revenues, including the alms-tax from Muslims and tribute from the protected minorities. The miscellaneous contents of this work include: criminal law, rules of fair trade, public order, fighting apostates and erecting administrative boundaries between parts of the Islamic empire.

Al-Mawardi places the caliphate within the jurisdiction of the Shariah, the only legitimate power system directly sanctioned by God. The caliph earns the sole authority to delegate power to his representatives because he sets the gold standard for political and economic justice. Having won the right to be sole custodians of the Shariah, the Muslim religious intelligentsia (*'ulamā'*) need not meddle in government affairs.

Al-Mawardi introduced a standard of political justice for assessing the behaviour of de facto absolute rulers by insisting that de jure rulers must provide political security, respect revealed religion, charge moderate taxes, and offer specified public services. He did not, however, impose an independent criterion of personal integrity on the ruler. Like other jurists, Al-Mawardi endorsed the authority of a tyrant who upheld the Shariah so long as he verbally accepted the jurists' right to be its sole custodians. He may have privately regarded such rulers as unjust but he gave no procedure for deposing them. In practice, tyrants controlled clerical opinion through threat and favour. The faithful community had no democratic mechanism for removing the ruler any more than Catholics do for deposing a Pope.

This situation still persists. Classical political theory is ambivalent and confused on the question of how to regulate the relationship between the autocratic state, represented by a caliph, and a disaffected civilian population seeking just reform or removal of a corrupt leader. How can the ruler of a theocratic empire be effectively held accountable by those he rules? There need not have been so many mundane mechanisms offered if scripture had already supplied the perfect one; and so many mechanisms need not have been offered if any of them had been any good. By contrast, post-Christian Europe and republican America developed effective and sophisticated accountability measures which, insofar as advanced capitalism permits their implementation, remain the envy of the world.

VIII

Muslim history is conservative. It is a tale of dynasties rather than revolutions since Islamic orthodoxy tried to maintain a peaceful society. The jurist–scholars dealt with civil unrest rather than with the maintenance of private confessional orthodoxy. The Hobbesian fear of tumult, civil war and public disorder (*fasād*; Q:5:33) motivated jurists to identify and oppose seditious (rather than doctrinal or dogmatic) heresy.

Muhammad advised his followers that the caliphate is to go to the man who does not desire it: 'Do not quest for authority, for if you do so, you will be destroyed by it. If you are given power without asking for it, you shall be made to succeed.' This intriguing hadith shows Muhammad's nuanced attitude to power. Critics would say that he himself was a megalomaniac, not a man ready to share power or work as one among equals in a committee. This criticism is unfair since he did delegate authority to his close followers and trained them thoroughly in statecraft. Otherwise, it is hard to explain the phenomenal expansion of the Islamic enterprise in the wake of his death.

Monarchy is still advocated by reactionary and conservative Muslims who accept the counsel of the (insecure) hadith cited above. A king does not seek power; he receives it, together with a sense of the honour and responsibility of his line. The Muslim tradition, as expressed by Ibn Khaldun, acknowledges that dynasties decay and become corrupt. They need an external injection of energy, often from some nomadic Übermenschen innocent of urbane and civilized instincts, men gripped by Dionysian ecstasy, eager to court risk. After the eventual and inevitable rehabilitation of this new force, its energies are dissipated; society must await a new man blessed with the requisite will to power.

It is the responsibility of the Muslim community, especially its scholar–jurists, to urge the king to reform and to uphold the holy law. If he does not reform, he must be disobeyed and deposed. Although the precise mechanism is left unspecified, the real threat of such coups keeps kings, sultans and caliphs in line. They may be corrupt privately. That is, up to a point, their business. If their corruption threatens to corrupt and oppress others on an intolerably large scale, Muslims must unseat them, provided that their attempt stands a reasonable chance of success. As elsewhere in Islamic law, God gives people the right to go to Hell but not to take others with them.

IX

Does the idea of a single caliphal leader invite a cult of personality? Like other ancient cultures, Muslims usually failed to create a civil society in which citizens obey the rules rather than the rulers. Muslim dynasties and imperial institutions have been unstable, rarely enduring beyond the death of the principal actors. Important institutions, free of the cult of personality, have seldom emerged. This problem plagues most Muslim cultures today, whether the institutions are legal, political, civil, voluntary or charitable. The Islamic ship flounders without a domineering charismatic figure at the helm of Muslim destiny.

The emergence of an Islamic cult of personality is puzzling. How can a cult of personality surround men who had abdicated originality and personal investment in the issue? Although the Prophet was the direct recipient of revealed law, his successors were saintly men simply administering God's law. They were only indirectly instruments of God's will. If they rejected the hubris of political individuality and legal innovation, how could the politics of such men become identified with their personae?

Relevantly, excessive confidence in the moral authority of one man's cause undermines intelligent management of dissent although, to complicate matters further, it is not seen as one man's cause but rather God's cause. To appoint even a saint as God's deputy is, surely, to invite him to become a megalomaniac. The Persian poet–monarchist Sa'di Shirazi, considered the Shakespeare of classical Persia, is famous for his sycophantic aphorism: 'Obedience is the secret of greatness'.[5] It epitomizes the political lethargy of Islamic rulers and of their docile people. King Louis XIV, an absolute monarch, said: '*L'état, c'est moi*' (I am the state). He was the last French sovereign to be able to say that without losing his head. Sensible citizens demand that their leaders, known to be fallible, should be elected democratically and held accountable democratically.

The requirement of a single absolute and, in the Shiite case, infallible, leader conflicts with modern notions of leadership. Shiites, even more than Sunnis, emphasize the superiority of individual inspired leadership over consensus and socially approved power. Democracies have one individual who is the final decision-maker but they do so in consultation with their cabinet. While the Islamic ruler has viziers – an Arabic word literally meaning burden-bearers (Q:20:29–30) – and a consultative experts' assembly (Fārsī: *Majlis-e-Shūrā*) to advise him, he is ultimately free to decide as he wishes. As in Western political and educational institutions, advisory committees lack executive power. Yet unlike Muslim institutions, their Western counterparts function well enough.

Muslims must replace classical Islam's elitist and charismatic ideal with the democratic pattern of leadership selection and removal. In the former, one individual, always a man, is selected for his absolute virtue – public and private. This was indeed so with each of the four rightly guided caliphs and in principle for all others. A report attributed to Muhammad claims that if two men run for the caliphal office, the just community must assassinate one of them. The hadith does not mention on what grounds one is to identify and execute the false pretender.

In any case, the report must be a forgery from the Abbasid era since no problem of this kind could have troubled anyone during Muhammad's life-time.

X

One may object that our discussion thus far relies on two false assumptions: that there is no charisma in the leadership of modern democracies and that there is no elitism in power that is accountable to an electorate.

A photogenic charisma is certainly present in modern politics; leaders are never judged solely on the adequacy of their policies, especially in America where the irrational voting preferences of ordinary citizens baffle non-American observers. Big corporate money is involved: the media is not a neutral party. Images must be sold. Like consent, charisma can be manufactured in order to make certain leaders acceptable to ordinary citizens. Charisma becomes a form of political superstition.

Leaders such as Ayatollah Khomeini, Nelson Mandela, Mahatma Gandhi and Pierre Trudeau, and Adolf Hitler, in differing ways, have been admired for their economy of physical movement as shown in that fixed radius of physical and moral vision. This contributed to the photogenic charisma of their political presence. Khomeini was a leader wielding an ancient Persian charm in the modern age. For a decade, the CIA tried, unsuccessfully, to find another Shiite cleric of equivalent charisma but one opposed to Khomeini's anti-imperialist policies for Iran and the Muslim world.

Islam requires a dramatic, perhaps sycophantic, ritual of oath of allegiance to a chief (see Q:48:10). A version of this happens in all cultures, including modern democracies. Westerners enjoying the gift of democracy still display a discrepantly sycophantic attitude towards those in power, especially towards sovereigns such as Queen Elizabeth II but also elected officials such as the President of the United States. Citizens in democracies worry as much about the health and prosperity of their sovereigns and leaders as did any victim of an oriental despot. The behaviour of Canadians and Australians at parades in honour of the Queen of England makes one wonder whether even constitutional democracy can reduce the idolatrous worship of undeserved absolute privilege – even among those whose forbears fought battles to replace sovereign contempt of the masses with a republican regard for the democractic rights of all citizens.

The Quranic vision can be adjusted to most models of leadership but it favours the charismatic model of authority suited to a tribal society. It contains only two isolated appeals for deciding affairs by 'mutual consultation' (*shūrā*; Q:3:159; 42:38) while obedience to infallible prophetic leadership is regularly emphasized. While *shūrā* as political term occurs only twice, related notions of mutual consultation in familial and communal contexts are found more frequently (see Q:2:233; 4:35; 49:9–10; 65:1–7).

The Quran links Muhammad's leadership and authority closely to God's authority. One reference to *shūrā* occurs in a verse (Q:3:159) recited obligatorily at progressive Muslim gatherings. It is, however, addressed solely to Muhammad as a man already in power. Such a man may engage in consultation with his inferiors.

But why should any man who receives guidance from heaven listen to a committee of human advisors?

XI

The Quran envisages a society united by a shared vision and rejects some types of diversity as deviance from revealed norm (Q:16:9; 51:8–10). Only one path is the right one; many are the gates marked 'Error' and 'Speculation' and many enter through them. This Semitic exclusivism is shared by the Bible and the Quran. If one has absolute and final truth, including political truth, what is the point of free inquiry or free contested elections? Muslims opposed to the multi-party system of democracy cite the fact that the Pharaoh, a symbol of every evil ruler, divided his people into castes and parties (see Q:28:4).

In democracies, people enter into debate to determine the common good before pursuing it. For most Muslim supremacists, especially the disciples of Sayyid Qutb, an activist we encounter in the last chapter, Islam contains a morally perfect and entirely self-contained system of revealed beliefs, laws and social practices requiring implementation and application, not innovation or dilution through contact with external stimuli, especially those from the decadent west. To be fair to the Quran itself, however, every scripture is compatible with the best and the worst of our impulses. Democratic and autocratic politics can both be located in the sacred volume. All world religions were founded in pre-scientific, pre-democratic cultures. (Who asks whether traditional Catholicism is compatible with democracy?)

In a mature democracy, we concede political difference as legitimate and thus pre-empt society's capacity to divide harmfully into factions. A committee of fallible prophets with incompatible opinions seeking compromise is not commended by any scripture. The pagans object to the revelation being given to one man (or a few men) among them (Q:36:14–5; 54:23–5; 74:52). Why not to all or many, perhaps to a committee of prophets? It is a modern objection: anti-autocratic and pro-democratic.

Theoretically, the demand for consultation prevents any single person from convincingly claiming exclusive legal or political authority. A liberal-sounding hadith report reads: 'The mutual differences among my people are a sign of divine mercy' (*ikhtilāf ummatī raḥmah*). One version replaces 'my people' with 'the learned of my community'. Along with consultation, this attitude enables a democracy. This admittedly insecure traditional saying reflects a felt political need during the Abbasid period, if not earlier. Often a Muslim will make camp by himself, especially where power is at stake. There are many leaders and few followers. Managing dissent peacefully yet justly while effecting efficient and eirenic transfers of power are among the chief benefits of a democratic society. One wonders, however, whether this is only possible where there is little to disagree about – as in most Western societies. Politics, at least at the domestic level, has ceased to matter while an uncritical consensus about foreign policy prevails.

In mature democracies, leadership emerges from consensus and coalition; it is never autocratic, unilateral or imposed. Therefore, it endows only temporary and relative rather than permanent and absolute power. In Islamic lands, many subjects move moodily from abject resignation to the arbitrary will of the tyrant to an anarchic and inscrutable defiance even of properly constituted authority. To find a balance where citizens obey what is just and disobey what is unjust is the pedagogic task for every democracy. Muslims should develop the habit of the dialectic as part of the intellectual and philosophical foundations of democracy. An Islam filtered through secular modernity's democratic mechanisms is alert to the legitimate divisions in society. As we experience the strong and independent pull of two opposed positions, we adopt the best approach as a dialectical compromise which deliberately avoids finally resolved stances.

Many Muslims view the management of communal dissent through multi-party elections and contests for the popular vote as a divisive way of dealing with selfish political interests. The real anxiety for the purists is that the majority is usually misguided and will, therefore, vote for an abrogation of the holy law. Muslim opponents of democracy reject *shūrā* and cite the Quran's elitism, its rejection of majoritarianism (Q:12:21, 103). The majority knows nothing; truth, like piety, is the privilege of the few. Democracy is dangerous since it elevates majority opinion and speculation at the expense of divine truth. 'Public opinion' is merely public emotion. Since anyone can in principle stand for election, ungodly but ambitious men (and women) may seek and wield power over the unambitious but pious. Democracies differ from other governments solely in electing a different set of scoundrels every five years. Most people know only their own ignorant wishes, the Quran often asserts, but not their true ideals. This view is a recipe for Platonic elitism. No wonder that while Aristotle was the preferred moral thinker, many Islamic thinkers, especially Al-Farabi, endorsed Plato's elitist authoritarianism.

After centuries of bloodshed, European political thinkers came to see the political community as autonomous: not all law is divine law. The notions of inalienable human rights, informed political consent and participation, rival parties and popular elections, and representative bodies and free assemblies were gradually institutionalized in increasingly secular democratic structures with little or nominal Christian input. By contrast, Muslims have generally rejected secular notions of independent reason and democratic political organization. Contemporary Islam has therefore often failed to manage peacefully the dissent and diversity of opinion inside its household. Leaders have prevented the emergence of a participatory politics representative of varied social groups.

XII

'Democratic', like other adjectives such as 'moderate' or 'radical', is ideologically charged, possibly propagandist. Maintaining power through consent, not coercion, is democracy. This requires institutionalized doubt about absolute or concentrated power in order to create and maintain an equitable government accountable to an electorate. The variety of democracies indicates the elasticity of the concept: the range is from presidential, constitutional, and republican democracy (America), to monarchical parliamentary democracy (United Kingdom). Like scriptural words, secular political nomenclature can be elastic enough to cover the aspirations of all contenders. Despite having an accepted usage, democracy is an essentially contested concept.

Factually, a democracy must contain an electoral system, a set of inalienable rights and due process and rule of law. Civil discourse creates a competitive ethos in which free exchange of ideas takes place without fear of retribution from the powerful. A loyal and tolerant opposition checks the hubris of the ruling party but supports the basic shared structure of government and law. A full cluster (polythetic) definition of democratic polity would refer to nine pillars supporting the democratic edifice: sovereignty of the people, consent of the governed, major-ity rule with minority rights, guarantee of basic human rights for all, free and fair elections, equality before the law, due process of law, constitutional limits on government, and some commitment to social and political if not legal and economic pluralism.

Democracy can be direct – as in rule by the people through referenda. This is possible only in small modern communities or in the first democracy in ancient Athens with its assembly of about 5,000 male adults. It is harder to establish in large modern populations although the internet may one day help to enable it. Representative democracy is indirect: representatives are democratically elected to make political decisions, formulate laws, and administer programmes for the public good. In practice, representative democracy centralizes power into the hands of elites who regularly abuse power with impunity. America is the best example of this pattern.

Evidently, democracies run the risk of majoritarianism – the dictatorship of the majority. An elected government can become a benevolent tyranny. Plurality can reduce to polarity since only two parties are ever likely to be in power. This can deteriorate into autocratic tyranny. Two examples are furnished by Margaret Thatcher's arrogant conservative government in the 1980s and George W. Bush's Republican decade-long tenure which fortunately ended in 2009.

Democracy has other types of limitations too. Its political freedoms need not entail economic prosperity. Post-communist Eastern Europe and India come to mind. However, a democracy, by decreasing corruption and nepotism, and through regular institutionalized threats of accountability, can consolidate existing trends towards wealth creation. A democracy need not create or fairly distribute eco-nomic wealth while an autocracy may, perhaps fortuitously, occasionally succeed in doing so. In democratic republics, especially India and America, spectacular wealth co-exists with spectacular poverty.

Democracies are not automatically perfect. Secular democratic states can fail to achieve their declared goals; a bad or compromised democracy is still a democracy. Conversely, rule of law and respect for rights can exist without democracy. An undemocratic society can uphold individual rights to liberties, due process, tolera-tion and guarantees against abuse. Conversely, democracies such as India, Israel and America employ extensive secret intelligence services whose operations are not only evil but incompatible with open government and democratic accountability. Indeed, India's democracy has been a hereditary or dynastic variant in which Mrs Gandhi's family ran the country like their own estate. And last but not least, democratically elected leaders are, especially in America but now also in Europe, increasingly guided by corporate interests.

Even mature democracies are compromised. Democracy is compatible with invading other sovereign nations, especially those peopled with foreigners with slightly darker skins. Left-wing critics mock America as the most backward democracy in the industrialized world, 'the best democracy money can buy'. Domestic interest groups drive its immoral foreign policy. Noam Chomsky calls it a form of corporate fascism, founded on exploitation of many nations. America's pre-emptive imperialism, in Iraq and Afghanistan, and its anti-communist evangelism, starting with Vietnam, dented its reputation as a force for global good. Indeed, American 'democracy' proves the truth of the party slogan in Orwell's *1984*, 'Ignorance is Strength', since only an ignorant citizenry would permit its government to behave as it pleases in its foreign adventurism.

'For the people, despite the people' was the creed of the 'enlightened' despot Kemal Ataturk, the father of Turkey's imposed secularism. Many an unalert and indifferent Western citizenry also enthusiastically endorses 'democracy by trust': we the people leave it to you the people – who know better. In imperial Islam, as in mediaeval Christendom, the just ruler is like God since he considers his subjects' true interests, not their wishes. In a telling irony that would delight Plato, paternalism increasingly motivates modern democracies no less than the theocracies of a bygone age.

Part III

The crucible of reason

Islam as contemporary religion

8   A rational religion

In Islamic history, ascertaining the right relationship between faith and reason was guided by primarily social, political and legal, not philosophical, individual or rational forces. It was initially motivated by the practical religious question of who wields legal–scriptural authority and was only deflected into the abstract philosophical dimension when conflicts arose between rival authorities claiming legitimacy. In all faiths, hierarchically organized religious sources gain, maintain or lose authority over time. The authority of Islamic doctrine ('aqidah) matured only after internal religious and political controversy in the hinterland supplied by the faith–reason tension.

In the core Western, mainly Cartesian tradition, ecclesiastical authority was banned, by fiat, from the project of purely intellectual inquiry.[1] Before Descartes, Locke and Hume, religious and secular thinkers alike assumed that spirituality and virtue are preconditions of philosophical knowledge. The human subject had to be good in order to know. Access to truth transforms us. This ancient philosophical and religious view was rejected by Descartes for whom the mind is self-sufficient. Moral and spiritual growth is not a prerequisite of intellectual eminence. In Islam, compassion and wisdom are preconditions of exercising legal discretion (ijtihād). The subject must be transformed morally before he or she can know the object. Wisdom, knowledge and good judgment are rewards for piety and virtue (Q:12:22; 28:14).

Descartes' magisterial ambition was to establish Western science solely on the autonomy of individual reason liberated from ecclesiastical strictures. He wrongly assumed that whatever is immediately present to the senses needs no external authority. One must still trust in the authority of memory and sense perception, the two sources of experience, and, moreover, in the stability of language as shared means of communication and therefore an axiomatic social truth. Even the two sources of direct experience are not unmediated or always self-authenticating. There is deception and self-deception. Nor is scientific inquiry actually grounded in the autonomy of personal reason: it is mediated through the testimony of collaborators. Indeed scientific rationality relies on expert opinion and historical accounts. Social authority is inescapable and fundamental to individual experience, a truth that escaped Descartes as he meditated in the cozy liberal atmosphere of Holland.

The vague dichotomy of *fides* and *ratio* is analogous to specific dualities that are not necessarily antagonistic: religion and empirical science, tradition and secular novelty (or innovation), theology and philosophy, revelation and intellection, nature and the triple opposites of art, super-nature and grace. The faith–reason dichotomy, as absolute and confrontational, is absent from classical Islam as it is absent from the patristic theology of the Greek fathers. In ages of faith, Christian reason itself had been successfully Hellenized and reconciled with faith; the Enlightenment ruptured the two and solidified the adversarial dualism of faith and reason as the latter scored a decisive victory over faith by giving birth to science. Any modern criticism of the initially European but now universally relevant Enlightenment is automatically viewed as an attempt to undermine that inaugural victory of reason over faith, achieved after almost two millennia of the Christian interregnum. Any modern faith therefore, eager to reach the world, must make its case in the universal context of a Western reason freed of Christian strictures.

Muslim thinkers, in their capacity as jurists, explored the limits of knowledge. They fortuitously established the office of independent reason through a practical concern with *ijtihād*, the liberty and necessity to exercise the legal mind beyond the limits of revelation and prophetic precedent. Such an exertion must oppose neither revelation nor unaided reason: the first in case it leads to blasphemy, the second lest it lead to paradox, absurdity and inconsistency. The jurists discovered something strange. Islam is a rational faith and reason is supreme but only because it is in the service of faith. God has honoured the creature's reason by choosing it to be the handmaiden of faith, cheerfully providing the means necessary to achieve the goals and ends established through revelation. Thinkers as varied as Al-'Ashari, Al-Ghazali and Ibn Khaldun would concur. This order of priorities limits the role of independent reason in the assessment of revelation to a hermeneutical one, making it conservative rather than subversive or anarchic. By contrast, for the Western (Cartesian) tradition, reason's task, once freed of ecclesiastical strictures, was substantive, constructive and occasionally destructive.

II

If we define theology as a religious discipline motivated by the Quran and the Prophet's sayings, its stimuli are indigenous. The subject dates to Muhammad's tenure in Medina. Such theology relied on the exegetical use of reason in order to extract new opinions from sacred texts and thus to understand and explicate scripture and to appreciate the rationale for the Messenger's actions. Theology as hermeneutics was systematically practised as early as Abu Hanifah (d. 767 CE) and Malik Ibn Anas (d. 795), founders of the two earliest legal schools. Reason's role was not ambitious since its stimuli were wholly internal to faith. Theology was formally subject to supervision by the controlling comprehensive discipline of *fiqh* (jurisprudence). Unlike Christian theologians, Islamic theologians have rarely engaged in esoteric debates except in the faith's formative past when the positions adopted were surrogates for legal and political stances.

The scriptural harmony between the exercise of reason and the data for reflection supplied by revelation was ruptured as a result of the encounter with Hellenic models of rational autonomy. This led to the rise of classical Islamic rationalism, in the guise of Islamic scholastic theology and Islamic philosophy. Dialectical theology (*kalām*, lit. speech), the precursor of Islamic philosophy, was founded during the Abbasid revolution of the 750s (CE). Mu'tazilite rationalism, the school which, as its name suggests, 'seceded' from orthodoxy, emerged under the impact of Greek writings which were, under Abbasid patronage, translated into Arabic.

During the heyday of the Mu'tazilah (from 833 to 848), the translation of Greek writings continued to provide the first external heretical stimulus. The Arabs quickly learnt about methods of Greek reasoning, syllogism and other techniques of logic along with some metaphysics and ontology. It encouraged a dialectical theology which reached controversial conclusions. Its aims, however, remained internal to Islam since it sought to resolve anxieties inherent in scripture: intractable worries about free will, human responsibility and divine justice. The Mu'tazilite school combined extra-Quranic methods of inquiry with a sincerely religious quest for finding truths embedded in a scripture which, for all its claims to clarity, also contained moral, legal and metaphysical obscurities. Sustained inquiry, however, always carries the risk of doubt.

Philosophy emerged late: the impulse was not latent in the Quran. Philosophy was not inspired by internal struggles with scriptural views on justice or during the attempt to solve the urgent legal question of excommunication (*takfīr*) of the reprobate sinner. Islamic philosophy, like all authentic philosophy, was born during an audacious bid for the autonomy of secular reason. In its impulses, methods and priorities, Islamic philosophy contained the germ of a foreign and potentially insidious intellectual radicalism. Orthodoxy felt obliged to abort it.

III

Most neutrally understood, reason is a human capacity whose *tēlos* is truth; arguments are means of approaching truth. Reason is imposed on mere thought as a way to correct the errors introduced by the senses and the passions. Reason, as systematic or critical orientation, is a faculty transcending unrefined common sense. Its application yields a priori principles (of logical consistency) for guiding our understanding of sense experience. At its broadest, theoretical and practical reason is our deposit of critically organized common sense; at its core lies a kernel of widely accepted moral values and shared intellectual ideals. For the secularist, reason symbolizes the intellectual self-sufficiency of human nature which presupposes an optimistic assessment of unaided human rational potential. The Quran, from its earliest revelations, vetoes as hubris any such autonomy (Q:96:6–7; 75:36).

The Quran rejects the autonomy of unaided human reason but accords it a major secondary role: it limits human knowledge and circumscribes the role of reason in acquiring it. All knowledge is revealed in the sense that God decides how much of it is to be 'revealed' to human beings (Q:17:85). Such knowledge is later appropriated and processed via our reasoning faculty. In this religious model of the uses and abuses of reason, faith and reason co-operate: reason enhances and reinforces faith but cannot judge it unfavorably. Islam is not unique in its decision to limit the scope of unaided reason. In the aborted enterprise of Islamic philosophy, the Muslim thinkers failed to note that the Hellenization of reason also substantially circumscribes its role. Under the sign of Socrates, the sage who drank the hemlock for the cause of reason, reason is intentionally self-limiting and unremittingly sceptical. Reason knew its place because sceptics put it in its place. It could not even refute doubt although, for ancient Western sceptics, doubt brought serenity, not mental turmoil.

The Quran's very first revelation reveals that we humans know little (Q:96:5). The scripture rejects the subversive potentiality of a liberated and therefore anarchic reason. Throughout Islamic history, theoretical curiosity, a central element in secular modernity's epistemology, was replaced by Islam's practical concern with the limits of knowledge. 'Shorten the sermon but lengthen the prayer' has always been a popular anti-theological and anti-intellectual slogan. Even the Muslim elite appointed by departing European powers were only nominally curious: they were false representatives of modernity's epistemology since theirs was merely a politically neutered and therefore ultimately frivolous form of inquisitiveness.

How we define reason will determine its relationship to faith and revealed knowledge. Reason can be interpreted in an atomistic way (yielding logical or mathematical rationality) as in Aristotle and Spinoza's schemes. As scientific empirical rationality, with physics as its paradigm, reason is associated with logical positivism which limited reason's radius to the sphere of the empirically verifiable. Westerners cannot escape the enduring and deleterious legacy of Cartesian rationalism and its associated implied atomism and individualism although the Scottish Enlightenment, in the form of David Hume and Adam Smith, diluted reason's Cartesian sovereignty by assigning a balancing role for the emotions and for the physical and social, including economic, environment.

The modern notion of reason, relevant to all faiths entering the arena of secularism, is expectedly conditioned by the Enlightenment. It conceals an absolute, indeed irrational, commitment to reason and to a finite and contingent human faculty of intellection along with all that can be empirically and cognitively deduced from the sciences it has enabled. The relationship between faith and reason deteriorates into an unrelentingly adversarial extremism. Only an enlarged sense of reason, generous enough to include revelation, could enable us to move beyond this impasse. Only then could special types of human subjectivity, particularly self-authenticating religious experience, be acknowledged as authentic, whatever the merits of the case for public verification of the alleged truth behind such experience.

Promoting intercultural, interreligious, and interdisciplinary dialogue requires reason to expand beyond the privileged and monological arena of scientific and logical reasoning. It must allow for the validity and retrieval of experiential, religious, pragmatic and intuitive types of knowledge now that a barren positivism has finally fully subsided. A pragmatic account of reality certainly allows for a coherent, comprehensive and persuasive presentation of reality. It demands only provisional, never absolute, status. It is, for that very reason, unappealing to the religious imagination which requires certainty to satisfy its spiritual craving for the absolute.

IV

No scripture is more dialectically presented than the Quran: protagonists engage in dialogue involving extreme, adversarial and existentially vital positions that require urgent resolution. Faith itself is a dialectical process involving certainty, self-critical introspection, doubt, self-inspection and repentance. Extreme and urgent confrontation is often didactic: it teaches us the true nature of our disputes and helps ascertain the correct limits of our ideological relationships, something easily overlooked or obscured by the false politeness of routine interaction. Augustine, Anselm and Aquinas, three mediaeval saint-thinkers who defined the mediaeval millennium, upheld a concept of reason as dialectical. Plato, Berkeley and Hume, the West's three philosopher–dramatists, did the same. As in rabbinic and Talmudic literature, reason was a method that was valued not for leading to the finality of resolved positions but rather for constantly refining views under the pressure of argument and the scrutiny of multiple intelligent challenges. This modest and progressive, tentative and probing, role for reason is also present in the Quran although the superior profundity of the Quran's author is never in doubt. (Do not human dramatists also privilege their mouthpieces?)

While being faithful to their deposits of faith, religious thinkers must construct a model of reason, based on cultural interchange with secular modernity. The result: a decolonized, universalized, intercultural and syncretistic notion of reason. Believing philosophers of religion must reconfigure our understanding of reason and thus create an international anti-colonial modernity. We must rescue our conception of reason from the hegemony of Eurocentric imperialism which was produced by an aggressive secularism imposed indigenously in Europe and then imported to displace and render problematic (by sheer juxtaposition) all non-western conceptions of reason, especially those prevalent in Islamic civilization.

Thus, for example, Western supremacist (orientalist) scholarship committed 'epistemicide' by cordoning off 'Islamic or Arab philosophy' as if it were inferior to philosophy proper (which is identified with Western philosophy). Muslims are reduced to being mere transmitters of the West's lost heritage of Greco-Roman knowledge. The Portuguese sociologist Boaventura de Sousa Santos coined the term 'epistemicide' to refer to the death of some forms of knowledge. He noted that powerful people preserve and privilege the kinds of knowledge that benefit them. 'Epistemicide' alerts us to the way that the conjunction of knowledge with power reduces the disinterested search for wisdom to self-serving ideology. Epistemicide can become the mother and brother of genocide wherever an imposed colonial epistemology underpins cultural imperialism with its accompanying linguacide and devaluation of indigenous cultures.

Secular legal, political and cultural modernity rejects revelation as reason's competent dialogue partner even though, in ages of fervent faith, the faithful embraced reason as a partner. The contemporary dialogue of reason is internal: reason is what produces truth and truth is what reason produces. This method yields disappointingly meagre results and spells the death of philosophy as substantive discipline. The secular exercise of reason is culturally and temporally conditioned. It is no more transcendent than the interpretation of scripture is transcendent of its age and context. To acknowledge the autonomy of empirical historical and scientific methods is not to endorse the *ahistorical* autonomy of the reason which supports those methods.

V

We use our reason, Muslims believe, in order to understand revelation. In the aftermath of the *final* revelation, this is the place reserved for reason. Its more anarchic pre-revelation role is domesticated and disciplined – disbelievers would say attenuated – so that it becomes largely exegetical. Believers think as they struggle to understand, explain and implement the verdicts and imperatives of scripture in a tradition where reason is both individually intuitive and socially participatory while always being subordinated to faith. It functions analytically and discursively in exegetical, legal (and associated analogical) employments as jurists expound and extract new judgments from revered old texts. The need for such rational exertion decreases as the corpus of traditional and contemporary authoritative texts increases. The consensual reason of all competent believers guarantees infallibility in the understanding of the revelation since collective, socially exercised, reason cannot err. This sociologically validated view of consensus is extracted from the Prophet's claim, related on the authority of the traditionist Muhammad Ibn 'Isa Al-Tirmidhi, in his collection (*Jamī'*): 'God will not allow Muhammad's community to agree on an error.'

Intelligent believers reject only the final self-sufficiency of unaided human reason; they endorse the integrity of its reduced (exegetical) role. Reason explains, develops and utilizes revealed ideas; it does not originate them. What is unknowable by reason is still believable by reason although one cannot believe what one cannot understand. Reason, post-revelation, is not the anarchic reason of the private individual under the sway of passion but rather the communal and consensual reason of the paradigmatic but nonetheless imperfect community which, according to Muhammad, cannot agree on an error but which, one should add, may also fail to agree on a truth.

Faith and reason can subsist in a reciprocal harmony but only if reason makes no bid for autonomy. The autonomy of reason is irreconcilable with the transcendence of divine revelation. Muslims are cautious about the correct uses of reason, especially in moral life. Many objections to revealed moral imperatives, as opposed to revealed dogmas, are not wholly rational. Often our passions and instincts are strong enough to be the real motivation behind an apparently rational rejection of God's word.

At the other extreme, if we reject all rationally grounded criteria for judging the truth of religious claims, we leave believers' wills vulnerable to the onslaught of false but emotionally appealing views. We cannot commend a faith of fanatically intense conviction lacking in resources for self-introspection and self-criticism. A faith, deprived of independent critical checks administered by secular reason, may evoke fanaticism, sentimentality, zealous defensiveness and isolationism, thus falling prey to the secularist's charge that religious conviction is ideological and insular. The political ramifications of this for an alert citizenry in a democracy hardly need elaboration.

VI

The Quran intends to make religion universal by distinguishing it from the superstition of paganism and Islam's two rivals, Judaism and Christianity. Jews, Christians and 'pagans' must wonder: Is Islam a rationally appealing faith? Can Muslims accept the fact that Islam too is subject to valid external rational critique? Intelligent Muslims also wonder: Is it religiously permissible, in a secular age, to assess and support one's faith using philosophical reason? If so, what is the religious authority for this essentially modern view?

These inquiries are components of the practical project of developing a rational attitude to politics, part of the presupposed attitudinal basis of modern democracies. The political organization of enlightened reason would bring utopia: that was the promise of the Enlightenment. To ask whether Islam is rationally appealing is also to ask whether those who accept it are obliged to understand and defend its credentials, not merely assert them with dramatic dogmatism. To recruit independent reason in the defence of faith is to recognize the importance of such reason in its own right too. And to debate the possibility, even desirability, of external critique is to recognize the location of our debate – inside a mature democracy where dissent and diversity are not objections to the possibility of politics but rather conditions of it.

While philosophers of religion probe and assess the consistency, coherence, plausibility and truth of competing religious beliefs, believers correctly challenge the value and function of such scrutiny. Some Muslims raise the charge of the alleged impiety of rational methods for assessing faith's credentials. Why do Muslims resist the right of reason to judge faith, even favourably? While reading the Quran's dialectical exchanges, Muslims become subliminally anxious about the subversive role of pagan reason: the interrogation of divine claims and imperatives reminds them of the determined original rejection of the Quran by Muhammad's aristocratic contemporaries. Many were neither rationally convinced nor psychologically persuaded. They died in their doubts in a whole decade full of battles. Muslims still cannot fully disengage from the revelation's polemical first context, its ideologically charged environment. Recent events make them view Islam besieged by even more powerful and derisive forces than those which trapped the Prophet.

Goethe thought that: 'Properly speaking, we learn only from those books we cannot judge.' Most believers would concur. Should a text, written in the spirit of faith and demanding a faithful response, be read and interpreted in a spirit of philosophical disputation and analytical detachment? Analytical prying seems inappropriate when examining sacred scripture. If pressed in the service of doubt and subversion, protests the believer, reason moves outside its proper domain. Like other human faculties, it should be recruited in the service, not destructive criticism, of faith.

Some Muslims, thirsting for certainty in our dislocating era, think desperately that the Quran must be either absolute or else obsolete. If absolutely true, it is supposedly an automatic safeguard against heretical deviation. If obsolete now, it was never true. We need not torture ourselves with this insoluble dilemma. If the Quran is found, after persistent rational scrutiny, to be false, we must relegate it to the crowded museum of religious absurdities and relics. If genuine, we expect it to withstand hostile probing and mockery in every age. In any case, believers must acknowledge reasoning (as opposed to reason itself) as our only agreed procedure for ascertaining truth and distinguishing revealed truth from portentous falsehood. Reason is the common heritage of our shared humanity. Even scripture bases some arguments on public – philosophically accessible and universally recognized – evidence.

VII

Through its threats of hell and the promises of heaven, Islam offers more rational motivation than rational evidence for living the ethically grounded religious life. As a rational religion, however, the Quran also argues its case. It offers reasons for foregoing the pleasures of this world in order to seek the pleasures of the permanent next world, including God's everlasting good pleasure. Earthly life is finite while the after-life is infinitely (or at least indefinitely) long. 'Consider! If we let them enjoy [this life] for [a few] years; then there comes to them at length the promised [punishment], the pleasures they enjoyed shall not [then] benefit them' (Q:26:205–7). Pleasure, unlike knowledge or virtue, is not cumulative. No matter how much pleasure we experience in the past, it cannot mitigate the pain of the moment of chastisement when it arrives in the present.

The Quran portrays prophets giving reasons for their trust in God and warning their people about the resurrection from the dead as a prelude to judgement of conduct. Abraham the iconoclast, exemplary prophet and Muhammad's role model, appears as a skilled polemicist who rather sceptically requests God to show him how he gives life to the dead (Q:2:260). The Hebrew iconoclast is an empiricist natural philosopher who concludes from observations of finite heavenly bodies that there must exist a single supreme infinite being. He rejects the infinitude of the sun and the astral deities (Q:6:74–9) studied by the Babylonian astronomers. He shows a disbeliever the divine first cause behind the sun's rising and setting (Q:2:258). Armed with an empirically grounded certainty of faith, he provokes his father and mocks the local temple's idolatrous guardians (Q:6:74–83; 21:51–71; 37:85–98).

Part of the Quran's teaching is, like that of Jesus, in parabolic rather than syllogistic or argumentative form although the Quran rarely portrays Muhammad preaching (see Q:62:11 for an exception). The parables are divine monologues; unlike New Testament parables, there are few characters and no development of plot. The diversity and scope of the parables merits a monograph. The parable of the fly mocks the false gods who cannot even create a fly or retrieve anything from the fly (Q:22:73) while the parable of the spider notes the frailty of the spider's house which symbolizes the choice of false gods as patrons (Q:29:41). The parable of the two slaves compares the slave of God (*'abd allāh*) with a chattel slave (*'abdan mamlūkan*) who owns nothing and behaves like an idiot bringing no credit to his master (Q:16:75–6). The good and evil word correspond respectively to a firmly rooted tree which bears its fruit in every season while its branches reach towards heaven, and a fruitless tree which lies uprooted from the ground, with no stability against the wind (Q:14:24–6). Finally, in a mystical parable, God's light (Q:24:35) can barely be (intellectually) understood, let alone visualized.

The Quran claims to have coined every type of parable to teach truth to human beings, the most quarrelsome of creation (Q:18:54; 30:58). The pagans carped that Quranic parables and verses referred to insignificant creatures (Q:2:26) such as the fly (Q:22:73) and the spider (Q:29:41), and to ants (Q:27:18) and bees (Q:16:68-9). The Quran responds that even a parable involving a gnat might guide someone (Q:2:26). Recent advances in natural history have alerted us to societies of ants and bees and other micro-creatures with minutely complex systems of communications.[2] More generally, the pagans pointed to the way we humans too live and die as victims of fate and chance, as small creatures enjoying some happiness mixed with much suffering and inevitably destined for death. Surely, there could be no transcendent meaning in the lives of finite and insignificant mortals (see Q: 25:43; 28:50; 45:24).

This objection about our size, temporal duration and spatial location, our finitude in the titanic immensity of the universe, is intuitively entertained as a pre-philosophical prejudice in many cultures, including modern secular ones. Consider: 'We are puny little creatures with a fixed lease of life on an insignificant planet.' This is raised as an objection to the possibility of life having intrinsic meaning beyond short-term goals we pursue within it. This is a confused objection. If we change the temporal and spatial parameters, does life suddenly and 'miraculously' acquire meaning? Let us suppose we were larger creatures – as large as whales or sharks – or as tall as giraffes. This would complicate our social lives and make interaction awkward but such increase in size, connected to the possibility of developing larger vertebrae, would not necessarily endow meaning to our lives. Again, if we lived to be as old as Noah, almost a thousand years (Q:29:14), such longevity would not by itself endow significance to our lives if such lives are otherwise judged (by us or a superior judge) to be empty.

Finally, if we relocated to a larger planet, would our lives acquire meaning? The meaning of life is logically unrelated to our size, location and longevity. This truth does not automatically imply that only God or that even God could endow human life with significance. It merely refutes one stale atheist objection to the idea that the significance of human existence could ever be externally imposed.

An external imposition need not be arbitrary or degrading if God is the one imposing it after creating and determining human nature.

VIII

Charles Taylor has argued that we no longer locate our place in the objective order of the *cosmos*, a religious and teleological word, but rather construct our position in the natural *universe*, a secular scientific replacement.[3] In the former, the order and purpose were God-given and permanent; in the latter, arduous human effort shaped and engineered human lives and transformed societies.[4]

A Muslim must add that traditional Islamic science differed from European science since Muslim scientists kept the cosmos a cosmos. It never became a mere universe, a closed system of natural causality. Islam rejects the disengaged agency of the observer, the critic, and the analyst, the lasting legacy of the Cartesian project of 'dislocated' and disembodied inquiry. This aggressively secular project conceals a scientific literalism which corresponds to the religious position of scriptural literalism. There is no purpose beneath or behind nature; scripture conceals nothing deeper and hence needs no interpretation, a view which authorizes intolerance of even opposed religious, let alone secular, views. The gradual attenuation of the teleological and transcendent orientation of nature led inexorably to agnosticism, deism and finally an atheism which pontificated that the emergence of autonomous sentience required no supernatural explanation. The atheist's instrumentalist and pragmatic view of nature contradicts the spiritual view which motivates us to celebrate nature and endorse ecological and aesthetic rather than economic, technological and exploitative objectives.

The natural order is the visible token of an invisible grace which suffuses nature with a sacramental quality. The earth's beauty and bounty disguise God's presence. Residing in nature and society, this presence is mediated through the 'signs of God' which attest to his sovereignty. We must interpret human phenomena consistently and continuously with the rest of nature. Penitent servants ponder these divine portents in the four loci of God's presence and activity: external nature and history, human nature and community. In this square, believers detect hints of God's gracious association with humanity but the divine reality is fully accessible only to faith rooted in obedience and surrender. Such faith and the purity that characterizes its possessors are gifts of grace by-passing human initiative but not subsequent human cooperation and contribution. New Testament claims such as 'Many are called but few are chosen' (Matthew 22:14) and the Calvinist doctrine of election would be rejected by the Quran as unjust elitism. The Islamic scripture sees itself as rationally comprehensible and egalitarian.

The signs of God *rationally* attest to God's sovereignty. Application of reason leads to faith, the basis of the design argument (see Q:50:6–11; 89:17–21). Natural events supply evidence of divine craftsmanship, not of undirected biological evolution. God is continuously evident in routine but dynamic processes in nature and society. He is not only merely a dramatically interventionist or capricious deity. Natural order implies the existence of the merciful one (*Al-Raḥmān*), not merely of an abstract deity (see e.g. Q:43:45; 67:3–4). One Quranic surah opens with this moral attribute of the creator (Q:55:1). Only philosophers have 'demoralized' God to a first efficient cause in a physical system and then sought to prove the existence of such an anaemic and irrelevant being.

Even repeated scrutiny of creation will reveal no flaws in the creator's handicraft (Q:67:1–4) although only 'the people of insight' (Q:20:54, 128) discern such perfection and therefore spontaneously offer praise and gratitude. Pagans invent lies about God and refuse to reason about him (Q:5:103–5; 6:138–9; 67:10). The context is often food taboos on classes of animals venerated by pagans who, in order to honour their idols, declared select animals exempt from slaughter or toil. Irrationally, disbelievers prefer ancestral superstition to the latest revealed guidance.

IX

The mystical, rather evasive, notion of God's signs will guide the future of Islam as it recedes politically but assumes the role of guardian of the environment and defends the good green earth against ecocide. The Quran encourages a rational perspective on nature, confident that any intelligent inquiry into nature's mysteries will strengthen faith. Believers are ordered to read from (and into) nature the spiritual meanings inherent in creation. That is the rational project of understanding the world 'in the name of God'. It opposes any scientific literalism that reduces nature to an object.

Both nature and human nature are marvels. Goethe boasted that he renewed his humanity often by learning a new language. The variety of human languages is cited among God's gracious signs (Q:30:22). Linguists believe that our native language is not acquired but rather, like our liver or heart, grows organically and unaccountably. The fundamental if common miracle of birth, the daily marvel that perpetuates the human heritage, is cited in the very inaugural revelation (Q:96:1–2). The stages in a baby's formation, growth and emergence from the womb (Q:22:5; 23:14) are offered as proof of divine power beyond all human competence, reducing to hubris any human disputation with the divine creator (Q:36:77–83).

The Quran inculcates an aura of inevitability but not the inevitability of predestination or tragedy. It endorses the unavoidability of the rhythm and periodicity of nature and of human nature: regularities, recurrences and patterns in external nature and inside our nature accumulate to permit a human life to exist and flourish through the pre-determined stages of conception, life, maturity, ageing and death, foreshadowing the renewal of resurrection. Nature and human nature both permit resurrection, a dual sign for the penitents. Typically, the Quran does not appeal to the miracle, the event occurring *para doxan*, opposed to what we could imagine or expect according to reason. Instead it cites the familiar and routine event and natural reality as evidence of a universal and supernatural providence. It argues from analogy with the empirically observed dead earth which, revived periodically by rainfall (Q:29:63; 30:24; 41:39; 43:11; 50:11), dons the green mantle of fertility. Finally, the God who creates human beings from nothing (Q:19:9) or 'a fluid emitted' (Q:86:6) can certainly resurrect them (Q:2:28; 36:77–83; 50:3–4; 75:1–6, 36–40).

The Quran alerts us to the regular emergence of one thing or medium from another. The causally determined emergence of X from Y is a ground for wonder. Change both as the progression of stages and as final transformation of one thing into another (Q:20:17–23; 53–55; 36: 39) delights the believer and leads to penitence. Water, pouring from the clouds, transforms the dead into the living and causes different levels of transformation in plants as attested by their differential yields of fruit and their varied colours (Q:13:4; 35:27). The growth and spurting of green vegetation from an earthy mineral ethos (Q:6:95; 86:12) and the emission of sperm from flesh (Q:56:58–9; 75:37) are reverently noted. The inanimate processes by which juxtaposed fluids emerge already separated – wholesome milk flowing between the excrement and blood in cattle's stomachs – are divine signs (Q:16:66–7).

There are spiritual processes to match these natural ones. God brings the living from the dead and the dead from the living (Q:3:27) just as he splits the dawn to separate its light from its darkness (Q:6:95–6; 79:29). Divine revelation takes humanity in its ignorance and darkness, by God's permission and through faith, into the light of faith and knowledge (Q:14:1). The Quran's focus is not on the development of the mind but rather the organic maturation of the disciplined heart as it passes through the channels of gratitude and repentance to reach faith. This is the sound and contrite heart (Q:26:89; 50:33), the aim of the ethical life on earth, foreshadowing the human spirit at peace, about to enter Paradise on the day of immortality (Q:50:34; 89:27–30).

X

Islam is a juristic monotheism which upholds reason as a legitimate source of the Shariah. Reason supervises religious affairs to ensure that no falsehood is attributed to God or his Prophet. Typically, the Prophet and Muslim jurists – not the Quran – give reasons for various prohibitions and discern the purposes behind the scriptural interdictions.

Traditional Islam recognizes no boundary between ritual religious duties and civil law. As Islam becomes a private faith, legal and moral rules must be justified more on rational than on revealed or dogmatic grounds. Take the absolute veto on the consumption of alcohol and other intoxicants, a prohibition that limits Muslim cultural integration into the West and is currently the main reason why Islam is less universally distributed than Christianity. Some entire nations, especially the Russians, would convert instantly to Islam if this absolute prohibition were removed.

The Quran offers several reasons for its absolute ban on drinking alcohol. It is implied to be impure: the vine yields wholesome food (the grape) which the Quran contrasts with the toxic intoxicant derived from it (Q:16:66–7). Drinking alcohol causes social discord, and most importantly, it prevents the remembrance of God at regular times throughout the day. Only a lifestyle of sobriety is compatible with the five separate canonical prayers. (Shiites combine them into three). According to the Prophet's custom, prayers are timed at dawn, early and late afternoon and early and late evening. The Quran forbids believers from approaching prayer while drunk since understanding the words of prayer is a prerequisite of valid prayer (Q:4:43), a condition unfulfilled, incidentally, for (sober) Muslims who do not understand Arabic. The Quran specifies the advantages and disadvantages of consuming intoxicants but reveals that it is, like gambling, on balance more harmful than good (Q:2:219) and therefore discourages it. Alcohol and its pleasures are deferred to heaven (Q:47:15) where there are no social duties or timed prayer requiring absolute punctuality, even during battle (Q:4:101–3).

Alcohol is unique in being forbidden absolutely but in stages. In its final revelation on the subject (see Q:5:90–1), the Quran calls alcohol the Devil's idea and abrogates its own earlier permissive ruling (at Q:2:219). Jurists cite the preservation of one's intellect and the allied moral capacity to fulfill divinely imposed obligations (based on Q:2:286). The ban is imposed absolutely since an intoxicated person would probably violate the other prohibitions. Moreover, someone who begins to become intoxicated is in no position to decide when (or if) he or she will become wholly intoxicated. In Muslim culture, this absolute ban has encouraged a sentimental and romantic attitude towards alcohol, evident in religious and secular poetry and in songs and films glorifying the forbidden spirit.

Purist Muslims believe that insofar as any moral and legal rule derives its authority from God's word, it does not need the support of an appeal to personal and societal benefits of obeying it. There is some Quranic support for this view. The prohibition on hunting game while in pilgrim garb and in holy retreat is admitted to be arbitrary in its content (Q:5:94). To build our character, God tests us to see who fears him in secret. Again, solely as a punishment for their sins, God prohibited Jews from consuming certain intrinsically clean foods (Q:3:93; 6:146) which were permitted to others. Traditionally, grounds for Islamic prohibitions were apologetically specified only when Muslims were challenged by rival monotheists.

Pork is prohibited and the reason indicated: it is filth (*rijs*; Q:6:145).[5] It is forbidden along with blood and carrion (Q:2:173; 5:3), indicating that hygiene was one ground. Believers may consume it if forced to do so; all unlawful foods are permitted in an emergency or under duress (Q:16:115).

For ablutions, the Quran specifies a precise protocol (Q:4:43; 5:6); no reason is given for the performance although removal of physical dirt may be an unstated ground. Since ablutions can be performed symbolically – with wholesome dust (Q:4:43) – the reason need not be solely the removal of dirt (which would require water). More broadly, God loves those who purify themselves (Q:9:108) although this must mean moral and spiritual cleansing. Idolaters are declared unclean (*najas*; Q:9:28). This is an unspecified metaphysical category of impurity which dictates countless ritual, sexual, moral and spiritual laws in the Shariah.

As Islam becomes a faith without legal sanction or enforcement, believers must use their own reason (and conscience) to fortify their resolve. In the case of alcohol, our most widely available and approved drug, opportunities for temptation abound. It is dishonest to pretend, as some Western apologists do, that consuming alcohol is only part of a tolerated sub-culture in the West rather than, as Muslim apologists claim, a ubiquitous and epidemic feature of Western civilization wherever it has spread. There is some exaggeration in the Muslim accusation but it is close to the truth. Let me be autobiographical here. From the age of eight, I was brought up in northern industrial England. I recall that the ratio of mosques to pubs in the Islamic ghetto where I lived was roughly one to ten. There were, in the 1970s, about five pubs for every one church, most of which were Anglican. While parental supervision, social pressure and even fear of violent reprisal might singly or together deter a young Muslim from drinking alcohol, no such restrictions apply when he or she goes to study, for a sustained period of time, in the secular university environment far from home. Reason, fortified by conscience, is the only guide for the perplexed but devout young man or woman away from home.

9   An ethical religion

I

Not all monotheisms are ethical; the earliest variant, associated with the Egyptian ruler Akhenaton,[1] was probably morally lax. God need not, solely in virtue of his numerical uniqueness, be a good being who makes moral demands on his creatures. Once self-qualified as 'ethical', monotheism becomes self-congratulatory; defeated paganisms are summarily judged as unethical. Muslims are merciless editors of their polytheistic past. They repudiated the pre-Islamic era of Arab infidelity as a time of unrelieved uncouthness and ignorance (*al-jāhiliyya*) and, as part of the detoxification of Arabia, they erased the residues of pagan poetry and virtually eliminated the secular poetic canon.[2] This zeal to obliterate the literary past resembles the Roman custom of *damnatio memoriae* (damn the memory), the Orwellian-sounding dictate which authorized the senate to blot out the very names of those, especially emperors, who were posthumously declared enemies of the state. The record of Akhenaton, incidentally, was also scrupulously erased from the Egyptian hieroglyphic chronicles because his short-lived and rudimentary monotheism proved an affront to orthodoxy.

The Quran condemned the ostentatious behaviour of Arab pagan men and women. It warned the Prophet's wives and other Muslim women to abjure lubricity, the wanton display of beauty (*tabarruj*; Q:33:33; 24:60), popular in pre-Islamic Arabia.[3] The Quran mocks pagan warriors who 'march boastfully to battle' (Q:8:47) and links such conceit to the Devil's ability to beautify ugly and vain realities and thus distract and mislead disbelievers (Q:8:48). This holy God was offended by those actions which were performed merely 'to be seen of men' (Q:8:47) or motivated by that pagan self-regard which the Quran condemns as anarchic and pretentious (Q:48:26). The Islamic scripture's notion of virtue was in content, though not, as we see presently, in mood, dramatically opposed to the disbelievers' reckless bravado and ostentatious courage. The Quran extolled meticulous[4] prudence, the linguistic meaning of *taqwā* (piety). The Greeks too valued prudence as the master virtue that enabled the virtues of justice, fortitude and temperance (self-discipline). Prudence, in both cases, was not caution but rather the practical wisdom that enabled one to recognize what is right and to choose it. And that required courage.

Courageous virility (*muru'ah*), not a Quranic term, was already indelibly imprinted on the pagan heart. Inveterate Arab traditions of chivalry demanded the single outrageous gesture, some act of magnanimity or machismo or spectacular generosity in which the hero squandered the accumulated wealth of a life-time or even his life. In that unique act, he yearned to be seen by the crowd. Armed with their pens, the poets eulogized it with ebullience and hyperbole. The third (final) part of the Islamic ode praised the tribe's magnanimous (large-minded) men, the heroes with *megalopsychia* in Aristotle's idiom.[5] Meanwhile, among the pusillanimous (small-minded) men was the *bakhīl*, the stingy one, a serious insult for a tribal chief expected to be generous and hospitable even to enemies. The Quran links salvation with freedom from miserliness (Q:59:9), a vice virtually innate to humanity (Q:17:100) and particularly marked among hypocrites (Q:33:19). The earliest revelations prohibit hoarding and note that it cannot make the pagan immortal (Q:104:1–4).

Despite its demand for prudence, Islam had its own dramatic and glamorous act albeit in the cause of virtue defined as awareness of God's sovereign's rights over humanity. It was self-sacrifice (martyrdom) for God's sake, a spectacular way to make good one's confession of self-surrender to his will. Tradition cites 21 ways of attaining martyrdom, among which a popular one is death caused by the rigours of the pilgrimage to Mecca. Ardent believers see martyrdom as their golden fleece; its pursuit finds firm and constant Quranic support (see Q:3:169–71; 9:111).

Muhammad's companions eagerly sought reassurances from him that they would achieve martyrdom. One companion, known by his patronym and title Abu Ayyub Al-Ansari (*c.* 576–674), fought countless campaigns until he participated in but fell fatally ill during an unsuccessful siege of Constantinople in 674. He was almost 100 years old when he achieved martyrdom. His mosque still stands in modern Istanbul and many pious Ottomans are buried in its proximity. One enthusiastic sect interpreted literally the promise that God, like a merchant, bought the believers' selves and goods in exchange for Paradise (based on Q:9:111). These were *Al-Mushtarūn*, the bought or forfeited ones. It was a good bargain since the believer bartered temporal and finite goods in exchange for the everlasting bliss of eternal life. It is a version of Pascal's wager and is weakened by similar objections – principally, the atheist rejoinder that the choices to be made rationally in this life are not restricted to 'Paradise or extinction' and 'Hell or extinction'.

While extolling martyrdom, the Quran despised the martial aura of internecine and continuous tribal violence epitomized in the indiscriminate blood-feud. As a concession to its tribal context, it sanctioned proportional restitution or reparation (*al-qiṣāṣ*; Q:2:178–9), a provision resembling the law of equality (*lex talionis*) but often incorrectly translated as retaliation. The Quranic ordinance applied only to intentional murder, not to manslaughter, and even then mitigation, via forgiveness, was encouraged (Q:5:45; cf. Q:5:32; for manslaughter, see Q:4:92–3). It limited the reach of the vendetta by encouraging unilateral pardon: letting vengeance belong wholly to God cut the endless cycles of carnage. But revenge within just reason was recognized as a human prerogative. The Quran issued no absolute commandment of non-violence; nor did it endorse any permanent sanctification of a state of peace or spiritual poverty (see Matthew 5:3–12). Islam is too pragmatic a faith to demand what is possible only for saints. Instead of the beatitudes, Islam aimed merely to anneal justice and mercy.

II

In this chapter, we note the emergence of Islamic ethics against its pagan background and discern the evolution of Meccan moral maxims into legal imperatives in Medina. With the advent of colonial modernity and Muslim decline, we note the opposite process whereby law is transformed into ethics: an empowered, formerly imperial, faith evolves into a voluntary private faith. Islam as religion quarantined in the private sector engages us in the next chapter. The objective and coercive externality of the Shariah, reflecting a divinely willed moral order, is replaced in Western cultures by an appeal to the intrinsic objectivity (or at least shared subjectivity) of ethical concepts such as justice and duty. This stance is fair enough but, like other theists, Muslims must reject the false humility in the more aggressively secular claim that that there is no moral truth and that nobody can aim for it. Islamic ethics are only possible on the assumption that moral truth is not merely, post-modernist cynics notwithstanding, the safest lie. Such epistemological cynicism leads to moral cynicism and hence injustice.

While one cannot coherently privatize a code of law, one can extract the independent ethical foundations of a law. In effect, we do so by removing the legal sanctions and penalities for unethical conduct. This is the converse of the (incoherent) notion of 'legalizing' intrinsically moral rules, such as those found in the New Testament (see Matthew 5:1–7:5) or embedded in the Quran's voluntary directives to mutual kindness and good manners (Q:2:263–4; 24:27–8; 49:11–12). Moral duties cannot be entirely enforced by law without losing their primarily ethical status.

Al-akhlāq (ethics) is the plural of *khuluq*, a word found only once in the Quran (Q:68:4). Possibly related to *khalq* (creation), it means character, something made or stamped. 'Ethics' comes from the Greek *ethikōs*; the Latin *mores* yields our word morality. All three are plural nouns, a linguistic hint about their communal significance: the correctness of customs derives from their social acceptance. Classical nomenclature conceals conservative undertones that suggest that morality is derived from a distrust of anarchic individuality.

Most of the Quran's ethical imperatives were later formalized into social custom and law at Medina although there was neither a police force nor army, only the Prophet's charismatic example and the believing community's subtle collective pressure urging conformity. For many Muslims today, Islam is an exclusively ethical religion since few believers are obliged by state sanction to live on a strict plane of ritual duty. This stage marks the de-politicization and secularization of Islamic imperatives, processes understood sociologically, though not judgmentally, as loss of regard for religiously authorized law enforcement. Originally, Meccan ethics solidified into law in Medina; the laws of Medina have now softened, for most Muslims, into purely ethical counsel. Thus, for example, the establishment of canonical prayer is now largely voluntary and private although some modern theocracies, like all early Islamic states, formally enforce it.

What makes an ethical system Islamic? Ethics became Islamic when norms of conduct derived their authority from the Quran or from the example of Muhammad, the recipient, bearer and interpreter of the Quran and first executive director of the social charter inspired by it. The link with Muhammad also explains why Islamic ethics is comprehensive enough to render artificial the distinctions between positive law, private morals and etiquette. Ethics can cover areas classed as mere etiquette in other belief systems because the authoritative basis of Islamic ethics is Muhammad's personality as God's apostle. This basis is broader than the authority of any book or legal system or precedent. Muhammad, as prophet, received God's immense grace (Q:4:113; 17:87; 33:21, 46, 56; 68:4) and thus became an excellent exemplar (Q:33:21). Imitation of his actions is a morally praiseworthy act independent of the contents of the action. Muslims classify as meritorious such neutral behaviour as drinking a glass of water by punctuating it with three pauses: Muhammad drank it in this way on the eve of a journey. Again, Muslims think they earn merit by, for example, refusing to use furniture since a secure hadith (reporting an omission) records a narrator saying baldly: 'I never saw the Messenger of God sitting at a table.'

The imitation of Muhammad makes sense since the quest for the historical Muhammad is no flight of fancy. Indeed Muslim reformers may regret that we know too much of his life and actions. In traditional lands, the result is a mental paralysis and an incubus on novel departures. If a narrative (hadith) about Muhammad's actions or beliefs is authentic, no dispute about the authority of its content can arise. If its content is moral, the believer tries to implement it; if legal, the believer is required to abide by it. Judging the Prophet's action, no less than judging the Quran, would be anathema.

There are naturally limits to this emulation of the Prophet since no-one can imitate his prophetic role. And many rightly doubt if they can achieve his level of piety. According to popular adoration, God created Muhammad out of special dust (or clay). The angels asked for further use of this clay in creating more human beings of exalted character. God answered that the clay was no longer in divine stock: all was used in the creation of one extraordinary man.

III

Muslims rarely distinguish ethics from holy law and neither from etiquette (*adāb*) and good manners. Two Islamic neo-Platonists, Abu Nasr Al-Farabi (d. 950) and Abu Al-Miskawayh (d. 1030), treated ethics as distinct from law. Both elevated Greek ethics to axiomatic status and then located Islamic equivalents for various virtues.[6] Unlike Islamic jurisprudence, the stimulus for writing ethical disquisitions was external to Islam. Most Muslims have never heard of these works and yet they would gladly purchase a multi-volume Quranic exegetical extravaganza or a voluminous legal compendium, both items displayed and sold in local markets in the Muslim world. Some believers would dismiss these ethical works since the Quran pre-empted the need for such manuals. Moreover, Greek ethics was secular, based on merit, with no room for grace. Islamic ethics, despite acknowledging grace as fundamental, are works-based. Its chief category is meritorious reward (*thawāb*; Q:28:80) calculated by using a calculus of the value of good deeds; detailed algorithms are supplied by the voluminous hadith literature. This concrete reference to quantifiable merit replaces a theoretical appeal to grace although God's gracious enablement of virtue remains a prerequisite of achieving it.

We must do the right thing and be on the right side. The dilemmas of duty and tragedy, which make both of two freely chosen actions equally wrong or equally right, are foreign to the Shariah. Islam does not recognize tragedy and has no word for it. The closest we get to it is the choice of the lesser of two evils (*akhaff al-ḍararayn*), a principle derived from the Quran: God prohibits Muslims from swearing at the idols of the idolaters in case the idolaters retaliate by swearing at God (Q:6:108), a greater evil that must be prevented. Some Muslim jurists see violent struggle against injustice as the lesser of two evils, a 'cruel necessity', to use Oliver Cromwell's verdict on seeing the corpse of King Charles I. Muslim radicals see it as a 'kind necessity' since defeating inequity is part of the prophetic representation of God as the merciful but just lord of requital.

Muslim jurists differentiate major from minor sins and both from moral trifles or peccadilloes (*al-lamam*; Q:53:32). Persistence in any minor sin is a major sin (Q:3:135). And sins committed by children, before they attain legal majority, are charged to their parents' account. Summaries of moral teachings occur in Meccan and Medinan chapters (see Q:2:177, 17:22–39, 23:1–11; 25:63–76, 31:12–19; 42:36–43; 51:15–19; 70:23–35). The content of Islamic morality is mainly original but, naturally for a reformist faith, some elements are simply a repudiation of existing pagan rules (see Q:17:26–7, 31). The scripture outlawed female infanticide (Q:81:8–9; see also 17:31; 16:58–9) and prohibited sacrifice of children at the altar (Q:6:137, 140), actions partly motivated by fear of poverty and famine (Q:17:31).

The Quran constantly commends and commands justice and kindness and outlaws evil (Q:16:90). It demands honesty, fidelity, patience and the honouring of oaths and promises (Q:16:90–1). The Meccan Code (Q:17:22–38) opens with the worship of one God followed by kindness to parents, giving in charity to the poor, and moderation in spending. It prohibits adultery, unjust killing, robbing orphans' property and cheating in trade. These laws correspond to the parts of the Decalogue (Exodus 20:1–21) minus the Sabbath observance which is mentioned in the Quran as binding only on Jews but not observed properly by them (Q:2:65; 7:163; 16:124). God did not tire of creation and took no rest (Q:2:255; 50:15, 38). Medinan passages alert us to the sin of believing false reports (Q:49:6) and giving false testimony (Q:2:283; 5:106–8). One Medinan verse commends restraint of anger and forgiveness of enemies (Q:3:134).

Vices include back-biting, gossip, slander and boastful behaviour (Q:49:11-12). The root cause is pride (*takabbur*), the sin known as hubris and *superbia* to the Greeks and Romans respectively. It was Satan's original sin (Q:7:13; 38:71–83). God does not love the arrogant or boastful (Q:31:18), a message captured in the

Talmud where God says of the proud man, 'He and I cannot dwell in the [same] world'.[7] For Muslims, humility includes humility in worship (*khushū'*; Q:2:45).

The earliest revelations excoriate our inordinate love of wealth (Q:100:8) and would concur with the New Testament that the worship of *māmōn* – Aramaic for the god of wealth (Matthew 6:24) – is the root of many evils for he is an only and jealous God. Greed and avarice motivate the callous and hypocritical denial of the rights of slaves and widows, the refusal to feed 'the orphan kinsman on a day of great privation' (Q:90:14–5) and the rejection of even 'a small act of neighbourly kindness' (Q:107:7). The Quran often urges charitable spending and urges believers to make a good bargain by lending God a 'good loan', on spiritual interest, as a corrective to the rapacious interest rates of usury (see Q:2:245, 261, 275–6). Both as *ṣadaqah* (voluntary charity) and as the obligatory alms called *zakāt* (meaning purification), charity is a social virtue central to the Quran's teachings. All wealth is unlawful until it has been cleansed by payment of the *zakāt*. Islam shares with Judaism this stress on charity. In the Talmud, charity is extolled as '*the* mitzvah', equal to all other mitzvot combined.[8] The charitable actions of Jews even hasten on the advent of messianic redemption.[9]

Finally, to complete our survey of the scope of Islamic ethics, some Islamic injunctions coincide with the wisdom literature recognized by the ancient Arabs. Luqman, a sage unknown to Jewish scripture, has a Quranic chapter named in his honour. The Luqman pericope (Q:31:12–19) is in the genre of the Persian 'paternal admonition' (Farsi: *pand-e-pider*) and resembles the book of Proverbs (*Mishle*). A virtuous and anxious father imparts wisdom to the young, giving counsel for living a good life in an evil world. Luqman tells his son to be grateful to God and not to associate partners with him. The dialogue is then suddenly interrupted, out of modesty, when God himself intervenes to advise the listener to honour parents (Q:31:14–15). Luqman resumes his speech to his son by commenting on God's subtle ability to illuminate matters that are craftily concealed. He concludes with the advice that a true believer must persist in patience and prayer and avoid ignorance and its twin sister pride which is often exhibited in loud speech, a trait associated with the donkey (Q:31:19).

IV

Islamic sexual ethics need a brief separate treatment. In the Quran, lust or desire (*hawā*, Q:45:23; *shahawāt*, pl. at Q:3:14) is more than an emotion or irresistible drive. It is a social force with anarchic potential for the communal fabric, hence the severe penalties for sexual transgressions. The Latin *lustus* similarly means any overwhelming emotion of which sexual passion is the best example, with anger a close second. Men are required to control their sexual prowess ('*irbah*; Q:24:31) but women must do their best not to cause male desire. In the charged sexual realism of the Quran and the Prophet's life, we note a frank recognition of the power of an inconveniently strong sex drive which distracts us from performing our religious duties.

The Quran is concerned to ensure that society is sexually healthy, given neither to excess nor to monasticism. Men and women are confidants and confidantes who console one another (Q:3:195; 9:71). Most Quranic injunctions impose limits on male excesses towards women, abuses such as inheriting widows against their will or denying them their inheritance or preventing divorced women from remarrying (Q:2:231–2; 4:19; 65:1–7). Only a few verses impose (paternalistic) restrictions on women's behaviour (Q2:228; 24:31; 33:59). It is a far cry from the Taliban's ban on loud female laughter and on wearing shoes with heels, their clicking sound giving advance warning of a terrifying female presence.

Feminists would argue, with some reason, that the Quran treats women as juveniles since they, like children and orphans, need to be saved and protected. Women need not worry about financial matters. Is that kindness or condescension? Certainly, Islam allowed women to inherit wealth but discouraged them to earn an income. A woman may, independently of her male relatives and husband, own property. Moreover, the Quran recognized women as legal persons with the right to give testimony. That was a revolutionary reform without precedent in ancient cultures.

Western feminists note the upward sexual mobility of Indian and other Asian women, seen as exotic and alluring and thus able to attact westernized and white partners. Many see Muslim women as oppressed and trapped in cultures where the demand for modesty is a second veil, hence the proverb, 'the eyes are the first veil'. Muslim women are, however, generally assured of marriage and a home within their own cultures and thus spared the humiliations of the free market search for love and romance which fuels the gender war in the West.

Islamic society is certainly under male leadership although Muslim women have played a role in Islamic history. Some served in auxiliary roles in the Prophet's army. The widowed Aisha led an army though she later regretted that decision since it contradicted a Quranic directive (see Q:33:33). Umar, as caliph, was once corrected by a female believer inside a mosque though admittedly only on a minor question of dowry stipulation affirmed in the Quran. The scripture mentions only one female ruler, the Queen of Sheba, and does so without adverse comment about her rule, condemning only her idolatry. When she criticizes (male) kingship (Q:27:34), the Quran makes no comment on her disapproval.

In a society under male leadership, women become particularly powerful on the domestic front. A wife is affectionately called 'lady (lit., lord, feminine form) of the house' (*rabbatu al-bayt*). As in Orthodox Judaism, women often control events behind the domestic scenes although Jewish wives are far more self-assured and dominant than their Muslim counterparts. As in Judaism, however, sexual satisfaction is a wife's right. Some Orthodox Jews and Muslims report that devout wives, happily married to observant men, exhibit a voracious, virtually insatiable sexual appetite. The Quran affirms sexuality as a delight but tactfully places it next to piety in the verse that permits sexual adventure and variety but only inside marriage as part of male initiative (Q:2:223).

Although family life and children are among the signs of God's favour, the Quran cautions believers that these can obstruct the pursuit of righteousness. No kinship, whether of family or tribe or matrimony, ought to obstruct the course of piety, a revolutionary view in a society in which even one's survival depended on tribal belonging and solidarity. The Quran once calls wives and children 'enemies' of the God-fearing; along with wealth, one's offspring is only a trial and temptation (*fitnah*; Q:64:14–15). Family life is a temptation if it discourages the believer from jihad (see Q:8:28). God cautions believers that children and wealth distract believers from their duty to God. Such Quranic injunctions (Q:9:23, 113–4; 60:1–4, 13) are not as harsh as directives in the New Testament where Jesus rejects his family of biological origin in favour of his disciples who seek the kingdom of heaven (Luke 8:19–21). Compare Paul's similar views (1 Corinthians 7:1–11, 29–40). Muslims would regard as extreme the verdict that true allegiance to God requires one to love him more than your own family (Luke 14:26). Again, Muslims find it disturbing to see Prince Siddartha Gautama abandoning his son Rahula since the little boy was allegedly an obstacle to enlightenment.

Despite the stress on our communal and social nature, the bonds of lineage and matrimony will dissolve in the face of divine judgment (Q:23:101; 25:54; 80:33–7). This was more shocking to Muhammad's audience than to us moderns since such bonds now hardly exist even in this life. The day of judgment becomes 'the day of mutual disillusionment' (Q:64:9) when sinners finally recognize the fragility and futility of human connections as though one had finally outgrown people and relationships, much as a teenage boy outgrows stamp-collecting. It is the day of decisive parting of the good and the evil just as the Quran is the decisive word (Q:86:13) separating truth from falsehood.

V

In this hiatus, we note the foundations of Islamic ethics in the Quran's protology, its doctrine of first realities. The contemplation of our latent nature, our self-experience, ineluctably leads to God. Humans are created as the zenith of creation, with uniquely human endowments of conscience and reason. The angels and animals reflect splendour and innocence respectively while plants signify simplicity. But all of these are subordinate to humanity for we alone are able to choose to do God's will on earth. Our human gifts, along with the prophetology that provides tuition and the eschatology that threatens sanctions, should enable virtue to triumph individually and socially. A bitter caveat must however intervene: God created humankind with a limited capacity for self-mastery.

God equipped human nature with (innate) ethical and rational dispositions so that human beings can abide by the sacred law. In this creation of original righteousness, God 'created humankind in the best of moulds' (Q:95:4). But, in Islam, as in Judaism, the good inclination (Hebrew: *yetzer ha-tōv*) combats the evil one (*yetzer ha-rā*). Muslim theology eulogizes human beings as the apex of divine creativity, custodians of the green earth and benevolent imperialists appointed to harness nature (Q:14:32–3; 43:12–13; 45:4, 12–13; 67:15). Since God breathed his spirit into Adam (Q:15:29; 32:9; 38:72), our endowment is divine though we remain *species humana*, a more modest self-description than the falsely self-congratulatory *Homo sapiens* (wise man).

How much of our natural endowment need we retain if we have God's spirit in us? While no robust divinity is immanent in our humanity, there is no purely human nature either since God is the subject hiding in and behind it. Since God is the light of the heavens and the earth (Q:24:35), every believer proclaims: *Lucem sequimur* (we follow the [divine] light; see Q:57:12–3).

Human beings must worship the God who only created them to worship him (Q:51:56–7) and to show him 'which among them is the best in conduct' (Q:18:7). God tests us to try our moral mettle (Q:21:35; 67:2; 76:2). The Quran stresses the morally serious purpose that motivated our creation (Q:6:70, 7:51; 21:16–17; 38:27; 44:38–9; 45:22; 67:2). God informs the pagans that the creation was neither pointless nor done for divine self-amusement (Q:3:191; 21:16–17; 23:115; 38:27; 44:38). Apart from Sufis and members of apolitical (progressive) Islamic sects, both of whom emphasize the aesthetic grounds of creation, all other Muslims register the primacy of the moral stress.

Some groups, especially the Salafis, Islam's self-appointed puritans, go to extremes by abjuring laughter and humour, insisting on constant repentance and remorseful weeping (based on Q:53:56–62). Many are suspicious of all beauty and decoration, even rejecting the ornate recitation of the Quran. Acknowledging that much frivolity is committed through the tongue, a view shared by James (James 3) who threatened stricter punishment for teachers and orators, some Muslim saints placed pebbles in their mouths to disable impetuous speech. The view that speech, like wine, intoxicates, was popular with some Sufis. 'He who keeps silent shall be saved' was attributed to Muhammad. The Quran emphasizes that pure speech is a feature of Paradise (Q:22:24). The blessed constantly hear divine praise and the salutation of peace (Q:14:23; 39:73–4). It commends sincere, just, truthful and kind speech on earth (Q:4:9; 17:53), especially to parents (Q:17:23). It condemns idle and boastful speech, gossip and argumentativeness (Q:2:197). The Companions of the Garden will hear no sinful, vain or false talk (Q:78:35; 88:11) while the sinners in Hell will wrangle and loudly accuse one another, the late arrivals the earlier ones, the weak the strong (Q:7:38–9; 14:21; 40:46–50).

While Muslims did not practise the spectacular variety of torments and self-mortifications of the flesh popular among Christian ascetics, they indulged in long prostrations and excessive fasting. Despite being more God-fearing than any of his followers, Muhammad enjoyed with wholesome zest the permitted pleasures while abstaining from excess. To Muhammad, the Christian view of pleasure must have appeared morose, mawkish and atrabilious.

Islamic morals are not, by religious standards, austere. Christian monks denied themselves even any vision of the beauty of the landscape and took refuge in barren places and deserts just as the Jain ascetics in India wore no clothes as a protest against the pride and comfort clothing gives to the naked body. Unlike these ascetic faiths, Islamic principles are, by contrast, rather secular, pragmatic and relaxed. Contemplative Islam, in heterodox mystical form, commends asceticism and solemn solitude while mainstream Islam merely steers believers between a tragic gravitas and a comic levitas.

VI

What are the eschatological (theological) foundations of Islamic ethics? A post-mortem chronology of supernatural events – called *maghībāt* (mysteries) – of the Garden and the Fire are allied to an apocalypse of the hour and the final day to render urgent the ethical outlook. The neologism *amām* (Q:75:5) denotes the portion of the future left for virtue as life decreases each day. Like Joseph's brothers, sinners take no thought for the morrow: after leaving Joseph for dead, they assure themselves that there will still be plenty of time to be 'a righteous people' (Q:12:9). The Quran advises us to be constantly alert to what we send forward for our souls for the morrow (Q:59:18). Some commentators explain 'the chain of 70 cubits' which sinners carry in Hell (Q:69:32) as symbolizing the seven decades of sin that comprise the average life-time. The Quran's moral system honours the irreparability of the creature's actions set in time's irreversibility. Underlying eschatology and ethics is the conviction that 'the sequel is only for righteousness' (Q:20:132) since evil-doers can never triumph (Q:12:23) and have no patrons (Q:47:11). The requital for goodness is inevitably either goodness or something better in the next life (Q:16:30; 39:10; 55:60).

A Meccan revelation (Q:90:1–20) typically weaves this ethical message with the Quran's expressive eschatology:

vv. 1–4 oaths, protology;
vv. 5–7 hubris attacked as an obstacle to the moral life;
vv. 8–10 divinely endowed human capacity for goodness and evil;
vv. 11–12 the ascent of man: the moral struggle;
vv. 13–16 ethical duties;
vv. 17–20 ethical eschatology: eternal consequences of mortal moral life.

The Quran subtly spurns the worldly life by calling it *al-dunyā* (the near or 'low life') which is easy to attain; only fools prefer this life to the enduring next life (Q:79:37–9; see also Q:29:64; 47:36). The Quran degrades this material life as transient and deceptive (Q:6:130; 13:26; 42:36; 17:18; 75:20; 76:27), as frivolous and falsely glamorous (Q:3:185; 6:32; 20:131; 28:60; 47:36; 57:20) and 'amusement and play and mutual rivalry in wealth and children' (Q:34:37; 102:1–2). We have a fixed lease on physical life in this lower world where we are placed on probation before death enables us to enter the permanent life. Death is neither a mystery nor a tragedy, only a preface to a state of immortality.

We can enter the higher life (*al-ākhirah*, the later or last one) only through constant and sincere struggle in God's path in this lower world. We must place our prudential fear of God above our natural desires for lavish wealth, above concern for business interests and property (Q:9:24), above gold, silver, horses of pedigree, cattle and fertile lands (Q:Q:3:14–15; 9:24), the last two being the measure of wealth in the pre-industrial age. Devout believers rise above the distractions of material possessions, family, spouse and progeny, especially sons (Q:58:22; 63:9; 64:14–15; 74:12–13), above the lure of illicit sexual pleasure, sensual comfort, above the lawless wish for freedom from divinely imposed restraints (Q:9:24; 75:36; 96:6–8).

Only a minority shall inherit the reward of the next world (Q:12:90; 28:80). Like Jacob and Muhammad, they must show 'beautiful patience' (see Q:12:18, 83; 73:10) and constant gratitude. Confident of the perfect alignment of virtue with reward in both worlds (Q:12:23; 19:76; 39:10), the Quran consistently, persistently, and confidently emphasizes the unbreakable link between doing good (works) and believing in the good (faith). The despair of many modern people is captured by the Artful Dodger in Charles Dickens' *Oliver Twist*: 'This ain't the shop for justice.' This urban lament echoes an ancient voice whose pedigree is biblical: upright Job in the whirlwind. Islam, however, with its confident and ethically effective eschatology, offers a convincing hope of final justice both for people of virtue and for those who are enemies of the human race.

The Quran calls death an inescapable certainty (Q:4:78). Funerary decoration is an undeveloped art in Islamic cultures. Simple graves mark the spot where, in the Prophet's bitter words, 'The son of Adam is content only when his mouth is finally closed with sand.' One can lighten this sentiment by adding that an epitaph such as 'A virtuous man and an oil sheikh lie buried here' would make non-Muslims wonder whether Muslims bury two to a grave!

The Hajj, the fifth pillar of Islam is optional since it is a duty owed to God and thus to be fulfilled once all worldly duties have been discharged. Yet it is spiritually the most basic pillar. Performed during the first third of the final month of the lunar calendar, it absolves any adult male or female Muslim of his or her accumulated wrongdoings. As the pilgrim packs for the journey, he is made aware of the futility of possessions: his worldly needs, including his two shroud-like white sheets, can be fitted into a small bag. The best provision for this long journey is the apparel of piety.

VII

For the rest of this chapter, I shall discuss the role of morals in society and the cultural politics undergirding it. We note the Muslim stance on the malaise of a secular society. These few sections may appear somewhat more ideological, even polemical, than is normal in an academic work.

Islam is an ethical project for transforming societies so that they can produce men and women of character – a Nietzschean programme, only more practical. In the Quran's typology, Pharaonic societies supply 'exemplars who invite to the Fire' (Q:28:41). The Pharaonic culture is the ignorant (*jāhilli*) society Muhammad encountered in Mecca and, centuries later, Qutb faced in modern Egypt. Khomeini preferred the adjective *ṭāghūtī* (rebellious), derived from one of the Devil's titles (Q:4:51; 39:17). If we forget God, he will cause us to forget our true selves (Q:59:18–20). The generic human defect is, despite Islam's social character, self-injustice (*ẓulm al-nafs*). This is the sin of wronging oneself through treachery to one's original higher nature.

The believer is in charge of himself and no-one can mislead him (Q:5:105). This stress on the believer's solitary stance as guided individual is related to the pursuit of character. Other people can seduce us from implementing noble ideals. Most of us yearn for attention, to be known widely but not intimately. We crave fame – the compulsion to live to impress strangers. Anonymity is anathema. The wise man or woman knows that *vita privata, vita beata* (private life, happy life). The laughter from a crowd of strangers is a drug taken by comedians; it keeps them young at heart. But all artists, serious or humorous, old and young, must return to a lonely room after the concert and the kudos of performance, after the transient thrill of the public gaze subsides: a thousand people staring with two thousand eyes. Even academics hanker for awards from colleagues in an intellectual version of a beauty contest. Its vulgarity does not strike them since they think the life of the mind is automatically noble and forget that character consists, as the Greeks knew, in deserving rather than possessing honours. Today often only the terminally ill and those awoken suddenly by turbulence in an aircraft register the vulnerability of our humanity in our unadorned state. Even they discern all too late the vanity of praise, the futility of our ambitions. And the young do not fear death at all thinking only the ripe apple will fall.

Being ordinary is no easier than being extraordinary. We need to be disabused of the false glamour of the imbalanced genius who has allegedly risen above the human predicament. Achievement without fame is commonplace. Fame without moral achievement is the life of most celebrities whose magnified ambitions are only hiding-places and props. Character relates not to the office but to the man himself – the human capital. Sadly, we no longer have artists, only stars. Most modern men and women pursue them thinking that they are remote and light-giving when in fact many are grounded on earth, with many personal problems to deal with. In the case of American celebrities, the result is one nation under therapy.

An inner fascism makes us slaves of the self via the market with its samsara cycle of endless desires which people take to be the result of free choice but which are designed for them by media and corporation executives. You must have a beautiful and preferably youthful body to be taken seriously. Most societies are now somatically fascist, shamelessly promoting the pursuit of the elixir of youth while showering contempt on the old and disabled. The body controls the whole person.

In such a world, secular humanism collapses into a misanthropic and cynical secularism, sceptical of all meaning, a harbinger of despair, ready to accept moral depravity under the guise of art. Nor can literature, notwithstanding the conceit of writers, console us for the pain of life and life sets us all up for some suffering. Formerly Christian nations have many inconsolable victims, pigeon-holed by the state, separated from each other by class, race and gender and wrapped in plural solitudes.

Despite the progressive humanization of religions, the alienation, division and violence of modern cultures distinguish our age. In advanced capitalist nations such as America, Japan, South Korea and India, people confuse moral value with material wealth as they make deals, not friends. The alienation caused by industrial capitalism gives us many products but destroys the human capital of its producers.

Nor is there any escape from this predicament. Many are lured by the myth that in the Catholic Americas in the southern hemisphere, we shall see the next epicentre of a practised Christianity. In fact, these nations are increasingly animated by national fanaticisms, for example, about football and sensuality.

VIII

Muslim critics, living in Muslim lands, note the desperate decadence and increasing vulgarity and frivolity of Western societies, the collapse of the family, the widening use of alcohol and pornography from subculture to mainstream culture, amid an undeclared civil war between the genders and the races. The cultural and moral deterioration of society is noted and lamented but not reversed or cured by secular critics of secular culture. People are atomized, alienated, even solipsistic, in their world of delusions, fed by internet messages and false bonding with others. In the uniquely isolating alienation of advanced capitalism, even sober individuals experience only the personal life while merely observing the social one. Contemporary Christianity no longer supplies the spiritual and moral, let alone political and legal foundations of Western secularized cultures. In no way does it challenge society's coarse laicity and capitalist vulgarization. By contrast, Islam offers to confront metaphysical secularism and its children: moral relativism and nihilism, excessive hedonism and self-absorbed indifferentism.

How does one eliminate the need for love and mutuality, two harbingers of vulnerability? Once post-Christian human nature has mutated into an alienating coarseness and coldness, sex is for recreation and self-assertion, not for procreation or bonding. How does one find love in such a world? Masturbation relieves temporarily the pressure of lust on the human frame. But there is no such release for the pressures of love and conscience. What do I live for? Whom do I live for? Do we live for ideas and ideals or for other people? Westerners find that they live in societies where neither faith nor love is possible to find. A fanatical notion of absolute personal freedom prevents even friendship since this relationship, universally valued as an antidote to the poisonous side of marital and domestic life,[10] creates expectations and loyalty and therefore limits freedom and is therefore unacceptable.

In late capitalism, for most people, all human possibility is distilled into a purely *economic* dream of freedom. This freedom is in fact an escape from human commitment and thus produces an impoverishment in human capital in the midst of material abundance. We are consumers, not human beings. Such a vision must not become our future: we must take the world back from Mammon, an only God, and reclaim it for an ethical vision that must be grounded in God.

We can conceal our condition – as a vain woman can hide her pregnancy or a terminally ill man denies his cancer. But we can never escape from our condition of suffering, sin, guilt and mortality. We have more leisure today but we spend it in the pursuit of hedonism, not spirituality. Sexual fantasy consumes much time as the video, DVD and internet formats make leisure, frivolity and pornography widely available. Technical time-saving gadgets were meant to liberate housewives for a higher function, not for making more time to watch afternoon soap operas fixated on glamorous sex lives. Religious thinkers join existentialists in critiquing the ethical implications of the spectacular triumph of a *techne* which represents a self-aggrandizing and therefore sinful intervention into an order that was created to be teleological, not technological. Technology opposes natural order and purpose and competes with the unassertive beauties of a divinely crafted nature.

IX

The Western humanism which matured with the rejection of Christianity was an exclusively and self-sufficiently secular one. Its goal was to ensure the flourishing of humans as purely rational, physical and biological beings. Theism is, according to new atheist critics, irrational and its imperatives are immoral. The focus shifts to the immoral consequences of faith as opposed to proving that there is no God. Believers must therefore now show that atheism is not merely false or irrational but rather that it lacks a stable and persuasive basis for doing good things and being good people. Atheists often disguise their failings through an ostentatious intellectual conceit.

The new atheists mock faith as a basis for morals. If God recommends an action because it is good, the divine commendation is superfluous: the action is morally right independently of God's authorization. And if an action is good solely because God recommends it, then we have left the arena of morality for that of authority. The Quran implicitly rejects this dilemma by making God the creator of a moral order that is objectively present in creation. It eulogizes it as the truth (*al-ḥaqq*; Q:47:3) from God; the world is created in truth (*bi al-ḥaqq*; Q:14:19; 30:18) with God himself as The Truth (*al-ḥaqq*; Q:22:6, 62). The moral order is thus guaranteed to be objective, real, just and complete, and readily discernible by humans who train themselves in the art of piety.

Atheists argue that religion, no matter how sophisticated and evolved, is indistinguishable from the crude superstition that proceeds from fear and produces in turn more irrational fear. The real reductionist fanaticism of modern life, however, is in the victory of capitalism which demands that everything reduce its value to the quantitative measure of money just as the ideology of scientism pontificates that all truth is reducible to the results discovered by the mechanisms science uniquely elucidates. The antique project of finding a short-cut to heaven, the biblical myth of the tower of Babel, is now replaced by the hubristic and utopian scheme of building heaven on earth through the social and political engineering of happiness. These were the supremely rational tasks emerging out of the European Enlightenment. Have we, however, built Hell where Heaven should have been built?

Many moderns complain that God begrudges human strength and self-reliance. Why should the highest religious virtues be identified with passive obedience to his will? We must kill such a demanding and autocratic God in order to be fully human. Marxism, secular humanism and existentialism together preach this dogma. Absolute human power is the key to human liberation. Human self-affirmation and autonomy leave no room for God. Marx rejects religion for the sake of economic redemption while Freud slays the divine father-figure for the sake of psychological liberation from sexual repression. Sartre joins Nietzsche in proclaiming absolute human autonomy for the sake of artistic and cultural freedom.

There was much morally serious indignation in the explicit atheism of Freud and Nietzsche, in the humanistic atheism of Feuerbach and Marx inspired by their moral and political idealism, and in the science-inspired atheism of Freud and Russell. The rational defence and the rational repudiation of religious faith are equally arduous. Traditional doubt, however, has now been replaced by a shallow atheism whose adherents are addicted to sensationalist and combative journalism.[11] The superficially clever and flamboyant erudition of the polemical atheists is allied to their conceit that they stand, in ecstasy, on mountains higher than Sinai and Hira, inebriated on science and evolutionary biology, the opiate of the intellectuals.[12]

X

In the West, humanism is seen as exclusively secular since it initially emerged in opposition to religion. There is no reason to extrapolate this into a universal pattern of history. We have reached a stage when ethical monotheism must re-emerge as the only humanism which can refute that counterfeit humanism contained in the modern consciousness of the world: an empty subjectivity cynical about objective meaning and moral purpose, frequently depressed by the inevitability of suffering, loss and death, and constantly in need of humour, irony and drugs to conceal its vast pain.

The Quran aims at freedom *from* the self, not freedom *of* the self. The latter is an illusion. To attain complete freedom, we need outer freedom from social constraints and inner freedom from forces agitating our personalities. The divinely ordained and imposed meaning of life is humiliating only if we forget that an inner force that imposes its will on us is no less humiliating simply because it is internal to our nature. Our drives are irresistible impulses, mysterious forces whose power is not attenuated by their internality. The religious law, with its coercive externality rooted in an independent sovereign will, does not degrade human nature any more than our natural passions do. Indeed the latter are, in the absence of moral restraint, strong enough to be autonomous. Think of the sexual pressure on our frame, especially during youth, a hot season in every land. Are we not all victims of our own natural bodies? We must suffer the body and suffer in it too. Nor do we need to be Buddhists to know this truth. A Persian proverb about repentance (understood culturally as sexual restraint) advises us: 'To repent during youth – that is the way of the prophets.'

Islamic theism was not accidentally a form of humanism, some nebulous concern for human welfare that was an unintended by-product of a refined concern for God. Islamic law salutes the common good (*maṣlaḥah*) and supplements it with guidance by the wise and virtuous in society, not by vulgarians at the gate, self-elected and self-indulgent artists who wish to impose a dictatorship of vulgarity under the pretence of freedom and art. We need a populist consensus but also an informed individual liberty. The Islamic ummah is defined in its moral, not inherited tribal, dimensions as that community whose members believe in God, promote good and prohibit evil (Q:3:110). Good actions speak louder than words while faith provides the straitjacket on our immoral impulses.

Islam, even as private religion, as we shall see in the next two chapters, is a moral force that stands for an equitable distribution of political power and of economic assets in place of the current domination of the monopolized market and the bureaucratic state disguised as liberal participatory democratic polity. It intends to recapture the market and political economy from monopoly capitalism and neo-liberalism. Islam repudiates the economic liberalism of the right and the moral liberalism of the left. It opts for a revolutionary combination of economic egalitarianism allied with conservatism about moral and religious values which are useful for educating the young. In place of a supinely ineffective representative democracy, it contends for the recovery of a democratic agenda which extends to the local and the civic to give us the transformative power of a politics which voluntarily refuses total autonomy in order to respect transcendent ethical controls that monitor and ensure mundane political humility.

10 A private religion

We are exploring Islam's continuing transition to a place inside an alien political modernity. How should Muslim minorities, about a third of the total Muslim population, live as citizens of non-Muslim nations? Muslim believers have no official theology of the minority position since historically they inherited only the undiluted legacy of religious establishment at home and imperial success abroad. The only certainty is that Islam will resist historicization and secularization of its absolute doctrines even as it becomes a private faith. It will probably retain some part of its political heritage. And while the military utility of jihad has permanently lapsed, its capacity for instilling moral discipline, control and training remains intact.

While dreaming of the universality of their faith, Muslims confront a universally powerful and secular west. Westerners, including Jews and Christians, cultivate a cultural and linguistic uniformity in the midst of unyielding and deepening global political differences. Hope lies in the opposite direction: a publically endorsed political unity based on social justice, sustained by respect for international legal standards and implemented by force. This will provide an atmosphere in which private religious, cultural and linguistic differences can safely flourish. The pursuit of this ideal must characterize the adolescent twenty-first century as it enters its second decade.

Colonial theorists and orientalists pontificated that the decline of Muslim civilization justified its subordination by a militarily ascendant Europe. Muslim activists and thinkers concurred with this assessment but added that there was no intrinsic shortcoming in Islam that had caused the collapse of Islamic powers. It was divine punishment for the Muslim betrayal of God's message. Muslims abandoned God; therefore he abandoned them. Thus, while Europeans thought that a tenacious attachment to Islam had led to the decline of Muslim civilization in the face of European assaults, the Muslims thought that it was solely their abandonment of Islam that had led to their demise.

This devout reading of Muslim history sounds implausible only to Western historians. Muslims note with pride and nostalgia that early Islam achieved the fastest (and largely permanent) conquest of recorded history. While Muslims obeyed the Quran's directives, they were virtually invincible. This religious reading of

history implies that the defeat of Islam by the West was the defeat of weak secularized communities by strong secularized communities. Muslims lost only after
Islam ceased to be a variable in the imperial competition. Unsurprisngly, we hear
Muslim preachers thundering that Islam is the solution, the missing variable,
which must be re-inserted into world history if Muslims are ever to again become
an empowered avant-garde community of faith.

Two problems plague this Muslim ambition. First, many nations and peoples
have built empires that finally crumbled. No-one has a second helping at the banquet of history. Why should Muslims hanker after their glorious past instead of
moving into their mundane present? The caliphate and Shariah jointly symbolized
the utopian ideal of the Prophet's just commonwealth. Although the Shariah outlived the caliphate, it did not survive the colonial onslaught intact. Can the ashes of
the holy law be revived so that Islam rekindles into a flame, a new empire of faith?
Secondly, the insertion of Islam into Muslim and world affairs has no known a
priori form. Re-insertion could mean the restoration of a universal caliphate or
the establishment of one or more Islamic states or perhaps an attenuated domestic
role for Islam in its humbler social posture as ethical watchdog within Western
democracies with sizeable Muslim populations.

Traditionally, the household of empowered faith supplied the paradigmatic
framework for discharging private and public duties since even individual duties
have social aspects. Thus the believer's canonical prayer, often called his 'daily
ascension into paradise' as opposed to Muhammad's dramatic and literal ascension (see Q:17:1; 53:7–18), is a non-transferable duty. Communally performed, it
earns greater merit, especially if the believer must walk on foot to the mosque,
each step being a station of virtue. Occasions of celebration and mourning require
congregational prayer. Most Quranic pleas and petitions, especially in Medinan
verses, are addressed by the community speaking to God, using the second person
plural (see Q:1:5–6; 2:286; 3:8–9). Indeed, communities will be judged communally on the day of reckoning (Q:4:41–2; 45:28–9). Islam's five pillars require a
community but not necessarily a state, the politically autonomous community.
Fasting in Ramadan and the collection of the alms tax are socially exercised duties
that do not need political sanction or reinforcement. The Hajj, like the Friday
congregational prayer, is a potentially political assembly. Unlike the Hajj, however, the Friday assembly is inquorate and invalid if the community lacks a caliph
as supreme leader.

Maximal implementation of the laws of the Quran and Sunnah began during
Muhammad's last decade of life and continued, at least in the area of family law,
until the eventual collapse of the Ottoman Empire in the early twentieth century.
There was no legal implementation during the Meccan period when Muslims
were weak, isolated and persecuted. Private duties such as prayer, the only pillar
of faith mentioned at that stage, apart from the creed, were not enforced. In
Medina, the community was charged with 'enjoining good and prohibiting evil',
an article of faith (see Q:3:104, 110; 9:71). This appropriately vague maxim
assigns moral duties to the individual and collective duties to the empowered
community.

In Europe and North America, Islamic political ambition is curbed by the restraints of mature democracies: a privately practised faith and a culture, certainly, but neither a divinely willed universal political order nor a caliphate committed to preserving an immutable core of holy legislation. How does a formerly imperial faith retreat into private belief, taking its place as one among many offers of truth and salvation in a pluralist world? In the next chapter, we determine Islam's residual role in the international political sector while here we debate its role as a depoliticized faith surviving in a ghetto in cultures which have canonized their doubts about political religion in particular and religion in general.

II

Tradition can be mined for patriarchal brutalities and for liberating creativity. Tradition is often simply nostalgia or our present wishes smuggled backwards into the glorious past. (In the modern American capitalist notion of time as a commodity, the past appears as a waste of time.) The Islamic tradition can no longer be selfishly guarded as an ossified set of rules and prejudices defended by an elite group of scholars. It must become an organic principle which informs and partly defines but not fixes an ideal Islamic identity. The interaction between inherited tradition and this ideal modern identity helps us to discern the faith's core message. What we cannot avoid inheriting is establishment, a power structure buttressed by the state. Tradition we can forge anew; establishment is law, order and power and it cannot be easily dislodged.

The received tradition can be mined for three political alternatives. The Prophet's Meccan career can be used to support an apolitical and quietist stance, the Medinan one an activist radical one. The former supports Islam as a private faith, the latter the public faith of a community empowered progressively from its chieftaincy origins to an empire. The third paradigm is the Abyssinian one named after the Muslim migration to that country when the Muslims were persecuted in Mecca. This exhibits an Islam of private conviction, practised in tolerant and humane non-Muslim states. It resembles the Muslim condition in modern Europe and North America.

Modern Islam has been reactionary. It has reacted to the hegemonic west. Before the abolition of the caliphate, Muslims wanted to modernize their legal tradition. After its abolition by triumphant European powers manipulating native collaborators, the trend was reversed. Muslims wondered why legal modernity should not be Islamized. Why should secular certainties in every department of life remain fixed and absolute while religious ones are forced to evolve? A narrow and intolerant modernity inspired a narrowly conservative Islam as Muslims clung to memories of their glorious past. Before the nineteenth century, Muslims were never fixated on the Shariah. They recognized and celebrated competing mystical, theological and even semi-philosophical currents. After experiencing colonial humiliation, all the currents converged on the legal tributary of the Islamic ocean. And even that was reduced to a stream in a backwater as the supple and complex Shariah was reduced to a catalogue of rules about the permitted and the forbidden.

Islamic ethics deteriorated into an algorithmic calculus of merit with no regard for the moral agent's underlying dispositions.

The result has been devastating for Muslim self-esteem. Islamic nations, post-revolutionary Iran apart, have not achieved even technological autonomy. Why are Saudi Arabia's petroleum experts mainly foreigners? Are the descendants of Averroës and Al-Kindi, Umar Khayyam and Avicenna, not smart enough to run their own oil fields? The identity crisis stimulated by Western colonization of Muslim territories inspired a wholesale return to tradition understood conservatively. Unlike establishments, traditions are formed retrospectively. Muslims opted to rewrite their history as an uninterrupted conservative deposit with no innovation or intelligent compromise. The ancient community now reappeared as brain-dead men and women. The formative and classical periods of Islam were in fact marked by supple and subtle achievements in law and politics. For the past half a millennium, the Muslim community is like the tired man who is trying to wake up and must finally wrench himself out of bed lest he fall asleep again.

III

The triumph of the West lies in its innovative conception of politics as a form of negotiated freedom for all classes of society. The utopianism of perfect statecraft was replaced by the empirically known and accountable workings of power operating inside the dialectical exchanges of citizens in a civil society protected by an empowered state. The first step was the separation of church and state.

In Christian Europe, this separation addressed a prior question. Should we bracket discussion of final ends, as prescribed by scripture, and thereby banish this subject from the political realm? After centuries of vicious sectarian bloodshed, Christians shelved this debate without resolving it – or rather doing so wholly at the expense of religion. Muslims have not emulated this pattern since they do not have a similar history of conflict between the two realms. In its origins, Islam co-opted the secular pretender by proposing the unity of religion and state as a religious doctrine about the ends of power, a doctrine that denied the autonomy of secular politics by making religion itself secular and political. The subordination of the secular realm to the religious imperial order is the clue to Islam's enduringly effective resistance to secularization. The Quran permits but co-opts the secular dimension as an operative and effective inoculation against the ideological process of secularization, the latter understood as the mechanism whereby all religious authority is actively subordinated to the secular state.

Secularism is the ideological claim that religious and political authority can and ought to be kept separate. Once Europeans realized it was possible, they thought it necessary. In this separate but unequal co-existence, the church was severed from the state which was set in authority over the church. This arrangement permitted the birth of a semi-autonomous middle region called civil society which administers with secular neutrality all non-political and non-legal activity, especially charitable and religious activity. Secularism is a viable solution to the destructive problem of the relationship between church and state: it prevented state officials from using religion to reinforce and extend state authority while preventing clergymen from using state power to impose their dogmas on others in society.

Unlike Christianity, however, Islam cannot be easily divorced from its political heritage inspired by the Quran. Islam's political institutions were only recently destroyed and then by European colonialists. As an imperial faith rooted in a tradition of legal coercion, Islam diverges from models of secularized religion derived from post-Enlightenment Christianity. A mosque–state separation cannot be an exact parallel of a church–state separation since 'The Mosque' is an abstraction constructed by comparison with a Catholic 'Roman' Church. In any case, the church–state separation was neither complete nor necessary even in the European case. Only Americans formally endorse constitutional separation of state and religion and even they do not observe it; most European nations observe it in practice but only a few, prominently France, explicitly accept it in theory.

Only the Turks (Ottomans), relatively late recruits to Islam and the only ones to formally renounce it, effected any formal institutional separation between the religious intelligentsia *('ulamā')*, called *ahl al-qalam* (people of the pen), and the ruling family and its military auxiliaries, collectively known as *ahl al-ṣayf* (people of the sword). The status thus assigned to Sunni scholars resembles that of modern Iranian clergy: funded by their inalienably held endowments of land and property, they are economically independent enough to discharge their primarily moral duty, namely, to condemn the ruler's injustices against the weak and dispossessed.[1]

IV

Islamic history is the record of late empires (Ottoman, Safavid and Mughal) and early empires (Umayyad and Abbasid caliphates). The legal, imperial and dynastic Islam of the classical period began in 622 and ended in 1258. The next 750 years mark continuous decline punctuated by ineffective revivalism.

When did Islam become a defensive political ideology? The pivotal event is the battle of Lepanto in 1571 when the Ottomans were defeated by the combined forces of Spain, Venice and the Papacy, terminating Ottoman maritime power in the Mediterranean and making way for the rise of Portuguese, Dutch, French and British naval supremacy. It ushers in four centuries of uninterrupted decline that ends in 1978 with Iran's Islamic Revolution. We shall now trace Muslim history from 1571 to 1978 and then return to this narrative in the final chapter to canvas events since the end of the cold war. There are three phases of decline opening with 1571 to 1798 (Napoleon's invasion of Egypt). Ottoman territorial contractions and economic and political concessions begin with the signing of the Treaty of Karlowitz in 1699. 1798 to 1924 and 1924 to 1978 mark two further phases of Islamic impotence. The fourth stage is Islamic resurgence from 1978 to the present, a revival movement that irrationally worries Western policy-makers.

Phase two opens in 1798 when Napoleon occupied Egypt and thus entered, with impunity, the heartland of early Islam. From then onwards, we witness 125 years' of irreversible decline and stagnation in the whole Muslim world. This phase ended in March 1924 when the caliphate was abolished by domestic modernist Turkish reformers seeking a submissive assimilation to foreign colonial ideals for the Islamic peoples. Historians note an uninterrupted domination of the Muslim world as it laboured under the potent influence, if not direct control, of the colonizing Christian west. This subjugation reached its greatest geographical extent in 1920 when the League of Nations, precursor of the United Nations, gave Britain and France mandates to rule the newly-created Arab states. When the last sultan–caliph was deposed, Egypt's King Fu'ad I (d. 1936) and other local potentates coveted his title but failed to attain it.

The climax of wordwide Muslim impotence was solemnly proclaimed by the abolition of the ancient caliphate, intended as a harbinger of the final demise of Islam itself. The caliphate, the symbol of Islamic unity, religious identity and political integrity for some 1300 years, died young: it was younger than the Papacy. From 1924 to 1978, the Islamic world was being officially decolonized. It was the beginning of Islam's defensive militancy in the face of overwhelming Western economic and military power. This continues until today. During the nineteenth and twentieth centuries, Islam motivated many nationalist movements for independence and stirred the masses, from Morocco to India and Indonesia, to revolt against Western powers. In 1923, the republic of Turkey became the first modern 'Muslim' nation-state, founded on the debris of the dismembered Ottoman empire. Most Muslim nations became independent of European rule, mainly British or French, between 1945 and 1960 (Pakistan, 1947; Algeria, 1962). Egypt had limited independence since 1922.

These newly created nations were placed in the custody of indigenous elites sympathetic to Western economic and ideological goals. The freedom granted was to prove Pickwickian. Sensing this, Muslim activists spurned indigenous nationalism and the Western import of Marxist socialism. They founded their own pan-Islamic, transnational, supra-ethnic movements reflecting a universal Islamic fraternity, a practised brotherhood and sisterhood. Two twentieth century examples will suffice. Abu Al-Ala Maududi wanted to convert a Muslim homeland into an Islamic state, a transformation of an empirical and flawed reality into a normative utopianism which copies the Prophet's perfect commonwealth. His Jamat-e-Islami has proved to be an embarrassment and a failure. Hassan Al-Banna founded the Muslim Brotherhood, a movement that has succeeded but only by disowning its original activism. We defer this discussion to the next chapter.

V

In this brief hiatus, compare the case of Christianity. It endured three stages in its gradual pro-liberal humanist shift of perspective, itself as an indirect consequence of internal changes Western Christianity failed to harness. The initial stage was a generalized and pragmatic, at times reluctant, sometimes supine, acceptance of post-Reformation and post-Enlightenment culture. This included a religious pluralism which eventually legitimized political pluralism with its associated paradigms (secularism and democratization or, in bad times, fascism and totalitarianism).

The second stage, especially prominent in Catholic thought, was the nineteenth century concern for the working class. At that time, the (secular) Marxist movement was monopolizing moral concern for the poor and deprived while the churches were sharply alienated from society at large in most Western European countries. Christians appropriated the Marxist claim that it is exploitative to treat workers as mere commodities; it contradicts the Christian law of love which demands that we treat individuals as ends, not merely as means. In his encyclical *Rerum Novarum* (Concerning New Things) promulgated in 1891, Pope Leo XIII addressed the moral problems created by the Industrial Revolution. He effectively endorsed the workers' movement by formulating a doctrine of economic justice (minimum wage, profit and healthy industrial relationships) in the light of absolute New Testament values. This was the orthodox precursor of the revolutionary initiative of Christian liberation theology which argues that divine justice is easier to secure in a socialist economy.

In the final stage, Christians articulated theologically and philosophically grounded ideas of the dignity, freedom and self-determination of the person in the context of social justice and its obligations. Christian thinkers, both Protestant and Catholic, appropriated the findings of modern thought; they salvaged whatever they could and stamped it with the imprimatur of Christianity. This was to ensure that Christians at least, unlike secular society at large, would humbly acknowledge that freedom and dignity were derivative and undeserved gifts of grace. Otherwise, like the sceptical existentialists and other cynics, one felt free – but free to do what? And did one deserve one's freedoms anyway?

VI

We now return to the Islamic narrative. The state in Muhammad's day was a civilian community while the modern state is an organization with enough resources of violence to destroy civil society. The Islamic community was founded as a civilian as opposed to a military grouping where the army is the sole source and instrument of coercive power. The Prophet and his caliphs did not employ professional soldiers or mercenaries. There were no standing armies, only voluntary militias composed of zealous men who banded and disbanded according to necessity, in response to the caliph's declaration of jihad. The caliph himself was a civilian although he commanded the army and, until Ottoman times, led his men in battle. A professional army emerged only by the second Islamic century when all the spectacular military triumphs had already been achieved.

No modern civil society has *internal* coercive authority, whether military or religious. As a sector of society that exists between the individual and family, on the one hand, and the army and the state, on the other, it provides an arena for private association where all initiative and social action is voluntary, determined wholly by currents of public opinion and interest, personal choice and private whim. Paradoxically, however, civilian society can only be sustained autonomously if it receives *external* support through the larger society's legal, military and religious authorities.

A typical Western civil society contains professional associations, voluntary charitable bodies, learned societies, clubs and lodges, sports teams, college boards, business corporations and trade unions. Islamic society has less of these associations and more of the kin-based groupings: family, clan, city neighbour-hood, tribe, religious sect, Sufi fraternity, in addition to craft groups in guild associations. Civil societies, mainly in the democratic west, also accommodate competing political parties sustained by a shared respect for decisions reached through consensus.

Unlike Shiite Islam, Sunni Islam was never organized from above by a clerical elite or theocratic hierarchy. It was arranged, on an informal self-help basis, at the level of community and civil society. The focus was the mosque (*masjid*; place of prostration). Muhammad ordered that a mosque be built in every Muslim locality and built his own mosque in Medina with his own hands. The Prophet's mosque spontaneously and rapidly evolved from place of prayer to political command centre. The institution of the mosque was at the interface of civilian and military subcultures within early Islam. Men left for jihad after the Friday prayer in the central mosque which was often constructed, like the ancient Ibn Tulun mosque in Cairo, to house the entire army at prayer.

Sunni Islam is centred not on the caliph or the theocratic power system but on a building – the mosque. Mystics see the whole world as a mosque, with nature as its main entrance. In the Prophet's day, mosques were small, fragile and func-tional, reflecting the transient futility of this life and pointing the way to the permanent after-life. The Prophet's mosque in Medina was originally a humble, dust-coloured and frail structure. Along with the Holy Mosque in Mecca, it was frequently extended by rulers paying homage to Islam and sometimes to their own self-image as feudal despots and autocrats who ruled in the name of a God who was beyond accountability. Outside of the Arab peninsula, early Islam rapidly became a military society, a community of resident aliens in foreign lands, housed in vast mosque compounds, constantly seeking to expand the empire of faith. The earliest grand mosque is Jerusalem's Al-Aqsa completed in 692 CE.

Civil society symbolizes political humility while the spectacles of Islamic architecture support autocracy. A vast mosque can be soothing since it offers sanctuary. Typically, however, the grandeur of the grand mosques, especially in imperial Turkey, built to rival the Meccan and Medinan shrines, subconsciously reinforced totalitarian and autocratic sentiments about God's irresistible domina-tion. Such despotic implications are unwelcome to modern Muslims since we want God's Kingdom to evolve into a democratic republic that befits the inalien-able dignity of our humanity.

Gradually, the mosque emerged as simply a place of learning and worship; it was allied to the madrasah, a boarding school for religious education, which sur-vives as the last bastion of reactionary scholasticism and isolationism. The mosque merges wholly into civil society only in non-Muslim democratic cultures of the West where it is often one voluntary body among many, perhaps in the shape of a sup-plementary school where, after the statutory school day, children learn basic Arabic and their own mother tongues. In the Muslim world, ancient mosque-madrasahs, such as the university-mosque of Al-Azhar, remain at the interface of civil and political societies.

Once completed, a mosque belongs inalienably to God. There is no land title or deed. Adjacent to the mosque is the *waqf* (pl. *awqāf*), a benevolent endowment association or philanthropic foundation, supported and maintained by local residents. Property could be donated or bequeathed, thus creating a reliable income stream and a source of mundane facilities for the living and continuous posthumous virtue for the original benefactor. In modern Arab Muslim societies, the mosque has been nationalized and thus absorbed into the state. The philanthropic funds tied to the mosque have been seized by the state. This explains the state of disrepair of mosques in poor Arab countries, such as Egypt.

The scope for independent and self-supporting associations and organizations has been reduced as modernizing secularized autocrats nationalized the *awqāf* and brought endowments under state control. The encroachment of the violent modern state has inhibited the emergence of a civil society. The state tries to manipulate schools, media, publishing houses and universities although the electronic media revolution of the internet has undermined absolute state authority. Nonetheless, every important madrasah appointment, like every university appointment in sensitive fields, needs state clearance.

The status of the mosque is the clue to Muslim political culture, today as in the past. Will the mosque remain a part of the state or be absorbed into civil society? If the latter is the case, it can become a potent source of independent critical comment on the state's failings. Islam's future as a robust faith in the private sector shall hinge on the evolution of the mosque into the chief institution of a dissenting civil society.

VII

Islam is now a player in the politics of mature European democracies. The Muslims, forcibly expelled from Spain about 500 years ago, have returned. It is no return of the barbarians. The new peaceful Islamic presence in a tolerant post-Christian Europe is part of an experiment in multi-cultural citizenship.

The British Muslim response to Salman Rushdie's *The Satanic Verses* dates to Christmas 1988, exactly a decade after Iran's Islamic Revolution. This literary controversy single-handedly integrated Islam into the domestic politics of Britain and then Europe, unifying disparate Muslims in the European diaspora into one community. During the Rushdie furore, Muslims first became Europeans. Islam was no longer a distant and exotic force located in a Semitic land but rather an institutional domestic player informing the politics of ethnic and religious diversity in God's own white Christian continent. It finally marked the end of 'the myth of return' for immigrants who did not intend to settle abroad but rather to return some day to their land of origin, with their pockets loaded with cash, ready to settle scores over land and escape the West. In the meantime, the countries they had left had become culturally more westernized, the elite mere lackeys of Western powers. The migrants were losing their children, born in the West, to a universal Western culture while their own homelands changed beyond all recognition. They learnt that one went west wherever one went.

In the aftermath of the Anglo-Rushdie affair, we find two opposed tendencies in European Islam. Many Muslims want to be part of Western society on condition that they can exercise the same right of dissent as any other citizen. Equally, however, the secular anger at Muslim indignation over the Rushdie provocation has further isolated and alienated Muslims from mainstream European society. Even two decades later, few Westerners sympathetically wonder: Why were otherwise reasonable people incensed enough to be willing to spill much more than ink over this matter?

Muslims feel that they won the Rushdie battle but without the support of any allies. The victory, when it came, was wholly theirs and some now think they can make camp all by themselves in a self-segregating Muslim bloc in European politics. Conservative Muslim leaders, suspicious of change and assimilation, advocate social and religious isolation. The result: self-segregated ghetto communities which now need trained professionals to negotiate and present their needs to the liberal state and its welfare representatives. Many European Muslims remain poor and unemployed, living on state benefits that infantilize citizens in what American critics mock as the 'Eutopian' welfare state.

In the immediate aftermath of the Rushdie affair, some British Muslims made unwise political gestures. For example, the late Kalim Siddiqui's Muslim Parliament, sitting in symbolic opposition to its Westminster counterpart, was a misguided, provocative and sensationalist move in the early 1990s. Other British Muslims naïvely launched an Islamic Party as an alternative to the major power groupings. The attempt was premature and unsuccessful but the gesture was pregnant with meaning. To those who fear empowered Islam, the endeavour confirms the impudence of a minority which behaves like a majority – an attitude that is, ironically, characteristic of white settler minorities in their enduring colonial scramble for Africa, Asia, the Middle East and Latin, North and South America. Such Muslim behaviour punctures the arrogance of some Westerners since Islam has a competitive colonial history in parts of the globe. Muslims see their attempt to enter the political arena as being inspired by an instinctive recognition of the irreducible risks of powerlessness.

In retrospect, we see that multiculturalism is a valid expression of moral good will but, as a political ideology, it has failed to combat racism and may even have exacerbated it. Since secular Europeans can no longer appeal to religion, they have drifted towards nationalism and tribalism. We note increased racist indignation at immigrants and asylum seekers. Muslims have at best nominal citizenship since having a passport is only the beginning of citizenship. In liberal cultures, withholding recognition from those who are different, usually by denying them jobs, is a subtle but pervasive and powerful form of oppression. Immigrants never become settlers. They are usually invisible men and women or else constantly asked about their real origin, even after several generations. As I can testify from experience, even linguistic courtesy is lacking in documents that exhibit snide or careless inaccuracies about their names and genders.

Taking universal white privilege for granted is part of the enduring racism of Western liberal societies.

Westerners wrongly interpreted the Muslim response to Rushdie to be evidence of Muslims feeling threatened about their religious identity. It was in fact a threat to Western identity and cultural hegemony. For all their talk of openness, Westerners are far more indifferent to other cultures than Muslims are to the West. Western universalism is imperial and hierarchical, motivated by corporate profit and strategic imperatives wholly internal to the West. Apart from areas such as cuisine and art, Westerners acknowledge the non-west only where they sense an obstacle to the westernization of the globe. Westerners rarely assimilate even when they are physically living in or visiting other cultures, let alone on home ground. Muslims are much more ready to assimilate to the West's culture, art and economics. As for politics, all the influence is one-sided. The West has ubiquitous interests. No-one speaks of, say, Indonesian interests in America. The West appoints leaders to rule Muslim lands and 'stabilizes' those nations. If some native in Pakistan or Saudi Arabia speaks what the West wants to hear, suddenly a nation, a whole faith is said to have found a voice as if no-one had spoken anything of value there before English became a universal language of communication.

The economic consequences of European imperialism continue to extend into today's world: immigration is an indirect effect of colonial exploitation of various lands. Immigrants were invited to Europe to fill cheap labour shortages. Family re-unification, marketable skills, and humanitarian compassion are grounds for asylum; all are being overridden by doubts about the assimilation of Muslims. The European birth-rate is falling as secular Europeans reject the rabbinic counsel that 'children and righteousness shall deliver us from death'. In Europe, Islam is now the second largest faith though cynics might say it is second only to the fear of Islam – Europe's largest faith.

VIII

Muslims have not produced any new indigenous moral or legal system after the Quran; the scripture remains the sole ethical register of Islamic civilization. Extra-Quranic legal and moral innovations, often camouflaged as cultural and educational reforms, were of Western colonial origin and therefore suspect. Turkey's secularization, to take a prominent example, was the opposite of a grass-roots revolution. It was an imposed elitist revolution since secularism did not mature as a social process with indigenous intellectual, cultural and political roots. More broadly, the continuing struggle between Europe's religious past and its secular present and future is organic while the Muslims' struggle is complicated by the colonial intervention and its legacy. We see it clearly in the interrupted and arrested development of the Shariah.

The call to reform Islam is not sufficiently indigenous. The spirited and brave Muslim stance against Rushdie taught Westerners that the Islamic Reformation will not be created by the Western liberal inquisition aided by renegade Muslims. Its main agents must be recognizably Muslim. Muslim academics in the West are usually secularized assimilators, not credible religious reformers. They are the brown sahibs in exile playing the same role as their native counterparts, those Trojan horses of cultural enslavement and inferiority to Western culture. Only an imposed westernization, as instant reform, offered by writers such as Rushdie, interests and impresses Westerners. Responsible but gradual internal reform is rejected. Thus, any 'Muslim' can attain instant fame by attacking Islam and Muslims. If a woman – even better! A healthy process of social change, however, involves adherence to part of the past.

An Islamic modernity emerges from a critical Muslim appreciation of the Islamic past. Muslims should argue for a reasoned, not dogmatic or wholesale, rejection of Western colonial modernity, especially its toxic implications for communal cohesion and personal belonging. Muslims have the advantage of knowing where reform in Europe ultimately led: the exile of God to the margins of society, and finally his death. Some liberties of thought lead, in a straight line, from faith to a militant and sterile atheism.

Islam has produced few intellectuals but many martyrs. The secularized Muslim intellectuals, trapped in the limbo and trauma of transition, have prematurely abandoned the whole of their tradition as retrograde and reactionary. As westernized assimilators, they increasingly encourage submissively adaptive secular lifestyles, some even giving their children Muslim names solely as an act of diplomacy. Their case cannot detain us, in view of strict libel laws. These intellectuals are west-smitten but lack the foresight and insight to understand the agnostic, even nihilistic, consequences of Western modernity. As for the secular but indigenous route to the reform of Islam, it is blocked by a religious assertiveness that rejects all doubt as satanic.

Muslim societies are typically feudal, traditional, falsely theocentric and stagant, fixated on a noble past. The only two choices seem to be integration with the West on partly Islamic terms or a one-sided unilateral assimilation to Western ideals during a total eclipse of Islamic autonomy. Let me conclude with an irony here. Starting with the European Renaissance, the West, currently the sole possessor of modernity, created its modernity by recapturing its Graeco-Roman heritage. An empowered Islam, the great modern symbol of evil and irrationality, helped to create the Renaissance and hence Protestant Europe's politically enlightened modernity.

IX

Henry Kissinger, supreme cynic that he is, has defined a moderate Muslim as a soldier who has run out of ammunition. Such cynicism can be matched from the Islamic camp which has its own definition of a moderate Westerner but cynicism would not suit our gentle style in this chapter. In an escalating terminological war on Islam, countless labels and adjectives are currently applied to Islamic stances. Islam can be reformed or progressive or reformist and hence modern (inevitably so since it has survived into the modern world). A determined Western attempt to make it 'liberal' is resisted by many Muslims. 'Liberal' is an adjective whose meaning differs even between European and American usage; its meaning and application in the Muslim context are entirely unclear. For Muslims, it has undertones of the sexually permissive and therefore decadent. It can be a synonym for 'enlightened' and 'progressive' but these are usually codewords for 'westernized'. This trio could, factually, mean scientific or experimental and thus opposed to superstition and magic. 'Liberal Islam' is virtually always a codeword for an apolitical and hence powerless Islam. 'Liberal' does however usefully emphasize the need for change that would update the faith. Muslims should make a decisive turn towards enlightenment. That need not mean, however, as I argue in the final chapter, that they should abandon their share of legitimately acquired and exercised power.

The opposed labels are propagandist too with 'traditional' and 'orthodox' being the mildest on the continuum. An intermediate one is 'revivalist'. The trio of 'radical', 'militant' and 'fundamentalist' is ideologically motivated and tendentious. Factually, it often indicates an Islamic system that is domestically coercive (determined to impose the Shariah without winning popular consent) and internationally anarchically violent. Finally, we should reject the false contrast implied by 'jihadi' versus 'ijtihadi' (militant versus liberal or secularized Muslim). The popular tradition about an alleged greater jihad (militant struggle) versus the lesser jihad (personal purification) is polemically useful to Sufis and progressive Muslims eager to please Western audiences. It is based on a forged hadith and is in any case implausible. Why should we suppose that fighting in a battle-field is, for most believers, any easier than controlling their appetites and lusts?

The moderate (or progressive or liberal) Islamic paradigm is propagandist since it is invariably defined as a faith conducive to Western geo-political and economic interests. Alert Muslims recognize it as an Islam made acceptable to powerful Westerners. Liberal Islam may be practised primarily in the private sector but it need not reduce itself to merely self-help. And it certainly need not be a powerless Islam. Liberal Islam is moderate in its doctrines. But 'moderate' is always a codeword for subservience to Western elites to whom Muslim rulers are directly answerable rather than to their own subjects. Liberal Islam, as defined by Muslims, connotes an equal and just civilization – equal and different in its views on polity, inter-faith relations, human nature, minority rights and women's rights and duties.

Only an intellectually confident Islam can properly assimilate the best of the West. Any wholesale submissive assimilation, a passive emulation of the European experience of modernity, without mastication or digestion, will be a betrayal of Islamic values. Muslims will endorse only a gradual and intelligent and therefore selective adaptation of a largely alien Western modernity.

X

Before we can address the question of an Islamic reformation, we must be clear about the difference between westernization and modernization. For Muslims, the former includes the Western style emancipation of women and may include the legalization of pornography. Modernization affects areas such as economics, weapons and technology. Westernization is about moral values. When I lived in

Malaysia in the early 1990s, I recall the Malaysian government's firm ban on importing pornography, easily available on the local black market economy which escapes the state's radar. Many Chinese (and some Indian) pressures for liberal reforms were readily accepted. Legalizing pornography, however, it was argued, no matter how widely available it was in practice, would be a formal and frontal attack on the family.

Muslims are not alone in being overwhelmed by Western cultural hegemony but they are virtually alone in opposing global cultural westernization. Take the world's two largest populations. Observers are often alarmed by the accelerated westernization of spiritual non-violent India[2] and of communist and Confucian–Buddhist China, both experiencing more change in the past 50 years than in the past 5000 years. As nations with inveterate traditions, both face rapid modernization, secularization and westernization. Culturally, young Indians and Chinese are increasingly anglicized and westernized Orientals who are happy to be docile pupils of the occident.[3] A few conservative Indian groups do protest against Western imports such as beauty contests and St Valentine's Day. Groups such as Sri Ram Sena, nicknamed the Hindu Taliban, are cultural vigilantes operating in large westernized cities such as Mumbai. Only Islamic nations, with few exceptions, remain culturally defiant and isolated. Tellingly, virtually all Muslim nations opt out of beauty contests while Miss World readily finds contestants from the rest of the world, including former communist states.

No Islamic reformation will be judged authentically moderate by Westerners unless it results effectively in a separation of religion from politics, at the expense of the former. This is the Western understanding of reformation since that was the unintended but welcome (from a secular point of view) consequence of the Christian Reformation. The following six pillars of Islamic reformation, partly addressed as imperatives to male Muslim readers, will pre-empt Western attempts to reform Islam. The first three are internal reforms, listed in order of importance, while the rest relate to changes that affect relations between Islam and its Western monotheistic rivals for the hand of grace.

1   To prevent Westerners patronizing Muslim women as weak and oppressed, Muslim men should give women their rights rather than encourage women, incuding Muslim women, to view Islam as the most comprehensive charter for their oppression. Do not be quick to judge and thus alienate women. They are morally no worse or better than men. Be lenient in matters of sexual ethics so that women, like men, make their own journey of self-discovery. For many Muslim women, Islam means patriarchy so that men are in control and 'God is great' translates into 'Men are great'. Eradicate honour killings and the disgrace of genital mutilation.

2   Reform requires freedom of belief. Conversion from Islam to another faith, including a revealed faith, or to no faith, is a capital offence against the dignity of Islam. It renders the converts and those who converted them equally liable to the death penalty. Apostasy is defined as defection from Islam and hence desertion of its global community. Heresy (*ilḥād*) is distinguished from

apostasy (*irtidād*). The Quranic verse 'Let there be no compulsion in religion' (Q:2:256) and Muhammad's tradition 'No allegiance (*bay'ah*) is given under under duress' can support reform of the laws governing the fate of conscientious apostates.

3   Manage internal dissent about political and economic liberty and its limits so that foreigners cannot exploit your political disunity. These developments in Western Islam will eventually help to topple the oil despotisms, imposed by Western capitalism. At present, these cannot be internally reformed, except through popular revolutions.

4   Treat non-Muslim minorities with justice and respect as Islam commands. Reciprocal freedoms of belief should be allowed since Westerners accord honourable treatment to their Muslim minorities. Public Christian and Jewish worship in Islam's land of origin should be permitted since these fellow monotheists also seek to honour God and walk in his ways. This will also discourage Western intervention or at least any excuse for it.

5   Strengthen Islam through peaceful proselytization and charitable works, philanthropy, donations to educational institutions and sponsorship of inter-faith initiatives. Inter-faith and inter-cultural coalition building must move beyond the motto 'Know your foe'. This task will begin with a veto on a disgracefully casual anti-Semitism which hinders Muslims from seeing Jews as potential allies and not necessarily as permanent political enemies.

6   Create a *theologically* moderate Islam with an appealing pluralist political outlook. We already have a pluralist jurisprudence which permits reciprocal recognition of multiple schools of law. Although Islam was born as a religion of authority, armed with a fully defined and fixed scriptural canon, its doctrinal orthodoxy permitted much inner pluralism, mainly owing to its lack of a centralized authority such as a pope.

This proposed reformation will assist sincere non-Muslims to view modern Islam as a truly ethical monotheism and thus help Muslims win the current war of (and on true) ideas. Unlike the Protestant assault on a sole monolith such as the Roman Catholic Church, (Sunni) Islam has no single central authority which can be reformed. Therefore we shall not see a single reformation movement. Local and regional reformations will create a new private Islam whose total contours can only be discerned in the near future.

XI

Can private faith suffice as a basis for community? The problem today is not how to live well but how to live well among others. Max Weber foretold that modernity heralds the legal–rational form of political authority – a form typified in the bureaucracies of modern states where legal power along with the institutional interactions of civil society replace personal and individual spheres of influence. This arrangement leads to effective government and management by replacing the rule of the charismatic leader with the rule of law and of institutions which enable legitimate and positive politics. Inevitably, it also engenders the atomization and alienation wintnessed in all consumer cultures, particularly America and Japan.

Isolation from others and one's true self is not the condition but the response of alienated modern humanity. That is the tragedy of our mature, urban and urbane humanist modernity whose advocates flatter themselves with the conceit that they have given us history's culminating humanism. We moderns live not among people but among crowds and masses. It is the end of effective community long before the end of history. The crowd is by definition random and transitory, even if it acts in the name of a coherent and unifying cause. It is never community for it cannot cohere except in its function and utility – and that only temporarily. We know no face except our own and even that is a stranger's face. Contact with people contaminates. 'Hell is other people' was the verdict of the depressed exis-tentialist Sartre. He promulgated it as a universal truth, arrogantly generalizing from his own French (and post-Christian European) experience to the whole of humanity. There are no neighbours since no-one knows any-one and no-one cares. The crowd that gathers for the joyful celebration is no different from the crowd that observes the common modern tragedy, the road accident.

A search for a blessed singleness consumes and consummates modern human-ity where the mobile phone and the television become the friends of every lonely heart. This terminates effective community as isolation is preferred to communion. The Christian message of universal brotherhood sounds incredible. This pattern of alienating isolation, including inter-generational, parental, familial, sibling and marital alienation, persists across the political spectrum. A complete dehumaniza-tion is found in America and Sweden, one a right-wing Christian state, the other a secular far left one, united in their inconsolable social malaise. This is the exile in which the alienated one shouts: 'Do not come near me!' It is not the cry of the ancient leper who sadly whispered, 'Do not touch me!' And he had a reason. The modern degenerate thinks of himself as no more than the life-carrying animal and the disease is life. Humans become inhuman while remaining merely biologically and physiologically human since they are exiled and alienated from their own nature as social beings. This primordial nature has mutated under the pressures of materialism, commercialism, and exaggerated freedom and sensuality.

This is not to idealize community or belonging. It cannot be part of any defen-sible case for community that its experiences for the individual are wholly positive. Lack of community in civilian life is, however, a major cause of war as many hanker for the alternative if temporary community created by war, the crucible of crisis, heroic struggle and camaraderie. War gives meaning, power and false glamour to the empty lives of young men who cannot cope with relationships. The most potent weapon in war becomes alcohol. Vietnam gave America its first 'heroes on heroin'.

Given its origins, Islam alone among religions faces the trauma of transition from empowered public to impotent private faith. During the past two centuries, the intersection and interaction of secular modernity with Judaism and Christianity has dramatically secularized both faiths. Christians and Jews side with secularism and demand Islam's secularization rather than salute the heroic Muslim stance of not conforming to the profane world. Judaism, a successful private faith for millennia, has become critically secularized as Jews have travelled over three millennia from ancient temple to synagogue and, in modern times, from the ghetto to the museum and holocaust memorial. Will Judaism be eventually reduced, as religious Jews always feared, to merely an American fund-raising mechanism for Israel? Can privatized and thus secularized faiths serve as a basis for ethical community?

The secular enlightenment was, like its firstborn political child called Marxism, a secular duplicate of Judaeo-Christian messianism: an earthly utopia, a secularized eschatology, a temporal climax to history. The devout hope is to create a private and enlightened faith which does not reduce to pseudo-spiritual self-help mysticism, a failed secular humanism in religious dress.

XII

Can a private Islamic identity be a basis for ethical integrity without the traditional legal sanction? Or can only an empowered collectivist faith resist the blight of sterile secularization? In this final section, I touch on a variety of related themes that coalesce around the future of Islamic identities and the cultural politics of misrepresentation of aliens and migrants in liberal societies, a theme for another occasion.[4]

Not all modern Muslims take pride in their Muslim identity. Some young Muslim women feign a stylish ignorance of basic Islamic rituals and practices such as daily prayer or burial (rather than cremation) of a corpse. The message is: 'I am proud to be ignorant of Islam because I am a Westerner, at most a Muslim by chance, not by choice.' A generation ago, such an avowal of ignorance of Islamic duties or dogmas would have been seen as shameful for oneself and for one's family.

Progressive Muslims, 'Salafi in worship, Sufi in society, secularist in government' declare that 'All we need is to be just.' The Quran, however, was not revealed solely as a call for equity in our private relationships but rather as a comprehensively directing amalgam of spirituality, ethics, politics and law. Islam was not founded as an Arabian version of Christianity.

Can Muslims manage multiple identities? Perhaps a few should be eliminated and the remainder unified. Social identity, as defined by class and education, is not equivalent to human worth. A complete Islamic identity requires Islamic community. A fully autonomous identity presupposes linguistic integrity: possession of one's own authentic tongue which is rooted in an organic relation to one's identity. For Muslims, English and other European languages serve as languages of communication, commerce and diplomacy but not of religious, cultural and literary identities.

Class concerns are also implicated in questions of reform and future identity Working- and middle-class Muslims understand the appeal of Islam in Islamic terms and inherited religious traditions. Only upper-class Muslims, who call themselves progressives, as if self-praise were a recommendation, along with most Western converts, require a secular, sometimes Sufi, way of appreciating and appropriating Islamic truths.

A continuing danger for many young Muslims is from the absolute aesthetics of modern polemical atheism, especially from literature and exaggerated claims on its behalf. Art as unbridled self-expression is anathema to Islam. Art is only a vehicle, a secondary goal. To think otherwise is idolatry of art. Most controversial affairs, especially the case of the Danish cartoons and the Rushdie affair, are not about Western Muslim identity as such but rather about the Western incapacity to face a culturally confident Islam that challenges the cultural hegemony of the Western artistic elite. Can we interpret a culture in which 'nothing is sacred', where it is impossible to blaspheme, to a culture in which only the sacred matters and it is all too easy to blaspheme?

In secular societies, modern literature, whether as literary achievement or merely entertaining gossip in print, provides an alternative to religion. The bromides and platitutudes of the illegitimate children of colonial modernity – writers such as Hanif Kureshi, V.S. Naipaul and Salman Rushdie – are heard only in the artistic wilderness of fellow artists such as Martin Amis. These artists display a healthy disregard for all forms of authority, especially religious and moral but, in their idolatrous attachment to art, they fail to question the authority of the established aesthetic tradition. Literature is in all forms, especially the literary novel, a subtle form of social criticism, not just entertainment. When stripped of its exaggerated self-status, the novel communicates and binds us by dramatizing values that inform our actions. But we cannot expect prose or poetry to offer solutions to our problems. Only political programmes, including those of a religiously informed politics, can solve communal problems and dilemmas that extend beyond our quotidian and personal life.

Part IV
Epilogue

11 The future scope of an imperial faith

I

In closing this book, we canvass Islam as a modern political faith, survey the varieties of contemporary Muslim governance, record and defuse the tension between Islam and the West and predict possible future trends for this confrontation. In the first half of this chapter, we explore contemporary Islam with a view to its past and present ambitions; in the second half, we assess the future potential of Islam as political faith. Muhammad as statesman runs as a theme through the chapter.

In the binary vision of Islam versus the Euro-American empire, a major component is supplied by indelible media images of a faith fostering apparently motiveless malice and terror. Islam is synonymous with a fanatical bloodthirstiness sustained by an overwhelming lust for power. The truth is not captured by this tabloid image of Islam which is in fact an imperial faith in continuous recession for some half a millennium, a faith leaving vulnerable Muslim minorities in lands where Muslims once ruled justly and gently for over a millennium. The Muslim ummah fragments as each faction puts its goals and grudges above principles and unity. Islam has scored few successes against Western powers despite constant calls for revolutions, jihad and intifadas. The proliferation of mosques today, cited as evidence of Islam being the fastest-growing faith, is evidence of ethnic sectarianism and disunity among the ummah. This standard alarmist myth about Islam camouflages the fact that evangelical Protestantism is the world's fastest growing religion. Why should a wounded and fractured Muslim community, externally attacked and internally disunited, be seen as posing a grave threat to the free world?

The modern history of the Islamic world is a byproduct of global power dynamics. It differs from recent European history which was propelled by internal European forces. Although the seven crusades (from 1095 to 1270) initiated the stalemate between east and west, the startling rise in Europe's expansionist power from 1789 to 1923 broke the deadlock and ushered in the virtually universal triumph of the ideologically defined west. It marked the end of Islam as autonomous civilization. In the heyday of Western expansion, only four nations were spared formal colonization although each was influenced by Western powers: Turkey, Iran, Saudi Arabia and Afghanistan. The last mentioned has been occupied by

American troops for a decade while Saudi Arabia is routinely manipulated by America and the United Kingdom.

The interest in Islam as a revolutionary faith dates from Christmas 1978 when Ayatollah Khomeini (1902–89), armed only with his golden nail-clipper, returned to Iran from exile, to become the first man since the Renaissance to create a theocracy. Westerners do not consider that progress but Muslims entertain different cultural memories of theocracy – a time of glory, not ignominy. Iran's elite are the only wholly free modern Muslim elite. Muslims, especially in the Middle East, resent that the Western imports of socialism and Marxism did not save them from humiliation at the hands of Israel. Created only in 1948, it defeated Arab armies and annexed land on three occasions in a mere 25 years. Interest in an empowered Islam – which the West unjustly dismisses as fundamentalism – is on the increase in the wake of defeats, massacres and even a holocaust of Muslims in places as diverse as the former Soviet Republic, Indian Kashmir, the Middle East and Eastern Europe, especially Bosnia and Albania. Since 1979, Muslims recognize that the West does not have answers for the woes of the Muslim world since even many Western leaders are puppets – not of foreign powers but of global but invisible economic forces and masters. The amoral ideology of corporate capitalism, fortified by fanatical market fundamentalists willing to kill worldwide, has shot down both Christianity and democracy, especially in America.

Islam was never a theocratic ideology which merely politicized an existing cultural universe. Founded as holy law and sacred politics in which the secular is not excluded from religion but rather fulfilled in it, it corresponds to Christianity, the private faith emerging post-Enlightenment, and to Christendom, a former empire based on it. Classical Islam integrates religion and government by making their liaison coherent, cohesive and comprehensive. Islam successfully made politics more ethical: Muslims rarely abandoned politics altogether to withdraw into cynicism and despair. The Quran transfers moral concerns found in private ethics to politics so that social justice becomes the paradigmatic public cause – no longer a private concern of charitable organizations. Accordingly, Islam opposes a political economics centred on the absolute power of capital, hence the Quran's determined and frequent assault on usury (Q:2:275–80; 3:130; 4:161; 5:41–3, 63; 30:39).

Westerners assume that power must always be an enticement which can only undermine the sanctity of a religion, never establish or enhance it. They cite the way that Muhammad rose from citizen of Mecca to ruler of Medina and hence of Arabia. Muhammad certainly ensured the survival of his faith by creating an empowered and autonomous community. He synthesized religion and state as his followers grew to constitute an independent community. Medina became a refuge for those seeking asylum from persecution. Muslims established a base from which they could bring all humanity under a universal faith-based brotherhood. Only such an order allowed Muslims to fully conduct their affairs in a way that did not demean their religious identity and conscience. Establishing Muslim rule in Medina reflected not simply Muhammad's political ambition but rather a compelling combination of his pious intention, diplomatic skill and sheer will, all visible in his prophetic charisma.Wedding faith to power unified the ethical, legal and doctrinal dimensions of Islamic monotheism.

At the end of its Medinan phase, Islam was poised on the edge of empire in a world where Jews had been defeated (Q:33:26–7) and Christians were viewed as effete rivals who could not resist the new faith's energetic confidence. This imperial Islam, originating with Muhammad and his deputies, remained the ambition of dynasties, monarchs and sultans until the caliphate was abolished in 1924. After that date, Quranic verses about conquering the world for Islam still spoke to individual readers: the mantle of empire was transferred to activists such as Abul Ala Maududi (1903–79) and Sayyid Qutb (1906–66). These were powerless individuals at odds with their secularized and pro-Western governments. With the emergence of Al-Qaeda, Islamic activism operates without any territory to serve as its base. Supra-territorial and supra-national entities such as Hizbollah and Al-Qaeda, operating as freelance states, take on Western powers as war is reduced to skirmishes and guerilla tactics. For all of the Islamic rhetoric and despite the unparalleled courage of Muslim fighters, reminiscent of Islam's glorious origins, the modern Muslim posture is only defensive militancy against overwhelming Western power. Muslims cannot win in the sphere of physical power. Nor do they own the means of producing propaganda. The fear of this just faith is the greatest irrational phobia in the age of reason.

II

There are religious religions and political religions. Christianity and Buddhism[1] offer private salvation while calling for humble service inside the acknowledged hegemony of public secularism. Official Christianity repudiates Islamic and Marxist estimates of 'the power of power' to attain valued moral ends. The New Testament contains nothing analogous to ancient Jewish or Quranic politics, only an interim politics and ethics suited to visionaries waiting for the world to end. As for the democratic institutions of modern Western nations, these were established mainly in protest against Christian political norms, especially the divine right of kings, which were judged juvenile and immoderate and therefore eradicated through revolution or reform.

The Prophet inculcated in Muslims a sense of their colossal social responsibility so that they cannot plead neutrality about political stances. It is every Muslim's duty to identify injustice and to call it by its name. Wherever religious obligation and the demands of professional detachment clash, the Mulim scholar is religiously obliged to indicate which loyalty comes first. Genuine religion – the qualification is necessary – entails political activity though not necessarily impulsively revolutionary activism. The Quran certainly does not legitimize the indiscriminate slaughter of innocents, no matter how understandable the temptation to engage in sensational acts of terror in order to force the callous world into caring.

Muslim preachers remind believers of their collectivist obligations, including the duty to preserve an Islam which resists annexation by oppressors. Despite the efforts of rulers to domesticate it, Islam has not become a nationalized industry.

Apart from Enver Hoxha (1908–85), an Albanian communist leader, no ruler has prohibited the Friday assembly mandated by the Quran (Q:62:9). This potentially revolutionary association, the weekly analogue to the annual pilgrimage to Mecca, threatens venal rulers. Brave preachers take their belongings with them on Friday afternoons since they know that their sermon will induce the regime, represented by plain-clothes agents hiding in the congregation, to arrest them at the end of the prayer. The Quran describes the Muslim community as just, balanced and moderate (Q:2:143). Believers forbid what is wrong and enjoin what is right (Q:3:104, 110) and walk on the middle path, the straight path of piety, patience and equity (Q:1:7; 20:135). Owing to the enduring power of this self-image, Islam remains, despite the material and military weakness of Muslim nations, a moral super-power.

Marxists taught Christians that private piety is futile if one cannot dismantle the structures of evil. Marxists can claim no such didactic favour with respect to Muslims. Far from dulling people's political consciousness, Islam agitates the masses, demands revolt and enjoins self-sacrifice and jihad against militant oppressors. It has outstanding credentials as a freedom movement against colonial occupiers. That the promise of heavenly compensation for earthly wretchedness imposes on religious societies a passivity in the face of gross injustice remains a hackneyed socialist criticism, incorrectly leveled at all theists. This reservation about the ideological use and abuse of revealed religion is nourished on data gathered from Christian Europe. Passivity is foreign to the instincts of a faith whose prophet was a man of action.

Muslims and Marxists concur that we need power because human suffering is partly avoidable. Contra the Buddha, it is a political phenomenon. Islam predates Marxism in the determined quest for an economically prosperous and legally just order on earth. This theoretical concurrence leads to cooperation among communists and Muslims. Secular nationalist and communist factions, notably in Algeria, Iran and Egypt at different times, have united with Islamic radicals against a common oppressor until the common enemy was unseated. The Egyptian dictator King Farouk was overthrown by the military regime of Gamal Abd Al-Nasser in concert with the Muslim Brotherhood during Sayyid Qutb's day. Again, in 1978, the Tudeh community party assisted Ayatollah Khomeini's supporters in the attempt to overthrow Shah Reza Pehlavi.

For Christians, sinful human nature aborts social justice in the earthly city. Our fallen state conceals an irremovable disability that no political order could eradicate. Christianity views human suffering as apolitical: transcending political resolution and requiring only transcendent grace. Islam and Marxism concur that power properly applied can eliminate some types of avoidable suffering. Despite fearing the imminent Day of Judgment, Muhammad constructed an order that survived him until 1924. While Christianity's *apocalyptic* eschatology condemned the world so fiercely that it left little room for a functioning political order to ameliorate our plight on this side of the grave, Islam's *ethical* eschatology demanded precisely a *political* order to rectify immediately the world's evils. 'Things are so bad that nothing can be done about it' is countered by 'Things are so bad that something must be done about it'. If redemption is meaningful in Islam, it can only mean redemption of the politically sinful world. The Quran requires Muslims to engage in the politics of righteousness by using limited violence but only for the sake of virtue. The only other option, given that we are only passing through this transient world, is to abdicate our mundane responsibilities.

I conclude this section by adding that the political vigour of politicized Judaism (as Zionism) and of fundamentalist American Christianity is overrated. Both derive their power from their support for capitalism, the world's dominant ideology that has shot down all faiths except Islam. Most Jews and Christians are secularized and humane capitalists who utilize their faith as a moral foundation for a hegemonic capitalist order even though their religious values are far more compatible with a socialist economy. The exception is the fanatical activism of Christian Zionism, an extremist organization largely restricted to America. Its members neglect the entire Bible in favour of its last book (Revelation) and see no contradiction in a violently established millennial empire of Jesus Christ, the prince of peace.[2] Irresponsibly and arrogantly, they propose that current tensions between the West and Middle Eastern Islam should be resolved with a cosmic battle between God and Satan in the holy land.

III

The intellectual, economic and political stagnation of Muslim peoples hardly needs advertisement. Muslim cultures worldwide are the detritus of imperial Islam's continuous recession. Politics has been replaced by dictatorship and terrorism while conventional warfare is rejected in favour of assassinations, coups and guerrilla wars. The few indigenous dictatorships are supplemented by countless western-imposed ones. Muslim nations are only rhetorically religious: the powerless masses are united but their leaders are united only in their subservience to the secularized Christian west. By contrast, Western nations (defined ideologically, not geographically) are united despite the collapse of Christendom: leaders and the ruled masses are wholly united in their core purposes. Politics at home has been either corrupted by the interests of the wealthy or trivialized. While domestically the liberal hour is over, a secular evangel motivates Western messianic fervour which helps to globalize liberal Western culture.

Let us survey the Muslim world and countries with large Muslim populations. Seventy-five per cent of Muslims live in Asia if we include Turkey (Asia Minor). Islam is the largest and most widely distributed Asian religion with more followers than either Hinduism or Buddhism. One-fifth of Muslims are in Africa (which includes the Levant, the Middle East proper and Iran). Five per cent are found in the ideologically defined west with three per cent residing in Europe.

The OIC (Organization of the Islamic Conference), created in 1969, has 57 member states (with three granted observer status). Two members still aspire to be European (Albania and Turkey). Surinam and Guyana, admitted in 1996 and 1998 respectively, are in the extreme Western hemisphere while most members are in North Africa, Asia and the Far East. The OIC effectively champions pro-western policy while rhetorically protesting it. It is utterly ineffective in international politics: its resolutions are not read even by the Western nations at whom they are aimed. Like the Arab League, it is a talking shop for powerless and frustrated, mainly third world, nations incapable of resisting total Western hegemony.

Islamic governments run the entire spectrum of political patterns, including a few stable monarchies such as Morocco, Jordan and Saudi Arabia. The last mentioned is feudal, dynastic, autocratic, capitalist, theocratic and reactionary and a Western ally. For Saudis, their state is their own estate: it is named after the Al-Sa'ud dynasty. (It is the equivalent of renaming Texas 'Bushland'.) Most Muslim nations are artificially stable under authoritarian military governments, often enabled and then actively supported by Western powers (especially America, Britain and France). Since political parties are banned, unelected soldiers, at the level of general,[3] often rule by decree and the threat of force. Unstable republics include Algeria and Pakistan which were created (after wars of independence) to be exclusively Islamic homelands. After 65 years of independence, Pakistan still awaits a return to democratic civilian life. Unyielding secular autocracy characterizes Libya, Syria and, until the war to oust Saddam Hussein, Iraq. Like the Iraq of Saddam's era, Turkey, Syria and Yemen are secular states governing religiously diverse societies. Other secular states with devout civilian populations include Turkey and Malaysia, both similar in that respect to America. Religion supplies social and political stability in most Muslim nations.

Egypt is among the world's oldest nations and one of the few Muslim states not created arbitrarily by European colonialists. It is the most populous Arab nation, setting standards in art, literature and music. Egyptians are often perceived as cunning and dishonest, qualities traced by some commentators to the Quran (see Q:12:23–35). Insultingly, Egyptians are called 'the Jews of the Muslim world'. Egypt is now as famous for its Al-Azhar University as for its pyramids and its pyramidal society: a corrupt few at the top and millions of innocent paupers at the bottom. In most Arab nations, rich and poor, state involvement in economic life continues even though few countries are officially socialist. Most citizens depend on the state for income. Apart from farmers and small business owners, most people are employees of the state, often as soldiers, officers and bureaucrats.

There are few constitutional or civilian governments but popular Islamic revolutionary governments rule Muslims in Iran and Sudan. Malaysia has a power-sharing government with ethnic, democratic and Islamic elements combined. Malaysians endorse technocratic economic liberalism combined with paternalistic but benevolent authoritarianism. Like neighbouring Singapore, once part of the Malay federation, they reject the political liberties of Western liberal democracy.

Iran is a case apart for several reasons. Revolutions in the West have been anticlerical; in Iran, the clergy rule. (Ataturk assassinated virtually all Turkish Muslim clerics.) Admittedly, from exhilaration to exhaustion turns the cycle of every revolution. Iranians are, however, in a Shiite version of revolutionary theocracy, governed by their own rather than foreign elite. Utopian Shiite revolutionaries replaced Iran's consumptive and venal secular aristocracy which has now deteriorated into a clerical aristocracy. Even so, Iran's revolutionary parties are democratically elected and the country is a regional superpower submitting a successful bid for equality with the West.

In looking at south-east Asian Islam, we cannot ignore India, once the centre-piece of the non-white British empire, now the subcontinent with the largest Muslim population by far (concentrated in India, Pakistan and Bangladesh which was East Pakistan until 1971). Western commentators rarely report the sharp rise of Hindu fascism and the daily communal violence and brutality against Muslims in India and Kashmir. Muslims are routinely victimized by Hindu extremists and taunted for their ancestors' rule of India. The dispute between India and Pakistan may escalate grievously given that both are nuclear-armed. Irredentist Hindu nationalist claims to all Pakistan, not merely Kashmir, fuel a continuous tension, making nuclear confrontation probable. Despite claiming to be a democracy – and one that showcases its commitment to non-violence – India is always ready to go to war with Pakistan and even fought with China once.

Finally, sizeable Muslim populations live in communist nations. In China, the Sunni minority of Turkic origin, the Uighurs, in oil-rich Xianjing province, is in violent conflict with the Han Chinese. In recent riots, many hundreds of both groups have been killed, some by the police. Again, the oppression of Muslims in the former Soviet Republic, especially Chechnya, is on daily display in the world's headlines.

A word about the leadership of the Muslim world will complete this sketch. The Muslim world's rulers, venal elite with no popular mandate, are actively supported by the West in the name of national security and global stability, code-words for Western economic, cultural, political and military hegemony. The Muslim world is ruled by ageing secular autocrats (answerable to America, Britain and France) and tractable puppets bribed by Western nations and by drug warlords. Virtually all 'Muslim' elites are house-trained by the CIA, taught the latest torture techniques and crowd control.[4] Muslim 'citizens' are reduced to mere proxies, their indigenous aspirations ignored, as Western elites try to control the whole world's natural resources.

Radical leaders can be religious nationalists (as in Iran) or radical internationalists (Al-Qaeda). Religious radicalism and secular democracy are often allies: examples include Hamas, Algeria's Islamic movement and Egypt's Muslim Brotherhood, also active in Jordan. Western powers, including Israel, must negotiate with the Islamic counter-elite. These are individuals who oppose the imposed secularization of their countries and cultures, a secularization correctly interpreted as a metonymy for Western cultural invasion, capitalist domination and even military occupation. Corrupt, self-serving, secular and elitist pro-western movements (such as Fatah) cannot justly be preferred to democratically elected, popular and largely incorruptible mass movements such as (Sunni) Hamas and (Shiite) Hizbullah.[5]

IV

In this second survey of the Islamic world, we note the geo-political tensions between Islam and the West. Despite being militarily defeated, few Muslims, apart from the imposed elite, envy the West's culture or seek to convert to its dominant (Christian) faith. What is new about the post-cold war's New World Order is resurgent Islam. In 1914, Islam was a defeated, dying, tamed force. Ottoman Turkey was about to reject its imperial past; European colonialists were celebrating. Revivalist Islam forged its credentials in the crucible of the anti-colonialist nationalist movements whose leaders were usually secular, often educated in the West and attracted to its ideals of universal freedom, justice and equality. Those who fought and died for freedom were ordinary Muslims. At the beginning of the twenty-first century, foreign imports such as communism, pan-Arabism, Arab nationalism and Arab socialism have failed to deliver the goods. Many Muslims are incensed by the injustice that while even good and smart people must struggle daily to survive in the third world, countless ignorant and bigoted people are safe and happy in a politically stable west. In this context, Islam, the indigenous faith, has returned; the radicalization of Muslims is a standing item on the Western and secular Arab agenda. The storms that blow across deserts can dethrone kings.

The Muslim peoples' right to freedom and self-determination conflicts only with Western, especially American, economic interests, not with the West's professed ideals. Distrust, tension and misunderstanding persist between Muslim majority states and the Christian west. American foreign policy since the presidency of Ronald Reagan is captured in the Roman military maxim *Oderint dum metuant* (Let them hate so long as they fear). America, the most immature Western democracy, is too ready to go to war, an atavistic reminder of its wild west past. It spends more on its military than the rest of the world combined. The land nicknamed Jesus-land shows little interest in the ideals of the Prince of Peace. It is a refined irony that while American Christians desperately seek, inside a pacifist New Testament, a mandate for their nation's propensity for war, American Muslims seek verses condemning jihad and political violence in a scripture that condones legitimate violence.

The delinquencies of Muslim fanatics apparently account for much of the daily news while Christians and secular liberals either sit comfortably on the moral fence pretending that they have washed their hands clean of the political muck or else only occasionally intervene to depose the odd tyrant in the third (or Muslim) world. The rebellious real world is not eager to support such self-righteous stances. The standard Western critique of the Muslim involvement with power survives intellectually because its producers exploit the ignorance and prejudice of partisan audiences. Political Islam is portrayed as a uniformly fascist or totalitarian ideology with no resources for self-criticism. Wrong indeed but Western policy-makers are defending this thesis at all costs. The realities of world power point an accusing finger at the ubiquitous west and its allies: pretentiously secular and democratic and yet, in the hour of war with the Islamic world, suddenly and proudly religious and authoritarian.

In the first decade of the twenty-first century, the political compass swings to Islam, as religious superpower, and to the West as secular superpower. The American defeat in Iran and the Russian despair in Afghanistan, both caused mainly by radical Islam, enabled the Cold War to end as it reached freezing point.

The termination of that conflict – a struggle inside the European family – highlighted the tension between the Muslim east and the militarily powerful west which absorbed Russia, the failed superpower. India, Japan[6] and China are, economically and in part ideologically, Western nations whose emerging economic might wrongly disturbs Westerners: money without a challenging ideology can safely be ignored. All three will be absorbed into a global capitalism head-quartered in America.

The Arabs will run out of oil and cash; they will not run out of Islam, their real wealth and only enduring contribution to the world's stock of moral, aesthetic and spiritual meaning. Muslim anti-colonialist radicalism secretly impresses and depresses Western policy-makers committed to their allegedly benevolent universal hegemony which, under the pretext of democracy and philanthropy, disguises their economic interests.

The Berlin wall came down in 1989 but some Western ideologues are busy building higher walls between themselves and the ancient enemy from Arabia. Israel has literally walled in the people of the occupied West Bank.[7] Each brick of prejudice is being carefully laid in place. Muslims are seen as vandals and barbarians, hyper-enemies of culture and civilization. Can we dismantle these new walls and thus terminate 'the war with the longest truce in history'?

Popular and sophisticated Western opinion identifies Islam as the new threat and this while Muslims are plagued with war, famine, disunity and military weakness. Westerners have transferred their fear and contempt of communism on to Islam. Muslims have become the new Jews of the West, the enemy of the future, waging demographic jihad against Western societies too lazy and self-absorbed to have babies to maintain their birth-rates. According to popular Western belief, all the most hated men in the world are Muslims. Why are there no Serbian dictators or Russian autocrats on this list?[8]

This Western hatred is inspired by perceived Muslim bloodlust and indiscriminate violence. But terrorism is partly the outcome of powerlessness and desperation, though not of poverty. Many rich and educated Muslims, aware of intolerable injustices against Muslims worldwide, are more likely to become 'suicide bombers'. Poor Muslims, trying to survive financially, care little about global injustices while professionally educated Muslims pay lip-service to their faith. People normally embark on the road to violence when all other avenues are closed. Terrorism by Muslims gives Westerners a conclusive reason for ending their oppression, not a fragile excuse for perpetuating it. The helpless and entirely human rage of an Islamic underclass of victims, created by the West as a residue of its continuing colonialist triumph worldwide, is never acknowledged. Muslims note the West's moral blind-spot, its crude and dishonest rhetoric implicit in the very choice of vocabulary: all Islamic resistance is Islamic terrorism as if Muslims had initiated the fight or had no cause worth defending or had a monopoly on such violence. Even rhetorical Muslim threats of violence are daily met by real Western violence.

Modern revivalist movements such as Hizbollah and Hamas focus their energies on social work, building health clinics, schools, orphanages and so on. Consumers of the Western media know only the political manifestations of such groupings.

Baffled by their indignant rhetoric and occasional activism, Westerners loathe socially empowered Islam as a force of aberrant evil which endangers the progress of values considered 'modern' – a synonym for 'Western' since the West has a monopoly on modernity. For their part, Muslims fear westernization as the harbinger of cultural extinction and social debacle, a malign cancer imposed by force by Christian armies and later by military juntas and regimes presiding over a Muslim world whose indigenous political processes were deconstructed by colonial policy, its territory divided by national boundaries not drawn by Muslim hands, and its devout masses suppressed by small westernized elites contemptuous of their own heritage and its moral and religious values and verities.

An enduring peace between Islam and the West is possible; confrontation is neither inevitable nor necessary. Muslims are religiously obliged to seek a mandate for peace. But such a peace can endure only if Muslims are treated as honourable equals, heirs of an equally worthy if wounded civilization. That non-Muslims need to be careful with Islam and its adherents is a plea for compassion, not for caution. Islamic revival is a symptom of a wounded Muslim community, victimized by Western Christian civilization for centuries. Muslims want to live with the West, not under it. Current Western occupation of Muslim lands and constant military threats of more attacks on Muslims have together caused the Muslim retreat from modernity into a narrow traditionalism. American and British neo-colonialism intellectually empowers Muslim extremists at the expense of moderates and reformers.

A psychic tension will persist between a west that suffers from a power-complex and an Islam that is too compulsively political to be secularized into a harmless spiritual mediocrity, the fate of other faiths. Like a meddlesome relative, Western powers, led by America, regularly interfere with Muslim nations while Western 'scholars' co-operate with novelists in locating Muslim locales and sites that satisfy a Western appetite for violence and sex. Muslims cannot be trusted to run their own societies; they must be controlled and guided by civilized Christian powers. It is the orientalists' agenda, brazen in its new confidence and shameless in its endorsement of double, even triple, ethical standards.[9] All talk of tolerating Islam, and then only its 'moderate' version, assumes Western superiority as if autonomy and freedom were deserved only by the peoples of Western and north Atlantic civilization.

V

One must be careful with grandiose titles such as 'Islam in the twenty-first century' when hardly a decade of that century has elapsed or with 'The Crisis of Modern Islam'[10]. In canvassing the near future of an erstwhile imperial faith, my aim is modest. I differentiate between two visions of Islamic activism, often confused in the minds of Western policy-makers: imperial or supremacist Islam and liberal democratic (or representative) Islam. In this and the next two sections, we examine the radical activist or aggressively militant version. In Sections VIII and IX, we examine the other variety.

The supremacist version is a corollary of Islam's self-image as final faith. Triumph over their enemies or worldly annihilation of themselves exhaust the options for militants such as Khomeini, Qutb, Maududi and Al-Banna. Maududi wanted to convert a Muslim homeland into an Islamic state, a move from the descriptive reality of mere Muslims to the normative reality of Islam. This type of ambition symmetrically confronts the aggressive paramountcy of Western powers who maintain tyrannical regimes in most Muslim lands. Muslim supremacists oppose the West precisely because it is a democratic society, not because it fails to be a truly democratic society. The radicals accuse it not of having double standards but rather merely human standards. This position is obscurantist, arrogant and deluded. Most Muslims, however, to record our second position, credibly accuse the West of double standards and maintain that Western governments are, despite being mature democracies, unfair in their foreign policies.

Muslim activists boast that it is not the moderates but rather Muhammad's uncompromised followers who, operating underground through tunnels and caves, without military might, armed only with faith, topple dynasties on the ground. Only the radicals have faced the lion in the den and been torn to pieces. Do American and Israeli airstrikes and drones target the moderates? They would do so if Muslim leaders, so moderate and diplomatic that their only concession to their faith is that they give Islamic names to their children, failed to sing from the same hymn sheet as their colonial masters.

Islam's amalgam of religious and political enthusiasms still inspires the highest rate of martyrdom of any living faith: it remains unaffected by the secular laxity and hedonism of our times. Such activism must not be despised or dismissed, though its excesses must be questioned. That revolutionary Islam is the star performer, argue the militants, is a fact, not a boast. Decades of patient preaching and years of strategic temporary acquiescence with oppression must end with a mature piety eager to show its quality. The disposition to struggle, denied an opportunity earlier, owing to fear of violent reprisal without chance of success, must redeem its past deferrals. If militant evil can only be dislodged by goodness in an equally militant posture, then the refusal to move from preaching to activism compromises one's vocation. No matter how noble the principles one preaches, the enemy must eventually be confronted in the sphere of physical power. Despite conveying the message of the noblest humanism, did not Muhammad have to face his Badr? The pen is mightiest with the sword.

This Islamic disposition is dismissed by Islam's detractors who mistakenly judge Muslim activists as simply seducing gullible people into paradise. If Islam were not inherently appealing to the masses, why would anyone listen to the ideologues whose sermons bring the Friday traffic to a halt outside the overflowing mosques? People have to be in the market for something if the charm is to work. A man cannot, for example, seduce a woman who is indifferent to sex.

Islamic radicals are not the darlings of the Western press but at home they have huge constituencies. By contrast, Western radicals address a hostile indigenous population and hostile elite who dismiss them as mere leftovers of the left. The intellectuals of most Western nations understand the realities of power and usually oppose their governments' unjust foreign policies. One exception is America's often thoughtlessly patriotic intelligentsia.

Muslim activists preach that Muslims who accept powerlessness in their own lands are abdicating their religious responsibilities and inviting foreign aggression. They cite the Quran. 'Obey God and his Messenger and those in authority among you' (*min kum*; Q:4:58–9; 6:165). The expression *min kum* indicates an organic and indigenous leadership, not a crew of corrupt rulers imposed by departing or meddlesome colonial power elites. If one acknowledges the real-politik in the clash between an impotent House of Islam and an ever-expanding occidental imperialism buttressed by global capitalism, one cannot credibly assail this activist stance from any angle.

Muslims see their thinkers as criminally secularized, their agendas too closely tied to Western interests to be intended for the good of Muslims. The popular progressive attempt to demarcate and privilege a liberal (that is, powerless) Meccan Islam over the later empowered (Medinan) Islam is judged to be an attempt to convince Muslims that their interests are best served when they lay down their arms and let Westerners rule the world. Such thinkers' excesses inspire a litmus paper test for assessing the credentials of Muslim intellectuals active in the West. Does this scholar's works empower or weaken Muslims? According to this criterion, there is not a single Muslim scholar based in the West since all of them are more proud of the noun than of the qualifying adjective. Westerners apply the same litmus paper test in reverse: it is no coincidence that only those Muslim thinkers whose views effectively emasculate Muslims are guaranteed to win countless Western admirers and secure more than the normal quota of opportunities to exercise free speech in the most widely read magazines and journals.

VI

No Western thinker has ever offered any cogent reason for rejecting empowered Islam or for dismissing all Muslim activists as villains. The only reason must be the unspoken and self-serving one that we Westerners must stay on top, no matter what the moral cost. For their part, the Islamic radicals are unconstrained by fear and undiluted by respect for the West's moral achievements. Muslim activists believe that they must resist the West, not justify their resistance through newspaper articles in which they complain of their impotence. One militant unreservedly admired by all authentic Muslims is the Egyptian martyr-exegete Sayyid Qutb Shahid (1906–66), Islam's Karl Marx though Marx was no martyr.

As he approached age 50, a time of deepened awareness of one's mortality, Qutb found his life gravitating towards a crisis. Martyrdom can be in vulnerability or in zealous struggle for imperial expansion of the witness. The duties of faith culminate in self-sacrifice as proof of self-surrender, a final measure of fidelity to God. Activists such as Qutb have imitated Muhammad's militancy: fruitless verbal preaching gives way to a confrontation with the power-structure that resists just reformation.

The pattern was already set: the Muslim Brotherhood, founded in 1928 by Hasan Al-Banna, was a revivalist faith movement supplemented by an eagerness to struggle against heavy odds, in imitation of Muhammad's early battles. The activist interpretation of Islam condemned oppression and offered personal, domestic, social, legal and political justice through a workable mechanism for effecting redress and curing social ills. It appealed to Qutb who argued in his writings that communism gave us social justice at the expense of personal freedom while capitalism gave us personal liberties while sacrificing social justice. Islam gave us both by balancing our material and spiritual needs. A few decades later, Khomeini reasoned similarly. Western technological expertise was injected into Iran, the prime example of Western development policy after the Second World War, the last uncontroversial war of modern history. Yet it failed to prevent a revolution in God's name because the Iranian revolutionaries rejected both Eastern communism and Western capitalism as equally materialistic civilizations.

Little has changed since Qutb's time. For despotic Arab regimes, supported zealously by America, Britain and France, there are two kinds of Muslims: those who support the pro-western status quo and those who should be in jail since they constitute an alternative power-base that spells sedition and conspiracy. The Muslims who stand up for justice, move beyond the comfortable catharsis of moral outrage expressed in newspaper articles, are jailed and tortured. Being in jail is an important rite of passage for an Islamic activist. A spell behind bars can act as a spur to scholarship and also confirms one's authenticity in the eyes of fellow believers. This aid to authenticity is now readily granted to Muslim activists by Muslim and Western governments.

In 1965, to return to our hero, Qutb was tried for plotting to overthrow the Egyptian regime. Qutb conceded the charge and expatiated on it by claiming that defiance of evil structures of power was a duty, not an option. Loyalty to God and the Muslim ummah superseded a profane fealty to the Egyptian motherland: *Allāhu akbar*. Qutb called injustice by its name and saw justice as his scripture's absolute imperative (see Q:4:135; 5:2, 8). Found guilty of treason, he was executed in 1966. His rare combination of moral excellence and intellectual genius has enriched the Islamic heritage.

The rigorous quality of Qutb's conviction singles him out as a martyr of the first rank. Having placed his bet on Islam, his patient endurance was exemplary as he relied on God's all-sufficient grace. Qutb had time to cultivate patience, that most Quranic of the virtues. He was admired by lesser brothers for his dignity of posture and the absolute trust in God with which he endured moments of eclipse. One looks in vain here for a trace of the tragic impulse. For Qutb, vicissitude is from God – to be borne with patience and gratitude even in prison, with its deprivations and torture. Qutb's equanimity was inspired by the Quran when it sets down complete indifference to profane verdicts as the final proof of the strength of the man of God (Q:5:54).

Activists still wish to copy the style of the Prophet's unified and sincere militancy: prayer and the pen in the private sector of piety supplemented by the sanctions of power and polity in the public domain. Islam's power dimension, central to a comprehensively religious ideal, can be sublimated but not ignored or discounted. The morally constrained employment of power is an intrinsic demand of all-encompassing faith, not a lapse from an initial integrity necessitated by later recalcitrant events.

The truly religious mind willingly sacrifices itself to absolute revealed authority. In some moods, we may feel moved to question or regret what such authority demands of us. The standards are set too high. For example, Islamic activists have had to watch their children tortured in front of them. Qutb's witness was self-sacrificial since it was within worldly defeat, without the signal triumph that crowned the Prophet's endeavours. Qutb stressed the preparatory value of preaching, the pen and education, but knew that the final battles are always in the arena of physical power. He took martyrdom to be an obligation, not an act of supererogation. It was, after all, virtually a sixth pillar until the end of the Ottoman empire.[11]

To preach martyrdom is not to preach a death wish but rather to preach that death is better than a life condemned to be temporary. 'Suicide bombers' intend to sacrifice themselves to become martyrs who remain alive – literally so in paradise and metaphorically so on earth (Q:2:154). In suicide, death is the goal; in martyrdom, the goal is to affirm the measure of one's loyalty to God's cause. Martin Luther King mused: 'If a man is not willing to die for anything, he is not fit to live for anything either'. Islam requires a proud, rational and courageous submission to the hardships entailed by the divine will, not the cowardly and superstitious surrender of a victim.

In a vignette of Sayyid Qutb, Kenneth Cragg condemns him for rejecting tragedy and brands it a failure of intelligence and sensitivity.[12] Cragg looks and fails to find any trace of it; he records it as a deficiency in the martyr. Despite Qutb's prodigious reputation, among Muslims, for his piety and erudition, Cragg questions Qutb's status as an authentic believer who might serve as an exemplar for fellow believers.

Cragg is distressed by Qutb's condemnation of his era as a post-Quranic age of ignorance: despite Islam and its countless adherents, he argued, most Muslims are lured, through Western influences, back into the age of barbarism before the light of faith first shone. Cragg is puzzled by the Egyptian martyr's eagerness to claim that the presence of unIslamic rulers is evidence that idolatry still flourishes within the citadel of official Islam after 14 centuries.[13] Many observers have, surely, noticed the blight of venal and compromised government in the Muslim world. Qutb merely identified it, called it by its name, and opposed it. In any case, Christian triumphalism is unwarranted: the same idolatry persists despite two millennia of Christianity, flourishing now in the very heartland of an erstwhile Christian Europe.

Cragg wonders about the identity of the real Muslims – Qutb and the Brothers or their opponents? Cragg wrongly suggests that this dispute may be intractable. Islam is a religion conclusively defined by the scripture which inspired the man who established it. Copies of the Quran are to hand; claims about latitude of interpretation, especially those made by outsiders, are liable to exaggeration.

Qutb's interpretation of Islam is wholly correct on a traditional reading of the Quran. Cragg admits that Qutb's attitudes are inspired by the Quran.[14] He concedes that his militancy resembles the Prophet's.[15] If so, what prevents Qutb from qualifying as a true, indeed exemplary, Muslim? And if it is granted that he was authentically faithful, then surely those who wished to destroy him cannot possibly qualify as better Muslims especially when they made no secret of their indifference to, and practical neglect of, fundamental ethical and devotional Islamic obligations.

For non-Muslims, this still leaves open the question of who is right. This question is not open for Muslims: if a position is genuinely Quranic, it must be substantively right. Any appeal to the complexity of tradition, to the varieties of empirical Islam, is contrived and suggests ulterior and undeclared motives. Certainly Muslims, as intelligent heirs of their faith, differ among themselves. This does not imply that that there are radical or intractable divisions of opinion over matters of fundamental self-definition and utopian idealism. Cragg's discussion is instructive: faced with Islamic positions that threaten Western hegemony, even intelligent inquiry can deteriorate into devious polemic that is a preface to apology for partisan interests.

VII

Gamal Abdel Nasser once taunted the imprisoned Qutb: 'If there were a God, I'd jail him along with you'. Nasser spoke with candour and wit on behalf of the secular elite in the Muslim world, those fellow conspirators with the West in their opposition to Muslim political ambition in their territories.

Who are Qutb's successors in modern Egypt, a central Arab Muslim nation? A mere 15 years after Qutb's execution, a dramatic event took place. In October 1981, in view of the television cameras, a military truck suddenly stopped during a parade in honour of President Anwar Sadat. Four men stepped down and opened fire at the review stand. Sadat was killed. In 1961, in an attempt to reduce the independence of Islamic religionists, Nasser, the successful version of Saddam Hussein, reformed and nationalized Al-Azhar university-mosque.[16] Two decades later, during a live televised debate in that citadel of Sunni Islam, Sadat launched a symbolic attack on the authority of the religious scholars by trampling on the cap of his Muslim protagonist. Six months later, Sadat was assassinated.

The leader of Sadat's assassins was a young Lieutenant, Khalid Al-Islambouli, who belonged to the outlawed Islamic Jihad movement. He shouted: 'I killed Pharaoh. I am not afraid to die'. (The Pharaoh of the Exodus oppressed God's people in ancient Egypt.) The daring Al-Islambouli seized the headlines but his radical ideas were promulgated by Abdal Salam Faraj in his banned pamphlet 'The Neglected Duty'.[17]

Faraj's predecessors also condemned Egyptian society as un-Islamic because it was ruled by a secular system of government. The accusation of *takfīr* (excommunication or declaration of infidelity) is invalid against a whole culture. Qutb's dismissal of modern Muslims as living in pagan ignorance also amounts to this blanket accusation. The radicals were influenced by Ibn Taimiyya (d. 1328) who took the Quran at face value: 'Those who do not judge in accordance with what God has revealed are surely evil-doers' (Q:5:44). Ibn Taimiyya argued for jihad within the Islamic community. Where ostensibly Muslim sultans and kings secularize the Islamic power-structure, it is incumbent upon their Muslim subjects to dethrone them. Similarly, Qutb had urged violent revolt and resistance to a regime he judged unworthy. Faraj argued that most modern Egyptians are believers but their rulers are apostates since they reject Islamic law and thus preserve Islam only nominally. *De facto* Muslim rulers remain inside the scope of the Quran's judgment. Al-Islambouli and Faraj were executed in 1982.

Rival Islamic factions compete for power and the stamp of authentic radicalism. Contemporary Egyptian radicals condemn the Muslim Brotherhood, founded by Hassan Al-Banna and firmly established by Sayyid Qutb, as having compromised with the establishment. Many Brothers have wisely opted for gradual reform through semi-secular structures. In doing so, they have repudiated a political Islam that reduces to a purist and isolationist ideology. The Brotherhood, still officially banned in Egypt, is in practice recognized there; in Jordan, its members hold seats in parliament. Only the radicals, like Joseph before them in biblical times (Q:12:35), continue to languish in prison.

Muslims, justly provoked, may refuse to entrust the current state of injustice, in the Quran's comforting words, to patience and prayer (Q:2:45). In Qutb and kindred patterns of sincere if hasty militancy, some young Muslims discern inspiring and trustworthy advocates. They look with pride on these Muslims who can be destroyed but not defeated. Western leaders should implement just policies in order to reduce the appeal of these models of self-sacrifice and courageous struggle against all odds.

VIII

If Muslim martyrs (such as Qutb) reject the West as total anathema, virtually all modern Muslim leaders are, culturally, submissively assimilated to Western ideals. This will change as Islamic counter-elite emerge world-wide. Inside Western democracies too, the state must deal with Muslims leaders who represent the interests of ordinary Muslims.

The Muslim peoples' legitimate desire to shape their societies, to harness and control their resources, is hampered by outside powers who resent the inconvenience that too much of the world's oil is under Arab and Iranian soil. (In Britain, the discovery of North Sea oil was almost a religious event: it was a relief to know that God was not an Arab Muslim.) Britain, France and now America, inheritor of the European colonial role, single out a few nominally Muslim rulers for special protection, ensuring their prosperity and absolute domestic power at the expense of their own people. A few spectacularly rich sheikhs, engaged in an endless orgy of vulgar displays of opulence and sexual adventure, provide materials for sensationalist European tabloids.

At home, Westerners fight over principles; abroad, they care only about the material interests of their elite. Muslims fight over principles only in their struggles against outside powers; on the domestic front, their leaders care solely about their material interests. In their own countries and in lands where they have no wish to control others, Westerners are thoughtful and restrained, caring about human rights' violations and securing the rights of ethnic minorities, women and homosexuals. In their dealings with Muslims, however, Western leaders usually behave unjustly and arrogantly. 'Do in Rome as the Romans do' is not a proverb any American or Englishman takes seriously. Cultural arrogance ranges from inappropriately dressed Western tourists to Western elites whose policies are designed to retard the progress of the recently manumitted brown and black races.

This moral schizophrenia, often called double standards, is a chronic disease whose symptoms include the tragedy of a devastated Iraq and the poison of the perpetual Israeli–Palestine conflict which persists partly because most American government officials, except for sincere Christians such as Jimmy Carter, work hard to deny justice to Palestinian victims. Young educated Muslims resent the West's interference in Islamic affairs, its determined attempts to place Westerners and their fellow 'Muslim' conspirators at the helm of Muslim political destiny. They see the Western penchant for arranging peace conferences as a diplomatic way of making the House of Islam an American protectorate.

For Western governments, 'moderate' Muslims are those who are happiest when they are governed from London and Washington. Muslims of all political leanings are convinced that Westerners cannot maintain a balanced and just view of the Muslim world since their vision is clouded by economic interests. The conflict between Islam and the West is therefore engaged daily in the sphere of physical power in deference to the maxim 'Might makes Right'. Can Westerners move beyond the platitudinous pieties that provide the public face of their foreign policy by preferring just policies to jejune platitudes? Can they seek friends rather than merely strategic and diplomatic allies? Can they change not their tactics but rather their unjust attitudes? Western foreign policy is decoupled from professed moral values. In their treatment of Muslims, Western leaders are unfaithful to their professed liberal moral traditions of justice and universal compassion, ideals derived from Judaism and Christianity.

IX

Does 'Islam versus the West' translate into 'theocracy versus democracy'? Is democracy the political religion of the West, a successor to Western Christianity and Marxism? Can Islam find its place in democratic cultures which value attaining consensus through intelligent compromise and negotiation? As Muslim societies become sovereign administrative states, committed to secularism and nationalism rather than universal Islamic brotherhood, the democratic option becomes more popular. Muslims have started to eagerly convert their largely autocratic legacy into an order of democratic nation-states. Muslim electorates in Algeria, Jordan, the West Bank and Gaza, and Iran have used the ballot-box to place their trust in leaders who sympathize with enlightened Islamic ideals of universal justice and prosperity.

Before Muslims can assess Western democratic procedure and learn from it, they must discover their own internal resources. Otherwise the impetus will be external and interventionist since the West is not neutral about the emergence of specific types of Islam. Democracy is unacceptable to Muslims if it is a powerful secular adjunct to an emasculated religious doctrine. Islamic doctrine will judge the fate of democracy in the Muslim world by preventing it from becoming an autonomously secular paradigm. In assessing the conditions necessary for democracy, we must acknowledge the strength of inveterate competing forces. What will emerge is a theo-democratic nomocracy whose motto is 'The people's voice is God's voice' (*Vox populi vox Dei est*).

Muslims readily endorse some patterns of government that bear a family resemblance to secular democracy. This issue is partly a verbal one but also a religious and political one. Any exegete can impose tortured interpretations on the Quran to extract a preferred verdict that impresses pro-democratic Anglo-American audiences. Revelation abounds with wise maxims elastic enough to cover the aspirations of all contenders. Since 'democracy' has acquired an approbative force that all factions wish to annex, the attempt to define it is now a political rather than academic endeavour. By contrast, 'theocracy' is for Westerners, owing to negative experiments in European Christianity, simply a dirty word, at best a pattern of government inspired by extreme hubris. I reject this verdict as unempirical and unfair though only in the case of Islam since it has patronized successful theocracies in its ages of glory.

Muslim activism does not envisage a theocratic fascism. The mainstream Islamic movement will never institute inquisitions because the duties of faith fall into two categories. Private duties that pertain to the individual's religious life include prayer, fasting, pilgrimage and the like. Public duties include the regulation and just ordering of the life of the believing community by arranging payment of the alms-tax, declaring jihad (defence of the realm) and so on. The Islamic state, properly and traditionally constituted, does not interfere with the former but dictates the latter. This distinction is ignored by puritanical groups whose ignorant enthusiasm alarms Westerners.

Private virtue becomes socially prevalent only if enough individuals are already virtuous. A paternalistic imposition of private virtue only leads to a hypocritical attachment to public virtue. In any case, the lust to institutionalize revealed certainties is the shortest route to fascism. Idealistic Muslims are paying a high and bloody price to learn the truism that no amount of religious idealism can guarantee the political humility necessary for successful statecraft.

X

I return now to a theme I broached above in section VIII, namely, the role of the powerful west in the political fate of Islamic nations. Universal democracy is compatible with modern Islam but not with Western imperialism. The perpetual war on terror camouflages imperialist expansion for the sake of economic and ideological interests of militarily strong Western nations, especially America, the most populous and powerful one. The opposition to democracy in Islamic lands usually stems from Western government policy: several Western powers actively prevent Muslim democratic self-determination lest this entail hostility to their economic and strategic interests in the Islamic world.

Some repressive regimes in the Islamic world are actively supported and sometimes installed by America, Britain or France. The French encourage many pro-western dictatorships in North Africa. Muslim nations are divided between west-dependent and west-independent dictatorships. Even Saddam Hussein was a friend of the democratic west until he raped Kuwait, a client state, and his Western friends revised their definitions of good and evil. The Americans and the British befriended the Shah of Iran. Savak trained its top torturers in America where they learnt the latest techniques. Guards were taught to watch pornographic movies, at loud volume, to drown out the screams of Muslim radicals being tortured in nearby cells.

The Arab secret intelligence services (*Mukhābarāt*) oppress their own people, using Western technology and active Western connivance. Western secret services oppress foreigners, mainly Muslims. Both are evil actions and equally so: oppressing foreigners is morally no better than oppressing one's own people though the former is more understandable.

Western experts used to claim that democracy cannot blossom on Muslim soil because Islam is ineradicably authoritarian, indeed fascist. This is a view which has everything going for it except evidence. Western experts, especially British orientalists, have dishonestly denied the democratic potential and impulses of Islam, an outstandingly egalitarian faith, just as they have naïvely promoted the myth of a non-violent and secular India. In the former case, hatred and fear are the motives; in the latter, nostalgia and sentimentality.

Since 2003, reversing previous Western thinking on Islam's alleged incompatibility with democracy, we have the ideologically motivated claim that democracy can flourish on Muslim soil! It is imperialism by another name: puppet regimes and pliant third world leaders submissive to Western command. We know this since the process will be coercive, involving unelected interim governments and violence against any who reject Western military intervention. The widows and orphans of Muslim men killed, as collateral damage, will reap the benefits of democracy.

Admittedly, traditional Islam discourages multi-party management of political differences. In Western democracies, currently the choice between rival parties is usually unimportant for most citizens and wholly trivial for Muslim citizens. The crucial task is to find a mechanism for making political authority accountable to an electorate, thus raising, beyond sterile rhetoric, the obligatory professions of political humility.

Since the 1980s, Muslims have used the ballot-box to place their trust in Muslim leaders who sympathize with Islamic ideals. They have rejected dictators, such as the late Saddam (literally firm-footed) Hussain, who aborted the democratic process of safe transfer of power between leaders. There are semi-democratic systems in the non-Arab Islamic world: Iraq's Kurdish north, Turkey, Malaysia and Indonesia. Observers note a steady move towards democracy in Algeria and Jordan. Iran is by far the most mature democracy in the Muslim world. The corruption levels among Iranian bureaucrats are far lower than among the bureaucrats running neighbouring Pakistan, an unreformed and undemocratic nation.

Nascent democratic movements in the Muslim world were opposed by Western governments and by 'the brown sahibs' – the indigenous westernized 'elite' who inherited colonial rule. In Algeria, to take a prominent example, Muslims peacefully acquired power and used it to implement the wishes of the majority but Western powers accused them of using the democratic route to acquire power once and for all as opposed to instituting a functioning democracy. The real reason for Western and indigenous secular opposition was fear of the popular demands, made in the early 1990s, for an approval of the law of 'total return to Arab (Muslim) culture'. In the Gaza strip, starting in December 2008, Israel assassinated the democratically elected Hamas cabinet. Finally, Pakistan's secular leaders oppose Islam as outdated superstition while their Muslim constituency overwhelmingly welcomes it as basic to their identity. Since 1991, Pakistan's Parliament has voted to adopt Shariah as supreme. The Senate passed the controversial legislation after rejecting 40 opposition amendments that denounced the Shariah Bill as undemocratic.[18]

Muslims must build democratic mechanisms for appointing, maintaining and removing political leadership in a safe, just and peaceful manner. They can learn this by observing the behaviour of mature Western democracies such as the United Kingdom, Sweden, Holland and France. Only democratic politics can reliably serve the interests of the majority of Muslims. Other forms of governance usually only pay homage to the abstract ideology of an unrepresentative but fanatically committed minority, whether Islamic or, more often, one in the service of upper class Western interests.

XI

Unlike Jews, blacks and Hispanics, Muslims remain, despite being a larger and more widely dispersed group, victims of vicious stereotyping and informal profiling. The strength and persistence of anti-Muslim stereotyping is not derived from personal experience, travel or study. Rather the omnipotent media and popular culture together reinforce it. Nothing redeems Muslims: they rarely produce figures in arts, music or sport. Let me give a glaring example of anti-Muslim prejudice at the political level. Would Turkey have been denied entry into the EU if it had been a nominally Christian nation rather than a nominally Muslim one, secularized at every level?

Since January 1979, tensions between Islam and key Western powers have escalated exponentially. Since September 2001, this is supplemented by a deliberately co-ordinated attempt to construct an influential stereotype of 'fundamentalist' Islam as a violent creed which must be militarily defeated. We must recognize this phenomenon of recurring war with Islam, the arsenal of clichés replenished by every new encounter. Muslims are stereotyped, stigmatized and criminalized as permanently and ineradicably violent and anarchic hyper-enemies of civilization; public debate on Islam is accordingly conducted through the bifocal lens of sensationalist journalism and ideological hostility.

The irony here is that, unlike other faiths, Islam has traditionally provided a coherent ideology of some political value, a system that should serve as a source of independent critical comment on the dominant secular international order. Although uniformly interpreted as no more than an ideologically sterile threat to it, Islam actually provides valuable commentary on a capitalist, free market fundamentalist secularism whose narrow political and economic certainties, unlike those of ancient faiths, are not expected to evolve. Islam aside, is there any external critical comment on this global, homogenized and aggressively secular world order? The political credentials of Christianity have been neutered while Marxism has collapsed.

If secularists want a penetrating moral critique of the secular liberal presuppositions of their system, they should listen to Muslim critics whose voices are heard only in late night television slots of the Western wilderness. Secularists are accustomed to criticizing, even abusing, religions but lack the political humility to listen to divergent opinions, especially if these originate among Muslims, the West's only articulate critics. Western secularists expect Muslims to learn from their political successes but think that they have nothing to learn from Islam. The Quran can boast the unique privilege of directly inspiring and determining, for some 1400 years, the course of a world civilization based on a religiously sanctioned quest for social and economic justice allied with respect for scholarship and personal moral excellence.

Should this achievement be dismissed as irrelevant on the sole ground that it is religious? Is there no place for the religious voice in modern politics? There can be no fruitful engagement between secular modernity and Islam on the basis that secularism has nothing to learn, only much to teach. Islam provides a dialogue partner for secular political projects since it can convincingly infuse religiously grounded moral concerns directly into politics.

The next paradigm in the House of Islam will be a theo-democratic nomocracy in which popular sovereignty will be reconciled with absolute revealed legislation. No new political model relevant to Muslims can emerge from the West. Marxism, the climax of Western political thought, has collapsed spectacularly. As private charity replaces politics, we may legitimately speak of the end of domestic politics in the West. Citizens are often 'doing their bit' only as a salve for their consciences. After the age of nationalism comes to an end in the Muslim world, the next paradigm will be an Islamic bloc like the European Union or the United States. Why not a United States of Islam, a pan-Islamic empire? But the accompanying new Islamic theology will not be opposed to the malleable politics of democratic consensus and negotiated compromise. The chiliastic theology of empire and absolute triumph will be replaced by moderation defined as the pursuit of justice for all peoples and a rejection of any culpable indifference to the consciences of any good human beings, whatever their creed.

XII

In this hiatus, we stop to abstractly explore power, a principal theme of this essay. It has provided a backdrop to the rivalry between Islam and Christianity, the religious superpowers with competing colonial histories in the past, present and future.

By acknowledging the need for power, we pre-empt a power-complex that leads us to overtly deny the need for it – only to seek it covertly and all the more aggressively. In the West, the tension between religion and politics, artificially removed from the public domain through the self-professed dogma of laicism, reappears elsewhere with greater force, often agitating the citizen's private conscience or permeating the world of international relations and suppressed quasi-imperial inter-faith rivalries. At best it is naïve, at worst dishonest, to pretend that the moral struggle of good against evil has no political or military dimension. Muhammad was a prophet–teacher and a ruler–soldier. This explains why Islam is an ethical system and a legal practice but also, more fundamentally, a religious identity buttressed by a political loyalty.

By contrast, Christian praxis is now openly co-opted by the ends of secular power. Little in modern Christianity enables political resistance against the hegemonic absorption of the churches by the guiding narratives of an unholy trinity: the secular state, civil society and the free market. This is true even in America, a powerful nation whose citizens loudly profess their Christian identity. To resist the secular colonization internal to the West, Christian theologians must urgently renew the ontological integrity of theo-political praxis as worthy of modernity by recovering the public witness of a Christian polity. How? They must challenge the domestication of the church and reclaim it as a *morally* subversive *political* force. As I proved in Part II, secularity proceeds by legitimizing as neutral or politically innocuous the most dangerous dichotomy of secular modernity, namely, religion versus politics.

Christians rightly insist that all life's departments, challenges and opportunities, including political organization, must be theologically interrogated. The duty to be socially just is rooted in the duty to love all regardless of their status, economic class, political affiliation, race, gender, disability and age. But this duty of justice, argues the alert Christian, is prevented from being merely political since it derives from an evangel that cannot be appropriated by politics. Personal salvation precedes social liberation since society and law derive from an order that transcends economics, politics and empire thus rendering the autonomy of politics a false and pernicious doctrine. Muslims can concur with this denial of autonomy to secular statecraft while rejecting the rest of the Christian agenda as evidence of misguided priorities.

The Christian rejection of the false politics of empire valuably questions the ready identification of worldly empire with universality, mistaking the conquest of cities with the conquest of souls. Paul's reference to 'powers and principalities' is intended to suspend the temporal question of imperial universality, the Roman ambition, by an eschatological re-orientation towards apocalyptic and apolitical notions of divine transcendence. The Apostle is seeking cosmic empire rooted in a new order (the New Jerusalem). Divine love (agape) is a political act with political consequences: a subversion of the dominant worldly and imperial pretensions to universality understood as universal territoriality. The Christian theology of persecution and powerlessness is not ad hoc: it has organically Christian roots in the eschatology of radical liberation which interiorizes and thus undermines the dominant Roman paradigm of empire as territorial possession. Muslims should note this profound critique of the theological foundations of religious, including Islamic and neo-Christian, imperialisms. It challenges Muslims proud of their imperial history. Must empire entail secular power over others? I have never despised the Christian accusation and have therefore, in Chapters 4 and 5, laboured to answer it on its own terms.

In the coming clash between militant secularity and monotheism, Western Christianity, apart from an inauthentic American variant, will be a minor player. Besieged by secularism for centuries, it is a spent force that has recently retreated further into secluded obscurity, torn away from its historical roots, and set on the secular landscape not as a beacon but as an excrescence and a warning. Islam stands proudly and decisively on the blood-stained landscape, the muezzin calling to peace and prayer in the midst of war and occupation. Islam's durability in Middle Eastern power calculations baffles orientalist experts who seek to understand but not appreciate the world's last anti-secular religion. Orientalism, irreverent and irrelevant as it is, need not detain us.

Islam's resistance to political and theological secularization ensures that there is at least one religious tributary feeding into the ocean of secularity. (If Islam had conquered Europe, would it have remained immune to secularism and still be God's continent?) A future Islam will be an applied Islam whose political passion will oppose injustice in order to secure our welfare. It will not feature a puritanical obsession with sex; it will deny the totalitarian vision which denies Islam entry into a democratic world order. It will not be Maududi's or Qutb's Islam which could innocently hope to imitate Muhammad's militancy. It will not be a faith equipped with the simple eschatology of the Garden and Hell, Jannah and Jahannam, exemplified in the utopia of the Shariah in this life and paradise in the next. The days are past when God spoke in only two languages: world conquest and paradise. Modern Muslims must learn to take eternity seriously but in a modern way.

No civilization has had more than one turn at the wheel of fortune. Islam is no different. We Muslims are humble heirs of a glorious age that has passed away. Our Islam remains linked to its past only as an amalgam of morally charged faith and responsibly exercised power which actively engages rather than culpably dismisses the consciences and ideals of its opponents. Inside the West, Muslims must strive for equality within democratic structures. It will be, as during the Rushdie affair, an affair of working- and middle-class Muslims creating an indigenous Western Islam.

XIII

External change plagues Muslims. It has been imposed by representatives of an alien modernity: disruptive and revolutionary (Iran and Turkey), transitional and disorderly (Algeria). It is rarely internal, constructive and engaged (Malaysia). Modern Europeans have never had to contend with any non-European culture or to take it seriously. Europeans have had an easy way with the rest of the world for some 500 years; their privileges are now universally taken for granted. The only opposition is from those Muslims who reject reform movements sponsored by Westerners trying to undermine the Muslim drive for political autonomy. Such movements receive too enthusiastic a patronage from the West for Muslims to think they are intended for their empowerment.

Why should Muslims voluntarily abjure power in their own lands? Nor are Western Christians in a position to cast the first stone. Since they allowed secular society to emasculate their churches, such capitulation permitted the canonization of the West's secular establishment. Like any other religion, and in practice to the same extent as any other religion, Islam is open to abuse by those seeking to clothe their political bankruptcy in the robes of popular religion. But the insistent Western demand that Muslims can only be modern by renouncing power is a hidden agenda for exploiting the wretched of the earth.

Westerners allege that Islam has a crisis of identity and authority. In fact its only crisis is that it has no power to implement even a modest version of its vision. Until recently, Islam was studied from a position of total and a priori rejection of its message, particularly its political component. Few Westerners view Islam as an honourable rival or endorse its moral message as essentially compatible with Judaeo-Christian values and indeed with some of the liberal humanist values which matured with the progress of secularization in the West. Few Western scholars entertain a neutral (or phenomenological) perspective that could mature into an open, reflective, possibly sympathetic stance.

If Islamic nations or the ummah as a supra-national organization were legitimately empowered, terrorist acts would not be perpetrated by non-state actors (such as Hizbullah and Al-Qaeda) fighting the West. Since political Islam is not an epiphenomenon but rather a natural growth from its theological roots in Quranic revelation, it must endure. By political Islam, I do not mean an imperial faith but rather one sufficiently empowered to resist Western encroachment, a religion legally enforced inside Islamic majority states, and everywhere revolutionary against oppression. An appropriately empowered Islam alone could prevent the persecution of Muslims in Bosnia, Chechnya, Kashmir and Palestine. Empowerment has countless benefits, especially the ability to prevent injustice rather than merely redress it. As in health, prevention is better than cure. That is why the body politic, like the physical body, must be empowered to fight its own battles.

Muslims wish to re-empower their communities mainly as a reaction against the excesses of colonialism which has apprised Muslims of their political impotence. A narrow and intolerant secularism has inspired a narrow and intolerant Islam. Some Muslims and all Christians propose a powerless and depoliticized Islam as the best dialogue partner with modernism. I believe the opposite: a politically confident Islam will be a more generous partner in the dialogue of civilizations, permitting Muslims to make appropriate concessions to secular modernity by shedding outdated parts of their ancient heritage and burdensome tradition. If Muslims controlled their destiny and enjoyed the sanction of power, this would limit the ability of powerful non-Muslim nations to mock and demean, with impunity, Islamic sanctities and sensibilities. Muslims would therefore feel respected by the community of nations. Most Muslims are currently powerless; and powerlessness corrupts. It tempts one to cynically and anarchically opt out of the social order.

Westerners too readily assume that an empowered Islam is necessarily a perverted faith, a disaster for non-Muslims. They forget Islam's experiment in convivencia, the harmonious co-habitation of Muslims with Jews and Christians in Muslim Andalusia for some 800 years. Admittedly, some Muslims preserve their glorious past to the point of being reactionary in places such as Saudi Arabia. Islam is, however, also a progressive emancipator, its political and economic paradigms just and liberating. Why should, for example, the Shariah's ban on inordinate interest rates not become universal legislation, especially in view of recent global recessions? Why should secularism and modern Christianity together exhaust the Western liberal paradigm? Islam could evolve into a liberal faith where 'liberal' need not mean an emasculated, merely mystical, faith.

An empowered Islam is the best hope for a just, peaceful and stable international order. Westerners need to be less ethnocentric: theocracy has a bad image mainly due to Western history. For Muslims, religious government secured peace, justice and prosperity. The Middle East saw almost 1000 years of continuous peace, the longest lasting period of stable rule supplied by a single system of government in the region. British Palestine, 'the twice promised land' (promised first to Arabs, then to Jews) enjoyed, from 638 to 1918, a virtually uninterrupted Pax Islamica that guaranteed peace, stability, and prosperity for all monotheists.

A powerful Islam indirectly inspired the European Renaissance and gave the Middle East a just peace for over a millennium; a powerless Islam gave us terrorism. The West must choose. The empowered ummah is not a guise for Muslim world domination, in any case hardly an achievable ambition. The unification of Muslims, achieved by superseding national and political boundaries, has political consequences if not political motives. Muhammad and his followers created a universal community flourishing in God's name. Why is that a threat to world peace? Islamic unity is bad news only for those who wish to maintain unjust universal hegemony.

XIV

The Judaeo-Christian component in the confrontation between Islam and the West cannot be ignored since the cliché of the Muslim universe as violent, irrational, barbaric, intolerant, uncivilized and anarchic, anti-Christian, anti-modern, anti-progress, and fanatically monolithic, is originally and even today, a religiously motivated one. Liberals inherit, unthinkingly, these originally Christian-produced stereotypes of Islam. The animus was not fortuitous: Christianity's nemesis was after all the rise of Islam, an external event which marked the end of early Christianity.

Muslim frankness about power leads Christians to accuse Muslims of being unscrupulous warmongers but then Christians are comfortably at the helm of the world's political destiny and therefore currently less in need of a vengeful God to avenge injustices against them. America, the world's sole superpower, represents and militantly defends Christian and Jewish interests worldwide. Six members of the G8, the club of major industrialized nations, are in some sense Christian powers. Since many European nations have Christian Democratic parties running for office, politically these nations may be called Christian. There are no Muslim members of the G8. The UN Security Council has five permanent members of which three are Christian (America, Britain and France) while two are communist powers. There are no Muslim members even though a quarter of the world's sovereign states are Muslim and about a fifth of the world's population is Muslim.

It is an irony never noted in the West that when Western writers and activists condemn certain states as illegitimate or oppressive, these Western commentators are widely admired as the vanguard of humanity. When Muslims condemn oppression in their lands, they are condemned as fundamentalists and militants before being liquidated, with impunity, by American, British or Israeli air-strikes. Westerners stipulate that they will negotiate with Muslims only after Muslims have been disarmed, pacified and made compliant. As long as they claim to be dissenting equals, they have no right to engage the West. The deadlock continues.

The roots of this political stalemate are religious. Muslims see Jesus, the pale Galilean, as their brother who was not pale in commitment, whatever racist pundits may say of his complexion. Christian apologists say that in the Christ of God, we have the whole truth. Unsympathetic theists retort that Jesus never grew old enough to find the truth about this sordid world. The idea that we humans will submit voluntarily to divinely ordained justice, in a world made precarious by human pride and perversity, is morally too innocent. Muhammad's political career can be read as a commentary on the reputation of a just and activist God. Islam is a virginal religion: it maintains its chastity in matters of dogma and morality by spurning the overtures of devious, worldly and duplicitous suitors. As a pre-Enlightenment consciousness in which good and evil are real categories of conviction, as they were for all proud and ancient races, Islam belongs to the purer half of our history when theism endorsed single standards of justice and when compromise was restricted to taste and triviality and did not extend to faith and principle.

History gives no example of a more honest statesman than the prophet from Mecca. Judged by modern Christian and liberal standards, Muhammad as prophet is bound to be a failure since for him violence, endured as persecution or inflicted as punishment, was inescapable. His frankness about the need for power is seen as a lust for domination, at best a misplaced fanaticism on God's behalf. The whole truth lies in neither of these verdicts, assuming that truth is what we seek and, in the case of believers, by God's grace, find. Islam builds a religious motive for political action, individually and socially, into the fabric of its dogma of God's rule as King. In this way, wise rulers could never claim that their merely human governments fully implemented a revealed Islam. God is King and dislikes other pretenders to the throne, unless they know their place.

XV

The American confrontation with Islam needs separate assessment. Many people see America as the leading cause of world problems ranging from climate change to war and depletion of resources. As a Christian superpower, it is seen by virtually all Muslims, outside America, as an oppressor of Muslims worldwide and the leader of rapacious first world capitalism. Islam's ban on usury opposes the financial infra-structure of a global industrial civilization led by America. Its foreign policy uniformly ignores or antagonizes Muslims. While European superiority is braided with an inveterate racism, the casual openness and innocence of Americans conceals a resolve of steel behind the superficially naïve and friendly façade. This artless American sincerity coupled with an exclusive, exceptionalist, militaristic and militant nationalism troubles even fellow Christian Europeans. Militarism is state terrorism by another name and is perfectly legal.

It is an innocent but chilling paradox that Jesus, the prince of peace, is most popular in the land of guns, a country where homicide is the second most popular national sport. War and Christianity provide two sources of patriotic cohesion in the United States. The agenda of far right Christians is the desatanization of the world as end-time messianic theology meets nuclear might. The American south is infected by Christian extremism and produces fatally dangerous bigotry. A domestically neutered but aggressively patriotic Christianity replaces the utopian politics of revolution, the chief anxiety for the capitalist elite. Even the American intelligentsia is patriotic, sold out to corrupt elites and interest groups.

American foreign policy is marked by a naïve and sincere Manicheism that sees the world in terms of our light and their darkness, a neo-Victorian messianic contrast. The self-satisfied and incoherent platitudes and jingoistic xenophobia of leaders speaking of the 'axis of evil' is rarely balanced by any redeeming xenophilia. Admittedly, Muslims who have suffered humiliation at the hands of Americans have also used hyperbolic language. Iranian leaders call America 'the Great Satan' and 'the global arrogance'[19] while Britain, in post-imperial decline, is no longer 'Great' and thus more kindly called 'the little satan'.

Americans deny American empire even though it is the most extensive in history, even extending into space. The ubiquity of American interests is obvious to non-Americans. One American writer argues that Americans should engage in pre-emptive strikes in 'anticipatory defence' of their global material interests.[20] He suggests that fear of collateral damage is merely modern moral squeamishness: '… killing innocent women and children shows the strength of [our] feelings'.[21]

The capitalist struggle against Islam's just economic policy provides the heart of American foreign policy although most Muslims regard as tolerable foreign intervention restricted to economic matters. America is the military Leviathan which enforces free markets worldwide. Democratizing the world is only a pretext for using military means to defend Western supremacy in a world of shrinking natural resources. Thus, democracy in Iraq is bound to mean sham elections in which American interests are given the veneer of local approval.

The defence of secular liberal democracy is a veiled defence of free market capitalism, an elaborate exercise in cheerleading for American corporations worldwide. Global capitalism is a universal ideology preaching 'profits bring prosperity', a religion whose prophet is profit. Although American capitalism is not pure – the state intervenes in economic policy – it is potent enough to have destroyed the morally restraining power of true Christianity, democracy and political idealism. Americans, including university students, are now the least progressive and idealistic among Westerners. The liberal hour that began in the 1960s is now over. Instead of courageous men and women speaking truth to power, we find a craven courting of those in power.

Europeans dismiss America as a teenager among the nations. Americans see Europe and the Middle East as senescent civilizations in search of a role – just as nutritionists dismiss vitamin E as a vitamin in search of a disease to cure. Unlike Islam in Europe, Islam is not part of domestic American politics since Americans can afford to decouple their foreign policy from their domestic policy towards their Muslim minority. Islam matters in European identity politics both for Muslims and for Europeans, especially for the purists who reject assimilation into the post-nationalist continental state of Europe (EU). Europeans, unlike Americans, cannot escape Islam, a geographically close neighbour for millennia. In the United Kingdom, the struggle between Islam and British society is a contest between two deeply held cultures. In America, neither the Muslims nor their American hosts tenaciously possess any culture of any depth since only a shared materialism unites them.

In concluding this section, I want to guard against a crucial misunderstanding. Critics of my stance could argue that I want it both ways: I condemn the way that Christianity has surrendered to secularism in Europe, leading to its emasculation. However, in America, Christianity is politically potent as a Christian nation implementing its vision of power in the world. And I condemn that too! My point is that in both cases *authentic* Christianity has surrendered to secularism. In the European case, it is obvious. The American use of power is secular and pragmatic, not principled or Christian. It is impossible to imagine a stance more treasonable to the cause of Christ.

XVI

Must politics tolerate the evil that power brings in its train? Can we eradicate the evil that power instigates? These questions express the rift between a Christian vision of a politically fallen world and an Islamic one in which we achieve redemption through politics. I disentangled this skein of reasoning in Part II by scrutinizing the work of Kenneth Cragg. Muhammad is not an Arabian Jesus – a more robust prophet, as required by his Arabian context. Such a Jesus would be as absurd as the Jesus mocked as 'the pale Galilean' by Julian the Apostate.

The vague mandate for peace is plentiful. Who would prefer war to peace? In peace time, sons bury their fathers; in war, fathers bury their sons. This wisdom is from Herodotus in *The Histories*. Daily life, history, world religions and secular ethics all advocate peace. Is it a peace that compromises with injustice? Jeremiah wistfully pleads for peace often enough, perhaps too often in its setting when Yahweh was virile – long before he subsided into obsolescence and irrelevance for his chosen people. Jeremiah's jeremiad: 'We hoped for peace (*shalōm*) but no good came of it, for a time of healing. But look! Only: Terror!' (Jeremiah 8:15). Many today pretend to be looking for universal peace and much evil comes of it (see Q:2:11–12). In their case, what I have said about them may be convicted of lacking in diplomacy and restraint; it will not be accused of lacking in frankness or sincerity.

It is reserved for modern Muslims to impart new life to the declining belief in the ethics of politics. Idealistic Christians remain fixated on a pernicious illusion: the militancy of oppressors shall wither away when faced with the accusations of the powerless private conscience. The truth is the other way: the private conscience is withering away. Evil is in the wrong but it is strong. To reject resistance to evil is to vote for the triumph of oppression. These are not academic thoughts. The struggle for social justice must be freed from the wrong kind of scruple. Where we find overwhelming injustice, we should jettison the principle of 'Turn the other cheek' since it is untenable as a principle of political morality and viable only in matters of private injury. Although Christianity's originating norms obliged it to avoid politics altogether, even this creed which strenuously aimed to remain powerless, was subsequently extensively empowered. Could there be a better indication of our instinct to embrace the political arm? The Christian attitude towards polity and power, since the compromise with Constantine and the adventurism of the Crusades, appears fraudulent to anyone reared on the honest realism of Islam.

I repudiate any supremacist, imperial or anarchically revolutionary (or reactionary) Islamic politics. Fortunately, classical Islam itself rejects the ideas of absolute political evil or absolute virtue. Power invariably limits virtue but need not destroy it. Muhammad did not merely fantasize about mending the world. By embracing the moral risks of direct action, he moved beyond the comfortable catharsis of merely moral outrage. Muslims are following him by participating in the *legitimate* violence of power for the sake of virtue.

Indeed the professed non-violence and powerlessness of victims can cause further violence. These attitudes can perversely arouse in oppressors a desire for inflicting more violence on the weak. Persecuted communities know well how their very vulnerability invites further oppression: perceived weakness is provocative. In the Quran, we read of communities of oppressed believers praying: 'Our Lord, do not make us a prey (*fitnah*) for disbelievers' (Q:60:5). Again, 'A falling camel attracts many knives', says the Bedouin proverb. One must not be so weak that one's weakness tempts the unjust. If unjust people know that their intended victims will forcefully defend their rights, they will think twice before attacking them.

Nor do Muslims see Christian principles of non-violence as high moral ideals. Rather, these exhibit an irresponsible refusal to address the pressing injustices of the real world partly because the human predicament is seen as hopelessly desperate. Christian pacifists are usually Christian pessimists who see hope as solely a theological virtue, never a political one. Hope is a moral and intellectual virtue in many cultures, especially among peoples who reject an after-life. If one sees the world as a transient passage, pessimism about changing it is an understandable stance. Most of us, however, would prefer to sing with the Latin poets: *Dum spiro, spero. Nil desperandum* (I hope while I breathe. Never despair.)

The adherents of non-violent creeds can, when empowered, prostitute power because, unlike the adherents of an avowedly political religion, they lack (and deny the need for) doctrinal guidance for regulating their innate belligerence. Since Islam is, unlike other faiths, by original design a political faith, it is *less* readily politically exploitable. We introduced nuance into such claims in Chapters 4 and 5. Here we note only the irony of a civilization in which peace prizes are patronized by repentant gunpowder merchants. If only all the paradoxes in this area were as innocent or sincere as this one.

We note in this context the ulterior motives for the West's regard for the Eastern religious proposal of non-violence. Endorsing the stance of Gandhi, the Indian utopian idealist,[22] is a devious way of condemning the violent option in opposing Western colonialism, the path chosen by Islamic and Marxist freedom-fighters. Unless undertaken in the right spirit, non-violence is a dignified word for cowardice.

As prophetic religion, Islam rejects a deferred messianic deliverance, the hope which animates soteriological (salvific) religions such as Christianity. It also repudiates an apolitical apocalypticism which marked Judaism in its depressed moods preceding the ambitious euphoria of the Zionist project born in the original sin of Arab exile and suffering and still colliding brutally with the facts of Palestinian demography. Islam opts for a mundane and temporal politics and then purifies it.

XVII

Islam's defensive militancy is called jihad by Muslims but condemned as terrorism by Westerners. Muslims want power to defend themselves against the militarily and intellectually ubiquitous West. Western capitals of thought and publishing encircle the globe: London, New York, Frankfurt and Sydney. Muslims concur with those critics of Western civilization who lament that the Westerners' welcome intellectual curiosity is the other side to their innate militancy and addictive need to control and possess and exploit others. All Muslim nations are militarily weak. A Western power can invade and rule virtually any Islamic nation until another Western power fights to evict it. Muslim government officials are usually answerable to Western powers, not to their own subjects. True: all nations are many nations; the West is many wests. But the only west with whom most Muslims must contend is the empowered west, ruthlessly imposing its economic and political will on them.

The Muslim response to continuing Western aggression is terrorism by individual actors. Terrorist acts by transnational actors and vigilante groups, directed against Western targets, are provoked by Western colonial policy which amounts to state terrorism. While there is much righteous indignation about the innocents killed by Muslim terrorists, one infrequently hears any corresponding outrage about the victims of Western aggression. Only the mode of delivery of the bombs varies: by a cruise missile, an unmanned drone or in person. What is the moral difference?

Too often, the response of American and British, like that of Indian and Israeli, forces is unbridled violence against a largely rhetorical act of symbolic terrorism by individual Muslims. Western audiences watch in colour television as Muslim infants are grilled to death in their sleep. It is merely collateral damage. The division of labour is: Westerners kill while Muslims die. When reversed, there is outrage and Western vengeance is not satisfied even after the killing of a disproportionately large number of Muslims. Even secularized Western democratic leaders are proudly religious in the hour of war: George Bush and Tony Blair claimed divine inspiration for their foreign policies.[23] Western and Israeli militarism and muscularity are noted by their Muslim victims. For Westerners, it is simply the price the free world must pay to maintain its superiority.

Terrorism is stodgily defined by American policy makers in such a way that it has no valid causes and can only be committed by those who oppose American interests. All too often, many Muslim observers would contend, one has only to call Muslims 'radicals' or 'fanatics' or 'militants' to justify killing them. It is easy to misrepresent those whom we wish to misunderstand.

Admittedly, terrorism is not due solely to poverty or lack of education. Desperation at the double and triple standards of international justice is more keenly felt by privileged youth since they entertain an educated view of world power. Increasingly Muslim women, largely indifferent to world politics, are starting to care about the atrocities routinely committed by Western powers. Thus, we see even young Muslim women wired as human bombs. Terrorist tactics have evolved into insurgency and guerilla warfare. In November 2008, we witnessed a small army of terrorists operating in an urban location, namely Mumbai, to commit a massacre.

All Muslims secretly note the empty flash of Western rhetoric about universal human rights. Muslim youth in European capitals shrug their shoulders and say: 'Bombs explode daily in Baghdad. Why shouldn't bombs explode in Western capitals?' One British charity's workers were traumatized by the sight of carts drawn by donkeys – used as rocket launchers by Palestinians – during the January 2009 Israeli invasion of Gaza. But they were worried about the fate of the donkeys: dead animals matter more than dead Muslims.

Even moderate Muslims are reluctant to condemn terrorism because they think that while the means are immoral, the means are no more immoral than those used by Western powers with far superior military prowess. In any case, the cause is just since the terrorists' strategic goals include justice for oppressed Muslim minorities. Can one fairly condemn the excesses of the Muslim resistance in occupied Muslim lands given the overwhelming odds against them in this asymmetrical war?

Adult citizens in a democracy, unlike in a totalitarian regime, are complicit in their government's policies since they freely elect it and are therefore not wholly innocent of its vices. Conversely, non-democratic nations blessed with vast oil revenues do not need to tax their citizens to finance their activities; therefore many buy out their citizens and thus remain autonomous, being neither demo-cratically elected nor subsequently accountable to their citizens. In this context, individual terrorists arise and organize since their governments cannot or do not petition for legitimate power on the global stage. Moreover, terrorists feel no guilt about targeting innocent Western travellers because they assume that democrati-cally elected Western governments, unlike their own western-supported autocratic tyrannies, must have the broad support of their citizens.

Western polemicists often note that Islamic terrorism, unlike all others, is global. They do not note that this is due to the West's ideological ubiquity, not to some innate feature of Islamic terrorism. If Muslims intend to oppose the universal west, they cannot oppose it locally since we all go west, wherever we go.

There were no Muslim suicide bombers until the late twentieth century. Once Islamic nations achieve military parity with the West, terrorism shall vanish since it is only a symptom, not a condition. A weak Islam gave us terrorism; a strong Islam shall give us peace and mutual tolerance on equal terms.

XVIII

Who has the right to decide the essence of Islam? Given that political religion is the only alternative to daydreaming, what will be the political entailments of that decision? For Westerners, politics has been reduced to private charity. For Muslims, politics is terrorism abroad – a stunt – and dictatorship at home. This prostitutes the noble art of politics. We can redeem politics by making the pursuit of an enduring peace, founded on justice and mercy, our most active duty. Nor is any area of human life entirely innocent of power. Even romantic love is not inno-cent of political intrigue. Wherever two meet, power is the third party; private relationships involve control and interpersonal force as loving becomes a political act which revolutionizes one's world. 'All is not fair in love and war' but the choices these realities impose cannot be avoided. Love must not lapse into tyranny: Caesar must not usurp what belongs to God alone.

Islam receives undue hostile scrutiny mainly because the question of its essence, unlike that of all other faiths, is a political one. Western monotheisms have expe-rienced internal pressures to define their orthodoxies. Early Christianity is famous for its proliferation of heresies during the attempt to define its creeds. Islam is unique today in that, apart from internal battles over its essence, outsiders also want to shape its profile. Unlike Christianity, Islam is actively debated by outsid-ers who claim to be greater experts on it than its own adherents.

Even in academic circles, political Islam is subject to a priori dismissal and deter-mined rejection. Only an apolitical Islam is acceptable. A political view is considered uncontroversial if the only people who take exception to it are Muslims. For Muslims, on the other hand, the political docility rather than the moral lenience of 'liberal' Islam makes it suspect and dubious. Politically docile doctrines encourage a 'moderate' Islam – a faith that poses no threat to unjust Western corporate capitalism.

The American commentator Paul Berman has argued that modern peoples behave predictably in pursuit of rational and identifiable interests. The only exceptions, he adds predictably, are those omnipresent villains, the Muslims: anarchic, unpredictable, irrational and pathologically unstable. It was the Nazis then, it is the Muslims now. Berman flatters himself with the conceit that Westerners, like him, are too rational, insufficiently motivated by passion and idealistic madness. He forgets that the deadliest conflicts of the past half a millennium continue to be initiated by Western Christian powers. Those who are most eloquent in castigating the sword of retaliation in their official ethics have been throughout history best known for their expertise in using it.

Berman, a pro-Zionist ex-left winger, offers a subtle apologia for Western hegemony.[24] Political Islam is, he argues passionately, a pathological variant of twentieth century European fascism and must be fought to the death. Such a provocative view fuels international Jewish–Muslim tensions that could easily mutate into communal violence even inside the West where Jews and Muslims live in harmony. Many Jews are at the forefront of continuing struggles for social and racial justice for minorities settled in the West. Although Muslims do not judge all Jews by the behaviour of the Israeli government or its army, Berman's polemic cannot aid the cause of international peace.

Berman has unforgettably defined anti-Semitism: 'Jews are at the centre of the world and therefore at the centre of the world's evil'. Muslim activists retort that in recent history Jews became victims only because they were oppressors at first; Palestinians are, were and remain simply victims. Some cynic might add that Jewish persecution begins with their own God terrorizing them in a closed desert circuit for 40 years (Q:5:26). The Quran is far less critical of Jews than their own prophetic (middle) division of the Hebrew Bible. But we accept criticism more readily if it comes from within rather than from hostile outsiders. Muslims should not add to the crude and cruel indictments of a people whose sufferings were undeserved, merely the result of their insisting on their own uniqueness. Communities which insist on their own uniqueness incite in others the desire for persecution. Hitler was offended that the Jews were still around, at least as a trace, when other ancient races had disappeared without a trace.

The only Islam acceptable to Berman, who speaks eloquently on behalf of Western policy-makers, is the kind offered by apolitical groups such as the Sufis and other Muslim moderates, liberals and progressives, as these labels are defined by Western commentators. Many prominent converts from Christianity to Sufi Islam have capitulated to a post-Enlightenment Western definition of religion as private solace. Such converts, notably the British convert Timothy Winter (Abdal Hakim Murad[25]), are in effect and possibly in intention apologists for a form of Christianity. Sufis flatter themselves with the conceit that their Islam is a truly moderate and spiritual variant that accidentally happens to fit Western definitions of religion. It is actually an impotent form of Islam which serves a conservative function by abdicating any claim to power. The choice of this politically indifferent Islam is itself politically consequential. It is not a politically neutral but neutered Islam. These writers are designing an Islam that suits the West's ubiquitous interests, hardly an innocent or neutral thing to do.[26] They casually dismiss easily verifiable truths about innate Western militancy in defence of Western interests worldwide as merely conspiratorial thinking as if conspiracies never happen. Every political discourse forcibly displaces in print (and, orally, silences) an alternative, usually more legitimate, power narrative.

XIX

We have arrived at the last turn of our long journey. The Quran articulately condemns injustice and calls for an ethical religious politics. Its language of equity and truth is invoked when Muslim rulers' professed ideal is detached from actual performance. No regime claiming Islamic credentials can safely ignore Quranic dicta on social justice. No government can harness Islam wholly to its own ends. Post-Enlightenment Christians tolerate secular national sovereignties that manipulate a Christian sub-culture for secular ends. When the instruments of social justice are distributed, Caesar acquired the things that matter while God and his spokesmen received only the scraps that fell from the table.

Islam offers a prophetic verdict and witness of dissidence. A faith seeking to perpetuate justice, truth and goodness must trade on a fund of fierce anger at the sight of injustice and evil. A temper of constructive but militant wrath is vital to the triumph of justice and truth in a world of sophisticated impiety, confident evil and vested economic interests. How do we warn the complacently unjust that there are forces greater than the human? Western Christianity, fixated on love, no longer appreciates the balancing function of fear, an emotion which effects not only personal rectitude but also social righteousness.

Alliances with Muslims have to be partly on Islamic terms. Arab governments contain Islam's *moral* energy by outlawing it as a *political* force in their lands. Politically, the freest Muslims live in the West and in Iran and Pakistan. The 'moderate' governments, headed by pliant 'Muslim' leaders are concealed neo-colonial nations cooperating closely with Westerners who also view Islam as a false faith with the power to endanger the West's ubiquitous political and economic interests. For ordinary Muslims, however, Islam is a source of emancipation from Western tyranny. A God of vengeance is appealing to those who are murdered daily by superior Western air power.

Will Islam survive as theology or ideology? This question masks the West's anxiety to remain the world's dominant political, economic and cultural ideology. Muslims suspect that the Christian west's true motive, disguised in politically correct language, is to re-engineer Islam in its own secularized image. Muslims are condemned because they offer an ideological challenge to a compromised Christianity. Liberal Judaism and Western Christianity have accommodated themselves to capitalist secularism to the point of assimilation without remainder.

Islam cannot be accommodated into frameworks of cultural and religious pluralism defined wholly by Westerners. In Chapters 4 and 5, we examined the Christian charge: the Caesar in Muhammad's nature took over at Medina and this betrayal of his humble vocation created the imperial prophet. Kenneth Cragg has expatiated on the Muslim failure to grasp the logic of divine triumph. The wiser patterns are Jesus in the enduring dignity of meek patience, Jeremiah who cried unto death in the Judaic wilderness, and Muhammad himself in the Meccan years of fruitless preaching, travail and defeat. Cragg omits Moses, Joshua, David and Solomon. The Arabian iconoclast wanted to see God's purpose win the day despite stubborn human persistence in error. Muhammad's aim was noble but, it is alleged, he misunderstood the nature of victory in spiritual matters where God's noblest aims are perfected more through temporal failure than success.

Christians claim that Jesus, unlike Moses before him and Muhammad after him, never founded a polity. Since the integrity of human nature was destroyed by original sin, we cannot establish an equitable order. Power cannot mitigate the political disability caused by radical sin; we cannot establish a just society. Although our portrait of the historical Jesus is fragile, he probably regarded the state as super-fluous.[27] There is equivocal support for the establishment of a Church, mainly in speeches perhaps attributed to him by later redactors (see Matthew 16:18–19; John 1:42; 21:17). That institution, however, was surely meant to proclaim the power of the spirit rather than the power of the state.

For Christians, justice is either immanent in the natural order since it is created by a just God or else impossible: original sin makes us congenitally unjust, as shown by our innate egoism and pride, two traces of the Fall. Christians therefore refuse to exact justice since it is always vengeance. For Muslims, since human beings are not inherently corrupt or fallen, every resource and facility is to be harnessed in the service of a comprehensive lordship. Muslims feel *religiously* obliged to establish a just order governed by a sacred law.

In the case of justice, pleasure and the appetites, Islam balances renunciation and celibacy, on the one hand, and the perspective of nature, on the other, by acknowledging our desire for power and the pressure of licit sexuality on the human frame. Islam considers both the rights of our natural constitution and the rights of the sacred law which represents God's rights. Thus in battle, the believer draws the sword without fear of perishing by the sword because he does it on God's behalf.

All is not fair in war; romantic pundits can legislate about love's duties. All resources and facilities, especially power, can be misused. Knowledge can be misused. No-one suggests however that we should cultivate ignorance: while knowledge can occasionally lead one astray, as in the case of Faust, ignorance never fails to do so. Like knowledge, power can be used for good or ill since pow-erful individuals can be good or evil. It is a moral truism that power should be used legitimately; it is a moral absurdity to claim that power should never be recruited even in the service of justice.

Force is often enough motivated by the lust for social domination and personal gain. Only an unempirical view of history and human nature could pontificate, however, that its employment can never be instigated by noble ideals in an imper-fect order rebelling against its own best interests. We are political beings whose pursuit of power is as instinctively powerful as the sex drive. Since every ideol-ogy and faith survives by courtesy of power, we must regulate it. It is a pious fraud to claim that God should simply ignore or disown the things of Caesar. We must embrace power as a means in a world of intractable conflict. We must do so without idolizing it since the end must remain peace, never power for its own sake. The mandate for reconciliation with enemies is in the Quran (Q:8:61) but, given its single standards of justice, it rejects peace contaminated with injustice. Without a just peace, Westerners and Muslims shall both remain, in both senses, prisoners of war.

Notes

1 A prophetic religion

1 Q:4:79 refers to the Quran's fourth chapter, verse 79. References to the Quran are given thus in the body of the text. The Lahoriyyah sect of Qadianis (Ahmadis) reveres Mirza Ghulam Ahmad (1835–1908) as a satellite prophet orbiting around the final Prophet. Orthodox Muslims interpreted this to be a denial of the finality of Muhammad's prophethood; Ahmadis were declared apostates. The real grievance against them was that they were seen as stooges of British colonialism as shown by their official abolition of jihad. While this was never a canonical sixth pillar, no-one had repudiated it explicitly.

2 To acknowledge the Prophet's centrality to Islam, Carl Ernst, a non-Muslim, has titled his mystically inclined monograph *Following Muhammad*. The late Annemarie Schimmel started this trend of referring respectfully to the Prophet Muhammad, in academic writings.

3 See my *Be Careful with Muhammad!*, London: Bellew, 1989, a response to Salman Rushdie. It derives its title from this cautionary proverb: *Bā khudā dīwana basho, Bā Muhammad hoshyār!*

4 A male child's first name is often Muhammad while his second name is a theophoric chosen from God's beautiful epithets. Mahmud (derived from Q:17:79) and Mustafa are also used to refer to Muhammad. Mustafa means 'chosen one' and derives from *istafā* (to choose). It is used of the family of Abraham (Q:3:33) who were preferred by God for the privilege of prophecy. It includes Muhammad, Abraham's heir.

5 Believers address him as 'O Muhammad!' In many mosques and homes, two large disks display the vocative address to God and to Muhammad. Some claim that he is present in their religious gatherings. The Prophet's birthday *(mawlīd al-nabiyy)* occurs on 12th of Rabī'Al-Awwal. It is a tenth (Christian) century Fatimid (Shiite) innovation to indicate that dynasty's consanguinity with the Prophet's family through his daughter Fatimah. It is harmless and popular but is opposed by purists worried about encouraging a cult of personality. The Fatimids founded Al-Azhar mosque seminary which subsequently became Sunni Islam's policy-making and legal centre.

6 Irving Greenberg, *Living in the Image of God*, Northvale, NJ, Jerusalem: Jason Aronson Inc., 1998, pp. xxv–vi. One might quip that such a joke is anti-Semitic only if Gentiles tell the joke: when Jews mock themselves, it passes for Jewish humour. Shiites indulge a similar sense of humour about the end of history. One Iranian politician wants to widen the streets of Teheran lest the hidden imam, about to arrive any time now, finds them too narrow.

7 All autobiography is concealed biography since the author is writing about someone else: a younger version of themselves, and therefore another person.

8 Sebeos, the seventh century Armenian bishop and historian, writes in the Armenian chronicles (c. 660 CE) that Muhammad endowed both Ishmaelites (Arabs) and Jews

(from Isaac's lineage) with a birthright to the holy land, based on a shared monotheistic genealogy via Abraham.

9 Using only non-Muslim sources, Patricia Crone and Michael Cook argue that Islam originated as a Jewish messianic cult. See their *Hagarism: The Making of the Islamic World*, Cambridge: Cambridge University Press, 1977. Scholarship is never above prejudice and partisanship, especially in the study of Islam.

10 *The Life of Muhammad: A Translation of Ibn Ishaq's Sirat Rasul Allah*, with introduction and notes by Alfred Guillaume, Karachi: Oxford University Press, 1955, ninth impression 1990. Ibn Hisham's Notes appear as an Appendix, pp. 691–798.

11 Ibn Isḥāq, *Sīrat Rasūl Allāh*, op. cit., pp. 161–2.

12 Abu Talib enabled a good cause but did not endorse it. There may be a reference to him in the Quran (see Q:2: 272; 28:56). Was he a conscientious disbeliever? Shiites claim that he became a Muslim on his death-bed.

13 Paul Cartledge, *Alexander the Great*, Woodstock, New York: The Overlook Press, 2004, p. 186.

14 Some frustrated Palestinians taunt Israeli Jews with '*Khaybar, ya Yahūd*', a little like a German insulting a Jew by reminding him of Auschwitz.

15 The word (*tathrīb*; Q:12:92) translated as blame means *deserved* reproach and is used only here. *Malāmah* simply means blame, whether deserved or undeserved. Its verbal conjugations occur often in the tale of Joseph (Q:12:32). On the Last Day, Satan will tell his disciples that they have only themselves to blame, deservedly (Q:14:22).

16 Barry Strauss, quoted by Cartledge, op. cit., p. 187.

17 Pickthall's Introduction, *The Glorious Qur'an*, Clarksville, MD: Khatoons Inc., 2001, p. viii. Muhammad Marmaduke Pickthall (1875–1936) converted to Islam and translated the Quran.

18 This tradition is found in Al-Nisa'i's collection.

19 Ali Mazrui, 'Claims that Islam suppresses freedom of speech are hypocritical' in Jennifer Hurley (ed.), *Islam: Opposing Viewpoints*, San Diego, CA: Greenhaven Press, 2001, p. 67.

20 In *The Satanic Verses*, Rushdie portrays the Prophet's wives in a brothel scene. Muslims interpreted that as a personal insult.

21 Cartledge, op. cit., p. 42.

22 Maimonides, *Guide for the Perplexed* 2:32,36, *Mishneh Torah, Hilkhot Yesodei ha-Torah* 7:7; Mishnah commentary, introduction.

23 The Quranic requirement that mothers suckle their young for two complete years (Q:2:233) is scientifically sound.

24 Justifiably, the conservative jurist Ibn Taymiyya (d. 1328) declared the Spanish mystic Ibn Al-'Arabi (d. 1240), a favourite among modern Sufis, to be an apostate.

25 See the early chapters of Peter Ackroyd's *The Life of Thomas More*, New York: Random House, 1999.

26 Peter Ochs, 'The God of Jews and Christians' in Tikva Frymer-Kensky *et al.* (eds), *Christianity in Jewish Terms*, Boulder and Oxford: Westview Press, 2000, p. 54.

2 A literary religion

1 For more on the contents and collection of the Adi Granth written in the Gurmukhi script, see *World Religions Today*, John Esposito *et al.* (eds), New York: Oxford University Press, 2009, third edition, pp. 332–4.

2 Daniel Madigan's, *The Self-Image of the Quran*, Princeton, NJ: Princeton University Press, 2001, explores the semantic range of *k/t/b*.

3 This Indian utopian idealist is the most influential Indian after the Buddha. See Ronald Duncan (ed.), *Gandhi: Selected Writings*, Mineola, NY; Dover Publications, 2005.

4 Antimony powder (*al-kuḥl*) yields 'alcohol'.

5 See Edward Said's *Covering Islam*, New York: Random House, 1997, revised edition, first published in 1981. The title's ambiguity implies that Westerners 'cover' Islam in order to 'cover up' the truth about it. For the limitations of the late Said's work, see my 'The corruption of the powerless' in *The Times Higher Education Supplement*, July 1994.

6 See Robert Lowell, *Selected Poems*, New York: Farrar, Straus, and Giroux, 1976, p. 163. 'The boys of the jihad on a string of unwitting camels rush paradise' only to find 'halls stocked with adolescent beauties, both sexes for simple nomad tastes'.

7 Plutarch's *Lives*, London: J.M. Dent and Sons Ltd., 1910, reprinted 1961, vol. 1, p. 9.

8 The Maliki jurist and Asharite theologian Abu Bakr Al-Baqillani (950 CE–1013/402 AH) is the leading expert on the Quran's inimitability.

9 Adnan Salloum (trans.), *Asbāb Al-Nuzūl*, Beirut: Dar Al-Kutub Al-Ilmiyyah, 1991.

10 'The harvest of the human tongue' in Ibn Wadan (ed.), *Sermons of the Prophet Muhammad*, New Delhi: Goodword Books, 2002, p. 26.

11 It occurs once inside a chapter (at Q:27:30).

12 Some Qurans have *Allāh* and *rabb* (lord), whether absolutely or qualified with possessive pronouns, printed in garish red. This is undertaken to emulate the Christian decision to highlight Christ's words. The undertaking is misguided since the whole Quran is the verbatim word of God.

13 In many cultures, horses are seen as noble and altruistic animals. Think of Boxer in George Orwell's *Animal Farm*. See Jeffrey Meyers, *Orwell: Wintry Conscience of a Generation*, New York: W.W. Norton and Co., 2000, p. 248.

14 There is no division of Meccan and Medinan in the hadith literature though the Medinan traditions are more practical, less theologically abstract, and therefore the basis of law.

15 Muhsin Khan (trans.), *Summarized Sahih Al-Bukhari*, Riyadh: Maktaba Dar Al-Salam, 1994, Part 56, Book of the Merits of the Prophet's Companions, chapter 47, hadith 1598, p. 754.

16 To lack such loyal faith was a capital charge. Accused of *apistia* (infidelity) to Caesar, Christians were persecuted for allegiance to Christ, the greatest emperor (Acts 17:7). John, writer of Revelation, was exiled by Domitian on the charge of *apistia*.

3 A universal religion

1 Modern Baha'is are members of an independent and universal faith. Like the Qadiani (Ahmadiyyah) sect, the Baha'i faith is now insufficiently Islamic to count as an Islamic heresy. The current generations of both sects are neither heretics nor apostates. Grand-ayatollah Hussein Ali Montazeri (1922–2009) campaigned unsuccessfully to grant Baha'is full rights of Iranian citizenship.

2 The Prophet compared an infant to an animal born without mutilation or defect. See Muhsin Khan (trans.), *Summarized Ṣaḥīh Al-Bukhārī*, Riyadh: Maktaba Dar Al-Salam, 1994, Part 23, Funerals, *ḥadīth* no. 680, p. 338.

3 In Eastern faiths, suffering is self-suffering. A dominant Western view of suffering is, as Winston Smith's torturer explains in Orwell's *1984*, power over others, expressed in the ability to make someone suffer.

4 See my 'Prophet Warning: Justification, Retribution and Salvation in Islam' in Peter Koslowski (ed.), *Endangst und Erlosung*, Munich: Wilhelm Fink, 2010, vol. 2.

5 For the letter accusing Paul of monarchian teachings, see Eusebius of Caesarae's *Ecclesiastical History*, book 7, chapter 30.

6 Arguably, this is a racist term which denigrates Palestinians. The Greek 'banausic' can replace 'philistine'. Similarly, 'pharisaic', meaning hypocritically self-righteous, offends Jews since the Pharisees were self-described as *Perush'īm* (ones set apart for holiness).

7 When Zionist writers such as Daniel Pipes abusively criticize Islam, then many modern Muslims resurrect the Quran's anti-Jewish verdicts. Such notices of ancient Jewish delinquency would lapse into irrelevance if Jews and Muslims were at peace.

8 Preface, Jon Stallworthy (ed.), *The Poems of Wilfrid Owen*, London: Chatto and Windus, 1990.

9 The aberrant rhyme of Q:17:1–2 coupled with the sudden shift to an unrelated motif in verse 2 indicate a late redaction for this verse (Q:17:1), albeit by Muhammad's own hand. This vision may be linked to Muhammad's other mystical experiences (Q:53:13–18).

10 Epithets were common in classical antiquity. General Scipio the Younger was renamed Scipio Africanus to commemorate the Roman defeat of Africa's General Hannibal at Zama in 204 BCE.

11 See my review of M.N. Pearson's *The Hajj in Earlier Times*, London: Hurst, 1994. My review is in *The Times Higher Education Supplement*, February 1995.

12 Mark Steyn, *America Alone*, Washington, DC: Regnery, 2006. Judging by their catalogues, these publishers publish only authors with right-wing leanings. White supremacists and alarmists claim that America is the last hope for white humanity since Europeans either abort or decline to conceive their future inheritors.

13 Turks ask Muslim-looking tourists whether or not they are *haji* (pilgrim), Turkish slang for 'Arab'. If one replies in the affirmative, one encounters racism. When I reply that I am Pakistani, I receive lavish praise and hospitality since Pakistan is the Islamic world's sole nuclear power.

14 Martin Luther, the Protestant reformer, was indelibly impressed by Paul's elevation of faith over works of the law, as shown in his substantial and authentic Epistle to the Romans. The Reformation is inconceivable without this Pauline epistle.

15 See Ismail Al-Faruqi, *'Urūbah and Religion*, Amsterdam: Djambatan, 1962, 2 volumes.

4 A political religion: Muhammad as statesman

1 Biblical scholars have disputed the historicity of the Israelite exodus. The Quran confirms the migration from Egypt (Q:2:61; 5:20–6; Q:44:17–32). The word for Egypt (*miṣr*) is used in the accusative indefinite singular (*miṣran*) at Q:2:61 and sometimes translated as 'settled land' as opposed to desert. It is used as a proper noun in its only other uses (Q:12:21, 99).

2 In terms of achievements, Umar's decade (r. 644–54) as caliph almost competes with Muhammad's decade (622–32) as prophet-statesman. Umar's decade is marked by spectacular imperial achievements and wise domestic reforms. Some have suggested that Umar was greater than Muhammad, the equivalent of saying that Paul surpassed Jesus.

3 The eccentric Libyan leader Colonel Ghaddafi has, in his 'Green Book', disputed the dating of the Islamic calendar. The Shah of Iran wanted to date Iranian history to King Cyrus.

4 Muhammad was a free man (*ḥillun*) in a land not under occupation by a superpower, a fact that crucially assisted the rise of Islam as political monotheism.

5 The Quran predicts his triumphant return to *ma'ād* (place of return; Q:28:85), meaning possibly Mecca or the after-life.

6 When Ayatollah Khomeini (1902–89) returned from multiple exiles to land on his native soil, a Western journalist posed the question, 'What do you feel about returning to Iran?' The Ayatollah replied in Farsi: '[I feel] nothing (*Hichi*)'. He meant that patriotism was not his motivation. One needs to know how the hijrah transcends patriotism in order to humanize this cryptic and cold comment. See Michael Axworthy's poetically sensitive *A History of Iran: Empire of the Mind*, New York: Basic Books, 2008. Axworthy ranges from Zarathustra to Khomeini. See pp. 259–61 on Khomeini's triumphant return.

7 *Muhammad and the Christian: A Question of Response*, London: Darton, Longman and Todd, 1984; *Jesus and the Muslim: An Exploration*, London: George Allen & Unwin, 1985, both reprinted by Oxford's Oneworld in 1999. Page references are to the original editions of both works, henceforth abbreviated to *M and the C* and *J and the M*. Cragg belongs to the last generation of theologians still permitted to use sexist language.

8 The title of Christopher Lamb's *The Call to Retrieval: Kenneth Cragg's Christian Vocation to Islam*, London: Grey Seal, 1996, implies that Cragg is a missionary to Islam. Charles Adams accuses Cragg of Christianizing Islam in his 'Islamic Religious Tradition' in L. Binder, (ed.), *The Study of the Middle East,* New York, Wiley, 1971.

9 Two documents from Vatican II commend Muslims as worshipping Abraham's God but neither mentions Muhammad or his prophethood. See *Lumen Gentium*, chapter 2, para 16 (November 21, 1964) and *Nostra Aetate*, para 3 (October 28, 1965).

10 Rabbinic Judaism resisted changes only to personal status law when Jews lived under Gentile rulers. The maxim *dīna de-malkhūta dīna,* absent from the Jerusalem Talmud, occurs in the Babylonian Talmud: Nedar'im 28a, Gittin 10b, Baba Kamma 113a three times, 113b, Baba Bathra 54b, 55a.

11 Cragg, *M and the C*, p. 18.

12 Cragg, op. cit., p. 14.

13 Cragg, op. cit., p. 23.

14 Cragg, *Jesus and the Muslim*, p. 154.

15 *Henry V*, Act IV, scene 1, ll. 149, 151.

16 Cragg, *M and the C*, pp. 43 ff.

17 Cragg, op. cit., p. 43.

18 See Fazlur Rahman, *Major Themes of the Quran*, Minneapolis, MN: Bibliotheca Islamica, 1980, passim.

19 Cragg, *J and the M*, pp. 126–7.

20 The South African Muslim polemical missionary Ahmed Deedat (1918–2005) was the worst offender although he deserved the King Faisal award (1986).

21 Cragg, *M and the C*, p. 48, 66.

22 See Montgomery Watt, *Muhammad at Mecca*, Oxford: Oxford University Press, 1980, and *Muhammad at Medina*, same publisher, 1981.

23 Cragg, *M and the C*, p. 51.

24 Ibid.

25 Tertullian, *Treatise on Idolatry*, section 19.

26 Ibn Wadan (ed.), *Sermons of the Prophet Muhammad*, New Delhi: Goodword Books, 2002, number 24, p. 56.

27 Cragg, *M and the C*, p. 44.

28 Cragg, *Jesus and the Muslim*, p. 154.

29 Cragg, op. cit., pp. 216–25, esp. p. 219.

30 Cragg, op. cit., p. 219.

31 Ibid.

32 Ibid. Cragg approves of the work of an Egyptian writer, Kamil Husayn, whose book *City of Evil* (*Qariyah Ẓālimah*) is a novel interpretation of the events of Good Friday.

33 Friedrich Nietzsche, *Ecce Homo* R.J.Hollingdale (trans.), Harmondsworth: Penguin Books, 1979, p. 45.

34 Cragg, *M and the C*, pp. 22–3.

35 Siegfried Sassoon arranged for publication of Owen's Collected Poems (1920). See Jon Stallworthy (ed.), *The Poems of Wilfrid Owen*, London: Chatto and Windus, 1990, Preface.

36 Allan Wade (ed.), *The Letters of W.B. Yeats*, London: Rupert Hart-Davis, 1954; New York: Macmillan, 1955, p. 851.

37 *The Arab Christian*, London: Mowbray, 1992.

38 Cragg, *M and the C*, p. 40.

39 Cragg, op. cit., p. 32.

40 Arab Christians use *kaffārah* for atonement and *badāliyyah* for substitution.

41 Cragg, *M and the C*, p. 45.

42 Cragg, op. cit., p. 23.

43 Cragg, op. cit., p. 50.

44 Cragg, op. cit., p. 144.

45 Nietzsche, *The Anti-Christ*, R.J. Hollingdale (trans.), Harmondsworth: Penguin, 1968, published in one volume with *Twilight of the Idols* (1888), Maxims and Arrows, 8.

46 Non-Muslim, agnostic, Jewish and Christian historians, with no sectarian axe to grind, think that the Shiite claim is absurd. Ali was merely 20 at the time of Muhammad's death. The ageing Abu Bakr, nearly as old as Muhammad, had the best credentials. Age is a relevant factor in holding political office since it tokens maturity of judgment. One might counter that we must respect achievement even in the young. As an Ibo proverb has it: 'If a child can wash his hands, he can eat with the kings.'

47 Cragg, *M and the C*, p. 48.

48 Muslims may have, however, persecuted some Armenian Orthodox Christians during the declining days of the Ottoman empire. India's Mughal Muslim rulers persecuted and assassinated several Sikh gurus.

49 Cragg, op. cit., pp. 132–3.

5 A secular religion: faith or ideology?

1 Ali Shariati (1933–77), the architect of Iran's 1979 Islamic Revolution, read the Quran through Marxist lenses. Like Moses, he never entered his promised land. The Shah's secret police probably assassinated him.

2 Tirmidhi's hadith collection, *Īmān*, 59. For more hadith on this subject, see Bukhari, *Aḥkām*, 6; Muslim, *Imāra*, 13, *Birr*, 55.

3 Dr. Samuel Johnson (1709–84) is claimed as one of their men by both conservatives and liberals – the fate of the politically discreet.

4 *Inside the Whale and Other Essays*, Harmondsworth: Penguin, 1957, p. 118.

5 Ibid., p. 118.

6 Ibid., p. 118.

7 The incident of the adulterous woman, unique to John, is a late and disputed addition. This pericope (John 7:53–8:11) is not found in the earliest and most reliable Greek manuscripts and other ancient witnesses.

8 This New Testament verse inspired the plot of Thomas Hardy's tragedy, *The Mayor of Casterbridge* (1886). Michael Henchard, nicknamed Hardy's King Lear, is a man with a shameful past. He repents and then rises to such prominence that his fellow citizens appoint him a judge. But a poor woman, on trial before his judgment seat, tells the truth to his face and challenges him to judge her when he is a worse sinner. He concedes the accusation and declines to judge her, only to decline into loss of reputation, poverty and a pauper's unnamed grave. Hardy was a master analyst of the ironic mischance that destroys human happiness in a malicious universe. But this novel can be read as confirming that the true cost of discipleship is necessarily high since the world will always persecute the Christian who follows Jesus in bearing the cross. The fact that most Western Christians, especially in America, suffer little or nothing for their faith indicates that they are merely speakers, not doers, of the word. They are not Christ's true disciples, notwithstanding their loud sermons. Among African Americans, the radical potential of Christianity has, much to the delight of the white elite, safely subsided into culturally harmless forms.

9 Sir Thomas More (1477–1535) believed that conscience was the right to be right about Catholic dogma. In 2000, Pope John Paul II declared him the patron saint of politicians. If only any modern politicians were ready for martyrdom!

10 See my review of Lee Levine (ed.), *Jerusalem*, London: Continuum, 1999. It appears in *The Times Education Higher Supplement*, February 2000.

11 *Summa Theologica*, Secunda Secundae Partis, Qn.11, art.3, objn.3. The translation is mine.

12 The quote is from an anonymous thirteenth century canon lawyer cited by James Muldoon in his *Popes, Lawyers and Infidels: The Church and the Non-Christian World 1250-1550*, Liverpool: Liverpool University Press, 1979, p. 16.

13 Muldoon, op. cit., p. 134. As for Christian outreach in South America, Muldoon mentions a short doxology (*Requerimiento*) which contained a statement of Christian convictions with a supplementary explanation of the Spanish presence in the Americas. A priest read this document to the infidels before troops attacked them. The text was never translated into any American tongue. Imagine a friar reading a statement to an audience of empty huts and trees, hurling his words at the backs of uncomprehending Indians terrified at the sight of armed strangers. Some Christian critics, notably Las Casas, condemned this procedure. See Muldoon, p. 140.

14 Duncan Forrester, *Theology and Politics*, Oxford: Basil Blackwell, 1988, p. 67. Few Popes deserved the title of 'Innocent'.

15 From the earliest times, along with polemical attacks on Islam, a tradition of fairness has also marked Western scholarship.

16 While Muslims have no theology of powerlessness, Jews have not had much reason to develop a theology of power. For the first time since the defeat of ancient Israel by the Assyrians in 721 BCE, Jews live in the officially Jewish state of Israel founded in 1948.

17 For an early statement of Cragg's position, see his *The Call of the Minaret*, published in 1956 and reissued by Collins in 1986. Few scholars can write for some 70 years without changing their minds about anything important.

18 Cragg, *Jesus and the Muslim*, London: George Allen and Unwin, 1985, p. 281.

19 Cragg, op. cit., pp. 281ff.

20 Cragg's competent and idiomatic translation, *Readings in the Quran*, London: Collins, 1988, omits a third of the text on grounds of repetition.

21 *The Pen and the Faith*, London: George Allen and Unwin, 1985, p. 6.

22 *Muhammad and the Christian*, London: Darton, Longman and Todd, 1984, p. 32.

23 Cragg, op. cit., p. 49. On the same page, Cragg quotes Hasan Askari: 'My deep conviction is that the Prophet of Islam did not create a state ... I believe that Islam can survive without political power, without a state.' Survive maybe but thrive? The omitted sentences refer to Askari's claim that the controversy between Sunnis and Shiites over the question of leadership of the community after Muhammad's death becomes baseless if we accept that he was not a politically motivated prophet-leader. Askari adds, correctly, that the Sunni Caliphate and the Shiite Imamate are both outside the Quran's scope. The caliphate has, however, some equivocal Quranic support.

24 Suicide is an insulting term. For more, see Chapter 11.

25 Gustavo Gutierrez, *A Theology of Liberation*, Maryknoll, NY: Orbis, 1973.

26 There is now, after the internet revolution, change at 'netroots' level.

27 Recent research on Jesus has rehabilitated him into his Jewish roots and, by implication, Islamicized him.

28 Peter Mayhew, *A Theology of Force and Violence*, London: SCM Press, 1989.

29 For example, 'public schools' are private fee-paying establishments independent of state control.

30 For discussion, see Dr John Habgood, *Church and Nation in a Secular Age*, London: Darton, Longman and Todd, 1983. Habgood offers no Christian argument for establishing a church. His contentions are secular, pragmatic and opportunistic but nonetheless valid: an established church is a force for moral good in a secular culture.

31 See Martin Marty's *Martin Luther: A Life*, Penguin, 2004, p. 192.

32 Think here of the Church of England's endorsement of the first Gulf war as a justifiable (though not just) cause as soon as the British government decided to join America in attacking Iraq in 1991. The distinction is too subtle to matter to those who were bombed.

6 A legal religion

1 Ibn Wadan (ed.), *Sermons of the Prophet Muhammad*, New Delhi: Goodword Books, 2002, sermon number 15, p. 38.

2 The Halakhah has only two aims: healing the world (*tikkun ōlām*) and maintaining our creation in the divine image (*tzelem elohīm*). See Irving Greenberg, *Living in the Image of God*, Northvale, NJ, Jerusalem: Jason Aronson Inc., 1998, p. 103.

3 During the upasammpada ceremony for the Buddhist novice, the silence of the Sangha implies approval. In English law, silence means consent (*Qui tacet consentire videtur*) if the party can speak. Thomas More invoked this statute during his trial for treason.

4 In his legal treatise *Marāqi Al-Su'ūd*, Sidi Abdallah Al-Shinqiti (d. 1855 CE) gives seven examples of promotion of the public welfare which cannot claim direct Quranic or pro-phetic support. Collecting fragments of the Quran into a book and its later vocalization, both done to preserve God's word, are evidently virtuous undertakings. Abu Bakr's decision to leave written instructions (that Umar should succeed him) prevented dispute over leadership of the type that occurred when Muhammad died suddenly. Others include innovations introduced by Umar: establishing a standard coinage and weights system to facilitate just trade, establishing temporary jails as administrative (though not punitive) detention centres for those whose cases were pending judgment, and taking a census to compile a state register indicating priority of conversion to Islam so that earlier converts could be materially rewarded more than the later ones (based on Q:57:10).

5 If a non-Muslim subject of an Islamic state insults the Prophet, the offence is the extra-Quranic crime of *shatm al-rasul* ('harsh speech about a messenger').This transgression must be individually defined, rules of evidence clarified and the penalty specified. The judge wants to determine whether the accusation is made by a Muslim plaintiff in order to exact private vengeance against a Jew or Christian. He must exclude this possibility before a verdict or sentence is pronounced. Typically, as in Ottoman times, flogging and a short prison sentence sufficed. If a Muslim subject insults Muhammad, he commits treason against the state. The protocol of arraignment, trial and conviction is dispensed: the accused is immediately executed. Apostasy (*irtidād*) is punishable only if the indi-vidual's stance becomes public and scandalous. In Muhammad's day, private apostasy was commonplace; the Quran specifies no worldly penalty for it.

6 The Prophet did not imprison anyone although his mosque served as a detention centre as we know from the case of the three detainees who were tied to a pillar in the Prophet's mosque while awaiting divine judgment (see Q:9:106). Since penalties are considered as purgatives to be administered immediately, Islamic law does not traditionally provide for imprisonment of criminals. Prisoners of war must be ransomed or graciously liber-ated once hostilities cease (see Q:47:4). Umar was the first to use empty houses and a well as temporary prisons. Indefinite incarceration as house arrest was the penalty for lesbianism (authorized by Q:4:15) and for female apostates. Activist Muslims argue that the Western prison system robs criminals of their liberty for countless years. The Catholic Church, incidentally, maintained its own prisons as shown by documents from the Inquisition, especially the detention and trial of heretics such as Joan of Arc.

7 Michael Durrant, *Theology and Intelligibility*, London, Boston: Routledge & Kegan Paul, 1973. See also Michael Martin's *The Case Against Christianity*, Philadelphia, PA: Temple University Press, 1990. He shows that Christianity contains the largest collection of highly implausible dogmas.

8 Kenneth Cragg, *Muhammad and the Christian,* London: Darton, Longman and Todd, 1984, p. 128.

7 An imperial religion

1 Alexander wanted to deport the Persian aristocracy to Europe.

2 An important communal duty is to hold a congregational funeral prayer over the body of a deceased Muslim before burial. In Hanafi law, a person is not considered legally dead until his or her debts have been discharged. A relative can offer to pay in order to facili-tate burial. 'He that dies pays all debts' said Stephano in Shakespeare's *The Tempest*, Act III, sc.ii, l.140. Not so in Islamic law which requires discharge of debts before burial of the debtor!

3 The Friday congregational prayer, a communal duty (Q:62:9), is invalid in the absence of a reigning caliph. Most jihad armies departed after the Friday assembly.
4 Al-Mawardi, *The Laws of Governance*, Asadullah Yate (trans.), London: Ta Ha, 1996.
5 Sheikh Sa'di quoted by Abbas Milani, *Lost Wisdom: Rethinking Modernity in Iran* Washington, DC: Mage Publishers, 2004, p. 39.

8 A rational religion

1 Galileo, a contemporary of Descartes, was found guilty of heresy by the Roman Inquisition in 1633 and rehabilitated only in 1992.
2 The spider is ingenious but it is a mechanical creature whose submission *(islām)* to natural laws, unlike human submission to God's moral laws, is involuntary and thus devoid of merit. All creatures glorify God in ways known only to him (Q:24:41).
3 Charles Taylor, *A Secular Age*, Cambridge, Mass.: Harvard University Press, 2007, p. 114.
4 Ibid., p. 125.
5 Although the New Testament permits the eating of pork, the pig was and remains a symbol of the Devil as implied in the titles of modern novels such as William Golding's *Lord of the Flies* and Mo Hayder's *Pig Island*. For George Orwell's hostility to pigs, as shown in his political fable *Animal Farm*, see Jeffrey Meyers, *Orwell: Wintry Conscience of a Generation*, New York: W.W. Norton and Co., 2000, pp. 248ff.

9 Islam as ethical religion

1 Amenhotep IV adopted the name Aton-Ra (servant of Aton) to become Akhenaton (d. 1334–6 BCE), Pharaoh of the 18th dynasty and father of primitive monotheism.
2 Islam denigrated pre-Islamic Arab history just as much as it dismissed the pre-Islamic history of colonized peoples. V.S. Naipaul is incensed by the Muslim erasure of the histories of peoples in Malaysia and Indonesia but he does not note the impartial reach of the Muslim imperial censor which erased the Arab pagan past too. See my review essay, 'A Grouse for Mr Biswas' in *The Times Higher Education Supplement*, May 1998.
3 In mediaeval Christendom, the monastic child's chief virtue was that he took no pleasure in female beauty or nudity (cf. Q:24:31).
4 The Latin *metus* means fear; doing something meticulously implies the fear of making an error. The Quran's neologism *taqwā*, translated as piety, means scruples caused by the fear of offending God's laws and limits.
5 For a heroic and manly but unsuccessful attempt, see Harvey Mansfield, *Manliness* (New Haven: Yale University Press, 2006). Academia excels in negative exemplars of emotionally weak men, both conservatives and liberals. This is unsurprising in the case of Eastern cultures and countries where personal liberty and assertiveness take second place to communal cohesion in all departments of life, including academic, intellectual and artistic endeavour. Surprisingly, such cowardice is also found among the Western intelligentsia, even in Britain and America, where one would expect more of the personal courage that befits a free mind.
6 Al-Miskawayh was an Islamic humanist who had greater regard for the Greeks than for the Quran. See his ethical treatise, *Tadhīb Al-Akhlāq* (*The Refinement of Character*), C. Zurayk (trans.), Beirut: American University of Beirut, 1968. Al-Miskawayh was a contemporary of Avicenna (Ibn Sina). Authentically Islamic ethics were developed by Abu Hamid Al-Ghazali. In his anarchic orthodoxy, ethics are rational but mystical, a semi-intuitive conception of a metaphysically knowable and fixed spiritual destiny for our species. Al-Ghazali, like Kant after him, rejected speculative metaphysics in favour of ethics. Al-Ghazali rejected rational metaphysics in favour of mysticism. To understand his mystical ethics, read his *Mīzān Al-'Amāl* (Criterion of Actions). *Mīzān Al-'Amāl* (Criterion of Actions), S. Dunyah (ed), Cairo: Dar Al-Marraif, 1964.

7 Talmud (Yerushalmi), *Sotah* 5a.
8 *Bava Batra*, 9a.
9 *Bava Batra*, 10a.
10 God gave us a choice in the matter of our friends as an apology for giving us no choice in regard to our families.
11 Journalism has been mocked as the first draft of history and as anthropology with a salary. Unlike poetry, it is always, literally speaking, reactionary since it reacts to events beyond its control. Philosophy, like poetry, is usually more ideologically original. For a Christian critique of modern polemical atheists, see John Haught, *God and the New Atheism*, Louisville, KY., Westminster John Knox Press, 2008.
12 After the collapse of communism, some humanist presses launched an aggressive campaign against Islam, a faith with a backbone, the only one refusing to surrender to secularism. Prometheus, with its new science fiction imprint called Pyr, has become the world's only publisher to specialize in both Islamic terrorism and futurist fantasy. It is hard to tell these two genres apart. Prometheus publishes the world's leading polemical atheists, including some prudentially anonymous, and allegedly formerly Muslim, critics of Islam.

10 A private religion

1 Ilkay Sunar discusses faith (*al-dīn*) and state (*al-dawlah*) separation in medieval Islam in 'Civil society and Islam' in Elizabeth Ozdalga and Sune Persson (eds.), *Civil Society, Democracy and the Muslim World,* Istanbul: Swedish Research Institute, 1997, pp. 14–5.
2 Paul Theroux's *The Elephanta Suite* explodes the myth of an ascetic India centred on the ashram. New York: Houghton Mifflin, 2007. It costs money even to be spiritual. And Rajneesh, 'the sex guru', once based in Oregon but since evicted for tax evasion, has popularized the erotic side of the Indian heritage. There is much Western naïveté and sentimentality about Indian civilization though it is steadily decreasing as Westerners realize that Hindu fanatics can be 'violent vegetarians' and that countless Indians eagerly search for material satisfaction through American green cards. We should however balance this image by listening to the compassionate message of Indian cosmopolitan humanists such as Deepak Chopra.
3 Queen Victoria, the Empress of India, could rely on anglicized Hindus to be loyal servants of the crown. The British humanitarian Malcolm Muggeridge joked that Indians were the world's last and perfect Englishmen. Muslims were then, as now, reluctant to assimilate totally to foreign ideals.
4 In the third book of my trilogy on Islam's confrontation with Western secular modernity, I explore minority issues, including the traumatic Rushdie affair and apostasy within a liberal secular state. I examine Muslim schooling in some European states which subsidizes the privileges of the few while neglecting the rights of their ethnic minorities. I scrutinize Christian–Muslim relations and dialogue. Inter-faith work must be respected but also corrected since inter-faith courtesy means respect for, not acceptance of, other people's religious ideals. Is dialogue even possible among committed Western monotheistic ideologues, especially given lack of parity in power? See my *The Call of Liberal Islam: Creating Authentic Humanism*, forthcoming. The trilogy opened with *The Quran and the Secular Mind: A philosophy of Islam*, London: Routledge, 2007.

11 The future scope of an imperial faith

1 Is Buddhism the preferred choice of Western intellectuals and artists alienated from their Jewish and Christian roots?
2 The level of religious illiteracy even in the 'bible belt' is appalling. For example, the majority of those polled thought that Joan of Arc was the wife of Noah; 50 per cent

believed that 'Sodom and Gomorrah' were not doomed cities but rather an ancient married couple. For further details of the poll, see Stephen Prothero, Religious Literacy (New York: HarperOne, 2007).

3 Despite being a democracy, Israel has sometimes been ruled by ex-generals.

4 In Andre Debus' American tragedy, *House of Sand and Fog*, New York: Vintage, 2000, we read of Savak torturing the Shah's opponents. To extract confessions, children were tortured in front of parents. The Shah was actively supported by America, Israel and Britain; the latest torture techniques were learnt in America. See pp. 61ff.

5 See Hala Jaber's excellent *Hezbollah*, London: Fourth Estate, 1997. My review is in *The Times Higher Education Supplement*, August 1997.

6 The Japanese occupiers in Indonesia and Malaya admired Islam as the only oriental force that could resist occidental aggression. Japanese academia has an honourable tradition of Islamic studies and produces outstanding Arabists.

7 Most Muslims see Israel as an imperial nuclear power, founded as a racist settler-state, no different from apartheid-based South Africa. Enlightened Muslims acknowledge, however, that Jews deserve a homeland, with agreed borders, in the Middle East. When Israeli scholars are not discussing modern political Islam, they produce some outstanding scholarship on Arab Islam and its history.

8 Two Arabs (Osama Bin Laden and Saddam Hussain) and the Iranian Ahmedinajed (who replaced the late Ayatollah Khomeini) are on the list. Why are controversial Israeli and Chilean generals or Serb demagogues not on the list?

9 The 1990 Iraqi invasion of Kuwait was unjustified aggression but it might have been reversed by Arab diplomacy and sanctions. The West's desire to interfere forcefully was motivated by economic interests although we need not here disturb the complacency of those Republicans in America and those Anglican clergymen and Conservative British politicians who pretend that the Western involvement was motivated by moral principles. The 2003 US occupation of Iraq is retrospectively acknowledged to have been illegal and immoral.

10 The Syrian-German secularist Bassam Tibi is the author.

11 The modern Egyptian Islamic Jihad Group, like the extinct Kharijite sect, claimed that jihad was the sixth pillar.

12 Kenneth Cragg, *The Pen and the Faith,* London: George Allen and Unwin, 1985.

13 Cragg, op. cit., pp. 60ff.

14 Cragg, op. cit., p. 62.

15 Cragg, op. cit., p. 54.

16 Al-Azhar maintains a canonical court which expels faculty deemed unIslamic. Founded by a Shiite dynasty, it has been Sunni for much of its 1000 years. Al-Azhar maintains a liberal tradition and formally recognizes the Jafari (Shiite) legal school.

17 *Al-Jihad: Al Farīda Al-Ghā'iba*, Amman: no publisher, 1982. See *The Neglected Duty*, Johannes Jansen (trans.), London, New York: Macmillan, 1986.

18 See Benazir Bhutto's autobiography, *Daughter of the East*, London: Hamish Hamilton, 1989. Many Pakistanis denigrated her as a daughter of the West.

19 Khomeini was partly anticipated by Gandhi who called Europe 'the kingdom of Satan'. See *Gandhi: Selected Writings*, Ronald Duncan (ed.), Mineola, NY; Dover Publications, 2005, p. 124. Gandhi was the last important non-Muslim critic of the West.

20 Richard Grenier, 'The United States should launch an attack on Islam' in Jennifer A. Hurley (ed.), *Islam: Opposing Viewpoints*, San Diego: CA.: Greenhaven Press, inc., 2001, p. 137, 141.

21 Ibid., p. 139. The original is 'their feelings'.

22 'Propa-gandhi' was coined to denigrate Gandhi's moral achievements.

23 'God bless the United Kingdom' was proposed by Tony Blair but removed by his advisors. I am personally saddened by Britain's relentless post-imperial decline confirmed in its status as a puppet state of America. It is a refined irony when a former colony becomes the master. Note how white nations are, once again in their history, beginning

to practise intra-Christian imperialist domination rather than subjugating only non-white peoples.

24 Paul Berman, *Terror and Liberalism*, New York, London: W.W.Norton and Co., 2003.

25 His last name in Arabic is unfortunately susceptible to a pun, currently very popular among radical British Muslim youth: Murad becomes 'Murtad' (meaning apostate).

26 Ed Husain's *The Islamist*, New York: Penguin, 2009, naïvely overlooks the West's desire to emasculate Islam. See Chapter 12 on 9/11, an event that is a permanent part of American political mythology.

27 Jesus was perhaps an Essene presiding over an esoteric mystical brotherhood which was never intended to be wrenched from the Law vouchsafed only to 'the lost sheep of Israel'.

Bibliography

Ackroyd, Peter, *The Life of Thomas More*, New York: Random House, 1999.

Adams, Charles, 'Islamic Religious Tradition' in L. Binder (ed.), *The Study of the Middle East,* New York, Wiley, 1971.

Akhtar, Shabbir, *Be Careful with Muhammad!: The Salman Rushdie Affair*, London: Bellew, 1989.

Akhtar, Shabbir, 'The corruption of the powerless', *The Times Higher Education Supplement*, July 1994.

Akhtar, Shabbir, Review of M.N. Pearson's *The Hajj in Earlier Times*, in *The Times Higher Education Supplement*, February 1995.

Akhtar, Shabbir, 'A Grouse for Mr Biswas' *The Times Higher Education Supplement*, May 1998.

Akhtar, Shabbir, Review of Lee Levine (ed.), *Jerusalem*, London: Continuum, 1999, in *The Times Education Higher Supplement*, February 2000.

Akhtar, Shabbir, *The Quran and the Secular Mind: A philosophy of Islam*, London: Routledge, 2007.

Akhtar, Shabbir, 'Prophet Warning: Justification, Retribution and Salvation in Islam' in Peter Koslowski (ed.), *Endangst und Erlosung*, Munich: Wilhelm Fink, 2010, vol. 2.

Akhtar, Shabbir, *The Call of Liberal Islam: Creating Authentic Humanism*, forthcoming.

Akhtar, Shabbir, Review of Jaber, Hala, *Hezbollah*, in *The Times Higher Education Supplement*, August 1997.

Al-Faruqi, Ismail, *'Urubah and Religion*, Amsterdam: Djambatan, 1962, 2 volumes.

Al-Mawardi, *The Laws of Governance*, Asadullah Yate (trans.), London: Ta Ha, 1996.

Axworthy, Michael, *A History of Iran: Empire of the Mind*, New York: Basic Books, 2008.

Al-Miskawayh, Abu, *Tadhib Al-Akhlaq (The Refinement of Character)*, C. Zurayk (trans.), Beirut: American University of Beirut, 1968.

Berman, Paul, *Terror and Liberalism*, New York, London: W.W.Norton and Co., 2003.

Bessenecker, Scott, *The New Friars: The Emerging Movement Serving the World's Poor*, Downers Grove, Illinois: InterVarsity Press Books, 2006.

Bhutto, Benazir, *Daughter of the East*, London: Hamish Hamilton, 1989.

Cartledge, Paul, *Alexander the Great*, Woodstock, New York: The Overlook Press, 2004.

Claiborne, Shane, *The Irresistible Revolution: Living as an Ordinary Radical*, Grand Rapids, Michigan: Zondervan, 2006.

Cragg, Kenneth, *The Pen and the Faith*, London: George Allen and Unwin, 1985.

Cragg, Kenneth, *Readings in the Quran*, London: Collins, 1988.

Cragg, Kenneth, *Muhammad and the Christian*, London: Darton, Longman and Todd, 1984; Oneworld, 1999.

Cragg, Kenneth, *Jesus and the Muslim*, Oxford: Oneworld, 1999.

Cragg, Kenneth, *The Arab Christian*, London: Mowbray, 1992.

Crone, Patricia and Cook, Michael, *Hagarism: The Making of the Islamic World*, Cambridge: Cambridge University Press, 1977.

Debus, Andre, *House of Sand and Fog*, New York: Vintage, 2000.

Duncan, Ronald (ed.), *Gandhi: Selected Writings*, Mineola, NY; Dover Publications, 2005.

Durrant, Michael, *Theology and Intelligibility*, London, Boston: Routledge & Kegan Paul, 1973.

Egendorf, Laura (ed.), *Terrorism: Opposing Viewpoints*, San Diego, CA: Greenhaven Press, 2000.

Ernst, Carl, *Following Muhammad*, Chapel Hill, London: The University of North Carolina Press, 2002.

Esposito, John *et al.* (eds), *World Religions Today*, New York: Oxford University Press, 2009, third edition.

Faraj, Abdal Salam, *Al-Jihad: Al Farida Al-Gha'iba*, Amman: no publisher, 1982.

Forrester, Duncan, *Theology and Politics*, Oxford: Basil Blackwell, 1988.

Gandhi, Mohandas, *Selected Writings*, Ronald Duncan (ed.), Mineola, NY; Dover Publications, 2005.

Greenberg, Rabbi Irving, *Living in the Image of God*, Northvale, NJ, Jerusalem: Jason Aronson Inc., 1998.

Grenier, Richard 'The United States should launch an attack on Islam' in Jennifer A. Hurley (ed.), *Islam: Opposing Viewpoints*, San Diego: CA.: Greenhaven Press, inc., 2001.

Grieves, Paul, *A Brief Guide to Islam*, New York: Carroll and Graf, 2006.

Guillaume, Alfred, *The Life of Muhammad: A Translation of Ibn Isḥāq's Sīrat Rasūl Allāh*, Karachi: Oxford University Press, 1955, ninth impression 1990.

Gustavo Gutierrez, *A Theology of Liberation*, Maryknoll, NY: Orbis, 1973.

Habgood, John, *Church and Nation in a Secular Age*, London: Darton, Longman and Todd, 1983.

Haught, John, *God and the New Atheism: A Critical Response to Dawkins, Harris, and Hitchens*, Louisville, KY., Westminster John Knox Press, 2008.

Helgeland, John, *Christians and the Military*, London: SCM Press, 1985.

Hurley, Jennifer (ed.), *Islam: Opposing Viewpoints*, San Diego, CA: Greenhaven Press, 2001.

Husain (ed.), *The Islamist*, New York: Penguin, 2009.

Ibn Wad'an, Muhammad, *Khuṭab al-Nabiyy Muhammad* (*Sermons of the Prophet Muhammad*), Assad Nimer Busool (trans.), New Delhi: Goodword Books, 2002.

Jaber, Hala, *Hezbollah*, London: Fourth Estate, 1997.

Jansen, Johannes, (trans.), *The Neglected Duty*, London, New York: Macmillan.

Karsh, Efraim, *Islamic Imperialism*, New Haven, London: Yale University Press, 2006.

Khan, Muhsin (trans.), *Summarized Sahih Al-Bukhari*, Riyadh: Maktaba Dar Al-Salam, 1994.

Kung, Hans, *Islam: Past, Present and Future*, John Bowden (trans.), Oxford: Oneworld, 2007.

Lamb, Christopher, *The Call to Retrieval: Kenneth Cragg's Christian Vocation to Islam*, London: Grey Seal, 1996.

Lowell, Robert, *Selected Poems*, New York: Farrar, Straus, and Giroux, 1976.

Madigan, Daniel, *The Qur'an's Self-Image*, Princeton, NJ: Princeton University Press, 2001.

Martin, Michael, *The Case Against Christianity*, Philadelphia, PA: Temple University Press, 1990.

Marty, Martin, *Martin Luther: A Life*, New York: Penguin, 2004.

Mattson, Ingrid, *The Story of the Qur'an*, Malden, MA: Blackwell, 2008.

Mayhew, Peter, *A Theology of Force and Violence*, London: SCM Press, 1989.

Meyers, Jeffrey, *Orwell: Wintry Conscience of a Generation*, New York: W.W. Norton and Co., 2000.

Milani, Abbas, *Lost Wisdom: Rethinking Modernity in Iran*, Washington, DC: Mage Publishers, 2004.

Muldoon, James, *Popes, Lawyers and Infidels: The Church and the Non-Christian World 1250–1550*, Liverpool: Liverpool University Press, 1979.

Nasr, Seyyed Hossein, *The Garden of Truth: The Vision and Promise of Sufism,* New York: HarperCollins, 2007.

Nietzsche, Friedrich, *Ecce Homo* R.J. Hollingdale (trans.), Harmondsworth: Penguin Books, 1979.

Nietzsche, Friedrich, *The Anti-Christ*, R.J. Hollingdale (trans.), Harmondsworth: Penguin, 1968, published in one volume with *Twilight of the Idols* (1888).

Ochs, Peter, 'The God of Jews and Christians' in Tikva Frymer-Kensky *et al.* (eds), *Christianity in Jewish Terms*, Boulder and Oxford: Westview Press, 2000.

Orwell, George, *Inside the Whale and Other Essays*, Harmondsworth: Penguin, 1957.

Paul, *Alexander the Great*, Woodstock, New York: The Overlook Press, 2004.

Plutarch's *Lives*, London: J.M. Dent and Sons Ltd., 1910, reprinted 1961, vol. 1.

Rahman, Fazlur, *Major Themes of the Quran*, Minneapolis, MN: Bibliotheca Islamica, 1980.

Ridgeon, Lloyd (ed.), *Islamic Interpretations of Christianity*, Richmond, Surrey: Curzon, 2001.

Robinson, Neal, *Discovering the Qur'an*, Washington, DC: Georgetown University Press, 2003.

Rushdie, Salman, *The Satanic Verses*, UK, Viking, 1988.

Safi, Omid, *Progressive Muslims: On Justice, Gender, and Pluralism*, Oxford: Oneworld, 2003.

Said, Edward, *Covering Islam*, New York: Random House, 1997, revised edition, first published in 1981.

Salloum, Adnan, (trans.), *Asbab Al-Nuzul*, Beirut: Dar Al-Kutub Al-Ilmiyyah, 1991.

Schedinger, Robert, *Was Jesus a Muslim?*, Minneapolis, MN: Fortress Press, 2009.

Spencer, Robert, *Islam Unveiled*, San Francisco, CA: Encounter Books, 2002.

Stallworthy, Jon (ed.), Preface, *The Poems of Wilfrid Owen*, London: Chatto and Windus, 1990.

Steyn, Mark, *America Alone*, Washington, DC: Regnery, 2006.

Sunar, Ilkay, 'Civil society and Islam' in Elizabeth Ozdalga and Sune Persson (eds.), *Civil Society, Democracy and the Muslim World*, Istanbul: Swedish Research Institute, 1997.

Taji-Farouki, Suha (ed.), *Modern Muslim Intellectuals and the Qur'an*, Oxford: Oxford University Press, 2004.

Thomas, David (ed.), *A Faithful Presence: Essays for Kenneth Cragg*, London: Melisende, 2003.

Tibi, Bassam, *Islam between Culture and Politics*, New York, NY: Palgrave, 2001.

Wadan, Ibn (ed.), *Sermons of the Prophet Muhammad*, New Delhi: Goodword Books, 2002.

Wade, Allan (ed.), *The Letters of W.B. Yeats*, London: Rupert Hart-Davis, 1954; New York: Macmillan, 1955.

Watt, Montgomery, *Muhammad at Mecca*, Oxford: Oxford University Press, 1980.

Watt, Montgomery, *Muhammad at Medina*, Oxford: Oxford University Press, 1981.

Index